Court and Family in Sung China

Court and Family
in Sung China, 960–1279

Bureaucratic Success and Kinship Fortunes

for the Shih of Ming-chou

———◆———

Richard L. Davis

Duke University Press   Durham 1986

Contents

ILLUSTRATIONS (following page 78)

To James T. C. Liu

Acknowledgments

ACKNOWLEDGMENTS NEVER COME easy. So many have contributed to my understanding of Chinese history and society, so many have encouraged me as I struggled to meet standards that were always high but never beyond reach. This book betrays, in varying ways, their influence. I have grown immensely thanks to teachers and friends in Princeton and Taipei, colleagues at Duke and elsewhere. I hesitate to name one for fear of overlooking another, but common decency necessitates that I name at least a few. A special thanks, therefore, to Professors F. W. Mote and Willard Peterson at Princeton and to Professors Ch'ü Wan-li, Mao Han-kuang, and Wang Teh-yi in Taipei, each of whom contributed, quite distinctively, to the development of this study during its formative years. The timely assistance of James Geiss, the selfless collegiality of Huang K'uan-ch'ung, and the scholarly discernment of Huang Ch'ing-lien have all meant much to me, personally no less than professionally. A long-overdue note of gratitude to Professors David Abosch, Laurence Schneider, and Constantine Tung, all of whom went far beyond the call of duty in giving of their time and guidance. Finer teachers and friends cannot be found and my debt, I fear, will be permanently outstanding.

I also thank the staffs at Princeton's Gest Library, Academia Sinica's Fu Ssu-nien Library, and Columbia's Starr Library. The resources of these institutions, human and material, made research a unique pleasure. As for making research financially possible, the Ford Foundation and the Fulbright program for research abroad both deserve special mention, as does the Duke University Center for International Studies Publications, which kindly contributed to publication costs.

Yet my greatest debt, a profound intellectual one, I owe to James T. C. Liu. It was his exemplary scholarship—so diverse in topic, so engaging in form—that first prompted me to concentrate on Sung history. I consider myself uniquely privileged to have studied under his direction in graduate school. It is only fitting, under the circumstances, that I dedicate this book to him. Whatever merits can be found in the effort owe much to his fine training and pervasive influence; as for the defects, they can only reflect my own deficiencies as a student still young and with much yet to learn.

Durham, North Carolina

1986

Preface

NOT MANY TOPICS in the study of Chinese society have attracted as much scholarly attention yet generated so little consensus as that pertaining to the nature and evolution of its traditional elite. There is little doubt that this, at least in part, stems from the considerable confusion about the genesis and function of the ruling class—the extent to which the term relates to community standing or political involvement. Early research tended to view traditional China's elite as largely a political one where social standing could be measured almost entirely through bureaucratic success. Finding the political life of most families to be short and the civil service to be highly fluid, a good many historians concluded that there indeed existed a high level of "social mobility" in late imperial China and that this reflected the openness of its bureaucratic order to "new blood." More recently, however, a younger generation of researchers have come to challenge this conclusion. They insist that, beyond the nationally prominent political elite, there also existed a locally influential social elite, considerably more entrenched and class-conscious than had been generally appreciated by historians. Through large landholdings, political alliances, and social ties, the larger social elite was able, in an almost conspiratorial fashion, to dominate the local scene for centuries, while effectively excluding outsiders from its closely knit circle. It is easy to see how entirely different conclusions can be drawn about the fluidity of Chinese society depending upon whether a researcher adopts a broad or narrow definition of "elite" and whether one's focus is on national or regional developments.

Few today would argue against the need to expand the earlier definition of elite and to correct the former tendency to speak of social mobility merely in terms of civil service involvement. Families which long had assumed roles of leadership in their communities and whose standing was reinforced by social and political ties were surely members of some sort of elite and should not entirely be neglected simply because they failed to identify with the bureaucratic order. At the same time, recent scholarship often exaggerates the cohesiveness of both family and community, while completely disregarding internal dissension and consequent fragmentation. The communal sharing of wealth and commitments of mutual assistance within the common descent group seem much more prevalent than was genuinely the case. Affinal ties appear to be not merely a reflection of attained social status, but often a major impetus behind upward mobility. This paints for us a well-ordered picture of elite consciousness, intrafamilial cooperativeness, and social harmony—none of which were ever dominant themes in the ordinarily uneven and conflict-riddled Chinese landscape.

Yet another inadequacy of studies with a regional focus is that they tend to neglect the impact of court politics upon local prosperity. No community lives in a vacuum. A native son who rises to a prominent position in the capital frequently carries on his coattails a host of kinsmen and neighbors, enhancing in the process the political stature of both family and region. An unpopular official, on the other hand, might generate considerable tension locally, even to the point of bringing ruin to those identified with him. It was no mean chore for those disfavored in the capital to protect their social status and financial resources at home. As for affinal ties, these were often an outgrowth of political alliances at court, not mere reflections of regional stature.

This study has relevance to such issues. First and foremost, this is the story of a family: its social and political obscurity during the Northern Sung (960–1126), its rise to empirewide renown in the Southern Sung (1127–1279), and its demise after the dynasty's collapse. The changing political fortunes of one scholar-official house in Sung China, while hardly an accurate barometer of social mobility in a broad sense, does provide insight into the dynamics of bureaucratic fluidity during this vital period, enabling us, at the same time, better to appreciate the impact of court policies and politics upon kinship fortunes. In a sense, the Shih of Ming-chou (modern Ning-po) provide an ideal case study. From extreme obscurity they rose, despite little land or wealth, to produce three consecutive generations of chief councillors, a virtual army of minor officials, and some of the most influential statesmen of the dynasty. Their extraordinary success at producing generations of civil servants might prompt the unwary regional expert to consider kinship status as somehow "hereditary." Nothing could be more untrue. On the contrary, there existed neither the institutional mechanism nor the kin group commitment to facilitate the maintenance of hereditary privilege in the fashion of early imperial times. Moreover, intralineal rivalries and antagonisms, the total absence of any spirit of mutual assistance, and the dramatic and unimpeded decline of the house over a relatively short span of time all suggest that turbulence within a highly competitive bureaucracy and tensions within a visibly discordant kin group made the long-term preservation of power, wealth, and status a virtual mission impossible.

This book is an analysis of the civil service experience of one common descent group: the methods it employed to climb the bureaucratic ladder, the factors influencing its decline, and the impact of court politics upon both movements. The story of the Shih can illuminate the times in which they lived. A kin group's success in the civil service cannot be discussed independently of Sung innovations in bureaucratic recruitment; its rise to prominence in the capital cannot be discussed independently of regional development; and its total experience cannot be divorced from the larger elite community to which it belongs. I have addressed such issues in the introductory and concluding chapters and, to some extent, in the body of the book itself. However, to generalize broadly about elites in Sung China based upon the study of one family would require a vanity far greater than my own, while addressing the full ramifications of the Shih experience in terms of social as well as political history would overtax the patience of author and reader alike.

When I first began research on this topic roughly nine years ago, my objective was to bring to Western audiences the history of a once-prominent, now largely forgotten kin group and shed light upon its times, its opportunities, and its challenges. Those objectives have not changed. Through the help of critics, I am now more aware of the relationship of this study to other scholarship, especially those with an anthropological or social history focus, and I have tried to draw out the contrasts whenever possible. Reflecting the civil service orientation of the Shih, their story is largely a political one, but it has important social implications that must be pointed out. Yet in so doing, I seek not to write social history from a political perspective and I am not denying the significance of the recent crop of social history scholarship for late imperial China. Quite the contrary, I am convinced that political and social history are, and must of necessity remain, complementary. Studies of the politically prominent assist the social historian to place regional elites in some wider context, while regional studies help the political historian better to appreciate the complexity of society and the dynamics of interaction between center and periphery.

This represents the first detailed study of a Sung dynasty kin group and the only work devoted entirely to the Shih. There remains so much yet to be done. Consequently, it will take some time before historians can generalize, with any conviction, about bureaucratic fluidity and social mobility in Sung China or the nature of its national and regional elites. This effort may raise more questions than it answers, but I have always preferred lingering questions to quick answers. It is often said that confusion always precedes understanding. With the paucity of secondary material that currently exists, it seems that I can offer my reader little more than confusion. But confused readers frequently make future researchers and nothing would please me more than future research.

NOTE ABOUT ROMANIZATION

In general, I have employed Wade-Giles romanization with some exceptions. When referring to modern provinces, more familiar forms have been used, such as Chekiang (instead of Che-chiang) or Kiangsu (instead of Chiang-su); familiar forms have also been used for a few other place names, e.g., Nanking, Soochow, and the Yangtze.

Introduction

IN THE EVOLUTION of Chinese society, there are no two themes that recur as frequently or are as pervasively influential as politics and family. Little in traditional China is not political and little in politics is uninfluenced by family. Interaction between the two often generates stories of glamorous spectacle and bewildering calamity. In this regard, the story of the Shih of Sung times is no disappointment.

Natives of the commercially prosperous and politically maturing Ming-chou, the Shih represent the popular rags-to-riches theme: starting from extreme obscurity, they manage to penetrate the civil service and eventually to run the empire. They enjoyed material wealth, political influence, imperial favor, and social status in a measure that few, if any, other kin groups of the time could match. Dominating the court for nearly a half century, their decisions even affected the fate of the dynasty. On the opposite side of the coin, it was success that ruined the Shih, and ruin came no less dramatically than success. The house soon became an object of wholesale ridicule at court, while at home it fell victim to intense factional strife and personality conflict. Under intense pressures, external and internal, it eventually fell apart. Before their story can begin, however, it is necessary first to place the Shih within the scholar-official context of the time, to understand how great families are often products of their age.

Few topics in the history of imperial China are as fascinating and, alas, as prodigiously confounding as the evolution of its ruling class. Despite many noble efforts, scholars have met with limited success in understanding the dynamics of this evolution. In what type of political, economic, and social environment are new elites most likely to emerge? Why is it that, during certain periods, political disunity and social turmoil appear only to enhance the wealth and influence of locally prominent families, while similar conditions at a different time can have the exact opposite effect? Conversely, what is the impact of political stability and centralized authority on traditional elites: do they serve to undermine such groups or facilitate further entrenchment? Such complex questions have no simple answers. As the political, economic, and social context for change is different for each period in Chinese history, apparently similar factors have a dissimilar impact depending upon the particular stage of an elite's evolution.

Students of imperial China have commonly assumed that political instability and popular insurrection tended to affect negatively the maintenance of social order and, implicitly, the preservation of the elite. This may have held true for late imperial China, when insurrection was often anti-establishment in character and dispersed throughout the countryside, but for most of the early imperial period rebellions were directed against the court and centered on the capital. So long as the locally prominent lived some distance from the seat of power and avoided direct involvement in the conflict, they tended to suffer little from the political somersaults that easily devastated a succession of ruling houses. Indeed, the absence of a central government frequently worked to their advantage by removing external obstacles to control of the local economy, including unabashed encroachment upon the land of the defenseless. The emergence of unified rule, on the other hand, always posed some threat to traditional elites, be they near or far from the political center. Retention of its newly acquired authority necessitated that a government act with utmost expedition to eliminate one-time rivals and to prevent the rise of any other group capable of challenging its suzerainty. Preeminent in its control over regional resources, the local elite was certain to suffer most from the court's centralization efforts.

Perhaps the earliest and most prominent example of elite repression in Chinese history occurred at the outset of the Han dynasty (206 B.C.–A.D. 220). The ruling Liu house, despite having received generous support from the nobility of the Warring States period (403–256 B.C.) in its drive to overthrow the Ch'in (221–206 B.C.), lived in constant fear that the same nobility might someday desert it, choose to ally with another upstart, and become a party to its own overthrow. Consequently, the most famous of noble families were forcibly uprooted from their native places and moved to areas within easy reach of the capital. Occurring during the first decade of Han rule, this well-known demonstration of imperial might reportedly involved over a hundred thousand people and met with remarkable success.[1] The old elite, separated from its former source of wealth and influence, was economically and politically broken; blending in with the Chinese landscape, it never again posed a serious threat to centralized authority. Later, the court found itself no less uneasy about the old nobility's successor as power-wielder in the countryside—clansmen of its own Liu house—and implemented an array of measures designed to leave them equally weak and dependent upon the center.[2] Thus, during the invigorated first century of the Former Han dynasty, it was clearly a strong imperial government determined to centralize authority that most effectively challenged and eventually undermined the old ruling class.

A new and more powerful elite emerged in the second century of the Han and gradually supplanted the regional influence of the old nobility, doing so largely because the court, by that time, had lost much of its former vitality. The court was no longer in a position to manipulate regional forces; these forces were thus free to expand untrammeled by central authority. Commonly referred to as "powerful families" (hao-tsu), the new elite owed much of its affluence to commercial activity, but it did not take long before commercial wealth was converted into landed wealth and this landed elite began penetrating the civil service.[3] Efforts by the government to harness society's rapid commercialization ended in failure and powerful families eventually overshadowed the Han nobility, both in economic and political status. Some indication of the preponderant influence of these families can be seen in the mid-Han crisis of the first century A.D. In the aftermath of Wang Mang's usurpation, Emperor Kuang-wu (r. A.D. 25–57) was able to revive the dynasty only after enlisting the support of the local elite; in effect, he owed his very throne to them.[4] After the restoration, powerful families rose to yet higher stature and the weak but grateful court in Lo-yang could hardly act against them. The end result was the entrenchment of an elite whose roots in the countryside lay so deep that its dominance would persist for nearly a millennium. Like no time since the feudal era, political power and social status had become principally a function of hereditary privilege.

Landholdings formed the foundation of powerful families, or "aristocratic clans" as they are sometimes called, while bureaucratic involvement generally served merely to enhance or confirm achieved status.[5]

Having failed to control commercial expansion, were the Han govern-ment able to curb land accumulation, perhaps it could have restricted the resources of the locally powerful. As it was, the various economic activi-ties of the rich went unchecked. In the political realm, rulers of Wei (220–64) and Chin (265–419) challenged the elite's manipulation of the bureaucracy by employing the "arbiter" system (*chiu-p'in chung-cheng*), whereby the government sought to make civil servants more responsive to the center by expanding its role in their assessment prior to recruitment and appointment.[6] Previously, candidates for office were largely recom-mended by regional officials, with the government playing the relatively passive role of sanctioning these recommendations. The arbiter system nonetheless ended in failure.

Most regimes of the post-Han/pre-Sui Six Dynasties period, having sway over a divided empire, were often chronically weak. Ineffective at asserting control over the bureaucracy, they were also unable to deny powerful families personal access to local taxes intended for national coffers.[7] With sprawling estates housing thousands of retainers and siz-able private armies, these lineages had assumed, in great measure, the basic functions of local government.[8]

Chinese society during this period of disunity represents the most rig-idly stratified in all of imperial history. Efforts by the Wei and Chin governments to attract to the bureaucracy recruits from outside the power-ful family cliques through the arbiter system, although yielding unimpres-sive results, did permit a modest number of outsiders to penetrate the bureaucratic elite. This was not so true for the fifth and sixth centuries, when dynasties both north and south of the Yangtze placed pedigree above virtually all other criteria in recruiting for the civil service.[9] That this should occur in North China seems reasonable enough. Rulers of the T'o-pa Wei (386–535), of alien extraction, were understandably insecure about Han-Chinese acceptance of their overlordship. Apparently to pro-mote such acceptance, the occupiers enthusiastically embraced the social and political values of their hosts, aristocratic traditions included. In this way, the new conservators of tradition took their charge of maintaining tradition far more seriously than Chinese leaders before them. T'o-pa Wei endorsement of powerful family dominance may also reflect its realiza-tion that elite influence in the countryside could not be challenged with-out creating a political vacuum which, in turn, would court a dangerous instability. The south, in contrast, should have been less steeped in the aristocratic tradition, as it initially imported that tradition from the north. The tradition's appeal, I would tentatively posit, represents a function of the competition between north and south for legitimacy. Lacking control over the cradle of Chinese civilization, the "central plains," the politically insecure regimes of the south anxiously sought to prove themselves genuine inheritors of heaven's mandate and this anxiousness may have prompted them to imitate, with meticulous care, elite society as they perceived it to exist in the north.

The maintenance of elite dominance in rural China probably provided an element of stability in times of political division. Yet, under unified rule, its effect could be the exact opposite: beyond threatening the flow of local taxes to central government coffers, locally autonomous groups also presented a formidable challenge to the political authority of the center. Consequently, the consummately manipulative rulers of the Sui (581–617) and T'ang (617–906), following in the footsteps of the Former Han centuries earlier, made every effort to curtail the wealth and influence of the regional elite. The first move in this highly sensitive scheme entailed reformulation of a regularized and objective civil service examination program that individuals of aristocratic background could not so easily dominate, one that placed literary skills above regional standing. With examinations being stressed at the expense of local recommendations, with the government assuming a more active role in bureaucratic recruitment, and with individual merit taking on an ever-greater importance, the civil service became more accessible to men of nonstatused background. Implemented under Han rule on a much smaller scale and achieving only moderate success, the examination system was expanded and formalized in T'ang times to become a major vehicle for recruitment.[10] No doubt, the greatest strides were made during the reigns of T'ai-tsung (626–49), Kao-tsung (649–83), and Empress Wu (690–705), for there emerged then a clear preference for scholar-officials of nonaristocratic backgrounds and the state assumed increased responsibility for their training.[11] Other measures targeted against the aristocracy included legal restrictions on marriage alliances between the leading families and a concerted effort to deflate their often exaggerated claims of noble ancestry through direct government involvement in the composition of once-private genealogies.[12] The forcefulness of these policies reflects more than just a pervasive uneasiness about aristocratic influence, but also the government's determination to humble the regional elite before the political center.

There is scant evidence to document conclusively success on the part of the T'ang government in diminishing either the wealth or cohesiveness of powerful families, yet we do know that changes in the bureaucratic selection process did alter the basic character of the old elite. With social status tied ever so closely to government service and high office increasingly the domain of degreeholders, these families became enmeshed in the competition to earn government degrees and secure high-level appointments.[13] They may have continued to dominate the civil service for the duration of the dynasty, yet they did so more through scholarly attainment and less by dint of hereditary privilege.[14] They had adapted, in effect, to the new demands of the day but, to their detriment, they lost the independence of government service that was once their trademark. That the old elite's relationship to the government should be transformed, so successfully, from one of independence and superiority to one of dependence and inferiority attests to the remarkable foresight of early T'ang rulers as well as the determination of their successors to strengthen central authority and to engage in contest even the most formidable of challengers.

With the inauguration of the Sung dynasty, the once indomitable powerful families had mysteriously, and permanently, disappeared from the political and social arenas. To some historians, this represents the well-earned fruits of two centuries of effort by an unrelenting T'ang government to divest the powerful of their regional clout.[15] Others view this as principally a by-product of the Five Dynasties (907–59), an age often characterized as one of extreme chaos and violence.[16] One writer concludes that powerful families were simply made "obsolete" or irrelevant to a changing society, gradually losing their former sense of identity and self-value.[17] Each explanation has its own considerable merit, yet none can stand entirely on its own. If the decline of powerful families occurred quite gradually over the course of T'ang and stemmed chiefly from professionalization of the bureaucracy, then why are modern scholars unable to document any significant diminution of their civil service involvement, even in late T'ang times?[18] If their demise is attributed to the "chaos" of the relatively brief Five Dynasties period, then how is it that the four centuries of disunity, and frequent turmoil, that preceded the Sui brought more prosperity than hardship to these families? Were the Five Dynasties somehow more intensely chaotic than the Six Dynasties? If powerful families simply became irrelevant to changing times, what is the precise nature of these changes and how did the movement gather the necessary momentum to destroy utterly a vigorous tradition that, for nearly a millennium, had outmaneuvered even the strongest of governments?

I have serious reservations about whether the government, in stressing the examination system, ever intended actually to eliminate the powerful families. To T'ang rulers, such a task must have appeared nearly impossible. Rather, the policy probably had the more limited objective of enabling Ch'ang-an to assert its own preeminence in the political realm by setting the criteria for civil service selection. Inevitably, this entailed some bureaucratization of the elite which, in turn, altered its basic character and left it more vulnerable to challenges from upstarts, or even "obsolescence." However, this alone would have been insufficient to destroy the aristocracy. Ultimately, its annihilation must be related to the emergence of some rival group or groups. Modern historians, almost invariably, have assumed that this new challenge came from civil officials of relatively "humble," nonofficial background (*han-men*), men whose role in the civil service had expanded significantly over the course of T'ang. Yet, focusing on political developments in the capital, scholars have failed adequately to explore changing trends in military organization at the local level and the extent to which these trends, by weakening the grip of the regional elite on the provinces, may have precipitated the powerful families' astounding fall.

In particular, it is well known that, in the aftermath of the An Lu-shan rebellion (756–63), political and fiscal control at the regional level fell into the hands of military governors (*chieh-tu-shih*) and, for all its effort, the T'ang government could never again assert its former control over the provinces.[19] This effectively created a new force to compete with prominent families for control over regional resources, a development that must have profoundly affected the ability of these families to perpetuate their dominance of the countryside. Despite the importance of this turn of events to understanding the shifting balance of power in rural China and the shifting equilibrium between center and periphery, specialists today have devoted scant attention to it.

In a fascinating essay on office-holding in North China during the Five Dynasties, Nishikawa Masao has observed that aristocratic families produced a declining number of civilian officials over the course of the period. Replacing them was a growing number of military men, individuals largely of humble origins. This development may simply indicate that the old elite had disintegrated even before the onset of the Five Dynasties era, or perhaps it reflects an unprecedented preference of the governments of the time for bureaucrats of martial bent. The dynamics of their ascendency may not be clear, but the eventual dominance of these military upstarts over the civil service appears irrefutable. Furthermore, the practice of using military recruits to staff the civilian bureaucracy, according to Nishikawa, continued throughout the Five Dynasties and well into the first two reigns of the Sung.[20]

Needless to say, such findings have important implications for students of Chinese society. First, it was not merely the "chaos" of the Five Dynasties that precipitated the decline of the powerful families. On the contrary, a local military presence, in all probability, ensured a good measure of stability. Far more crucial to elite standing is the fact that the military had substantially broadened its role in the civil service of the tenth century, thereby challenging the former dominance of the aristocracy. Second, the continued preeminence of military elements in the civilian bureaucracy long after the Five Dynasties suggests that the policies of early Sung rulers T'ai-tsu (r. 959–76) and T'ai-tsung (r. 976–97) played a critical role in permanently debilitating the old elite. Contrary to popular myth, the founders of Sung did not abruptly replace military with civilian officials; had they done so, perhaps powerful families could have regained some of their lost influence. This did not happen and these families—struggling with an increasingly awesome military clique for control over the limited resources of the countryside and dependent on office-holding to retain their status at the same time that progressively fewer posts were available to them—found themselves retreating both at home and in the capital.

Nishikawa and others also note that centralization of political and military authority, which is often identified with the Sung, actually has its roots in the Five Dynasties.[21] The various regimes of the time, while short-lived, nonetheless could claim impressive results in wresting power away from influential military governors—a problem that the T'ang government frequently tackled without much success. This suggests, again, contrary to widely held beliefs, that the period witnessed a remarkably high level of social order and competent political leadership. Interestingly, rulers of the Five Dynasties appear somehow less pressured than their Six Dynasties predecessors to strike a compromise with aristocratic power. If not a testimony to the unusual vigor of leadership at the time, it clearly attests to the weakened position of the old elite. Low-level military personnel had become sufficiently professionalized to assume civilian posts, providing the state with a pool of administrative talent outside the less reliable powerful families. With the emergence of Sung rule, reunification of the realm and centralization of authority only served to dim still further the prospects for elite recovery of its old privileges. Not only did the first two emperors of Sung continue to employ military men in staffing the civilian bureaucracy, but even after there evolved a policy of replacing military professionals with civilians at the turn of the eleventh century, it was clear that the new order would no longer accommodate an arrogant hereditary elite.[22]

The class of professional scholar-officials of Sung times owed its ascendancy to success at competitive recruitment examinations. Lacking the wealth and status of aristocrats, its identity became closely bound to bureaucratic service. The origins of this group, however, are virtually impossible to determine. In all likelihood, the powerful families of the past had not been annihilated. They had lost their former wealth, status, and cohesiveness as a group; fragmented and geographically displaced, they were no longer identified with the old choronyms (region-based prefixes to the surname that automatically identified one with an eminent house), but physical extinction probably did not occur. Thus, the Sung elite may well represent little more than the old elite masked by a new identity and, indeed, a good many Sung officials did profess to be descendants of the once-esteemed aristocracy. Recent research, however, has exposed many such claims as bogus.[23] It is also possible that many in the later professional elite descended from families that represented, in T'ang times, a social substratum of literate but nonstatused men—individuals once confined to minor bureaucratic or clerical posts—who came into their own under Sung rule.[24] Still others may have descended from professional military families of the tenth century, a group that had increasingly assumed civilian posts in the transition from Five Dynasties to Sung. Whatever its origins, the scholar-official elite of Sung times possessed little of the wealth, status, or security that characterized the powerful families. Growth in the size of the civil service and the careful division of power therein served to deflate the political influence of the individual civil servant. Meanwhile, the competitiveness of the examination process, combined with increased restrictions on the privileges afforded the offspring of civil servants, made it exceedingly difficult for scholar-official houses of the Sung to maintain prosperity over an extended period of time, as the aristocracy had once done. Rather, as the rate of personnel turnover in the bureaucracy was high, mobility within it was greatly accelerated. The consequent impact upon family fortunes was undeniably profound.

For most of the early imperial period, politically mobile kin groups commonly required at least ten generations to reach the summit of their climb, with another ten generations passing before decline set in.[25] It was not unusual then for a prosperous house to produce a long line of bureaucratic executives and for kinsmen to proliferate in the capital.[26] This was not likely to occur under Sung rule. The population of China from the eleventh through the thirteenth centuries was significantly larger than before, education was accessible to a wider segment of society, and the government made a more concerted effort to attract to its civil service the meritorious of nonofficial background. In essence, the pool of educated men had so grown that competition for office could be quite intense. Kin groups of the Sung tended to rise from obscurity to political prominence and back to obscurity, completing an entire cycle, within ten generations or less.[27] In this respect, mobility within the Sung civil service bears striking similarity to that of Ming (1368–1644) and Ch'ing (1644–1911) times, while differing markedly from the earlier period.[28]

This research explores the rise and fall of one highly prominent common descent group in Sung China. The Shih of Ming-chou were chosen for several reasons. First, they produced what is probably the dynasty's most astonishing success story. One of only two houses in the three hundred years of the dynasty to sire three consecutive generations of chief councillors, the Shih also produced some two hundred other civil servants.[29] The extraordinary nature of their success, beyond its inherent appeal to the inquisitive historian, has ensured an unusual abundance of source material. Second, the method employed by the Shih to win initial access to the civil service and to ensure their subsequent rise therein differed little from the approach of most politically aspiring contemporaries. They used the examination system. In this respect, their experience has implications for a large segment of scholar-officialdom. Third, unlike many highly successful and controversial families, the Shih remained in the good graces of the throne for the duration of the dynasty, so their decline followed a fairly natural course and was not the outcome of any abrupt political shift at court.

Focusing on civil service involvement, this study makes frequent reference to official rank (*kuan-p'in*) in assessing the political achievements of Shih kinsmen. When new recruits entered the mainstream of the civil service, they were generally assigned rank based upon the classification of their post or sinecure, with adjustments later being made to reflect promotions and demotions. Beyond simply indicating an individual's standing in the civil service, rank also influenced social status. Frequent reference in genealogies to bureaucratic rank leaves little doubt that it did indeed become reflected in community standing. Many historians have used rank as a convenient gauge in measuring civil service attainment in late imperial China.[30] In this volume as well, rank is indicated when describing the fortunes of Shih kinsmen in the bureaucracy.[31]

The reader should be reminded that the Sung civil service had a total of eighteen ranks; they were numbered 1 through 9 and then subdivided into "grade a" (*cheng-p'in*) and "grade b" (*tsung-p'in*). High-level, executive posts were largely included in categories 1, 2, or 3. Midlevel posts, often with administrative responsibilities, were included in categories 4, 5, or 6. Low-level, often secretarial, positions were generally confined to categories 7, 8, or 9. Except under special circumstances, recent recruits to the bureaucracy were assigned the lowest rank (9). For an official subsequently to rise to the middle level implied the passing of several promotion examinations and the notable accumulation of experience. The highest category was the domain of only a select few (the chief councillor was on top at 1a or 1b) and implied an extraordinary set of credentials—almost always the *chin-shih* degree. Due to its exclusiveness, penetration of this level easily brought empirewide renown and signaled an official's initiation into his empire's political leadership.

While useful in measuring civil service attainments, the charting of ranks denotes only one aspect of an individual's trek to power or his fall from it. After gaining entrance to the bureaucracy and achieving some level of imperial recognition, the future mobility of a kin group was commonly affected by the favor of the emperor, special contacts within the palace, personal influence among scholar-officials, and, of course, good timing. Probably the greatest shortcoming of most studies on bureaucracy and family is their general neglect of court politics in assessing family fortunes. Just as the policies of Han and T'ang had a lasting impact upon the current composition and future promise of elites during those periods, so political developments at the Sung court could be decisive in triggering the rise or decline of scholar-official houses. This was especially true for the Shih. Developments on the national level brought unimagined opportunity at times and extreme peril at others; on the personal level, a timely liaison of a kinsman with the palace or bureaucracy, however weak initially, could reap impressive rewards for both individual and kin group over the long haul. For this reason, this study focuses on *court* and *family* in Sung China. It is foremost a political history, an examination of one common descent group's evolution from disesteemed paupers to rulers of the empire. From one generation to the next, we explore the movement of Shih kinsmen within the bureaucratic hierarchy, their interaction with eminent personalities of the time, their role in formulating court policy, their affection as well as disdain for fellow kinsmen, and the ultimate effects of these various factors upon the kin group's overall political standing.

Reflecting this political focus, I have devoted little space to the material wealth of the Shih or their affinal ties with other prominent families. Quite apart from the limits of time and space, this was necessitated by the inadequacy of source material. References to wealth in historical works are generally so scant, scattered, and vague as to offer the modern researcher no real insight. In addition, unfortunately, references to the wives of Shih kinsmen rarely provide more than a simple surname, making them equally useless. In the absence of reliable genealogies for the Ming-chou Shih, it is impossible to draw any significant conclusions about marriage patterns.[32] As for those interested in the kin group's cohesion as a community, the social history component, I would direct them to my essay in *Kinship Organization in Late Imperial China*, edited by Patricia Ebrey and James Watson. In this book, I have addressed such issues only to the extent that they relate to the success or failure of Shih kinsmen as civil servants.

Throughout this volume, several major themes will appear and reappear. First, the Sung was a period that, relative to the past, offered far greater opportunity for civil service aspirants. Due to the demise of the old hereditary elite, full implementation of an impartial and competitive examination for official recruitment, proliferation of publicly supported schools, and dogged determination on the part of the government to attract talent from as wide a social spectrum as possible, the avenues for bureaucratic access had noticeably expanded. Moreover, this expansion was enhanced during the late eleventh and early twelfth centuries by innovations in the government's various recruitment policies.[33]

Second, the Sung civil service was largely a meritocracy and the Shih success therein derived largely from their extraordinary ability to produce an uninterrupted succession of degreeholders and proven officials. This contrasts sharply with earlier periods, when many if not most members of the scholar-official elite owed their ascendancy either to family reputation or some personal contribution to the dynasty's founding.[34] Admittedly, once the Shih had achieved a certain level of success, many kinsmen could penetrate the bureaucracy, in a fashion almost resembling the past, without first proving themselves through the examinations. However, while the Sung civil service was open to the offspring of high-level officials who lacked degrees, the status given them was generally low. Lacking *chin-shih* credentials, an aspiring official from a privileged background faced the even more rigorous test of proving himself in office—a much slower means of advancement that, in the end, offered less promise. This, complemented by various qualifying examinations, virtually ensured that the incompetent and unaccomplished would not rise far above the level at which they entered. Denied the privileges of office once afforded their accomplished forefathers, it did not take long before families that failed to produce new generations of degreeholders were excluded from the bureaucracy altogether.

A third theme is the relationships of Shih kinsmen with key palace figures. In addition to a man's credentials as degreeholder, advancement to the very top of the civil service during any period in Chinese history inevitably required imperial recognition. For a politically obscure house with no special influence in the capital or the palace, this was most often gained through official service there. Posts such as tutor or advisor to the heir-apparent, while relatively low in rank, could provide just the right exposure for rapid promotion. In time, a bureaucratic aspirant could exploit imperial goodwill toward his family to advance his own career. Even under a system based upon individual merit, bureaucratic exposure and family reputation undeniably affected career promise.

In the final analysis, these several themes serve to underscore the highly precarious existence of the Sung dynasty's bureaucratic elite. Official success or failure ultimately rested upon two factors—a competitive examination and imperial favor—both of which lay beyond a scholar-official's ability to control. Members of the hereditary elite of the preceding period could easily withdraw from the civil service, maintain their local prominence, and then stage a political revival many generations later.

This was not true for Sung families. In their case, temporary political withdrawal might easily result in permanent eclipse; the decline of the Shih in Yüan times provides sufficient proof of this. Government service had become the key both to penetrating and to remaining a member of the empire's elite. Without it, kin groups lacked not only social prestige, but also the material wealth afforded civil servants and the political clout to protect that wealth. Many historians have discussed, in general terms, the sweeping character of the political and social changes that accompanied the Sung—the changing role of bureaucracy in Sung society and the unique qualities of the Sung elite—yet until now there existed no comprehensive case study of a prominent Sung kin group and its changing political fortunes.[35]

As will become increasingly apparent, I owe much to Professor E. A. Kracke and his seminal work on the Sung civil service. He was the first to illustrate, at least to Western audiences, the ascendancy of merit over heredity in Sung government.[36] Yet I am focused where Kracke was broad; I concentrate on politics where Kracke was concerned chiefly with policies; I have applied the development of a particular region and the peculiarities of a specific time to bureaucratic fluidity in a way that was not possible some thirty years ago. This is a different, perhaps more eclectic, approach to some of the problems raised but never resolved a generation ago.

Historians always strive to generalize broadly based upon a specific study and I am no exception. Yet, it would be imprudent to claim that the experience of the Shih was necessarily representative, either of most or of even a significant portion of politically and socially aspiring kin groups of the time. Their extreme obscurity for most of the Northern Sung, their sudden rise to a position of political preeminence during the Southern Sung, and their abrupt decline after the dynasty's collapse can hardly be considered typical. On the other hand, the factors contributing to their rise and fall were undoubtedly the same factors affecting the fortunes of many around them. In this respect, the experience of the Shih does have applicability. Besides, it makes for a great story!

1

The Setting

As those familiar with traditional China well know, not a few modern scholars have in various ways touched upon the structure of the Sung bureaucracy, the nature of its sundry recruitment programs, and the extent of its true accessibility to persons of humble origin.[1] I am hardly inclined to test the reader's patience with a reiteration of their findings. At the same time, the political success of the Shih cannot be understood independently of certain specific civil service recruitment practices during the eleventh and twelfth centuries. The relationship between institutional reform and family fortunes is quite intimate, so some review seems unavoidable. For purposes of manageability, and out of a pious devotion to the virtue of brevity, the discussion that follows is confined to practices immediately relevant to the Shih story.

BUREAUCRATIC ACCESS

Much like the T'ang government that preceded it, the Sung maintained an extraordinarily flexible policy in its selection of officials, combining several, often contradictory, programs. On the one hand, it administered an array of competitive examinations, the most revered of which culminated in conferral of the *chin-shih*, or "doctoral" degree.[2] Competition for this could be exceedingly keen. During the first stage of the elimination process, the prefectural examinations (*chieh-shih* or *kung-chü*), a mere 1 to 10 percent of the candidates could expect to pass.[3] This select group subsequently went on to the capital, first to take departmental examinations (*sheng-shih*) and then court-conducted palace examinations (*tien-shih*).[4] Another 80 or 90 percent were eliminated in these metropolitan examinations; the remainder became *chin-shih*.[5] It was a terribly competitive process that required extensive training and offered no guarantee of reward for years of effort.

Yet success at the examinations represented the ultimate scholarly distinction. For those with *chin-shih* status, the degree not only brought social prestige but, more important, access to the upper reaches of the bureaucracy—a realm otherwise immensely difficult to penetrate. Small wonder that aspiring candidates, despite the odds, flocked to the prefectural seat and then to the capital to try their luck. Generally based upon literary achievement and not noticeably affected by family background or personal ties, even at the dynasty's outset, the examination system contributed significantly to opening the civil service to a much wider social spectrum than in the past. In the eleventh century, the proliferation of state-operated local schools served further to enlarge the size of the candidate pool, while subsequent innovations in the examination and recruitment processes helped remove some of the more formidable barriers to civil service involvement for the socially obscure.

On the other hand, the Sung government also maintained an assortment of less competitive recruitment schemes alongside its insensitive examination system in an effort to ameliorate the potentially destabilizing effects of competition upon the families of accomplished scholar-officials. The most well known and widely employed among these was "recruitment through protection" (*yin-pu*).[6] In order to "protect" the descendants of civil servants against sudden exclusion from public office for lack of a degree, the government allowed official status to be partially heritable. The sons and grandsons, and sometimes more distant kin, of a meritorious official could receive civil service rank and bureaucratic assignments almost independent of personal merit.[7] With chief councillors frequently permitted to draw as many as ten relatives into the bureaucracy through this process and midlevel officials allowed two or three, the size of this group must have been enormous.[8] One researcher estimates that nearly 40 percent of the entire civil service in the year 1213 represented men who had entered through "protection," rather than success at the examinations.[9]

Needless to say, more than simply overloading the bureaucracy with unnecessary weight, the practice must have also dispirited examination hopefuls who lacked such privileges. Each post taken by a "protected" individual meant one less for those without such advantages. Nonetheless, the government did impose restrictions on protected recruitment to blunt somewhat its negative impact. First, annual quotas were devised to limit the total number of individuals entering the civil service in this way, while other regulations required that both the official and his protectee exceed a prescribed age before exploiting the process.[10] The government also conducted regular evaluations (*mo-k'an*) of men in office to identify and eliminate those proven delinquent or incompetent.[11] Finally, most offspring of ranking officials were given low rank and protected for only two generations.[12] Their failure to secure degrees and adequate rank for themselves made it highly unlikely that the privilege would be available to later generations.

In addition to the protection process, the Sung government's promotion or placement examination (*ch'üan-shih*) represented another vehicle for recruitment that favored individuals from established families.[13] This special examination was administered by the Ministry of Personnel and designed for those already admitted to the bureaucracy who sought to accelerate their rise within it, especially from low- to midlevel posts. Emphasizing moral conduct and official deportment, as opposed to the *chin-shih* examination's stress on literary skill, the *ch'üan-shih* proved in character to be far more subjective and less academically rigorous. It was also not especially competitive. For most of the Northern Sung, examinations were held twice a year (as opposed to once every three years for the *chin-shih* degree) and as many as 70 percent of the candidates passed. No doubt, this served to increase the competition for promotions and to make bureaucratic advancement difficult for all, protected and nonprotected alike. After 1165, however, the court made a major effort to reduce the size of this group; it administered promotion examinations only once a year, permitting just one of three candidates to pass.[14] This could have meant a new quota representing one-fourth the previous number. Unfortunately, historical sources do not indicate the number of examinees per sitting either before or after 1165, so we cannot know how great an impact promotion examinations had upon bureaucratic fluidity. In terms of the Shih, the change is important because it suggests that rapid promotions, especially during the last century of Sung rule, were not so easily won as in the past. This may have encouraged those entering the bureaucracy without degrees to enhance their competitiveness by taking the *chin-shih* examination. Consequently, those with *chin-shih* status who, lacking family ties, entered the civil service somewhat later, at least had the consolation of knowing that not all midlevel posts had already been gobbled up by younger bureaucratic entrants from established families.

Quite often, the protection and promotion programs were used conjointly: those admitted to the lower level of the civil service through protection often employed the promotion scheme to receive advancements. For some, this was an intermediate step before proceeding to take the *chin-shih* examination; for those destined never to hold a degree, it was just another means of exploiting family status to the fullest. The negative effects of the promotion scheme on bureaucratic access were many, the most important being that it helped further to entrench the civil service elite.[15] However, there was a positive side. Promotion examinations helped to ensure that those entering the bureaucracy through protection did not get promoted without proving a minimum level of competence. Meanwhile, the prestige attached to the *chin-shih* degree and the difficulty of receiving executive appointments without it prompted most men of ambition to aim for the degree.[16] In the final analysis, both protection and promotion merely functioned as brakes to reduce the speed of both bureaucratic fluidity and downward social mobility. They never performed, nor were they ever intended to perform, as vehicles for maintaining a hereditary elite of scholar-officials similar to the powerful families of pre-Sung times.

One factor that attests to the Sung government's determination to avoid the formation of such an elite is its commitment, and it appears to have been a noble one, to single out for recruitment the socially obscure but talented novice. The ideal of maintaining a bureaucracy open to as wide a social spectrum as possible had existed long before the eleventh century. As early as the Han dynasty, the government supported a variety of institutions and programs designed to canvass the empire, near and far, for the talented and promising.[17] Under the Sung, this ideal was advanced through decree examinations (*chih-k'o*), whereby local officials were responsible for recommending the "wise, genial, forthright, and veracious" to be sent to the capital for examination and subsequent appointment to the bureaucracy.[18]

Also designed, ostensibly, to recruit the morally upright yet socially obscure for government service was the "eight virtues of conduct" (*pa-hsing*) program. Implemented in 1107 and continued for the remainder of the Northern Sung, the program required local officials to identify exemplary individuals whose conduct was "filial, fraternal, compassionate, endearing, trustworthy, beneficient, loyal, and harmonious." At the recommendation of authorities at home, these men were granted special permission to enroll in the prefectural school, advance to the Imperial University, and eventually join the bureaucracy, entirely bypassing the usual series of examinations.[19] In this way, individuals without the academic training to compete for the *chin-shih* degree and whose nonofficial background precluded exploitation of the protection process might still gain access to the civil service by dint of personal conduct. Meanwhile, bureaucratic aspirants from financially modest families with the courage to bet against the odds in search of *chin-shih* status received similar encouragement; once ready for departmental examinations, the government would pay their travel expenses to and from the capital.[20]

For those outside the scholar-official elite, access to the civil service came most easily, it appears, through the prefectural school (*chou-hsüeh*). This represents an institution, perhaps founded upon the inspiration of antiquity, yet clearly unique to the Sung. A brief discussion of its evolution in Ming-chou will follow presently.

One other important development relevant to the issue of official recruitment that deserves mention here is the inauguration in 1071 of the "three-levels" measure (*san-she fa*).[21] It was the objective of political reformer Wang An-shih (1021–86) to modify the criteria for official selection so that an individual's overall character and career promise, even bureaucratic expertise, took precedence over sheer literary skill and examination success. The measure enabled students at the Imperial University (*T'ai-hsüeh*),[22] upon graduation from the university's third level, to become eligible for *chin-shih* status and an official appointment, thus entirely circumventing the regular examination process. To Wang An-shih, an extended stay at the university would provide considerably more insight into an individual's suitability for office than performance on a single set of tests. Thus, the university came to be viewed, for the first time, as critical to enhancing the quality of the pool of bureaucratic talent; formal literary training was subordinated to practical knowledge. This approach, it would appear, tended to favor bureaucratic aspirants of nonstatused origins, for adeptness at composing the highly stylized essays and poems of the examinations came through rigorous and prolonged training, whereas practical knowledge is as much a function of native intelligence as formal education.

The objective may have been noble but, like most of Wang An-shih's reform measures, this one met with stiff resistance from the forces of opinion and was implemented only in part during his own day. Interestingly, the "three-levels" scheme did appeal to Emperor Hui-tsung (r. 1101–25). Revived in 1104, it was also expanded to include state-supported schools. Under the new arrangement, promising students at the subprefectural and prefectural schools could go on to attend the Imperial University and, upon graduating, receive degrees and official assignments. For nearly two decades, in fact, the government scrapped altogether its *chin-shih* examination system in favor of the "three-levels" innovation. With both the prefectural school and the Imperial University representing publicly funded institutions, this meant that the government, for the first time in Chinese history, had assumed chief responsibility for virtually the entire cost of a scholar-official's training. Needless to say, this commitment had the potential of thoroughly altering the social complexion of scholar-officialdom. Unfortunately, its potential was never fully realized, for bureaucratic resistance forced a restoration of the old examination system in 1121. Criticism notwithstanding, it appears that the Imperial University retained certain elements of the scheme until the very end of the Southern Sung, including the recommendation of exceptionally qualified students for *chin-shih* status.[23]

By maintaining such a varied and often contradictory set of recruitment programs, the Sung government sought to make its civil service more professional and responsible; placing limits on hereditary privilege, it helped undermine the old notion of social exclusiveness. Bureaucratic idealism of this sort had special appeal to Hui-tsung, although the reason for this particular emperor's idealism remains largely a mystery. Despite these laudable efforts, it would be naive to think that the Sung bureaucracy was suddenly transformed into a full-fledged meritocracy where family background counted for little and all had an equal chance to succeed. The protection and promotion prerogatives were only available to the privileged. Even schemes that might well benefit the humble, such as decree examinations and the "eight virtues of conduct" and "three-levels" programs, could easily be manipulated by the elite to their own advantage. In fact, contemporaries often criticized recruitment efforts ostensibly designed to assist the underprivileged that, in practice, were more often exploited by the prominent than the obscure. In addition, as so many programs—including ordinary promotion to metropolitan posts —required the recommendation of officials, bureaucratic aspirants short on family contacts were at a distinct disadvantage. Nonetheless, idealism could occasionally prevail and the programs did, at times, benefit the socially obscure; each played a special role in transforming the Shih from servants at the local sheriff's office to leaders of the empire.

ECONOMIC AND POLITICAL SHIFTS

No less crucial to social advancement is regional development. Regardless of government efforts to broaden the social base of the bureaucratic community by making opportunity available to a wider group, opportunity can only be exploited to the extent permitted by an individual's environment. An area lacking in material wealth and good educational institutions offers scant promise of official advancement, even to its most privileged residents. For the Shih of Ming-chou, mobility is closely tied to the blossoming of their native place as an economic, political, and cultural center. Yoshinobu Shiba and others have written extensively on the economic development of Ming-chou in T'ang and Sung times as well as on its growing importance to Sung China's Liang-che circuit (representing much of modern Kiangsu and Chekiang and part of Anhwei).[24] Without unnecessarily duplicating their efforts, a few points should be made here about these changes insofar as they relate to the success of Shih kinsmen.

The prefecture (*chou*) of Ming-chou (modern Ning-po), also known in Sung times as Ssu-ming and Ch'ing-yüan-fu, sits halfway down China's long Pacific coast, at the rim of Hang-chou Bay. About 150 kilometers east of Hang-chou, Ming-chou was for long the gravitational center of northeastern Chekiang. Some 700 kilometers in the other direction, on the opposite side of the East China Sea, lies the Japanese island of Kyūshū. When the Chinese imperial order was still young and the "central plains" its political and cultural heartland, Ming-chou was of only peripheral importance. That the area did not formally become elevated to a prefecture until the year 738 is sufficient testimony to this.[25] Yet, the gradual shift southward of the Chinese economy during the T'ang and the Five Dynasties period, first to the Huai and then to the Yangtze valley, brought the promise of prosperity to the region. Once the Grand Canal was extended to Hang-chou, thereby linking Ming-chou with markets to the north and west, the area quickly became a terminal for foreign and domestic trade. Through commerce, Ming-chou connected the Chinese interior with its coast and China with Japan, Korea, and even Southeast

Asia.[26] By the beginning of Sung, the prefecture's economic foundation was already firmly laid. Still, a century or more would pass before Ming-chou finally emerged as a densely inhabited and thriving metropolis.[27]

The importance of the eleventh and twelfth centuries as a period of unparalleled growth for the region is documented through population statistics. In the year 742, the prefectural population is recorded at about 42,000 households.[28] According to contemporary sources, this represented over two hundred thousand individual inhabitants, which suggests that Ming-chou was long capable of sustaining a reasonably large population. A source from the Sung period, on the other hand, indicates that the local population at the outset of the dynasty, rather than increasing, actually decreased to 27,000-odd households.[29] While very probably an underassessment, the figure does imply a relatively static population from mid-T'ang to early Sung, over two hundred years.[30] In contrast, the eleventh century brought unprecedented growth. Ming-chou of the Yüan-feng era (1078–85) could boast 115,000 households and that number climbed to nearly 123,700 by the year 1116. The population had tripled in slightly over a century.[31] With such a secure economic and demographic base, only one development would temporarily interrupt further expansion: the devastation of war.

When the Jurchen sacked the Sung capital of K'ai-feng in 1126, they took most of the imperial family hostage. The recently abdicated Hui-tsung and his son, Emperor Ch'in-tsung (r. 1125–26), were among their noble captives. Prince K'ang, the twenty-year-old son of Hui-tsung and younger brother of Ch'in-tsung, escaped a similar fate through his fortuitous absence from K'ai-feng at the time. Once proclaimed successor to Ch'in-tsung at a sanctuary only one hundred kilometers east of the fallen capital, he fled south, where he reigned over the southern half of the Chinese realm. From the very outset, the throne of the future Emperor Kao-tsung (Chao Kou, r. 1127–62) was most precarious and remained so for nearly a decade. The Jurchen frequently launched forays deep into the south, threatening not only the lower Huai valley, but also the lower Yangtze region. On more than one occasion they menaced his "temporary capital," Lin-an (modern Hang-chou), compelling Kao-tsung to take refuge still farther south.

One such episode occurred in the twelfth month of 1129 (January 1130), when a major Jurchen assault drove the emperor out of the capital. He initially found sanctuary in Ming-chou.[32] Within ten days word reached the port city of enemy movements away from Lin-an and in the direction of Ming-chou, the apparent plan being to trap Kao-tsung at the coast. A weary emperor and his entourage then hastily set sail for the ocean, drifting for weeks along the southern coast of Chekiang as they awaited further news about developments on land. Aware of the imperial departure, dispirited local and central government armies subsequently abandoned their defense efforts and permitted Ming-chou's prefectural seat at Yin *hsien* to fall to the Jurchen with virtually no resistance. The victors did not stay long; they had no intention of permanently occupying the area. Instead, they pillaged and destroyed everything in their path. Once their armies withdrew and the smoke cleared, it became apparent to all that Jurchen armies had effectively obliterated more than a century of progress in just two weeks. An early thirteenth-century gazetteer described the setting most vividly:

> Only a few Buddhist temples in the southeastern corner and residents of secluded alleys happened to survive. As the city began to fall, defending forces fled en masse to the southeast. Some descended its walls on ropes; others crossed the [Yung-]chiang [River] on wooden rafts, with half of them perishing [in the attempt]. Those who fled to the villages [inevitably] met with [the Jurchen] bandits [along the way]. In this manner, in every part of the prefecture, [even] its dense mountains and abysmal valleys—places where there is usually no trace of mankind—men were being snatched up by [these] plunderers. The murder and pillaging is beyond reckoning.[33]

This may seem an exaggeration, but I suspect not. Reports about Jurchen invasions elsewhere in central China allude to similar levels of destruction.[34] Perhaps it was the circulation of such reports that induced many of Ming-chou's prominent families to flee the area even before the enemy had arrived.[35] Those who chose not to flee, or for some reason were unable to do so, paid dearly. Nearly half of the well-known Lou kin group, for example, perished during the rampage.[36] Their loss appears to have been common for those left behind, a conclusion verified by population statistics.

Although the only records of population date from nearly four decades after the invasion, certain inferences can still be drawn from them. According to census reports of 1168, the population stood at roughly 136,000 households, just some 12,000 more than in 1116.[37] In light of the area's unusually high and sustained growth rate for the preceding two centuries and the massive immigrations to the area that followed the Jurchen incursion into North China, such a modest increase is most curious.[38] Shiba suggests that Ming-chou had, by this time, simply reached a point of economic and demographic saturation whereby it became incapable of supporting much more than 130,000 or 140,000 households.[39] Unfortunately, he does not adequately assess the impact upon the twelfth-century population of the Jurchen invasion.

Statistics for the beginning of the Yüan dynasty (1279–1368) place the population of Ming-chou at 241,450 households, a 77 percent increase over the figure for 1168.[40] From this it is clear that the region's growth continued unabated for the duration of the Southern Sung and into the Yüan period. The population of 1168, therefore, is not a stagnant but an expanding one. That it appears to be stagnant can only be explained by a sudden depopulation, one that is surely related to the war of 1130. The magnitude of this depopulation is uncertain, but considering growth rates before 1116 and after 1168, it is quite possible that Ming-chou could claim a postwar population of only about 80,000 households. This would suggest that it lost as much as one-third of its population in 1130. Meanwhile, such an estimate is also consistent with previously mentioned reports of families losing half of their kin and of evacuees dying on a massive scale.

In the short run, the founding of the Chin dynasty in the north meant disaster for Ming-chou; in the long run, it came as a blessing in disguise. With the Sung capital now safely located in Lin-an, neighboring Ming-chou suddenly gained strategic importance to the empire. It had provided the emperor sanctuary when the capital came under siege in 1130 and might be needed for future refuge as well.[41] Consequently, the court was most generous with investments in the recuperation and continued development of the area.[42] The high commodity demand of an imperial capital also ensured Ming-chou an expanded market for its many local and imported wares. As the population of Lin-an swelled from about 200,000 households at the beginning of the Southern Sung to nearly 400,000 at its close, this market also grew.[43] Finally, the Sung loss of North China prompted large segments of the imperial Chao clan to migrate south, with a sizable contingent settling in Ming-chou.[44] Beyond the added prestige the Chao lent the area, their presence also served to increase capital accumulation, enhance cultural refinement, and further the arts.

EDUCATION AND OFFICE-HOLDING

Just as the economic foundation for Ming-chou was laid during the mid- to late T'ang period, so was its educational base. An early thirteenth-century gazetteer for the region alludes to the proliferation of Buddhist and Taoist monasteries as institutions of higher education, many antedating the eleventh century.[45] A number of private academies of Confucian learning that prospered under the Sung have similar roots in the T'ang and the Five Dynasties period. Even the area's prefectural school can be traced to pre-Sung times.[46]

When the government ordered all prefectures to establish publicly supported schools in 1043, the most recent addition to Ming-chou's school system was already a quarter-century old.[47] Although promulgation of this and similar edicts did not serve to inaugurate public education in the area, it did stimulate the growth of existing facilities.[48] The earliest major expansion occurred in the late 1040s, when a youthful and energetic Wang An-shih served as chief administrator of Ming-chou's prefectural seat at Yin. It was largely through his efforts that the prefectural school began to build up and employ a sizable body of locally distinguished teachers, while developing a reputation for scholastic excellence.[49] Contemporary writers are uncharacteristically parsimonious in providing information about the actual size and wealth of the local school at the height of its development in the late eleventh and early twelfth centuries. Local gazetteers nonetheless contain general statements about the school's overall evolution in Ming-chou and these suggest a high level of prosperity during the latter half of the Northern Sung. Indeed, by the reign of Hui-tsung, Ming-chou emerged as the center of education for the region.

With the expansion of educational opportunities, there began to develop an identifiable regional elite. Interestingly, its emergence appears to have had few direct links to the growing commercial wealth of Ming-chou. There is no indication that the more prominent of its members were originally of merchant background, although they inevitably benefited from the economic activity taking place around them. There is also nothing to suggest large landholdings among elite families. Wealth was clearly to be found among the socially privileged, but not conspicuous wealth. The key to their ascendancy was instead their training, first as scholars and then as officials. For the vast majority, this training was either secured at or enhanced by their identification with the prefectural school.[50] Following full implementation of the "three-levels" measure under Hui-tsung and with expanded opportunities for education, the local elite grew at an astounding speed. It is not mere coincidence that the political genesis of an important part, perhaps a majority, of Ming-chou's community of scholar-officials, can be traced to this era. Shattering this optimism, however, was the Jurchen invasion of 1130, which swept away so many of the political and intellectual accomplishments of preceding decades.

It was noted earlier that a good many of Ming-chou's leading families fled the area just prior to the Jurchen assault. Having lost their homes and valuables, most returned to begin anew. Except for a single structure, the entire prefectural school had been destroyed.[51] More important, in the chaos of flight and siege, officials lost track of vital school records pertaining to landholdings, without which it could not provide the usual salaries to instructors and stipends to students.[52] The school system, like the local elite, had incurred a heavy loss and it required at least a generation or two to recover. By the latter half of the twelfth century, however, the two resumed their former promise as Ming-chou came to assume a position of leadership in the empire.

Just as the political center of the empire shifted to the southeast during the Southern Sung, so intellectual activity also gravitated in that direction. Prior to this time, philosophers and classicists of Ming-chou were rarely known outside their own region. They instructed only a handful of local youth and had few ties with nationally renowned intellectuals or schools of thought.[53] This changed dramatically toward the close of the twelfth century, as the area gained increased political and intellectual exposure. During the reign of Hsiao-tsung (Chao Kuei, r. 1162–89), locals such as Shih Hao and Lou Yüeh (also read "Yao," 1137–1213) developed empirewide reputations for both their erudition as scholars and their influence as court officials.[54] From this point on, Ming-chou no longer remained on the empire's periphery; in fact, it would soon occupy center stage.

The intellectual fervor of the eleventh century—which ultimately inspired the Neo-Confucian (*Tao-hsüeh* or *li-hsüeh*) revival of the Southern Sung—had originally bypassed Ming-chou and, for that matter, most of the empire's southeast. Chou Tun-yi (1017–73), Shao Yung (1011–77), Chang Tsai (1020–77), Ch'eng Hao (1032–85), and Ch'eng Yi (1033–1108) were all natives of either northern or central China and their intellectual impact during the Northern Sung was concentrated in that region.[55] By the latter half of the twelfth century, there developed a renewed and invigorated interest in these masters and the larger issues that they had raised about the fundamentals of Confucian ideology. Unlike the earlier period, however, the geographic focus of this new intellectual movement had shifted away from the Chinese interior and toward the coast. It was here that the two most prominent figures in the Neo-Confucian revival, Chu Hsi (1130–1200) and Lu Chiu-yüan (1139–93), spent many of their mature years and exerted their greatest initial influence.[56]

Lu Chiu-yüan's idealist school was contemporaneous with the rationalist one of Chu Hsi, both beginning to flourish during the 1180s and 1190s. This coincided with the rising political prominence of Ming-chou and its sons. To the prefecture's good fortune, Lu Chiu-yüan acquired a home at Hsiang-shan subprefecture and taught in the vicinity for some time.[57] Not only did his presence attract scholars from near and far, but it also helped to stimulate the formation of an identifiable community of disciple-philosophers. Among the more accomplished of these were Yang Chien (1140–1226) and Yüan Hsieh (1144–1224), both of whom subsequently played leading roles in enlarging the impact of the idealist school upon the local as well as the national intelligentsia. Both Yang Chien and Yüan Hsieh had either studied with or served as minor officials under Master Lu, a native of Kiangsi, and may have even been responsible for initially drawing him to Hsiang-shan.[58] While in residence at Ming-chou, they were among his most respected disciples; after his death, they became major philosophers in their own right. Owing much to their efforts, the idealist school came to be centered at Ming-chou and eventually dominated its intellectual landscape. Private academies grew up around its teachings and students flocked there to study. The introduction of a new and vibrant philosophy contributed not only to the flourishing of education and the arts, but further enhanced the region's standing in the empire. From obscurity in the Northern Sung, the larger Ming-chou area was transformed a century later into a hub of intellectual activity. By the middle of the Southern Sung, its extraordinary success at producing both statesmen and philosophers of the highest caliber gave Ming-chou a reputation that few other cities could rival.

Among the most convenient measures of the social and political stature of a family or region is its *chin-shih* output.[59] In the case of Ming-chou in Sung times, these statistics reveal so very much about the timing and magnitude of its rise to prominence that a complete tabulation has been made. Appendix 1 contains a list of the total number of *chin-shih* from the region for each examination year beginning with 1057 (with summary totals for the pre-1057 period) and the *chin-shih* yield for Ming-chou is compared with yields for six other prefectures of comparable size and affluence in the same Che-tung/Che-hsi region.[60] The chart readily demonstrates several points.

First, with the exception of Ch'ang-chou, the *chin-shih* output of each prefecture realized a dramatic increase in the transition from Northern to Southern Sung. The yield for Soochow, Shao-hsing, and Hu-chou during the later period was virtually double its earlier yield. Lin-an tripled its previous output, while that for Chia-hsing quadrupled. Exceeding them all was Ming-chou: ending the Northern Sung with a mere 124 *chin-shih* (less than all its neighbors except Chia-hsing), it could claim almost 750 for the subsequent period—a sixfold increase. Even the imperial capital of Lin-an, with a population twice the size of Ming-chou, produced substantially fewer degreeholders. In the thirteenth century, these seven prefectures alone could represent as much as twenty percent of an empirewide examination list. It was unquestionably during this period that the central coastal area came to surpass most other regions in its production of *chin-shih*, a distinction that it continued to claim well into the sixteenth and seventeenth centuries.[61]

Second, only toward the end of the twelfth century did the *chin-shih* output for Ming-chou begin to accelerate to the point of eventually overtaking its neighbors. In this respect, its experience differed markedly from most other prefectures examined here, where degree yields suddenly increased from early in the Southern Sung and then were maintained at those high levels for the duration of the dynasty. In the aftermath of the war, Ming-chou entered the race with a handicap and required nearly a half-century to stake its claim to the many bureaucratic vacancies created by the loss of North China and the withdrawal of many northerners from the civil service.

Another salient point revealed by our tabulation is the ratio of Ming-chou's *chin-shih* output to empirewide totals. During the brief period of the Northern Sung for which there exists complete data (that is, 1100–1124), we know that the region's yield was never more than 1 percent of the empire's total output. A century later, it had so swelled that Ming-chou residents sometimes occupied as much as 10 percent of one examination list.[62] The exaggerated position of its influence is better appreciated when one considers that Ming-chou probably contained no more than 1.5 percent of the total Southern Sung population.[63] That a minority of this size should rise to such political and intellectual supremacy is as puzzling as it is inspiring.

A further indicator of Ming-chou preeminence is its yield of high officials. During the Northern Sung, not one of its inhabitants received advancement to the highest levels of the bureaucracy, chief councillor or assistant councillor. This stands in stark contrast with its performance at the southern court, where five chief councillors and ten assistant councillors are identified with this single prefecture.[64] In fact, the political influence of these men became so preponderant that Ming-chou natives, for nearly half of the thirteenth century, held a firm grip on the top leadership positions at Lin-an, with power passing from one provincial to another in a fashion quite uncharacteristic of Sung civil service practice. To a great extent, a region's *chin-shih* and high-official outputs are interrelated: without the degree, advancement to top posts in the bureaucracy is extremely difficult. In the case of Ming-chou, it produced high officials mainly because it first produced a large body of men with credentials to hold high office. All of the chief councillors and all but one of the assistant councillors from the area held the all-important *chin-shih* degree.[65]

The extraordinary success of Ming-chou natives in the Southern Sung capital relates, additionally, to a much larger trend that set in following prolonged separation of north and south: the trend toward regional provincialism. Inevitably, the loss of North China was certain to affect, in some measure, the geographic representation of officials in Lin-an's civil service—unless, of course, the government chose to intercede to turn the tide. This it did not do and, as a result, the bureaucracy came to be overrun with southerners. The trend is well documented in appendix 2. Chief councillors during the reign of Kao-tsung came from various parts of China, including the north, southeast, and even the southwest. The principal reason for their diversity appears to be that many of Kao-tsung's early appointees were northerners who once served his predecessors at K'ai-feng and after 1126 chose to join him in the lower Yangtze. To the extent that their mere presence at Lin-an lent legitimacy to the Sung government in exile, such immigrants were afforded considerable prestige and readily advanced to visible posts in the bureaucracy. Yet, they must have been short in supply. The rapidity with which the Jurchen seized control no doubt mitigated against a mass exodus of Chinese from the north and later treaty commitments made migration after 1141 extremely difficult.[66] By the next reign, southerners had already come to monopolize the bureaucracy's top post; the court of Hsiao-tsung had not even one chief councillor who can be identified as a northerner. For the duration of the dynasty, in fact, only a single councillor had such ties;[67] the remainder were all natives of the south.

More important than merely the "southernization" of the bureaucracy's leadership is the emergence of another trend that is far more difficult to explain. Beginning with the Hsiao-tsung era and continuing throughout the Li-tsung (1224–64) and Tu-tsung (1264–74) reigns, men from the single Liang-che region came to dominate, even monopolize, the chief councillorship. The court of Kao-tsung may have contained an exceptionally large concentration of councillors from the southeast, but they were distributed rather evenly among its several circuits. Already by the reign of Hsiao-tsung, more than one-third of the councillors were natives of Liang-che; subsequently, at least half came from this area. Beyond sheer numbers, it can be observed that the tenures of Liang-che natives also tended to be exceptionally long. For roughly twenty-one of Ning-tsung's thirty years (1194–1224), for thirty-three of Li-tsung's forty years, and for all of Tu-tsung's ten years on the throne, at least one of the two chief councillor seats were occupied by men from Liang-che.[68] Even Fukien, which produced a good many degreeholders and prominent statesmen in Northern Sung times, wielded noticeably little influence at the court in Lin-an. To some extent, this development may have surfaced as an outgrowth of power politics; certain chief councillors were infamous for exploiting their influence at court to secure the future advancement of fellow provincials.[69] The pervasiveness of the trend, however, suggests that responsibility does not rest with the personal influence of just one or two men. Quite probably, this is related to a much more sweeping regionalism that began to emerge at the very outset of the Southern Sung, the central government being so preoccupied with military matters that it tolerated a far greater measure of local autonomy than had ever been possible during the Northern Sung—note the high incidence of regional officials serving in or near their native places. And local autonomy can well induce isolation of court and bureaucracy. Although a more definitive assessment of the reasons for this development must await future research, one important impact is already quite clear. The tendency of the court at Lin-an, in selecting bureaucratic chiefs, not to look much beyond the circuit in which the capital is located gave officials from that circuit an unfair advantage over others in the competition for advancement. Certainly, this applies to natives of Ming-chou. The proximity of their home to the capital at this special period in Chinese history virtually ensured them a place of prominence at court.

Ming-chou was the home of many promising families during the Southern Sung. The Lou and Shih houses counted among the most nationally renowned, yet the imperial Chao clan clearly surpassed them all in sheer numbers. Originally immigrating from North China amid the chaos accompanying the collapse of the Northern Sung, the Chao did not become especially noteworthy in their new home until the 1150s. It was about this time that the clan began producing a noticeable number of *chin-shih*. The output grew with time and, by the end of the Southern Sung, the Chao could claim over 140 degreeholders.[70] The royal blood and literary attainments of the clan certainly made it the "first family" of Ming-chou but a long-standing policy that discouraged the advancement of imperial clansmen to top positions in the bureaucracy prevented them from ever wielding much political power in the capital.[71]

The Lou house also prospered, although on a different scale. Its progenitor, Lou Yü, was an immigrant from K'ai-feng who later became a noted teacher at the Ming-chou prefectural school during the middle of the eleventh century.[72] The Lou produced seven *chin-shih* in Northern Sung times and over thirty in the subsequent period;[73] Lou Yüeh even rose to empirewide prominence as assistant councillor. The house commanded the respect of many locals for its various attainments in literature and the classics but, much like the imperial Chao clan, its literary accomplishments were not matched in the political arena.

In contrast with the Chao and Lou houses, the Shih were socially and politically quite insignificant for most of the Northern Sung.[74] Initially as poor as it was small, it did not produce its first degreeholder until the close of the Northern Sung—and even then almost by a miracle. After gaining momentum, however, the Shih eventually produced the greatest success story in Sung history. When the dynasty came to an end in 1279, twenty-eight kinsmen held regular *chin-shih* degrees; in turn, the Shih supplied the court with three consecutive generations of chief councillors and over two hundred ranked officials. Members of the Shih house dominated the court at Lin-an for much of the early thirteenth century and the political power they wielded had few parallels in their time. Although not necessarily as large, at least initially, as some other well-known kin groups in the area, the Shih surpassed them all as civil servants. More than any other member of the local elite, it was the Shih who made Ming-chou the political nucleus of the empire. Unfortunately, fame easily breeds resentment and infamy. These too were part of the Shih legacy.

2

Dredging the Stream

THE ORDEAL PERHAPS most oner-
ous and least fruitful for the researcher of families in Sung times is that of
uncovering their roots in earlier periods. The disappearance of the hereditary elite during the ninth and tenth centuries and their subsequent
replacement, at least in the political arena, by professional bureaucrats
effectively undermined the once-flourishing tradition of compiling
genealogies. With family background no longer so crucial to bureaucratic
access and social standing, few felt the need to maintain detailed histories
of their kin group. This writer knows of no extant genealogy dating from
Sung times; either they were rarely compiled or simply not preserved.
There is evidence to suggest, especially during the tenth and early eleventh centuries, that most lineages bothered neither to preserve old genealogies nor to compile new ones. Reflecting this pervasive indifference, one
writer has observed that even specialists of genealogical inquiry during
the Northern Sung frequently could not trace the ancestry of a contemporary much earlier than the Five Dynasties period[1]—there simply existed
too little material to draw upon. With genealogical nescience so prevalent
in the north, the former hub of China's aristocratic tradition, it must have
been even more pronounced in the south, where immigrant concentra-
tions tended to be higher and society more fluid.

MIGRATION

For more than half of the tenth century, China was politically divided.
The north suffered from almost incessant warfare, as five major dynasties

rose and fell. Devastated in its aftermath, the region lost its long-standing position of economic and social preeminence, one that it never regained. South China, in contrast, remained relatively stable throughout this period. Leaders of its ten kingdoms appear to have lacked either the will or the wherewithal to challenge neighboring states; the consequent tranquility enabled the economy to prosper.[2] Small wonder that one migrant wave after another fled the war-torn north in search of refuge there. For the noble and ignoble alike, abandonment of their ancestral homes symbolized a decisive break with the past. It led to a severance, not merely of communication, but also identification with former kinsmen and lineal traditions. In the absence of any meaningful contact with the old home, it became much easier for these migrants to perceive themselves as genuine southerners, not just northerners residing in the south.

Like recent immigrants from the north, long-time natives of the south also tended to know little about their ancestry. Prior to the T'ang dynasty, official appointment south of the Yangtze represented cruel punishment, the farther south the more severe. Admittedly, this attitude did begin to change during the late T'ang, when an ever-widening flow of migrants made their way south out of choice, not coercion. However, the region continued to be regarded as remote and inhospitable, with many of its residents either disfavored officials or hard-pressed peasants. From all appearances, the aristocratic families living there during the Six Dynasties period lacked both the political influence and the social esteem of their counterparts in the north. Further exacerbating the identity problem of southerners was the fact that, even within the lower Yangtze region, migration could be uncommonly frequent, as families might well be uprooted several times over a relatively short span of time. This must have been especially true for Liang-che circuit during the tenth and eleventh centuries, where population pressures created by the steady flow of immigrants from the north compelled many families close to the border to move progressively farther south. Also encouraging geographic mobility was the higher concentration of commercial activity in the area and fluctuations in the demand for labor inherent to such an economy. For these various reasons, a cohesive and stable "regional elite" should have had far more difficulty prospering in the lower Yangtze, at least prior to the Sung. By the end of the eleventh century, however, local communities of scholar-officials did emerge and its members, anxious about community acceptance, often identified themselves with some illustrious house of antiquity in order to enhance their own prestige. Most such efforts proved utterly futile. Lacking the meticulousness that once characterized genealogical inquiry, the tracing of a kin group to its pre-Sung roots could be unabashedly haphazard and presumptuous. The Shih of Ming-chou are quite representative in this regard.

Tradition has it that the Shih of Yin subprefecture (*hsien*) descended from the esteemed Shih house of Li-yang *hsien*, located just southeast of present-day Nanking in western Kiangsu province. The Li-yang Shih of early imperial times were undeniably aristocrats. Although not especially prominent in court politics, they claimed a history of official service and prestigious ennoblements dating back to the Han dynasty.[3] Sometime during the transition from Five Dynasties to Sung, Shih Wei-tse, an official of the T'ang court and an accomplished literatus, reportedly migrated from Li-yang to the Ming-chou region, with the prefectural seat at Yin *hsien* eventually becoming his home. He fathered Shih Ch'eng (generation one); Shih Ch'eng fathered Shih Chien (generation two); Shih Chien fathered Shih Chao (generation three); and so forth. Thus, it is alleged that the Shih of Ming-chou represent an offshoot of an old and established house with a tradition of literary excellence and official service spanning more than a thousand years. The boast, not a modest one, may well contain an element of truth, yet there is good reason for suspicion.

The only link between the Li-yang and Ming-chou houses is the "famous" Shih Wei-tse. Sources on the early history of the Ming-chou Shih—the most detailed of which were written nearly a millennium later —assert that Shih Wei-tse once served as Han-lin academician during the last years of the T'ang and gained an empirewide reputation for his literary achievements. A thorough combing of extant historical works nonetheless fails to document the existence of such an individual at that particular time. Needless to say, this is curious, especially in light of the individual's alleged prominence. There does exist, however, mention in an eleventh-century source of a well-known writer by that name who lived a few centuries earlier. In a collection of colophons to T'ang dynasty inscriptions, Ou-yang Hsiu (1007–70), an accomplished historian and master poet-calligrapher, makes frequent reference to Shih Wei-tse, the master of *pa-fen* (eight part) calligraphy. These colophons leave little doubt that the calligrapher in question lived in the mid-eighth century, not the tenth, and resided in southern Kiangsu, not coastal Chekiang.[4] It is thus humanly impossible for him to have founded a family in Ming-chou during the tenth century, as some writers insist. At the same time, the name is most uncommon and the possibility of there existing two different men sharing the name Shi Wei-tse—both accomplished literati from the southern Kiangsu region—is next to nil. It may be assumed that there existed only one Shih Wei-tse, not two, and that the Shih of Sung times, in their impetuousness to latch onto a prominent name, unwittingly placed an eighth-century figure in the tenth.

An error of this sort has two important implications. First, the Ming-chou Shih either knew little of their true origins or had reason to conceal this information; in any event, the claim of descent from Shih Wei-tse represents an act of desperation. This suggests a dearth of reliable documents on the pre-Sung origins of the kin group. Second, such imprecision in tracing ancestral roots implies that the art of genealogical investigation had declined to an all-time low in Sung times, and especially in the Northern Sung. So obvious an error of placement could hardly have occurred during the aristocratic age of the past.

Others share my conviction that the Ming-chou Shih were genuinely ignorant of their origins prior to the eleventh century. Cheng Chen, a native of Ming-chou during the fourteenth century and an individual with close ties to Shih kinsmen of that time, states, "It is reported that [only] when the Sung was in its eastern capital [of K'ai-feng] did the Shih house of Yin begin to record that it actually descended from the famous Wei-tse of Ch'ang-an [subsequently Li-yang]."[5]

There is not a shred of evidence linking the Ming-chou group to either Shih Wei-tse or the Li-yang Shih; then again, this may not completely justify rejecting outright their claim to be related, however distantly, to the once noble family. It may well be that the Ming-chou Shih descended from a less eminent scion of the Li-yang house. In either case, the new house clearly does not represent a part of some "hereditary elite." Researchers have proven that dispersion usually occurs when an extended kin group has grown beyond its ability to support itself, causing less successful kinsmen to seek a livelihood elsewhere.[6] It is poverty, not affluence, that propels this fission. The Ming-chou group, if genuinely related to the Li-yang house, was probably founded by one of its more destitute members, surely not a successful scholar like Shih Wei-tse. In the final analysis, the existence of ties between the two houses is a moot point. No less than other immigrant households, the burden of beginning anew was a heavy one for the small household at Ming-chou. Having broken former ties with the outside, it faced an uncertain future alone.

FACING EXTINCTION

The earliest Shih kinsman who can be traced to Ming-chou is Shih Ch'eng.[7] Little is known about him save that he first married a woman of the Ch'en family and subsequently one surnamed Jen. Historical and genealogical sources tend to be equally uninformative about his life, occupation, or community standing, stating merely that the merit of a great-grandson led to the posthumous conferral of official rank. That he was not a man of much social importance seems irrefutable. While the name of Shih Wei-tse may have preceded Shih Ch'eng in the kin group's ancestral temple, Shih Ch'eng was the first kinsman to receive posthumous honors from the court. For this reason, he is taken here to represent the progenitor of the Ming-chou house. According to genealogical sources, Shih Ch'eng was the father of three boys.[8] The eldest, Shih Shu (n.d.), died without issue. Youngest son Shih Han reportedly had one son and two grandsons, but they all abandoned Ming-chou early on—for reasons not altogether clear—never to be heard from again. The entire Shih community of later times thus represents descendants of middle son Shih Chien (1034?–58), the earliest figure for whom a sizable body of material exists.[9]

With reasonable certainty, it may be said that Shih Chien served in some clerical capacity at the local sheriff's office. He died rather young, apparently in his mid-twenties, leaving behind an ailing son, a young daughter, and a pregnant wife, née Yeh (1033–1118). The death of the son followed soon after that of Shih Chien, at which point biographers portray the widow as extremely distraught, tormented by the prospect of the Shih line meeting an untimely end. Relief came a few months later when she gave birth to another boy, Shih Chao (1058–1130). Upon his shoulders then fell the heavy burden of perpetuating the family.

Beyond the brief outlines of this melodramatic account lies much historical discrepancy and debate about the nature of Shih Chien's clerical duties and the reasons for his premature demise. Two sources from the Sung period contain references to Shih Chien, but they mention him only by name and provide no detailed information about his life and background. One is an imperially sponsored tomb inscription for a fifth-generation descendant (Shih Hao) and the other a biography of his wife in a local gazetteer.[10] The first dates from the closing years of the twelfth century; the second was written some three decades later, at a time when Shih kinsmen had reached the pinnacle of power and prestige. That both sources should avoid discussion of Shih Chien, despite their lengthy biographies of his wife and great-grandson, certainly justifies suspicion. Interestingly, a rather detailed colophon to a tomb inscription extolling the virtues of the widow Yeh, written during the early thirteenth century, refers to the widow's great-great-grandsons without so much as mentioning the name of her husband.[11] Could it be that these writers simply knew nothing about Shih Chien, or did the Shih kinsmen at the time insist upon the omission for some reason, perhaps out of shame? A source from the Yüan dynasty suggests that the latter motive was indeed the prevailing one.

An early fourteenth-century gazetteer for Ming-chou compiled by a native of the area and an accomplished historian, Yüan Chüeh (1267–1327), provides the earliest known account of Shih Chien's life.[12] In the biography of the widow Yeh contained in his Yen-yu gazetteer, he reports that husband Shih Chien was no ordinary clerk, but a flogger at the sheriff's office. The sheriff, we are told, was a strongman of sorts who customarily accepted bribes from locals to intimidate their enemies or to prosecute personal vendettas on their behalf. After engineering the conviction of his victims on fictitious charges, he would order subordinate Shih Chien to administer the appropriate flogging. Unlike the sheriff, however, Shih Chien is portrayed as a just man whose uncompromising conscience led him to sympathize with his hapless prey. At one point, sentimentality got the better of him and he refused to obey instructions. Replacing heavy with light blows, he attempted to deceive his superior by covering his club with a blood-colored substance and making his intended victim appear to be suffering miserably when actually he was not. The sheriff, although blindly wicked, was sufficiently clever to uncover the ploy and ordered instead the flogging of Shih Chien. A few days later, he reportedly died from the injuries sustained. Thus, according to this account, Shih Chien was no more than a "stalwart man" who lived and died in humiliation.[13]

The controversial story of Yüan Chüeh did not go uncriticized, especially among Ch'ing scholars (1644–1911). Ch'üan Tsu-wang (1705–55) is perhaps most prominent among these critics.[14] Like Yüan Chüeh, he was a native of Ming-chou and a noted historian. While admitting that

Shih Chien probably served in some clerical capacity at the sheriff's office, Ch'üan Tsu-wang refutes the whole notion of his being a common flogger. On the contrary, he asserts that the Shih founder represents a locally acclaimed scholar and the "able disciple" of the prefectural school instructor Lou Yü (n.d.). The explanation that he offers for the untimely death of Shih Chien, however, is hardly a convincing one. He records, "[Shih Chien] served his mother with utmost filial devotion. He once spent his [entire] savings to rent a boat and [take her] sailing along the [West] Lake; but his superior was a common man who became angered at finding that he [had taken leave] without permission and fired him. Consequently, Shih Chien became despondent and died."[15]

No historian before Ch'üan Tsu-wang is known to have put forth this version of Shih Chien's life and death. He does not reveal his source, yet similar interpretations appear only in genealogical material, strongly suggesting that this represents an oral tradition preserved by eighteenth-century descendants of the Shih and then told to him.[16] The close association of Ch'üan Tsu-wang with several Ch'ing descendants of the Sung kin group also serves to confirm the suspicion that the Shih house is the source of this account.[17] As for the account in the Yen-yu gazetteer, it may well be based upon an oral tradition as well. Bibliographers of the mid-Ch'ing, in their *Ssu-k'u ch'üan-shu tsung-mu t'i-yao* (Annotated Catalogue of the Imperial Library), note that Yüan Chüeh was reputedly *the* most avid compiler of anecdotes in fourteenth-century Ming-chou.[18] No doubt, from this collection derived much of the information used in his Yen-yu gazetteer, including the biography of the widow Yeh. Consequently, reports by Yüan Chüeh and Ch'üan Tsu-wang must be held equally suspect.

It should be no surprise that post-Sung information on the ancestry of the Ming-chou Shih is of such dubious quality for, even in Sung times, Shih kinsmen knew little of their forebears just a few generations removed. In his colophon to a newly composed tomb inscription for the widow Yeh, author Lou Yüeh indicated that her original tombstone was destroyed during the Jurchen invasion of 1130 and never seen again.[19] In fact, all family memorabilia reportedly disappeared at that time. The only record of the widow and her life that had been preserved into the early thirteenth century consisted of one recently uncovered book, which itself had been reduced to virtual ashes when examined by Lou Yüeh and was barely intelligible. The tidbits of information contained in this work gave the Shih community its first, and seemingly only, glimpse into her life and times. Lou Yüeh's colophon to the inscription, like the inscription itself, was based in part upon this record and in part upon an oral tradition maintained by the kin group for over a century and then conveyed to him by one of its members around 1206. With sources on the kin group's early history of such limited quantity and questionable authenticity already by the middle of the Southern Sung, there is little to warrant our confidence in the conjecture of later historians.

Setting aside questions about Shih Chien's profession and the circumstances surrounding his death, it is fairly certain that he was poor and left behind little personal wealth. Both Sung and Yüan gazetteers for Ming-chou allude to the widow Yeh, in the aftermath of her husband's death, working long hours at home as a seamstress to support her children.[20] She ate and dressed simply, while rejecting the advice of friends to lighten her burden by remarrying. "Whereas others found her anguish unbearable," we are told, "the widow was self-possessed [in spite of it]."[21] Yet the thirteenth-century Pao-ch'ing gazetteer implies that, although financially pressed, the widow was nonetheless reasonably literate, for she allegedly taught son Shih Chao to read.[22] The Yen-yu gazetteer makes no mention of this, attributing Shih Chao's education instead to a local teacher.[23] The distinction is an important one due to its obvious implications with respect to the social background of the widow, and implicitly, her husband.

Rather than historical data, it is probably the future standing of the kin group that divulges most about the social origins of Shih Chien. Stalwart men were at the lowest end of Sung China's subbureaucracy, with clerks at the prefectural or subprefectural office near the top.[24] Their duties necessitated that clerks be at least semiliterate. Scholar-officials may have held them in contempt because they had no classical training, were not steeped in the moral precepts of Confucianism, and held no official degree, yet their literacy set them apart from the common man and this gave them distinct advantages in the struggle for upward mobility. As an urban group afforded the opportunity to interact regularly with the scholar-official elite, clerks could more easily gain admission to the local school or win the favor of a local teacher and thereby be trained for the regular civil service.[25] Stalwart men, in contrast, were almost invariably illiterates with few prospects for bettering their lot. Under ordinary circumstances, a woman like the widow Yeh—possessing some measure of education and strong convictions about Confucian morality—is not likely to have married such a man. Later, the son of Shih Chien, encountering little apparent objection, was able to study under a locally prominent teacher and become a respected member of the community. The offspring of a mere flogger is not likely to be so readily accepted by the local elite.

Balancing these various factors, our composite picture of the Shih family during the latter half of the eleventh century is as follows. It possessed a smattering of education, but probably not very advanced. It remained outside the local elite, but was nonetheless set apart from mere peasants by virtue of its limited literacy. It had a history of service with the subbureaucracy, perhaps even in a demeaning capacity, but such service was probably just temporary. Its members were relatively poor, but not to the extent that the widow Yeh had to compromise her virtue and remarry. Most dubious are allegations that Shih Chien was a mere flogger, because they fail to explain how such an outcast could sire a family capable of such rapid mobility. No less incredulous are assertions that he was extraordinarily learned, for they fail to explain why he should stoop to work as a clerk for the sheriff. His real identity will never be known, but it probably lies somewhere between these two extremes.

FROM CLERK TO LOCAL NOTABLE

With the demise of Shih Chien, the fate of the Shih line rested with a baby, Shih Chao. The single surviving brother of Shih Chien, Shih Han, is never mentioned in historical sources and he may well have already migrated elsewhere by this time. (The naming pattern adopted for his sons suggests as much.) With the widow Yeh functioning as head of the household, whatever rudimentary education the son received at home must have come from her. Once an adult, Shih Chao became more involved with the literati of his community, the most prominent of these associates being an instructor at the prefectural school, Lou Yü.[26] There is nothing to indicate his formal identification with either this school or, for that matter, any local academy, yet, from his association with Lou Yü it may be inferred that Shih Chao was not simply literate, but reasonably well educated. Perhaps, as Yüan Chüeh asserts, the widow paid Lou Yü to tutor her son. Or maybe, as Ch'üan Tsu-wang suggests, it was through his father's former relationship with the schoolmaster that the younger Shih was able to turn to him for training.[27] In any event, he gradually became a learned and respected member of his community, enjoying a status well above semi-literate clerks. Although a promising youth, Shih Chao's perennial devotion to his mother precluded exploitation of the growing opportunities around him for further education and official advancement. He refused to follow in his father's footsteps and work for the local government. In fact, he is said to have meticulously shunned most involvements outside the home for fear of being separated from his mother.

Spending much of his life in near seclusion, Shih Chao's occupational means of support is a mystery. Even more mysterious are allusions to the economic standing of the widow Yeh having dramatically improved in her later years.[28] How can a single woman with two young children, apparently without other kin and living in virtual isolation, manage to accumulate wealth? There is no indication that the family either began with or later acquired parcels of land, the traditional source of wealth in imperial China. Yet, for an urban family, this is hardly surprising. Being a man with a modest education, Shih Chao may have occasionally worked for hire, accepting temporary employment as a local scribe, a composer of burial inscriptions, or a tutor for local youths, but odd jobs of this sort tended to generate little wealth. Interestingly, local gazetteers do allude to the widow having raised several girls, in addition to her own daughter, ostensibly to help out with weaving chores.[29] While this is portrayed as largely an act of charity, it is tempting to cast the widow in the mold of a petty entrepreneur who runs a small weaving enterprise at home and adopts girls to secure cheap labor. That family riches might thereby be related to the enterprising resourcefulness of one woman, the widow Yeh—beyond its implications with respect to the role of women in traditional Chinese society—also suggests that neither speculation in land nor civil service involvement were responsible for the early ascendancy of the Shih house. Even so, the family appears not to have retained this commercial orientation for long, as it is never again associated with weaving and crafts. Furthermore, the wealth generated by the weaving business must have been modest, for the widow's eldest great-grandson, born during her last years, was once described as "destitutely poor."[30] The widow became well-to-do, therefore, only in relation to the straitened circumstances of her past.

Beyond his economic standing, the social standing of Shih Chao also improved with time. In 1107, when the Sung court ordered that local exemplars of the "eight virtues of conduct" be recommended for eventual promotion to the Imperial University, regional officials at Ming-chou enthusiastically supported Shih Chao.[31] This nomination raises yet another insolvable question. Shih Chao never took an official examination, never produced a scholarly work, and never studied at the local school. He had proven himself as neither a scholar nor a community leader. By what criteria did local authorities decide to select him as Ming-chou's model of Confucian morality and its most promising son? Could it be, as biographical materials insist, that his unusual filial devotion was alone responsible for enhancing his status locally and winning the recommendation? This seems so incredible yet, lacking evidence to the contrary, the incredible must be accepted as containing some kernel of truth.

The lure of office and prestige notwithstanding, Shih Chao refused the offer. Nearly fifty years old by this time, he remained true to his creed, vowing never to leave his mother's side.[32] In the process, he relinquished an opportunity that could have given him official status. Despite his declination, the selection alone did much to enhance Shih Chao's standing in Ming-chou. Fellow villagers subsequently referred to him as "Pa-hsing hsien-sheng" (Mr. Eight Virtues of Conduct), a term of reverence that continued to be identified with the man for centuries to come.

Shih Chao had five sons, most of whom became not just good students, but also promising aspirants for the civil service. As the Shih house grew, it flourished as none other in the region. Moralistic biographers credited later prosperity to the virtue of its progenitors. The widow Yeh's enduring loyalty to her husband, despite the personal sacrifice that this entailed, made her the region's earliest and most noted "woman of virtue." Similarly, Shih Chao's lifelong devotion to his mother earned for him the admiration of community leaders and their recommendation for government service. To contemporaries, heaven rewarded the widow and her son by making their descendants successful. Nearly a century after their deaths, eulogist Lou Yüeh wrote, "When [a tree's] roots are firm, then its leaves will abound; when a stream is deep, then its flow will be long."[33] Apart from heaven, it is clear that society also rewarded the morally upright in a tangible way. Virtuous conduct served to enhance community standing that, in the case of Shih Chao, also provided an opportunity to enter the civil service. The flow of the Shih family, therefore, did indeed owe much to the moral dredging of the widow and her son.

Shih Chao's selection under the "eight virtues of conduct" program gave a major lift to his family's social and political climb. Had he chosen to enter the Imperial University in 1107, the leap from the ranks of clerks to scholar-officials could have been made within just one generation. A tiny household without a degreeholder or an official, the Shih of the late eleventh and early twelfth centuries were still on the fringes of the local elite, but this would not last for long.

GENERATION FOUR: THE EARLY YEARS

Chronologically, the five sons of Shih Chao were: Shih Shih-chung (1082–1124), Shih Ts'ai (d. 1162), Shih Mu (d. 1130), Shih Ho (n.d.), and Shih Kuang (n.d.).[34] Each of the five achieved some modicum of education yet, unlike their father, did not shy away from but eagerly pursued community involvement and government service. To their good fortune, political and institutional changes occurring in a distant capital brought unforeseen opportunity to their home.

The sons of Shih Chao matured during the reign of Emperor Hui-tsung, when the government had abandoned its official examination in favor of the "three-levels" program. As mentioned earlier, this was designed to place the prefectural school at the center of bureaucratic recruitment by allowing its best students to be promoted to the Imperial University, there to qualify for a *chin-shih* degree and to receive official appointment.[35] The change must have been a welcome one for families with limited resources. With both the prefectural school and the Imperial University being publicly funded institutions, the burden of educating sons and preparing them for government service was appreciably lessened, enabling many to become bureaucratic hopefuls for the first time. This is confirmed by the Shih experience. Despite its political obscurity and lack of great wealth, in a short span of time the family was able to train each of its five youth for the civil service, all during the Hui-tsung era.

Eldest son Shih Shih-chung, like his brothers, initially received instruction from father Shih Chao before going on to attend the prefectural school.[36] Success there led to his promotion to the Imperial University, where we are told Shih Shih-chung was elevated to its upper division, just one step short of conferral of an official degree. A promising future, however, was cut short by death at the age of forty-two. Unfortunately, little else is known about him.

Second son Shih Ts'ai similarly took advantage of the "three-levels" program to enter the Imperial University, where he surpassed his elder brother and earned *chin-shih* status in 1118.[37] The family's first degree-holder also became its first official. Immediately after obtaining the degree, Shih Ts'ai was appointed assistant subprefect of Ch'u-chou in southern Chekiang. This apparently represents his only assignment under the K'ai-feng government. Following Jurchen expulsion of the Sung court from North China, he returned home to serve briefly as sheriff (*wei*, 9b) in nearby Yü-yao subprefecture. Then came the Jurchen invasion of Ming-chou.

The exact whereabouts of Shih Ts'ai at the time is uncertain; it may be that he was busy with his chores as sheriff. What *is* known with certainty is that his younger brothers were with the family at home. In fact, Shih Mu played a prominent role in organizing local rescue efforts. One late twelfth-century biographer records that the younger Shih spent his entire savings to rent boats in the vicinity to carry family and friends from the endangered Ming-chou to safety on the high seas. As a result, some two thousand lives were reportedly spared.[38] While the personal contribution of Shih Mu to the mission may be a bit exaggerated,[39] the account remains useful for its revelations about the size and character of the mass exodus that took place. Not only did the entire Shih family flee Ming-chou, but one of its sons helped coordinate the rescue mission. This suggests that the Shih had already begun to play a leadership role in their community by 1130, even though, as novices to the civil service, they were lacking in political status.

Shih Chao's youngest sons—Shih Mu, Shih Ho, and Shih Kuang —returned to Ming-chou after the enemy had withdrawn, no doubt to help in the rebuilding of their home and to restore stability to the family. Although Shih Mu and Shih Ho probably studied for awhile at the prefectural school during the Northern Sung, its destruction in 1130 prevented them from continuing their education there. Meanwhile, reinstitution of competitive examinations for official recruitment under the southern government required readjustment to the old system, with its emphasis on literary skill. These setbacks notwithstanding, the two subsequently attempted to secure degrees by taking the prefectural examinations. Both succeeded, with Shih Mu's performance so distinguished that his name appeared at the top of the list, but fate was against them, for neither cleared the elimination process in the capital.[40] It was not long after the Jurchen invasion and Shih Chao's death that son Shih Mu also died.[41]

This apparently thrust upon the shoulders of Shih Ho and Shih Kuang the entire responsibility for educating the next generation, some thirteen males in all, a responsibility made all the more weighty by the demise of the prefectural school. Consequently, the younger Shih brothers spent the remainder of their lives with a new generation of kinsmen in Ming-chou, never to be heard of again. In the interim, brother Shih Ts'ai was away advancing his career.

SHIH TS'AI IN THE CAPITAL

The death of his father in 1130 prompted Shih Ts'ai temporarily to return home for the customary two to three years of mourning. Upon fulfilling his filial obligation, he was restored to government service as subprefect (*chih-hsien*) for Yü-hang (8b), located in the Lin-an metropolitan area, and subsequently for Yung-chia, administratively subordinate to modern Wen-chou.[42] It was apparently while serving at Yung-chia (in the late 1130s) that he came to know the prefect for the region, Li Kuang (1078–1159).[43] Their association must have been quite brief, as the prefect was soon summoned to the capital to serve as assistant councillor, but fateful nonetheless. Shih Ts'ai, having left a positive impression with his superior, readily won the sponsorship of Li Kuang, and this was indispensable to further promotion in the civil service.[44]

To the misfortune of Shih Ts'ai, Li Kuang held onto his new post for no more than one year when factional strife culminated in dismissal and eventual disgrace. This was undeniably a setback for Shih Ts'ai, who simply disappeared from the political arena for most of the 1140s. Nothing is known of his whereabouts at that time; perhaps he withdrew from the bureaucracy to wait out the political war in the capital. When he resurfaced in 1151, it was as registrar at the Directorate of Education (*Kuo-tzu-chien chu-pu*, 8b),[45] a post with rank no higher than that held by him in the 1130s. Being a metropolitan post, however, it enabled him to interact with influential figures at court and to try his hand at power politics for the first time.

There is some discussion in the preceding chapter of the disruption caused by the Jurchen occupation of North China and the serious threat they posed to the southern empire. Needless to say, a desperate Lin-an was willing to pay most any price to end hostilities, including permanent relinquishment of the sacred mission of regaining the north. Without broaching a prolonged discussion of the evolution of the war-peace controversy, let it simply be said that Emperor Kao-tsung, by the mid-1130s, obviously favored a negotiated settlement and endorsed Chief councillor Ch'in Kuei (also read "Kuai," d. 1155) in his efforts to secure this.[46] In 1138 the chief councillor finally lured the Jurchen into a peace pact and, in the process, served his own interests by undermining the position of his critics at court, represented by revanchists Chang Chün (1097–1164) and Chao Ting (d. 1147). Faced with a fait accompli, much of the opposition chose to resign, while many others were humiliated with dismissal. The pacifists prevailed.

Despite his growing stature in the capital and the throne's unequivocal support for the peace agreement,[47] Ch'in Kuei still drew much personal criticism. To offset this and to lend an element of legitimacy to his policies, he anxiously sought out reputable officials to serve under him in high office. These were generally men who favored peace, but not necessarily mere lackeys. Apparently, the chief councillor would accept limited criticism from subordinates to the extent that association with these men had something to offer him in return. Li Kuang, the sponsor of Shih Ts'ai, is a good case in point. He was an outspoken advocate of peace and contemporaries also knew him as a man of integrity worthy of their respect —factors that, for Ch'in Kuei, made him a highly attractive recruit. The marriage, however, was one of convenience and it disintegrated after scarcely one year. Coming into conflict with Ch'in Kuei over the methods of implementing peace, Li Kuang was summarily dismissed from his post. Before long, the political conflict between the two men degenerated into a personal squabble, with the chief councillor launching a highly vindictive campaign against his former subordinate.[48]

Once a new and lasting peace was concluded in 1141, a more confident Ch'in Kuei began to tighten his grip on the bureaucracy. Although still interested in attracting competent and reputable officials to high office, he became less tolerant of those with differing opinions, cynically concluding that such persons were acting more out of personal ambition than political idealism. He also jealously guarded his relationship with the throne, permitting no one to get close enough to the emperor to win his confidence. Thus, Ch'in Kuei insisted on limiting the tenure of high-ranking officials who, with regular access to the throne, might conceivably undermine his influence. Bureaucratic turnover during these years was especially high. To remove from office potential threats, Ch'in Kuei regularly turned to the Censorate or related agencies, where he could always trust his allies to build up a case for indictment. In turn, those censors who rendered loyal service were often rewarded with promotion to executive posts in the bureaucracy, often replacing the same individuals they had been responsible for unseating. Before long, the quickest route to advancement came through indictment of the chief councillor's perceived or potential enemies, and high officials became popular targets. It was a game that many an ambitious official learned to play, including Shih Ts'ai.

As noted, the first assignment given to Shih Ts'ai in the capital was with the Directorate of Education. Although his position there as registrar carried little political weight, it did provide a platform for expressing his views on government and Shih Ts'ai did not pass up the opportunity. After addressing the throne on a minor issue relating to official etiquette at court,[49] he caught the eye of Censor Sung P'u (n.d.), who later recommended his advancement to a low-level post at the Censorate.[50] This was followed almost immediately by promotions to policy monitor of the right (yu cheng-yen, 7b) and, concurrently, lecturer at one of the many imperial palaces (7a). Upon becoming a censorial official, Shih Ts'ai had a higher platform from which to be heard and, again, he exploited it. It was his forceful indictment of the Ministry of Personnel's top executive, just months after his own appointment as policy monitor, that led to the executive's dismissal.[51]

On the one hand, Shih Ts'ai attacked his fellow officials to curry favor with the chief councillor. On the other, he was tireless at submitting policy proposals to the court and thereby demonstrating his dedication to improving bureaucratic management. One proposal, made in mid-1153 and designed to curtail the siphoning of tax revenues by local authorities, received the court's full endorsement.[52] This proposal, complemented by his successful completion of a promotion examination, led to his further advancement as policy advisor of the right (yu chien-yi tai-fu, 4b).[53] This was followed by other recommendations, the most noted of which related to abuses of authority by military men. Pointing to their illegal confiscation and misuse of land in Che-hsi circuit, Shih Ts'ai requested that the government double its efforts at monitoring the military and its excesses.[54] Acceptance of this proposal was followed by more indictments. First to come under the policy advisor's scrutiny and to be dismissed was an instructor at the prefectural school in the capital, who Shih Ts'ai accused of incompetence.[55] The second was his one-time sponsor, Sung P'u.

Sung P'u himself had risen from censor to assistant councillor (*ts'an-chih cheng-shih*, 2a) and concurrently signatory official at the Bureau of Military Affairs (*ch'ien-shu shu-mi-yüan shih*, 2b) by indicting prominent targets of Ch'in Kuei's wrath. Following the established pattern, he was rewarded for his efforts by being selected to succeed one of his victims. In office for only one year, the assistant councillor in turn came under attack by Shih Ts'ai, who alleged that his behavior in office was "rude and perverse." This led to the prompt dismissal of Sung P'u. Just four days later the court announced his replacement as assistant councillor: Shih Ts'ai.[56]

As assistant to Ch'in Kuei, Shih Ts'ai passed ten uneventful months before being cut down himself. Another censor accused him of being closely allied with his former sponsor, Li Kuang, and forming factions at court centering on the disgraced official. Not only did this lead to his immediate dismissal, but also the divestiture of all official responsibilities. On the very next day, critic Wei Shih-sun (n.d.) replaced Shih Ts'ai as assistant councillor.[57]

From the brief accounts contained in primary materials, it could appear that the ties between Shih Ts'ai and Li Kuang, as demonstrated through the latter's sponsorship, were chiefly responsible for the political demise of the former.[58] In reality, it was not so simple. Both Ch'in Kuei and the throne must have been aware from the outset that Shih Ts'ai held the recommendation of Li Kuang and chose to elevate him despite this. Although the recommendation undoubtedly had a negative impact upon the advancement of Shih Ts'ai in the 1140s, the passage of time should have defused this issue. From the above narration of events leading to his political ascendancy in the 1150s, it is apparent that bureaucratic activism, and not the origin of his sponsorship, provided the key to advancement for Shih Ts'ai. Similarly, dismissal in 1154 also seems to be intimately related to court politics.

Again, Ch'ing historian Ch'üan Tsu-wang offers some interesting insights into the matter. During his tenure as policy monitor, he asserts, Shih Ts'ai actually did the bidding of the chief councillor and relied heavily upon this to rise to the second spot in the bureaucracy. Later, perhaps because he had lost his political usefulness or had come to represent a personal threat of some sort, Ch'in Kuei employed another censor to eliminate his assistant.[59] Thus, Shih Ts'ai was no more than a political minion of Ch'in Kuei. This assessment stands in sharp contrast with a late twelfth-century biography of a nephew, which alludes to the difficulty of serving under the domineering councillor and implies that Shih Ts'ai came to power, not because of, but *despite* the presence of Ch'in Kuei at court.[60] As has been shown here, ingratiation of the chief councillor was not the only factor in his advancement but, as Ch'üan Tsu-wang asserts, it was certainly a significant one.

Other factors similarly suggest that Shih Ts'ai exploited his position in the Censorate to further his own career. The allegations of misconduct that he leveled against fellow officials were often unsubstantiated, ambiguous, and even frivolous. How does one substantiate accusations of "rudity" and "perversion"? The targets of Shih Ts'ai were carefully chosen to suit the whims of Ch'in Kuei, even though this sometimes involved forsaking old friends.[61] There is no better illustration of his opportunism than the indictment of Sung P'u, a man who had recommended him for promotion just months before. It is perhaps the shamefulness of his political maneuverings that explains why the compiler of the Pao-ch'ing gazetteer for Ming-chou, compiled when the kin group was at the height of its political influence, chose conveniently to ignore Shih Ts'ai, despite conspicuously extensive biographies of the controversial official's grandmother and nephew.[62] No doubt, later kinsmen preferred that the details of his career not be widely publicized lest his opportunism and complicity with Ch'in Kuei become all too apparent.

In balance, it is important to remember that the times in which Shih Ts'ai lived were difficult ones for an aspiring official. After 1141, Ch'in Kuei was undisputed overseer of the bureaucracy and those who stood in the way of his political machinations held little hope for future advancement. Under the circumstances, the decision by Shih Ts'ai to cooperate is understandable. How was he to know that Ch'in Kuei would later be cast as a villain and his associates held in disdain? Meanwhile, the many proposals relating to vital matters such as fiscal and military policy demonstrate that Shih Ts'ai had much to offer the court beyond mere indictments of colleagues. There is little question that he was both conscientious and imaginative while in office.

After his fall from power, Shih Ts'ai was never heard of again. Presumably, he spent his last years in retirement at Ming-chou. With his stay in Lin-an lasting a mere three years from start to finish and in the absence of any obvious ties with the palace, his political influence was inevitably limited; still, from the standpoint of kinsmen at home, the career of Shih Ts'ai was an astounding success. For the kin group's first degreeholder and official to land the second spot in the bureaucracy was no mean accomplishment and this says as much for the personal talent of Shih Ts'ai as it does for the extent of the bureaucratic access during his time. He entered the civil service through scholastic merit, not protection or imperial favor. He had no family connections to exploit in either furthering his career or shielding him from the powerful. Being entirely on his own, it is remarkable that he survived as long and achieved as much as he did.

SUMMARY OF GENERATION FOUR

The Shih community during the early twelfth century was small —generations four and five represented no more than thirty or forty persons, including women and children—and only of modest means. There is no indication of a strong literary tradition in the kin group. Shih Chao never attended a school, relying instead upon his mother and local notables to receive rudimentary instruction. No doubt, he initially trained his sons, but the shortcomings of his own education eventually prompted them to go on to the prefectural school for more advanced training. There, they were prepared to become a part of Ming-chou's scholar as well as official elite. Upon entering the civil service, it was a combination of bureaucratic merit and political manipulation that enabled the kin group's first official to climb so high. For subsequent generations, it was probably less difficult. First, the merit of Shih Ts'ai entitled certain members of the Shih house to enjoy the privileges of protection for the first time. In this way, official appointment no longer had to wait for conferral of a degree. Second, the career of Shih Ts'ai transformed his kin group into a serious contender for a place of prominence within Ming-chou's growing group of high-status families. This, in turn, provided an array of academic and professional contacts that positively influenced the education of its younger members. As the Shih house prospered in both size and wealth, as educational institutions expanded, and as Ming-chou was transformed into a hub of political activity, the opportunities for individual kinsmen multiplied. The path that Shih Ts'ai cleared to the capital would become well trodden in coming generations.

3

Setting Roots in the Capital

A s of generation four, the Shih family consisted of five male heirs. Shih Shih-chung, Shih Ts'ai, and Shih Mu all fathered highly prosperous lines. While the younger sons—Shih Ho and Shih Kuang—were not so prolific as their brothers, their lines proved nonetheless enduring. For the sake of convenience, future discussion of the Shih collectivity will be made with reference to its five principal divisions: branch A, representing the descendants of Shih Shih-chung; branch B, descendants of Shih Ts'ai; branch C, descendants of Shih Mu; branch D, descendants of Shih Ho; and branch E, representing heirs to Shih Kuang (see appendix 3, Genealogy of the Shih). The patriarch of the fifth generation—that is, the eldest male in the senior branch—also produced this new generation's greatest success story and is consequently the focus of this chapter.

ASCENDANCY OF SHIH HAO

The eldest of the five heirs to Shih Shih-chung, Shih Hao (1106–94), was a youthful eighteen when his father died.[1] Prior to this, he apparently studied under his father, whose affiliation with the Imperial University suggests a good measure of erudition. Shih Hao later came to rely for further training upon uncle Shih Mu, an aspiring official himself who never managed to get beyond the prefectural examinations.[2] To the family's great loss, Shih Mu died only six years after his brother.

When Shih Hao was a teenager and his father alive, the prefectural school still played a leading role in educating Ming-chou's growing community of aspiring scholars and officials, yet there is no indication that the younger Shih ever studied there. By the 1130s, when the family's personal loss made the school an important alternative source of education, Jurchen armies had already razed its buildings. Exactly what persons or institutions he turned to for more advanced study and intellectual stimulation are unknown; historians fail to identify him, during this formative period, with a specific private academy or noted scholar.[3] This is not to say that Shih Hao was self-taught or that he had few academic ties beyond his own kin group. The diversity of interests and breadth of exposure that characterize later literary productions suggests a broad scholastic inheritance, one unlikely to have derived from family traditions alone.

Shih Hao did not emerge as a scholar-official until 1145, when he ranked among the top ten candidates in the departmental examinations and went on to receive *chin-shih* status.[4] Already approaching forty by this time, he was hardly a young initiate. In all likelihood, this represents the last of repeated attempts at the examinations and Shih Hao's persistence betrays considerable self-discipline and determination. With rank of 9b, he became sheriff of Ming-chou's Yü-yao subprefecture, the same post held by uncle Shih Ts'ai some two decades earlier.[5] Another minor assignment, again not far from home, followed this.[6] Then came a move to Wen-chou, along the southern coast of modern Chekiang, where he served as instructor at the prefectural school.

For Shih Hao the appointment was quite propitious, for here he came to know Chang Chiu-ch'eng (1092–1159), then prefect of Wen-chou and a man closely identified with the Neo-Confucian revival that was gathering momentum in southeast China.[7] The acquaintance was very likely Shih Hao's first with so powerful a philosopher and its impact upon his subsequent intellectual development can well be imagined. The length of their association or, for that matter, his tenure as instructor, are equally uncertain, but Shih Hao probably remained at Wen-chou some seven or eight years. In 1157 he finally received another assignment. Having secured the sponsorship of Wu Ping-hsin (n.d.), he was summoned to the capital.[8]

Wu Ping-hsin was also a native of Ming-chou, an individual who rose to a prominent position within the Secretariat following the death of the ubiquitous Ch'in Kuei in 1155. His reason for sponsoring Shih Hao is not altogether clear. There is no indication that Shih Hao ever served under him, so perhaps his interest grew out of their acquaintance as fellow provincials. In any event, the sponsorship facilitated Shih Hao's advancement to the post of instructor at the Imperial University (*T'ai-hsüeh cheng*, 9a) and, before long, professor of the same (*T'ai-hsüeh po-shih*, 8a).[9] The second appointment augured especially well for his future in Lin-an; beyond the prestige associated with a professorship, the new post also afforded Shih Hao an opportunity to address the throne on policy matters. Just as Shih Ts'ai exploited his position as policy monitor to air his views and thereby to attract the attention of the powerful, the younger Shih did much of the same at the Imperial University. Unlike his uncle, however, Shih Hao exhibited little interest in fiscal policy or the conduct of fellow officials. He focused instead on moral issues, such as ordering the palace and molding the personalities of its occupants.

The earliest mention of Shih Hao that caught the attention of the throne was in 1159, when he petitioned for the speedy installation of an heir-apparent.[10] Kao-tsung obviously regarded his concern as genuine, for he named Shih Hao instructor for his two adopted sons and, concurrently, collator of the Imperial Library (*Pi-shu-sheng chiao-shu lang*, 8b). Once inside the palace, Shih Hao's integrity and forthright character impressed both the emperor and his favored choice for heir, Prince Chien. With time, the prince and his tutor became quite close and this gave the career of the latter a special lift. In scarcely a year, Shih Hao had moved on to become primary lecturer for the prince (*chih-chiang*, 7b) and then lesser lord of the Court of Imperial Family Affairs (*Tsung-cheng shao-ch'ing*, 7a). In effect, Kao-tsung entrusted him with a major share of the responsibility for grooming the future emperor.[11] Elevation of the prince to heir-apparent in mid-1162 witnessed yet another promotion for Shih Hao, this time as chief advisor to the heir (*t'ai-tzu yu shu-tzu*, 5b).[12] Within days of naming an heir, Kao-tsung abdicated after thirty-five years on the throne. The end of an era, perhaps, but for Shih Hao the transfer of power marked the beginning of heretofore unknown opportunities.

In his various capacities as tutor and advisor, Shih Hao's association with Prince Chien did not exceed three years, yet the future Emperor Hsiao-tsung came to place in him a confidence both pervasive and lasting. Merely four days after the accession, Shih Hao was elevated to drafting official in the Secretariat (*Chung-shu she-jen*, 4a) and Han-lin reader-in-waiting (*Han-lin shih-tu*, 7a). Within another two months he leaped to an esteemed executive post as assistant councillor (2a) and acting coadministrator of the Bureau of Military Affairs (*t'ung chih shu-mi-yüan shih*,

2a).[13] By the beginning of 1163, only a half-year after the installation of Hsiao-tsung, Shih Hao reached the summit of his political climb with his nomination as chief councillor of the right (*yu ch'eng-hsiang*, 1a) and concurrent commissioner at the Bureau of Military Affairs (*Shu-mi-yüan shih*, 1b).[14]

Commenting on the unusual pace of Shih Hao's advancement from instructor at the Imperial University in 1157 to chief councillor in 1163, biographer Lou Yüeh wrote, "To reach the chief councillor's seat within just six years [of becoming a court official] represents [a feat] unknown to recent history!"[15] To be sure, Shih Hao's race to power was at least partially fueled by the emperor's special fondness for his former teacher, but this stemmed not from sheer ingratiation of the throne. Hsiao-tsung was not so gullible and Shih Hao was not the ingratiating type. That the experienced Kao-tsung should single him out from the various other tutors of the prince to serve as chief advisor and that the discriminating Hsiao-tsung should trust him with the bureaucracy's top post, suggests that his qualifications were widely recognized. Inspiring imperial advancement appears to have been his powerful intellect and indomitable sense of personal conviction, traits that served the councillor well, at least initially.

A New Emperor and a Fresh War

Emperor Hsiao-tsung (r. 1162–89) is held in uncommonly high regard by modern as well as traditional historians. Writing in the mid-fourteenth century, compilers of the official *Sung shih* (History of the Sung) depicted his twenty-seven-year reign as the finest of the Southern Sung.[16] A modern historian similarly refers to the era as Lin-an's "Golden Age."[17] Already thirty-four years old upon inheriting the throne, the new emperor was considerably more mature than Kao-tsung at the time of his own installation some three decades earlier. Sharp of mind and determined in spirit, he tended to be frugal like few emperors before him and filial to a fault.[18] Most Southern Sung rulers alarmed the bureaucracy by permitting individual chief councillors to maintain virtual lifetime tenures and, in the process, monopolize the entire political process—not Hsiao-tsung. His great esteem for men such as Shih Hao notwithstanding, he allowed no one to detract from his own autonomy as decision maker. He epitomized the strong and assertive monarch. While not taking lightly the counsel of officials, he rarely accepted their advice uncritically. Although not prone to be rash, once his mind was set, he acted decisively. It was undoubtedly Kao-tsung's recognition of these special qualities of leadership that inspired him to select Prince Chien as heir and then promptly to abdicate in his favor. An additional factor inducing Kao-tsung to step down related to developments along the border.

As previously noted, the peace so desperately sought after and finally won by Kao-tsung and Ch'in Kuei in 1141 stood unbroken for the next two decades. During this period, the Sung government enjoyed both political stability and economic prosperity, but the price for peace was high. The Sung had surrendered to the Jurchen certain strategic parts of central China, areas that had previously provided an important buffer between north and south. In addition, the government had become obliged to deliver to its former adversary an annual "tribute" of 250,000 ounces of silver and 250,000 bolts of silk. Without question, the most disturbing concession was Lin-an's acceptance of a "vassal" status in its diplomatic relations with the northern empire.[19] The court of Kao-tsung apparently found it easy to rationalize concessions of territory and wealth, for these constituted only a small part of the empire's total resources, yet the last concession represented no less than an affront to the very sovereignty of the Chinese state! Understandably, this became the most contemptible item in the peace pact and a source of much anguish for citizens of the south.

For better or worse, twenty years of tranquility between the two powers was suddenly shattered toward the close of the summer of 1161. It was then that the temperamental Prince Hai-ling, an upstart of the Jurchen ruling house who seized the throne through intrigue and assassination, launched a full-scale invasion of the south.[20] The Sung, having been at peace for an entire generation, proved militarily unprepared for Hai-ling's strike into northern Che-tung and thus suffered some major setbacks. Fortunately for Lin-an, the troops of the Jurchen prince staged a mutiny only months after the eruption of war, culminating in his assassination. Hostilities subsided in the aftermath of the coup, but the expected cease-fire did not follow. Scattered border fighting persisted for nearly a year, while rebel armies in Shantung, heartened by the chaos and hoping to intensify it, rose up against Jurchen rule and proclaimed their loyalty to the Sung cause. Although war persisted, a semblance of order was nonetheless restored in the summer of 1162 and an aging Kao-tsung, weary after having led the empire through two wars, willingly surrendered his throne.

The border conflict remained largely unresolved when Hsiao-tsung came to power and there is little to indicate that either side aggressively pursued peace. Lin-an considered itself entitled to some form of atonement for the enemy's violation of the treaty. Reflecting its dissatisfaction with the previous treaty, it demanded an upgrading of diplomatic status, but the Jurchen would not accommodate. With the two sides deadlocked over such sensitive issues and border incidents still a regular occurrence, many statesmen feared that tensions might mushroom into another full-scale war.[21] Hsiao-tsung initially handled the dispute with meticulous caution, which suggests a genuine desire for a negotiated settlement. At the same time, as a new ruler anxious to prove himself to his father by adoption, he was in no position to compromise on so vital an issue.

Within one month of coming to power, the emperor accepted the advice of Shih Hao and dispatched a Sung envoy to the north.[22] It was a stipulation of the treaty of 1141 that official notification be made upon the installation of a new emperor and Hsiao-tsung, by complying with this even during a time of war, signaled to the Jurchen his desire to restore peace. Still expecting concessions from them, however, he refused to employ established protocol in the documents given to the envoy. The mission was thus declared illegal and turned back at the border. The Jurchen soon lost patience and, as the winter of 1162 approached, they initiated a vigorous assault upon South China.[23] Aggression of this sort should have convinced Hsiao-tsung of the futility of further negotiations, but it did not. Rather, he responded by entrusting administration of the bureaucracy to the court's most vocal exponent of peace: Shih Hao. The selection, especially at such a critical juncture, demonstrates quite unequivocally that the emperor continued to cling to the hope for a peaceful settlement of the conflict.

SHIH HAO ON WAR AND PEACE

Before proceeding to discuss the war and its unfolding, some exploration of Shih Hao's stand on war and peace seems appropriate. It must be stated from the outset that he can be identified with no recognizable faction at court. Following the death of Ch'in Kuei, Kao-tsung effectively uprooted the partisan supporters of his former councillor and subsequently allowed no other chief minister to retain power long enough to form similar alliances. Hsiao-tsung guarded against the political alliances of court officials with even greater vigil. For the duration of his reign, there existed no clearly defined factions at court. Rather, men such as Shih Hao became articulate spokesmen for certain policies due to their political prominence and, at the same time, their recognized proximity to the throne. In 1163 Shih Hao truly represented the most conspicuous advocate of peace at court, but this emanated from his special relationship with the emperor and not factional support.

Shih Hao favored negotiation over war, yet this does not justify labeling him a "pacifist." Contrary to the alleged views of Ch'in Kuei, he never proposed that the Sung abandon its mission to unify the realm and be content to remain a southern empire forever.[24] He rose to power at a time when leading statesmen widely assailed the defeatist policies of Ch'in Kuei and thereby made way for the purge of his supporters. For Shih Hao, or for that matter any promising official, to make proposals that too closely resembled those of the former councillor would have been tantamount to political suicide. On the contrary, he frequently expressed his desire to "redress the great shame" inflicted by the Jurchen in 1126 and to "regain the central plains."[25] He differed from the militants mostly on timing and strategy.

Shih Hao was convinced that the Southern Sung lacked both the military readiness and the economic resources to launch any successful offensive against its northern foe. Writing toward the close of 1162, he warned the throne against acting too rashly: "Today, the might of [our] armed forces is not yet efficacious, that of [our] people has yet to be rejuvenated [from previous wars], and [our] resources are still inadequate. Were we suddenly to neglect the internal while engaging the external, even if [it led to] restoration of the entire realm, it would still be of no benefit."[26] Clearly, there is an overriding concern here with the possible effects *upon the south* of any major military effort against the north. Insisting that more time was needed, he called upon the court first to invest in the economic and military development of South China. Only after strengthening the southern base did Shih Hao consider it feasible to take on northern enemies: "In this way, when [our forces] advance, they will be successful at enlarging the country and expanding its territory; when [our forces] retreat, they will avoid the calamity of tiring [our] soldiers and [thereby] becoming unprepared [to react to Jurchen retaliation]. This is the best plan for the real world."[27] Such a "realistic" plan, however, might require decades, even generations, before being implemented. Writing some twenty years later, Shih Hao admitted that yet another decade of preparation was necessary for the Sung to so much as *consider* military action against the north.[28] In retrospect, it is apparent that the chief councillor's extreme caution virtually precluded any Sung attempt at ever recovering North China. The emperor, he soon realized, did not share his pessimism.

Shih Hao called for the gradual expansion and careful deployment of the military for two reasons. First, as earlier statements reveal, he was troubled by the high cost of expansion and the added strain that this would inevitably place upon the economy of South China. Second, and perhaps more important, he harbored a deep-seated distrust of the military in general and military leaders in particular, fearing that enhancement of military authority unavoidably caused a decline in political authority. To him, military expansion was an invitation for political and social disorder. It is important to remember that Shih Hao was an official of the civilian bureaucracy and the closest he ever came to filling a military post was as civilian administrator at the Bureau of Military Affairs. Shih Hao shared with uncle Shih Ts'ai a profound distrust of military leaders and an uneasiness about the power they wielded. Thus, he insisted that the military be carefully controlled and the authority of its leaders be properly checked, fearing that inadequate supervision could leave military men arrogant and unwieldy. In selecting generals, he called upon the court to choose only those strict in discipline.[29] When members of the armed forces violated military ethics or the civil code, he insisted upon severe punishment.[30] Preoccupied with the maintenance of discipline within the military, Shih Hao also vigorously opposed the policy of incorporating into Sung armies "loyalist refugees" (*kuei-cheng-jen*, literally, "persons returning to the just [government]") from the north.[31]

The 1141 peace treaty had stipulated that the Sung neither encourage the migration of refugees from the north nor support the activities of rebel groups operating in Jurchen-controlled areas.[32] Inevitably, the agreement fell through with the eruption of hostilities. Partly to blame for this was the displacement that accompanies war, for this resulted in a swelling of the refugee population and made border control near to impossible. In addition, many border officials, wishing to exploit refugees to strengthen inadequate armies, were little interested in control and often encouraged migration south. Shih Hao, on the other hand, remained optimistic about a peaceful settlement to the conflict of 1162 and petitioned the throne to honor its treaty commitments by stopping the flow of refugees into the south. Independent of political considerations, he considered it militarily unsound to recruit men for the Sung armed forces from among the home- less and disaffected. The concept of "snatching up" refugees to serve in a hastily organized and poorly disciplined army, he held, was both naive and reckless. He likened it to "discarding the real, while engaging the nominal; neglecting the near, while pursuing the distant; seeing the advantages, while ignoring the drawbacks."[33] A unit of such recruits could hardly be as effective or reliable as a conventional force of army regulars. Like many contemporaries, Shih Hao also suspected that refu- gee groups contained large numbers of enemy spies.[34] Once incorporated into the Sung army, they could easily sabotage its actions by providing the enemy with vital information on troop positions, their strength, their movements, and the like. Basically, he preferred an army of time-tested southerners.

Of equal concern to Shih Hao was the fiscal burden entailed in repatria- tion of loyalist refugees and the consequent alienation of southerners. Loyalist commoners who fled south customarily received special govern- ment stipends and land grants, while loyalist officials were assigned posts exceeding in rank and salary those formerly held in the north. Such generous court treatment could well ruin the Sung government. A contem- porary reports, in the prefecture of P'ing-chiang (modern Soochow) alone, some one hundred thousand strings of cash devoted to supporting refu- gees there.[35] We can only imagine the cost empirewide. Beyond exces- sively draining the Sung exchequer, such special treatment understanda- bly angered natives of the south. Shih Hao wrote:

> Loyalist-officials already exceed five hundred, all of whom are high officials with elevated titles eagerly seeking to enhance their assign- ments by looking for vacancies. Loyalist-commoners are of unknown number, all of whom drain the fat and blood (that is, the resources) of the people, fearing only that their stipends may not arrive. In this way, the empire's resources will be exhausted after [just] a few years. [Consequently,] scholar-officials of the southeast cannot obtain trans- fers for long periods, while peasants of the southeast do not get to spend their personal [tax] remittances on themselves. [Under these circumstances,] how can we ensure that they will not rise up as bandits in search of the wherewithal to feed and clothe themselves?[36]

Further stressing the inequities of this policy from the standpoint of southerners, he added:

> As for scholar-officials of the central kingdom (that is, South China), even those who have joined the ranks of degreeholders and are [from] families which have held noble rank for generations, [nonetheless] are forsaken for the balance of their lives after [just] one misjudgment or oversight. In the case of loyalist-officials [who are so accused], no questions are asked whatsoever. In this way, how fortunate is he who [once] served in the north and how unfortunate is he who serves [this] celestial court![37]

Through these statements Shih Hao emerges as a staunch defender of southern interests, a statesman who placed the welfare of his native south before the larger political goal of regaining the north. His warning to the throne that its efforts at accommodating loyalists might create difficult-to-bridge cleavages in the south, indeed, more closely resembles a threat than an admonishment. Although research is still inadequate to speak with any certainty, the strength of this assertion suggests that large segments of the Chinese population in the south—scholar-officials and commoners alike—had become alienated by court policy toward refugee groups and this alienation had reached crisis proportions by early 1163. For Southern Sung rulers, such migration represented an important boost to their own legitimacy, as it underscored the repressiveness of Jurchen rule in the north and the urgent need to subvert it. There was thus a vital political incentive for encouraging at least modest migration. Natives of the south, however, saw things differently. Not only did immigrants stake unwarranted claims to the limited resources of the south, but their claims were disproportionately large. Meanwhile, the educated among them exploited their added prestige in Lin-an to receive premature promotions within the civil service and then to protect themselves from the scrutiny of censors. While the career of Shih Hao appears to have suffered little from the preferential treatment afforded loyalist-officials, his comments undoubtedly reflect empathy with fellow southerners who did suffer. By verbalizing such opinions before the throne—opinions that the emperor clearly did not share—Shih Hao readily became a leading spokesman for likeminded officials in the capital.

Chief among the antagonists of Shih Hao during the 1162–63 period was Chang Chün (1097–1164).[38] A native of modern Szechwan, he descended from a house that produced a long line of civil servants. Initially, he too entered the civilian bureaucracy, but soon switched to a military career. From the very beginning of the Southern Sung and for the duration of his life, Chang Chün held only a few civilian posts; the vast majority were military-related. Besides representing one of Kao-tsung's leading generals during his first and most trying decade of rule, he also served as chief councillor prior to the dominance of Ch'in Kuei. With the eruption of border hostilities some two decades later, he was among the first military leaders to whom Kao-tsung turned for help. Chang Chün was already an elder statesman when Hsiao-tsung ascended the throne, a man whose proven loyalty and long record of distinguished service commanded the respect of many. When a man of such stature petitions the throne to adopt a more militant stand against the Jurchen, the emperor cannot easily ignore him, nor was *this* emperor so inclined.

Upon learning in 1161 of the death of Northern Sung Emperor Ch'intsung, after a quarter-century of captivity in the north, and amid reports that the enemy was rearming itself for a resumption of hostilities, Chang Chün urged Kao-tsung to prepare for imminent war. The emperor refused to act, not wanting to provoke a conflict.[39] Once fighting erupted, Chang Chün agitated for the replacement of a fundamentally defensive strategy with an aggressive one. Again, there was no constructive response.[40] Not until his appointment in early 1163 as chief administrator at the military bureau, a seat that he shared with Chief councillor Shih Hao, did Chang Chün and his proposals begin to receive more serious attention at court. Hsiao-tsung had, after all, simultaneously appointed both Shih Hao and Chang Chün to executive posts in the Bureau of Military Affairs intentionally to maintain a balance between war and peace advocates. Apparently, this was still a period of indecision for him, but the two proved so contrary that even as a temporary arrangement it seemed totally unworkable. Regarding Shih Hao as cautious to a fault, Chang Chün devised his own set of policy proposals that called for swift action; he advocated seizing the moment to overthrow Jurchen rule and reunify China. For reasons of expediency, he pressed for the immediate induction of loyalist refugees into the Sung army. In fact, even without the expressed permission of Lin-an, he had moved to incorporate loyalists into his own forces as early as 1161.[41] Although in his midsixties, Chang Chün was hardly wanting of ambition or fortitude and he did everything possible to undermine the position of Shih Hao.

Conflict between the two finally came to a head in the early spring of 1163, following a dispute over "loyalist armies" (*chung-yi-chün*, literally, "loyal and righteous armies") and their recruitment.[42] Chang Chün insisted that the Sung government's support for and direction of these generally small, privately organized rebel bands whose operations were confined to North China could add sufficiently to the strength of a regular offensive to clinch for the Sung a rapid victory.[43] Assuming the Jurchen to have been significantly weakened by the power struggle within the ruling elite, he seemed certain that a combination of internal insurrection and foreign invasion would utterly paralyze them. The scheme, perhaps excessively optimistic, was not altogether unrealistic. Inevitably, Shih Hao countered with pleas for moderation, but the emperor had finally lost his patience. The chief councillor's peace initiative had produced no concrete results and, even if the venture of Chang Chün failed to achieve total victory, it might at least force the enemy to the bargaining table, perhaps in a weakened position. Throwing its weight behind the revanchists, the court issued secret orders for Chang Chün personally to supervise the formation of troops in the Huai valley in preparation for a major campaign.[44] For the first time since fighting broke out nearly two years before, the Sung had seized the initiative.

It was probably because Hsiao-tsung wished either to surprise the enemy or temporarily to avoid a confrontation with his former teacher that he issued orders to Chang Chün in secret. Whatever his motives, he chose completely to circumvent regular bureaucratic channels; he informed neither the Bureau of Military Affairs nor the chief councillor's office of the offensive then underway. When he finally learned of the action over a month later, Shih Hao flew into a rage. He exclaimed to Ch'en K'ang-po, his counterpart as chief councillor, "Among [the offices] with which I am entrusted is councillorship of the right, yet I was not informed in advance of troop movements. Of what use then is a chief councillor?"[45] He immediately tendered his resignation. Initially rejected—whether out of sheer ceremony or a genuine desire to retain his services is uncertain—the resignation was eventually accepted by the throne after several appeals. He had served in the high post for only five months.

Once it became apparent that Shih Hao's influence over the emperor was on the wane, the militants at court launched a caustic verbal campaign against him and his policies in the hope of undermining the position of moderate elements in general. Just days after resigning, Shih Hao came under the scrutiny of Censor Wang Shih-p'eng (1112–71), a protagonist of war and an ardent supporter of Chang Chün.[46] The indictment of Censor Wang accused the former councillor of crimes so great as to parallel those of the infamous Ch'in Kuei. Although he failed to substantiate most allegations, the forceful and sweeping character of the indictment, combined with the support lent Wang Shih-p'eng by the waxing prowar group, were sufficient to deny Shih Hao another metropolitan assignment for many years to come. More important, the charges also reveal much about the uniqueness of his relationship with the throne and the threat this represented to the militants. A brief summary of his "eight great crimes," therefore, is in order.[47]

First, by relentlessly expostulating a peace policy, Shih Hao reportedly impeded every attempt to recover the north. In this way, he was portrayed as a second Ch'in Kuei. Furthermore, by engineering the forced withdrawal of General Wu Lin (1100–1165) from modern Shensi, where he was directing a major thrust into the southwest corner of the Jurchen empire, Shih Hao was blamed for the loss of thirteen prefectures and tens of thousands of lives.[48] Third, Wang Shih-p'eng charged him with organizing his own faction for the sole purpose of manipulating court policy —members of the clique reportedly were so intimate that they employed terms of close kinship in referring to one another.[49] Fourth, he accused the chief councillor of abusing his power. Appointments to high-level posts, the distribution of noble ranks, even the administration of official examinations were all manipulated by Shih Hao to advance men of similar political persuasion and thereby to tighten his own grip on the court. Fifth, there were charges of intercepting the transmission of memorials critical of him and his policies, thereby denying the throne access to differing opinions. Sixth, through his constant obstruction and aspersion of Chang Chün, Shih Hao was said to have undermined imperial efforts to devise a strategy for regaining the north. Seventh, Wang Shih-p'eng censured Shih Hao for having "cheated his ruler" through the unauthorized alteration of imperial rescripts and his naked violation of commonly accepted rules of etiquette when in the presence of his majesty. Finally, Shih Hao allegedly "reviled the throne" by taking personal credit for every accomplishment, while blaming the emperor for every failure.

So serious are many of the allegations that the indictment against Shih Hao—at one point, the emperor's most trusted official—must have sent tremors through the capital. Apart from what they reveal about major issues being debated at the early court of Hsiao-tsung, these charges also imply a good deal about the stature of Shih Hao at that court. First, he clearly represented the single most influential exponent of peace at the time. It was for this reason that Wang Shih-p'eng held him personally responsible for all imperial decisions that fostered peace. In addition, the political sway of Shih Hao appears not to have been confined simply to the palace, but also extended to a sizable body of colleagues who shared similar views. This made him vulnerable to charges of forming factional alliances. The allegation of arbitrarily modifying imperial rescripts seems a bit farfetched, for it implies passive imperial leadership and the delegation of considerable authority to the chief councillor, which is not at all characteristic of the assertive Hsiao-tsung. Nonetheless, the freedom to dispense with ordinary proprieties when in the imperial presence—a courtesy we know to have been afforded Shih Hao—underscores the unique character of his relationship with the emperor. Hsiao-tsung expressed his great respect and affection by granting Shih Hao rare privileges such as sitting rather than kneeling during an audience. This caused some to be jealous, but it was the imperial goodwill reflected in such favors that most concerned the opposition. If their views were to receive a serious audience, the moderate Shih Hao had to be discredited.

To assess the accuracy of each charge is nearly impossible and it would not be terribly productive. While undeniably serving the opposition's short-term objective of eliminating moderate influence in 1163–64, the allegations of Wang Shih-p'eng had little impact over the long haul.[50] With time, Shih Hao was politically revived and imperial goodwill confirmed. This implies that Hsiao-tsung, although unable to reject outright the accusations of treachery leveled against his councillor in 1163, attached little credulity to them. Meanwhile, developments along the border following Shih Hao's departure only confirmed the superior wisdom of his counsel.

For the revanchists, the battle at court against Shih Hao proved easier to win than the war against the enemy to the north. With the removal of Shih Hao, Chang Chün held a free rein over border policy and his long-awaited offensive shifted into high gear. Its focus was Su-chou, a prefecture located just beyond the Huai River in the northernmost part of modern Anhwei. The move represented an important demonstration of Sung strength—a warning to the enemy—so Chang Chün invested heavily of men and matériel. When his forces flooded the city, it fell "like the splitting of bamboo," but Jurchen reinforcements soon reached Su-chou and the two sides became engaged in prolonged and intense exchanges. In the end, the Sung was repulsed. Excluding uncounted fatalities on the battlefield, which probably exceeded a hundred thousand men, the enemy "captured the armors" of some thirty thousand Sung troops (perhaps deserters) and decapitated another four thousand.[51] Lin-an responded to the defeat with alacrity. In less than a month, Chang Chün was reprimanded and the court resumed its peace overtures to the Jurchen.[52] In the process, Shih Hao was vindicated.

RESURGENCE OF THE CHIEF COUNCILLOR

After 1163, Shih Hao temporarily disappeared from public service. He spent the next five years in semiretirement at his native Ming-chou, where a concubine of his had recently given birth to twins.[53] In 1168, he received an appointment as military commissioner of Szechwan, but declined due to his mother's advanced age and the area's long distance from home. Another offer followed, much more to his liking, and he readily accepted the post of prefect of Shao-hsing, a large metropolis halfway between Ming-chou and the capital.[54] He held the position for only two years, the death of his mother compelling him to withdraw for the traditional mourning. Upon fulfilling his filial obligation, Shih Hao moved on to become prefectural vice-administrator (t'ung-p'an) of the port city of Fu-chou. He remained there until his two-year term expired and in 1174 retired once again.[55] He had spent only four years in service as regional administrator.

The career of Shih Hao focused more on the capital than away from it, yet his brief but productive tenures in Shao-hsing and Fu-chou contributed significantly to enhancing his stature within the bureaucracy, no doubt permanently dispelling lingering shadows of ignominy. Innovative approaches to social relief not only betrayed a beneficent conscientiousness, but attracted for Shih Hao empirewide acclaim. At Shao-hsing he led the local government in establishing "charitable estates" (yi-t'ien or yi-chuang) to assist families of official background suffering from financial hardship.

The scheme, a popular one during Sung times, involved renting publicly owned estates to local peasants and then using the rent income to maintain a charity fund. The fund at Shao-hsing had the specific objective of aiding the families of deceased officials, largely widows, who could no longer afford proper marriages and burials for kinsmen.[56] According to reports, the project generated such extraordinary goodwill that a grateful community dedicated a temple to their prefect.[57]

As vice-administrator of Fu-chou, Shih Hao inspired a similar scheme for social relief. In contrast with Shao-hsing, the project at Fu-chou was designed for the common people, not the scholar-official elite. In overpopulated Fu-chou, where many were afflicted with poverty, unwanted pregnancies commonly ended in either abortion or infanticide, a practice especially prevalent among recent widows. Driven, perhaps because of his great-grandmother's own hardship as a widowed mother, to curb the incidence of abortion and infanticide, Shih Hao applied the income from the Fu-chou government's charitable estates to provide poor, pregnant women with monthly stipends.[58] The longevity of his program and the extent to which it succeeded in addressing the problem remains uncertain, but the effort alone made him something of a celebrity among locals and an exemplar among colleagues.[59]

It may well have been Shih Hao's spreading reputation away from the capital that prompted the emperor finally to revive him as a court official in the spring of 1178. Once again, he became chief councillor of the right.[60] Fourteen years had lapsed since his last stint in Lin-an and the new political landscape did not resemble the old one. North and south were no longer at war; in fact, the border had been quiet for over a decade. Chang Chün was long dead and the war-peace debate had died with him. The emperor, now about fifty, had become more sober and less impassioned with age. Times had changed, but the chief councillor had not. Retained intact was his incorrigible distrust of the military establishment and its leaders. Hsiao-tsung, moreover, tended still to indulge that group. Such fundamentally antithetical orientations made future clashes a certainty. No doubt, the emperor anticipated few problems, times being so tranquil, and gave more thought to the happy reunion of teacher and student.

Shih Hao, a generally liberal scholar, was not without biases and his antimilitary views come through clearly in a memorial submitted to the throne just prior to his recall in 1178. In it he discussed the long-standing Sung tradition of revering men of civilian rather than military background, the origins of this policy in the Northern Sung, and its current importance to the maintenance of social order.

> In the Five Dynasties [era], military [men] were employed exclusively [as officials]; there were no scholars at court. As a result, they rivaled one another in fomenting tyranny, with turmoil persisting until [the time of Sung] Emperor T'ai-tsu. Founding the empire with valor and force, he [nonetheless] humbled his own ideas to conform to [those of] the literati. The *Way* of the "two Emperors" (Yao of the T'ang and Shun of the Yü dynasties) and the "three Kings" (Yü of the Hsia, T'ang of the Shang, and Wen of the Chou dynasties) has never been entrusted to persons [wielding] long lances and huge swords; [rather,] it must be discussed [with reference to] the scholars, [who wear] round caps and square[-toed] slippers.[61]

It is puzzling that Shih Hao should raise this issue some fifteen years after Hsiao-tsung had ascended the throne and at a time of peace. Historical records allude to no major policy dispute at court that might explain the timing of the remonstrance, so this may simply relate to some personal exchange between the two men. What is clear is the emperor's partiality for the military which, in the eyes of Shih Hao, was inconsistent with dynastic traditions. Some eight months later, this issue triggered another dispute. This time Shih Hao and Hsiao-tsung crossed one another over an originally minor incident involving a palace guardsman and a civilian.

The affair began with a low-level official in the Bureau of Military Affairs requesting the filling of some six thousand vacancies in various military units throughout the capital.[62] Before the court could respond, an overzealous officer in the Palace Guard rushed off to the marketplace with the intention of forcibly rounding up men for military induction. This touched off riots in Lin-an. Many prospective conscripts, desperately trying to evade service, went so far as to break or sever their fingers, which drew a good deal of public sympathy. There are reports of some resisters being threatened and others having their valuables seized by unruly soldiers. The incident created an uproar not only among the populace, but within the civil service as well, an uproar not easily quieted. To aggravate matters further, the inquest that followed seemed less concerned with justice than politics, all parties involved being well aware that this represented a contest between the privileges of the military and those of civilians. Undoubtedly under political pressure, judicial authorities deemed it most expedient to mete out sentences of capital punishment to the one palace guardsman and the one civilian accused of inciting the riot, while dropping charges against all others. This greatly displeased the chief councillor.

Convinced that the sentence was unjust and certain that the throne was somehow responsible for it, Shih Hao submitted a strongly worded memorial of protest. He agreed that the palace guardsman deserved the extreme punishment for transgressing his authority by impressing civilians into military service and confiscating their property. Yet, he contended, the largely innocent civilian—whose only crime was that of self-defense—deserved compassion, not death. Furthermore, he criticized the emperor for tolerating such an injustice and insisted that excessive sensitivity to the military community had created a dangerous insensitivity to popular opinion. Alluding to the story of two peasants of the Ch'in dynasty who responded to the severity of their empire's laws by rebelling, Shih Hao warned Hsiao-tsung of the grave consequences of alienating the people.[63] The sheer force of the memorial was sufficient to infuriate the throne, quite independent of the argument being presented. A more compromising official would probably have toned down the rhetoric at this point, but not Shih Hao. Tensions mounted for nearly a month as the controversy raged on. Before year's end, the chief councillor had tendered his resignation.

Despite strikingly different views and frequently heated exchanges between the emperor and his former teacher, Shih Hao never fell from favor. About two years after surrendering his post as bureaucratic chief, Hsiao-tsung sought his reappointment as vice-administrator of Fu-chou.[64] Shih Hao declined, possibly due to advancing age, and instead received a high-ranking sinecure.[65] A string of honorary titles also came his way, culminating in 1189 with the most venerated of all, that of "grand preceptor" (T'ai-shih, 1a).[66] He held a succession of ennoblements, including several as "duke" and eventually "prince."[67] Hsiao-tsung further demonstrated his abiding favor with an unprecedented court banquet in Shih Hao's honor.[68] The emperor often sent unusually generous gifts as well. Shortly before resigning in 1178, Shih Hao was presented with a mansion and attached private garden in a large and prominent section of his native Ming-chou.[69] Birthday gifts of gold, fine silks, and fragrant tea came every year.[70] In addition, he received a multitude of salary supplements, or "fiefs of maintenance" (shih-yi or shih-feng).[71] Beyond regular privileges under the protection program, his special merit led to official assignments for a younger brother, a son, and two sons-in-law.[72] Commenting on the emperor's largess, one Sung contemporary noted, "The magnitude of [the throne's] esteem and beneficence is without equal in recent times."[73] To be sure, Hsiao-tsung could be annoyingly stubborn and sometimes intolerant of those differing with him, but he was always a steadfast friend.

Shih Hao once likened his relationship with the emperor to that of a son to his father.[74] This represents a rather obvious allusion to their mutual respect and affection and the extent to which this created an intimacy resembling that of kin. The analogy is nonetheless revealing in another regard. As "son of heaven," the emperor represented the paternal overseer of the people and Shih Hao, being his subject, was nominally a mere child; in reality, the roles were reversed. About twenty years the emperor's senior, Shih Hao's position as imperial instructor afforded him the high esteem customarily due teachers in traditional Chinese society. Like a father, he constantly admonished the prince for improprieties of action, deportment, and attitude. He insisted upon restraint whenever his student wished to act.[75] He was the prince's virtual superego, always there to remind him of what not to do. Initially overwhelmed by the widsom of Shih Hao, it seemed only natural for the prince-turned-emperor enthusiastically to promote him to the highest posts in the bureaucracy. In time, however, the arrangement became totally unfeasible. Shih Hao was a man with strong personal convictions about imperial conduct and court policy, not at all given to compromise or indulgence. As chief councillor, he could be overbearing and contentious, expecting his student to be no less complaisant as emperor than he had been as prince. For a new ruler anxious to assert himself, domination of this sort must have seemed insufferable.

No less than Shih Hao, Hsiao-tsung could be highly individualistic and self-confident. Although attentive and even submissive as a student being groomed for the throne, he refused to remain so as a mature ruler. With the accession, Shih Hao would have to learn the art of accommodation, something quite out of character for him. When differences emerged over politically vital issues, neither man proved receptive to the other's outlook. The incidents leading to Shih Hao's two resignations as chief councillor both represent confrontations between individuals endowed with similar personalities but antithetical political views. That Shih Hao held onto the councillorship for a total of only fourteen months stems principally from this.

A modern historian, Wang Teh-yi, in praising Hsiao-tsung for his assertive leadership, discusses his adept manipulation of the bureaucracy as one case in point.[76] While Kao-tsung permitted Ch'in Kuei to hold onto the chief councillorship for an uninterrupted seventeen years and to dominate virtually every aspect of political activity at court, Hsiao-tsung jealously guarded his own authority against bureaucratic infringement. Determined to avert the emergence of bureaucratic bullies at his court, Hsiao-tsung permitted no chief councillor or assistant councillor to remain in office for long. The tenures of the majority, Wang notes, did not exceed one year.[77] Only four of a total of sixteen chief councillors held onto the reins of power for more than three years; these were men whose political views closely resembled those of the emperor and whose overall passivity made personality clashes highly unlikely. In addition, most individuals with more lasting tenures held the almost nominal post of councillor of the left, thereby enabling them to shun sensitive policy debates.[78]

Another of Hsiao-tsung's ploys designed to keep his top bureaucrats in line was to appoint a potentially threatening official twice to the same high post, instead of permitting a single, more lengthy tenure. By prolonging the interval between the two assignments, the bureaucrat in question tended to lose control over many old bases of support and thereby become all the more dependent on the throne itself. This was especially useful in dealing with rigidly moralistic types, men who the throne respected and anxiously sought to employ but could never expect to manipulate. Besides Shih Hao, the emperor handled two other councillors in this way.[79]

Such preoccupation with bridling top-level bureaucrats may, in part, reflect Hsiao-tsung's antipathy for Ch'in Kuei and his dominance during the preceding reign,[80] but other factors also help to explain this policy, the personality of the emperor being chief among them. Hsiao-tsung's initiation of a large-scale military campaign in 1163 without consulting or even notifying his top civilian officials—an act unprecedented in Sung history—underscores the capriciousness with which he sometimes reached major policy decisions. His inflexibility in the 1178 affair of the palace guardsman similarly betrays a strong sense of self-righteousness, an inclination to reject quite whimsically the counsel of chief advisors whenever it suited him. A close examination of the conflicts between him and Shih Hao suggests pronounced autocratic tendencies in the emperor. To reduce his dependence on civilian officials like Shih Hao, he strengthened ties with the military and later, finding few to trust there, turned increasingly to eunuchs. Hsiao-tsung thus represents not only the most manipulating emperor of the Southern Sung, but also its most arbitrary.

In time, the emperor developed an almost insatiable thirst for power. On the one hand, he expanded the authority vested in the chief councillor's office by eliminating the top administrative posts in the three ministries and making subordinate officers directly responsible to the chief councillor.[81] On the other, he emasculated his councillors to the point that most became virtual sycophants; he regularly drove from office less pliant individuals. By moving on these two fronts, the emperor sought, first, to eliminate as many intermediaries in the bureaucratic hierarchy as possible and consequently to enhance the responsiveness of lower executives to the top. In addition, with pivotal posts occupied by individuals easily manipulated by Hsiao-tsung, personal command over the entire bureaucratic machine was effectively the emperor's. His ultimate ambition was to become both political leader and chief administrator of the empire, and for awhile he became just that. From 1175 to 1178, the emperor refused to install even a nominal chief councillor and administered the bureaucracy largely on his own. In the absence of executives at the three ministries, he finally realized his ambition and, in the process, proved that the spiritual leader of the empire could also function quite well as its administrative chief.[82] Exactly what developments prompted a restoration of the chief councillorship in 1178 with the appointment of Shih Hao are not entirely clear; perhaps Hsiao-tsung found his many burdens simply too much for one man to bear. The sheer attempt nonetheless vividly illustrates the strength of his autocratic drive.

In the final analysis, Hsiao-tsung and Shih Hao shared a special relationship principally because they held several important personality traits in common, namely, an exaggerated sense of self-righteousness and self-worth combined with a general intolerance of contrary views. At the same time, it was precisely these characteristics that doomed any long-term collaboration between the two. Interestingly, despite his many criticisms of the throne, Shih Hao never directly admonished Hsiao-tsung for being an autocrat. So close to him in personality, this represented the emperor's one trait that he was hardly in a position to criticize.

LEGACY OF SHIH HAO

Although Shih Ts'ai holds the distinction of being the first Shih kins-man to hold high office, Shih Hao must be given credit for creating its empirewide reputation. The position of respect and influence afforded him at the court of Hsiao-tsung undoubtedly contributed much to enhancing his overall stature among scholar-officials both at home and in the capital. In turn, this provided an array of contacts, some of them political, but a good many of them intellectual as well.

Mention has already been made of Shih Hao's identification with Chang Chiu-ch'eng during his early years as instructor at Wen-chou. This became the first in a long list of scholarly associations that included many of the most prominent philosophical figures of his time. For example, the eminent Lu Chiu-yüan, a man later hailed as founder of the idealist school of Neo-Confucian thought, owed his early promotion in the civil service to the sponsorship of Shih Hao.[83] Chu Hsi, founder of the rival rationalist school, owed a similar debt to Shih Hao, having received his recommendation for promotion to a metropolitan post.[84] A leading disciple of Lu Chiu-yüan and a fellow native of Ming-chou, Yüan Hsieh, was also sponsored by the chief councillor,[85] as was the noted literary and political figure Yeh Shih (1150–1223).[86] Even in retirement, Shih Hao actively sought out talented men for the civil service. Despite his uncompromising attitude as bureaucratic chief, when it came to sponsoring men for office, he could be uncharacteristically liberal. Individuals of varied and often conflicting political and philosophical persuasions, including his own personal critics, owed their careers to his sponsorship.[87] In this way, Shih Hao became a popular figure in his later years, widely regarded as generous and principled. It was a record that few contemporaries could match. Furthermore, his original commentaries on such classics as the *Ch'un ch'iu* (Spring and Autumn Annals) and *Yi-ching* (Book of Changes) evince an unusual breadth of scholarship that further enhanced his standing among contemporaries.[88] When death came at eighty-eight, he had already provided his kin group with a foothold in the empire's political as well as intellectual domains.

The varied accomplishments of Shih Hao greatly profited the house as a whole, and not merely in terms of more kinsmen becoming eligible for bureaucratic appointment through protection.[89] Once in the civil service, being the offspring or close relative of so esteemed a statesman as Shih

Hao is certain to have made it easier, first, to win the sponsorship of a high official and, second, to attract the attention of the throne—the two most crucial hurdles in official advancement. Moreover, Shih Hao's special relationship with Lu Chiu-yüan and Yüan Hsieh stemming from his one-time sponsorship must have helped bolster his kin group's overall standing within philosophical circles in general, and especially within the idealist school. No doubt, the active involvement of subsequent generations of Shih in this particular school owes something to the early links established by Shih Hao.

SUMMARY OF GENERATION FIVE

In addition to Shih Hao, Shih Shih-chung sired four other sons. They all entered the civil service, but none received an official degree or attracted much public attention. Second son Shih Yüan (n.d.) reportedly ended his career as prefect of Chiang-yin commandary, in the southern part of present-day Kiangsu province.[90] Clearly, the imperial favor enjoyed by brother Shih Hao had been responsible for Shih Yüan's early penetration of the bureaucracy, yet his rise to an administrative post suggests a reasonably lengthy and distinguished career. Unfortunately, historical sources offer few details.

Third son Shih P'u (n.d.) reached the summit of his bureaucratic climb as vice-administrator of northwestern Chekiang's Hu-chou.[91] Again, the merit of Shih Hao had facilitated the initial conferrral of civil service rank, although little else is known about the development of his career.[92]

The two youngest sons, Shih Yüan [II] (n.d.) and Shih Chüan (n.d.) both held low-level posts: the former as a minor inspector in Ming-chou and the latter as assistant to the staff supervisor of Nan-k'ang commandary (8b), in the northern part of modern Kiangsi.[93] They similarly owed their official status to Shih Hao, yet neither appears to have done well in the civil service.

The eldest son of Assistant councillor Shih Ts'ai, Shih Chün (1129–1203), won the respect of his community as a devoted son, yet this yielded little fruit in the political realm. Entering the civil service in 1160 through the merit of his father, he went on to receive commissions, first as sheriff of Fu-chou (9b) and then as subprefect of Shao-hsing (8b).[94] Shih Chün also served as prefectural vice-administrator for Wu-chou, in the heart of present-day Chekiang, before retiring with the rank of 6b. While accomplished in his own right, he never penetrated the metropolitan bureaucracy and lived in the shadow of his father's glory. The younger son of Shih Ts'ai, Shih Jo-shui (n.d.), had no issue.

Turning to branch C of the kin group, Shih Mu was father of three boys.[95] Little is known about the two eldest sons, Shih Jo-ch'ung and Shih Chan, save that they posthumously received low-level bureaucratic rank. The youngest son proved, in the end, the most prosperous and in his case considerably more information exists. Shih Chien [II] (1124–94), according to reports, studied for some time at the Imperial University. Having failed to pass *chin-shih* examinations by forty *sui*, he decided to retire to his home. Interestingly, he represents the only kinsman of generation five to be identified with the university, which suggests that the institution—so vital to the education and bureaucratic advancement of an earlier generation—had a declining impact upon the subsequent rise of the Shih community. It was perhaps his long identification with the university, or maybe the reputation of cousin Shih Hao, that explains the decision by Emperor Kuang-tsung (r. 1189–94) to summon him to court. Shih Chien [II] declined the throne's offer of bureaucratic appointment, but he did accept the honorary conferral of official rank (9a).[96] Having concentrated much of his youthful energies on the education of his eight sons, he was not inclined to leave home and embark upon a new career in the civil service in his late sixties.

The heirs to branches D and E, quite unlike their cousins, were of no great accomplishment.[97] Of the two sons of Shih Ho, Shih Chi held bureaucratic rank; elder brother Shih K'o did not. The same holds for branch E, where Shih Ch'eng [II], a prefectural examination candidate, held rank but not office; Shih Hung, who seemed unusally promising in his youth, died before the opportunity came to prove himself. To the extent that the ancestors in the preceding generation for both groups were without civil service status, Shih Chi and Shih Ch'eng [II] undoubtedly penetrated the bureaucracy through the merit of kinsmen in other branches.

Except for Shih Hao, historical information on members of the fifth generation is generally limited to only a few fleeting passages. Although source materials are scarce and the career reviews presented above may be somewhat superficial, they nonetheless reveal several salient points about the mobility of the kin group at this time. In comparing the official career of Shih Hao with those of his brothers, the reader is first struck by the disparity. Shih Hao held the coveted *chin-shih* degree; his brothers held nothing. He rose to the highest posts in the bureaucracy; his brothers failed to rise beyond middle- or low-level posts. He served chiefly in the capital; his brothers were confined to the prefectures. He was a classicist who wrote extensively on complex philosophical issues; his brothers wrote virtually nothing.[98] Should it be concluded that the disparity existed simply because Shih Hao was far more intelligent than his brothers? This is always a possibility, but there are other factors that may also help to explain the phenomenon, chief among them being family finances.

When Shih Shih-chung died in 1124, eldest son Shih Hao was only eighteen years old. Although the exact ages of his brothers are unknown, the younger of them must have been small children. By Shih Hao's own admission, his family was still quite poor at the time and responsibility for educating the children ultimately had to be assumed by his mother.[99] Although uncle Shih Mu made a major contribution to the training of Shih Hao, his own death when the youth was only twenty-four did not permit him to help educate the younger of his nephews.[100] It is indeed probable that the deaths of their father and uncle, compounded by ensuing economic pressures, precluded the advanced training of the younger members of branch A. To this extent, it was just a matter of good fortune that the family's loss did not occur until after Shih Hao had reached maturity, thereby sparing him a similar fate.

The career prospects of his brothers and cousins initially trailed behind his own, yet once Shih Hao became a high official, he helped them to advance. The promotion of brother Shih P'u and the summoning to court of cousin Shih Chien [II] are two documented examples of this. They should not be viewed in isolation. As has been suggested earlier, a good many if not a majority of kinsmen appear indebted to Shih Hao for whatever inroads they were able to make into the civil service. The political achievements of Shih Ts'ai had no noticeable effect on bureaucratic access for kinsmen of his own generation and only a limited effect on the next generation. In contrast, when Shih Hao swept the capital, he carried many kinsmen on his coattails.

Another vital point revealed by comparing the career of Shih Hao with those of his relatives is the generally limited effect of recruitment through protection upon an individual's prospects in the civil service. The son of Shih Ts'ai, Shih Chün, theoretically occupied a far more advantageous position for official success than any other fifth-generation kinsman. No doubt, he was educated by his father, the kin group's first and only *chin-shih* recipient before Shih Hao. As principal heir to the former assistant councillor, he must have also been given priority in utilizing the protection scheme. Despite these advantages, it was not he who ultimately became the most successful member of this generation, but Shih Hao, a man whose own father never held an official degree or bureaucratic rank and who himself entered the civil service through examination success, not protection. That this should occur serves to illustrate the limitations of the protection privilege. While providing access to the bureaucracy for Shih Chün, it did not guarantee his subsequent achievement within it. Correspondingly, although the merit of Shih Hao could positively influence the careers of his close relatives, it did not make them the success that he was.

Shih Ts'ai was the first member of his kin group to hold a *chin-shih* degree and to enter the civil service, yet he rose to the second spot in the bureaucracy. Shih Hao was only the second member of the group to earn similar credentials, yet he became bureaucratic chief. Not only were they stars among their own kin but, almost overnight, they were transformed into the most politically accomplished members of their commmunity as well. Shih Ts'ai was only the second native of Ming-chou to become assistant councillor and Shih Hao was its first chief councillor.[101] As previously noted, the Shih lagged far behind other major kin groups in the region in terms of scholarly or official achievement.[102] It was among the last of Ming-chou's prominent houses to produce degreeholders and officials. Perhaps recognition that it was the underdog served to motivate kinsmen to double their efforts at competing with neighbors; perhaps it was just a string of fortuitous circumstances that made them a sudden success; or, maybe, as the widow Yeh's biographer insists, it was simply the work of "heaven." (In many respects, the Shih climb from the bottom of the local elite to the very top in only one or two generations does indeed appear to be somehow *super*natural.) Whatever the cause or causes of its phenomenal rise, the mere fact that so small and obscure a kin group could actually be so successful demonstrates that wealth and numbers represent not the only keys to bureaucratic attainment during the Sung.

In the aftermath of Shih Hao, the house grew dramatically. By the sixth generation, the Shih community became truly great, producing scholars and officials in numbers and prominence once beyond imagination. Its reputation, its connections within the bureaucratic elite, and its wealth were all carefully nurtured by Shih Hao for future generations to draw upon.

宋太師右丞相衞國忠獻王 諱彌遠像 第三十六世

1. Portrait of Shih Mi-yüan.

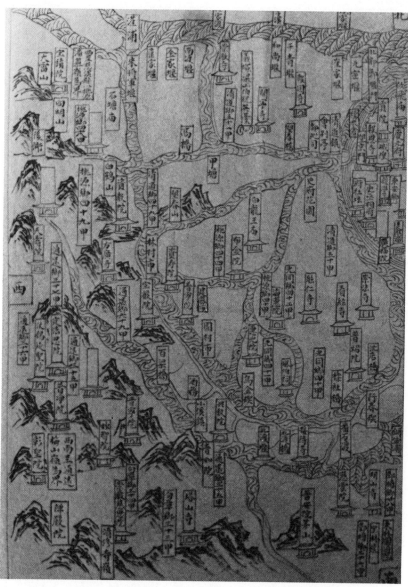

2. Map of Yin *hsien* and environs. *Pao-ch'ing Ssu-ming chih* (1228).
Note the Shih gardens to the west of the walled city, a gift to Shih Hao from
Emperor Hsiao-tsung. Courtesy of National Central Library, Taipei.

鄞縣境圖

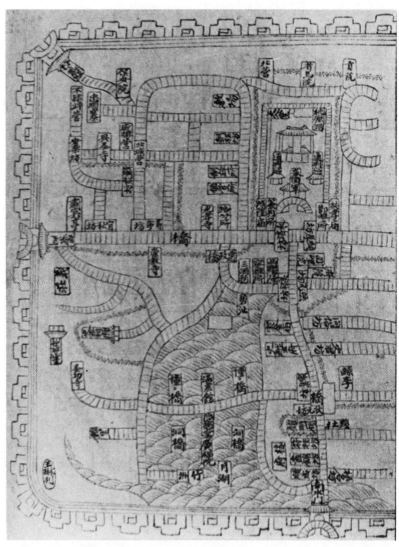

3. Map of the walled city, Yin *hsien*. *Pao-ch'ing Ssu-ming chih* (1228).
Note the mansion of Chief councillor Shih Mi-yüan, the mansion of Shih Hao,
and the Shih "ward," all in the city's southwest corner. Courtesy of National
Central Library, Taipei.

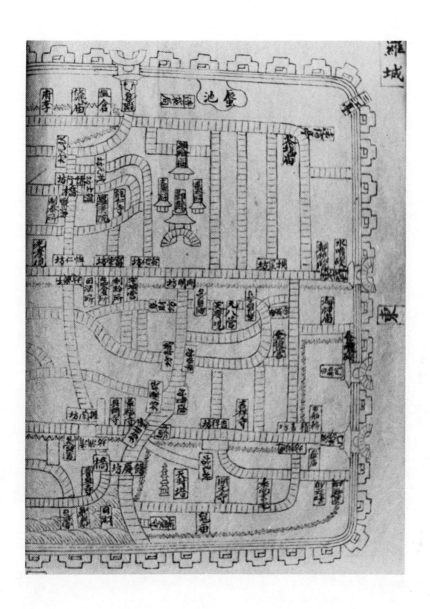

4. Portrait of the Widow Yeh. *Ssu-ming jen-chien, ch.* 3.

宋太師忠定王越王㳟

5. Portrait of Shih Hao. *Ssu-ming jen-chien, ch.* 1.

4

Blossoming in Autumn

THE FORTUNES OF the Southern
Sung, once so astonishingly secure, were destined to decline rather dramatically with the close of the twelfth century. The regime's first six
decades, under Kao-tsung and Hsiao-tsung, witnessed a good measure of
political and economic stability. The Jurchen challenge notwithstanding,
the border separating north and south was surprisingly tranquil for nearly
fifty of these sixty years. Admittedly, court officials virtually came to
blows, on countless occasions, over the war-peace issue, but Lin-an had
few real options. Men in the mold of Ch'in Kuei and Shih Hao, despite
their vast differences otherwise, could agree on the need to retain peace,
painfully aware of the high political cost of their unpopular stand. Chang
Chün and Wang Shih-p'eng advocated a bold policy of aggression toward
the north, acknowledging all the same that the bitterness of defeat might
well seal their own personal fate as well as the fate of the revanchist cause
in general. The fundamental question was whether to embrace war or
peace and then its optimal timing. Fortunately for Lin-an, only one enemy,
the Jurchen, posed a serious and persistent threat. Options being few,
policy decisions, however difficult to accept, were relatively easy to make.
Yet as time wore on, order and simplicity gave way to chaos and confusion.

With the early thirteenth century and the Mongol intrusion into the
Chinese realm, the very context for conflict was gravely, and permanently,
altered. Besides invading Jurchen territory in northwestern China, the
Mongols also roused the Hsi-hsia, western neighbors of the Jurchen whose
military inactivity over most of the twelfth century had enabled the leading antagonists in the area largely to ignore them as a significant factor in

North China's balance of power. The Mongol presence, therefore, suddenly transformed a once bilateral conflict into a four-dimensional melee. The speed and seriousness of the military power play to the north utterly bewildered Lin-an. Court officials well recognized the urgent need to respond to these developments, yet few could agree on the specifics of that response. To become actively involved in the conflict in the remote hope of expanding its own territory might well leave the Sung fighting a war on three major fronts. However, complete neutrality appeared equally dangerous, for greedy and vengeful neighbors might interpret this as an unfriendly act and exploit it to justify further expansion of the war. The times were difficult, both for an emperor to reign and a statesman to lead.

In addition to shifts in North China's once delicate balance of power, political leadership in the capital is another factor distinguishing the first and last decades of the Southern Sung. Despite Kao-tsung's inexplicable indulgence of Ch'in Kuei and Hsiao-tsung's unfortunate inclination toward absolutism, the contribution of these two rulers to the revitalization of their war-shaken empire cannot be denied. Punctual and regular at holding court, they were predictably conscientious about their imperial responsibilities and reasonably effective at keeping high officials under a tight rein. Although not always readily apparent, government policy generally emanated from the palace, not the chief councillor's office. Contrasting with such assertive leadership is the passive, sometimes derelict, character of succeeding rulers. Kuang-tsung (r. 1189–94) was given to mental illness, Ning-tsung (r. 1194–1224) to emotional insecurity, and Li-tsung (r. 1224–64) to licentiousness. Often unwilling or unable to make important political decisions themselves, they deferred most of these to the judgment of chief councillors. Thus, bureaucratic chiefs of the later period could be invincibly powerful, enjoying lifetime tenures and unflinchingly dismissing all who dared to challenge their dominance. In turn, the factional strife stemming from one-man dominance drove court intrigue and literary repression to levels unmatched since the last decades of the Northern Sung. Also reminiscent of K'ai-feng during its last years is the expanded role of empresses and dowagers in court politics, a development similarly stemming from the listlessness of imperial leadership.

The latter half of the Southern Sung is distinctive for yet another reason: after several generations of political division, decision makers at court were all born and raised in the south. Neither the emperor nor his high officials had much if any personal knowledge of the north, save for what could be gathered from brief visits to the border or travelers' tales. This was certain to affect their political views. The vast majority of statesmen—be they long-time residents of the south or descendants of early twelfth-century migrants, pragmatic politicians or idealistic philosophers—gradually came to terms with the likelihood that the Sung would remain a southern empire for the indefinite future. The thirteenth century yielded few militants in the mold of Chang Chün, or if it did, their views failed to attract a serious audience. Debates on war and peace reminiscent of the Hsiao-tsung era, while they did occasionally resurface, tended to be far less heated. Admittedly, the upset in North China's strategic balance during the Ning-tsung reign did give rise to a heightened concern for border defense. A growing number of officials demanded more aggressive involvement by their government in the widening conflict, including some limited expansion, but full recovery of the north seemed wildly ambitious to most. The views of the empire's political leadership had changed substantially since the time of Shih Hao.

This provincialization of the Southern Sung coincided with the growth in stature of Ming-chou and the maturation of the Shih kin group's sixth generation. As the Sung government came to turn increasingly to south-erners and then to southeasterners to staff its bureaucracy, the Shih house offered up progressively more of its sons. During the Ning-tsung era, the Shih blossomed into the empire's leading family of statesmen, a distinc-tion they maintained for much of the thirteenth century.

SHIH MI-YÜAN: THE EARLY YEARS

Perhaps the most visible indicator of a kin group's wealth and status is the size of its individual families. Prior to the fifth generation, Shih kins-men tended to keep a single wife and only one or two sons. All this changed with the ascendancy of Shih Hao. In addition to his legal wife, née Pei (1109–55), Shih Hao had at least two concubines.[1] Together, they gave him four sons and five daughters.[2] His legal wife gave birth to elder sons Shih Mi-ta (fl. 1169–85) and Shih Mi-cheng (n.d.). Younger sons Shih Mi-yüan (1164–1233) and Shih Mi-chien (1164–1232) were born, apparently as twins, to a concubine when the chief councillor was already sixty *sui*.[3] In time, each of the four became accomplished officials in their own right. However, outshining all three brothers, and indeed every other kinsman of his generation, was Shih Mi-yüan. This chapter thus focuses on him.

Shih Mi-yüan was born shortly after Shih Hao's resignation as chief councillor in the spring of 1164.[4] For most of his youth, his aging father stayed with the family at their residence at Ming-chou, serving the government for only five of his remaining thirty years. There is no evidence of the younger Shih formally studying either at the prefectural school or privately with some prominent local teacher. He relied, it appears, upon a leisured father, learned kinsmen, and older brothers to secure early literary training.[5] As it was, he learned fast and was ready for the civil service quite young.

In 1179, while merely a teenager, Shih Mi-yüan capitalized on his father's merit to enter the civil service through protection, whereupon he was given the rank of 9a and then 8b.[6] Two years after gaining official status, he took the Ministry of Personnel's promotion examination and placed first among the candidates. Considering the increased competitiveness of the examination, his high placement at only seventeen years old gives clear evidence of an exceptional precociousness. This led to early official appointments, first with Chien-k'ang prefecture's Commission of Provisions (*Liang-k'o yüan*), and then with Ming-chou's Military Commission for the Coastal Region (*Yen-hai chih-shih-ssu*). Although away from the capital, these assignments provided the regional experience normally required for promotion to more prestigious and influential metropolitan posts. This was followed in 1187 by Shih Mi-yüan's successful completion of the palace examination leading to conferral of *chin-shih* status at only twenty-three—some sixteen years younger than his father had been when he received the same honor. It seems undeniable that the younger Shih, beyond being simply precocious, had been well prepared from early on for the rigors of the examination process.

By this time, father Shih Hao was already over eighty years old and had long retired from government service. Emperor Hsiao-tsung was over sixty, soon to abdicate in favor of his son. The Shih house, like the Sung court, was on the verge of changing hands and this would have to pass before new opportunities presented themselves to a younger generation of bureaucrats and rulers. In the interim, Shih Mi-yüan was busy accumulating additional experience in the civil service. Making his debut in the capital, he served as auxiliary official at the High Court of Justice (*Ta-li-ssu chih*, 8a) and, subsequently, intendant at the Court of Imperial Sacrifices (*T'ai-she-ling*, 9a) and then registrar at the Court of Imperial Sacrifices (*T'ai-ch'ang-ssu chu-pu*, 8b). When his father died in the spring of 1194, Shih Mi-yüan took the traditional leave of absence to observe mourning. Up to this point, his father's good standing at court had had no appreciable effect upon his own advancement, for Shih Mi-yüan had held only minor posts. In fact, his presence in the capital appears to have gone largely unnoticed. Upon reemerging some two years later, however, his career took a dramatic and irrepressible upswing.

From 1196 to 1207, Shih Mi-yüan received over a dozen distinguished appointments, with promotions coming at such a pace that completion of tenure in any one post was scarcely possible. Quite fortuitously, a fair number of these provided access to the imperial palace and exposure to its most influential residents. These include instructor at the Multilevel School for Imperial Princes (*Chu-wang kung ta hsiao hsüeh chiao-shou*, 8a), executive assistant at the Court of Imperial Family Affairs (*Tsung-cheng ch'eng*, 7b), chancellery of imperial recorders (*ch'i-chü lang*, 6b), and auxiliary lecturer at the Tzu-shan School for Imperial Sons (*Tzu-shan-t'ang chih-chiang*, 7b). He held several secretarial posts as well, including recorder for the Bureau of Military Affairs (*Shu-mi-yüan pien-hsiu-kuan*, 8a), collator of the court's veritable records (*Shih-lu chien-t'ao*), deputy compiler at the Institute for Veritable Records (*Shih-lu-yüan t'ung-hsiu-chuan*, 6b), and vice-director of the Imperial Library (*Pi-shu-sheng shao-chien*, 5b). Away from the capital, he served as prefect of Ch'ih-chou (in modern Anhwei) and, concurrently, intendant for Che-hsi circuit's ever-normal granaries and monopolies for tea and salt (*t'i-chü ch'ang-p'ing ch'a yen kung-shih*).[7] Finally, in 1206, he penetrated the bureaucracy's executive level. After a brief stint as vice-president at the Ministry of Justice (*Hsing-pu shih-lang*, 3a), he moved on to the vice-presidency of the Ministry of Rites (*Li-pu shih-lang*, 3a).

Few officials could claim so extraordinary an array of esteemed assignments over a scant ten-year period. Shih Mi-yüan had accomplished in a decade what most promising officials devoted a lifetime of government service to achieve. Success in high office and the relative ease of his ascendancy can be explained, first, by his considerable administrative talents and imperial recognition of these. Historical sources provide few details of his early performance as a civil servant, yet in the absence of any evidence tying bureaucratic promotion to family contacts or political favoritism, we must conclude that the overriding factor was an exceptional official record. Second, and perhaps more important, such advancement suggests that the politically astute Shih Mi-yüan had succeeded in navigating around the intense disputes that so bitterly divided the early court of Ning-tsung. Yet, given his growing stature in the capital and regular interaction with the palace, neutrality could not be maintained for long. In time, Shih Mi-yüan too would be doused in the murky waters of palace politics.

DEMISE OF HAN T'O-CHOU

The decline in imperial leadership in Southern Sung times, while often traced to the Kuang-tsung reign, actually has its roots in the last years of Hsiao-tsung. The adopted son of Kao-tsung, so exceptionally energetic and conscientious for most of his twenty-seven years on the throne, fell victim to an incurable depression following his father's death at the close of 1187. For the next year and a half, he rarely held audiences and turned most of his responsibilities over to the heir-apparent.[8] Hsiao-tsung never regained his former vitality and this threw the court into near chaos. Not until the beginning of 1189 did he finally surrender to pressure from scholar-officials by agreeing to abdicate.

Chao Tun, Hsiao-tsung's successor and the future Emperor Kuang-tsung, was forty-two upon inheriting the imperial mantle. Officials initially welcomed his installation in the aftermath of his father's lengthy incapacity, yet he fell far short of his Confucian model. Kuang-tsung had long suffered from mental illness, for which he reportedly received regular medication.[9] The exact nature of his infirmity is uncertain, but it became so acute that he, like his father before him, was incapacitated, this time within months of ascending the throne. Ordering high officials to appear at court only once a month, he chose to spend most of his time locked away in the inner palace.[10] Following the emperor's immobilization, Empress Li emerged as a prominent force in court affairs. To the torment of all, she proved irresponsible, arrogant, and highly temperamental —behavior that alienated no small number of officials from the very outset. Making matters worse was her implication in the assassination of her husband's favored concubine in 1191, an incident that further aggravated Kuang-tsung's mental problem.[11]

Finding the emperor's disability permanent and Empress Li's antics insufferable, a growing body of high-ranking officials despairingly concluded that another abdication was in order. Repeatedly, requests were made that the emperor name an heir; the throne ignored them. The death of Hsiao-tsung in the summer of 1194 and the further deterioration of Kuang-tsung's mental health and his continued failure to respond to their requests finally convinced high officials of the need to act independently. Consequently, Chief councillor Liu Cheng (1129–1206), Administrator of the military bureau Chao Ju-yü (1140–96), and Palace Postern official Han T'o-chou (1152–1207) enlisted the support of the Dowager Wu and Empress Li in resolving the succession crisis. With the dowager having affixed her seal to the proper decrees, the emperor's eldest son, Prince Chia, was elevated to heir-apparent and almost immediately named emperor.[12] From beginning to end, Kuang-tsung was scarcely aware of the events leading to his own dethronement.

Chao K'uo, the emperor known to history as Ning-tsung, was a young man of twenty-six at the time of his accession. No doubt, the youth was much more physically and emotionally fit than his father to withstand the rigors of imperial leadership, but he appears only slightly better off intellectually. Historical records have described him using adjectives such as "humane, filial, and precipitately mature"; never is he referred to as intelligent.[13] One prominent compiler of anecdotes during the late Southern Sung, in fact, stated explicitly that he was rather dim-witted. Chou Mi (1232–1308) candidly noted, "Some say that Ning-tsung was not intelligent and had a slowness of speech. Every time an envoy from the north appeared [in the capital] for an audience, a eunuch would secretly be employed to speak on his behalf."[14] From this passage alone it cannot be readily determined whether the emperor had a serious speech impediment or merely a stammer.[15] Serious or not, such an impairment helps to explain his passivity as ruler.

Standard historical works rarely contain information about Ning-tsung's personality or leadership qualities. In contrast with narratives of earlier reigns, accounts for the Ning-tsung era contain few descriptions of verbal exchanges between the emperor and his chief advisors. He seems never to have differed with them over policy matters nor, for that matter, did he hold an opinion of his own. This is especially startling in light of the length of his rule, the complexity of the problems besetting it, and the abruptness with which policy could change. Ning-tsung, "the tranquil," may well represent the most unopinionated and passive emperor of the entire dynasty, a character trait that helps explain why he gave officials a free rein over the bureaucracy and court in a fashion unprecedented in Sung times. Entrusted with sweeping authority and secure about the favor that was theirs, chief ministers often felt little need to strike the usual compromises with colleagues; indeed, they could be outlandishly arbitrary, even authoritarian, as decision makers. Ning-tsung retained the throne for over three decades, the duration of which the court was controlled by only two men, both of them awesome ministers who held the bureaucracy and emperor tightly within their grip. The first of these was Han T'o-chou.[16]

Lacking an examination degree, it was principally by being nephew of Kao-tsung's influential Empress Wu that Han T'o-chou was initially selected to serve as supervisor of the Palace Postern (*Ko-men shih*).[17] The Postern, a quasi-military office, was responsible for securing the doors of the palace and, in this way, its chief supervisors could control access to the throne. Han T'o-chou readily exploited this privilege, as well as his family ties, to emerge as an important liaison between the palace and court officials in the delicate deliberations leading to the abdication of Kuang-tsung in 1194. With the installation of Ning-tsung as emperor, his first empress, née Han, was none other than the grand-niece of Han T'o-chou.[18] Such preponderant influence among imperial consorts ultimately enabled the Postern official to eliminate his major competitor for court dominance, Chao Ju-yü, and to win the imperial favor needed to become irreversibly entrenched.[19]

Although never officially appointed chief councillor, Han T'o-chou nonetheless functioned as one. From 1197 to 1207, he reigned as undisputed decision maker at court, the sole formulator of government policy, arbiter of bureaucratic disputes, and shepherd of official advancement. Yet even before coming to dominate court politics, an obviously ambitious Han T'o-chou drew heavy criticism from the bureaucracy, even contempt.[20] His lack of scholarly credentials, identification with the disesteemed Palace Postern, close ties to consorts and eunuchs—all combined to make him, in the eyes of officialdom, undeniably undeserving of the throne's confidence, let alone worthy of commanding the entire civil service. With good reason, they feared that his presence, in the long run, would strengthen the hand of palace women—the inner court—against themselves, the outsiders. With the treachery of Empress Li still a vivid memory, they were determined to guard against the rise of another powerful courtesan in the person of Empress Han; this also applied to her surrogates. As Han T'o-chou amassed ever greater political might, his critics grew in number. In response, he resorted to increasingly authoritarian measures to silence them.

Han T'o-chou originally employed the Censorate to eliminate individual critics, just as another autocrat, Ch'in Kuei, had done so successfully some two generations earlier. In time, however, he lost patience with this slow and tedious process. Having decided to eliminate all in one stroke, he moved to condemn the one school of thought with which a sizable portion of his opposition was allegedly associated: *Tao-hsüeh* Neo-Confucianism.[21] Through strategically placed civil service allies, he accused the school of philosophical heresy: "perverting the teachings of the ancients." Worse yet, they had reputedly formed "death-defying factions" at court for purposes of amassing political power. The defenseless opposition fell quickly, forced out of office under a cloud of controversy. Having made his case, Han T'o-chou then ordered the compilation of lists of more prominent *Tao-hsüeh* adherents, fifty-nine in all, among them some of the most respected political and intellectual figures of their day. Former Chief councillors Chao Ju-yü, Liu Cheng, and Chou Pi-ta (1126–1206) were among the accused, in addition to such philosophical luminaries as Chu Hsi, Ch'en Fu-liang (1137–1203), Yeh Shih, and Yang Chien.[22] Once included on the list, scholar-officials not only lost their jobs in the bureaucracy, but found their interpretations of the classics banned as sources of authority for official examinations. Designed to destroy his opponents both politically and intellectually, this repressive act proved wildly ambitious and baseless, exceeding Han T'o-chou's ability, in the long run, either to justify or to enforce. Yet the ban, however senseless, does betray the desperateness of the Postern chief and the extent of his unpopularity—apart from being quite numerous, his enemies were also highly influential. The proscription remained in effect for only a few years when, at the instructions of Han T'o-chou himself, it was gradually lifted.[23] While not enforced for long, the enmity it created for him was lasting.

The ban on *Tao-hsüeh* may have discredited Han T'o-chou among colleagues in the bureaucracy, but the emperor's confidence was not easily shaken. Rather than domestic policies, it was a foreign war that ultimately was his undoing. With the Sung-Chin border tranquil since the early years of Hsiao-tsung—nearly two generations—political division won increased acceptance. Even those officials who continued to embrace hopes for a reunification of north and south were nonetheless cognizant of Sung China's overwhelming military inadequacies and the implausibility of aggressive military action, at least in the foreseeable future. Han

T'o-chou differed from most bureaucratic chiefs of the late Southern Sung in that he was identified as a northerner.[24] Whether this was a factor in his decision to reopen hostilities against the Chin we will never know; he left nothing behind to make his case. But in light of his mounting failures in the domestic realm, I am convinced that this foreign policy offensive was politically motivated, not an outgrowth of revanchist idealism. As for timing, it was undoubtedly related to the widespread, and apparently erroneous, belief in Lin-an that the enemy, beset with an array of internal and external problems, was highly vulnerable.[25] Whatever his motives, in his new capacity as special councillor, literally "executive of military and state affairs" (p'ing-chang chün-kuo-shih),[26] Han T'o-chou initiated a war with the Jurchen in the spring of 1206 that would cost both him and the Sung empire dearly.[27]

The thrust of the Sung offensive initially focused on Ch'in-chou, the southeastern portion of modern Kansu. The special councillor planned, it appears, to use the west as a testing ground of enemy strength, conveniently enabling him to avoid endangering the heart of his empire in the lower Huai region. To this end, he entrusted to a prominent military leader with a long record of service in the area, Wu Hsi (1162–1207), control over the entire western flank. It was a fatal error. As assistant frontier commander for Szechwan, the politically ambitious Wu Hsi amassed increasingly more power until he was finally in a position to rebel. This he did at the beginning of 1207, proclaiming fealty to the Jurchen.[28] Fortunately for the Sung, his support among subordinates was anything but firm; scarcely a month after the insurrection, Wu Hsi was killed in a mutiny led by elements within his own army loyal to the Sung. Although short-lived, the rebellion doomed any plans of Han T'o-chou to make major inroads into the northwest. It also illustrated, to the court's considerable embarrassment, the extent to which the entire war effort had been poorly planned and carelessly executed.

Even before the Wu Hsi rebellion, Jurchen retaliatory moves in the northeast and military setbacks there proved equally troubling for Lin-an. As defeats on the battlefield mounted, an insecure Han T'o-chou began to forsake allies at court, seeking to blame policy failures and military defeats entirely on them. A close confidant who succeeded him as supervisor of the Palace Postern, Su Shih-tan (d. 1207), was among his first scapegoats.[29] At the same time, military leaders, including those in strategically vital areas, were quickly replaced for daring to differ with the special councillor over policy or for suffering a single defeat.[30] In this way, military leadership fell into inexperienced hands at the most untimely juncture. The Jurchen were clearly on the offensive by the close of 1206 and, with each victory, Han T'o-chou's political standing at home declined. Afraid of becoming the next scapegoat, previously loyal supporters began to desert him. Even neutral elements at court joined ranks with longtime opponents in the face of impending disaster. By 1207, the special councillor was vulnerable as never before to a political challenge.

The enemy must have sensed this, for when the Sung emissary, Fang Hsin-ju (1177–1222), visited their camp to open peace negotiations in the summer of 1207, they demanded no less than the special councillor's head.[31] Understandably, an infuriated Han T'o-chou abandoned his peace initiative, allegedly with the intention of escalating the war.[32] It was at this point that neutral elements at court, in alliance with the palace, were stirred to action. First, Ning-tsung's empress of five years, née Yang (1162–1232), joined her adopted son, Prince Jung (1192–1220), in pleading with the emperor to dismiss the special councillor.[33] The two then importuned Yang Tz'u-shan (1139–1219), the empress's adopted brother and prominent palace figure, to enlist the support of several eminent court officials in eliminating the special councillor. These included the vice-president of the Ministry of Rites, Shih Mi-yüan, and Assistant councillors Ch'ien Hsiang-tsu (n.d.) and Li Pi (d. 1222). Together, they were responsible for ordering the commander of the Palace Guard, Hsia Chen (n.d.), to assassinate Han T'o-chou. On his way to court on the morning of November 24, 1207, he was seized by guardsmen, dragged to a garden just beyond the walls of the main imperial palace, and bludgeoned to death. For the first time in Sung history, a leading court official had been slain, purportedly at the orders of the palace.

An incident of great controversy during Sung times, it has generated as much confusion as controversy among later historians grappling with contradictory primary sources. First, historians are at odds over the level of involvement of the various participants in the conspiracy. Second, they remain uncertain about the nature of the emperor's role in the affair. Among contemporary Sung and post-Sung sources alike, there are those that charge Empress Yang with single-handedly masterminding the entire assassination conspiracy.[34] Pointing to Han T'o-chou's alleged support for the elevation of the Lady Ts'ao to succeed his niece as empress following Lady Han's death in 1200, they contend that Empress Yang, the underdog, had reason to hate him from the very outset. This reportedly led her to be especially critical of the special councillor's performance in office and eventually to take steps to have him removed.

Many other sources, on the other hand, identify Shih Mi-yüan as the principal conspirator and portray the empress as a mere tool in his hands.[35] They point to his pro-peace inclination, open criticism of Han T'o-chou's war policy, and political ambitiousness as factors in his decision to have the special councillor eliminated.[36] Rather than merely assisting Empress Yang, Shih Mi-yüan is charged with having directed the entire scenario on his own.

Of the two versions, the former is far more convincing. Empress Yang made no effort to conceal her antipathy for Han T'o-chou and tension between them was incessant. Moreover, her status in the palace, combined with a long record of political activism, makes her a much more likely suspect. Shih Mi-yüan, after all, had no real motive for wanting the special councillor dead. In contrast with *Tao-hsüeh* adherents, his career was not noticeably affected by the dominance of Han T'o-chou; in fact, it skyrocketed during this period. Even after openly denouncing the war policy, civil service promotions continued to come his way. There is also no evidence to suggest personal animosity or political rivalry between the two men. Surely, a simple difference of opinion on foreign policy is insufficient motive for organizing a conspiracy to assassinate the most powerful man in the capital. In addition, Shih Mi-yüan's post in the Ministry of Rites gave him no authority to deploy the Palace Guards, especially for the highly irregular mission of executing the special councillor. Such orders could only have emanated from the palace or, alternatively, the chief councillor's office.

Finally, assertions that Shih Mi-yüan was sufficiently courageous both to organize and to execute an elaborate assassination plot is not consistent with what is known about his personality. An extremely cautious individual, he uniformly refused to take any action where the risks were high, except when compelled by extraordinary circumstances. Chou Mi, in fact, wrote that he had no intention of becoming an accomplice to the conspiracy and consented only after being subjected to much pressure from the empress's brother. Furthermore, when he sensed that Han T'o-chou was becoming suspicious, a frightened Shih Mi-yüan reportedly sought to abandon his fellow conspirators. It was only after additional prodding, so the story goes, that he finally agreed to remain with them.[37]

This pervasive indecision and timidity were virtual trademarks of Shih Mi-yüan's political leadership from beginning to end, in both the domestic and foreign policy arenas. Needless to say, these are hardly the traits of a murder conspiracy's prime mover.

Meanwhile, there is the issue of imperial involvement in the affair. Some historians portray Ning-tsung as totally ignorant of developments at court, only learning of Han T'o-chou's elimination sometime later. In support of this, they refer to an imperial edict ordering the dismissal of the special councillor; it was dated three days *after* his death.[38] There are other accounts that claim that the dismissal order was issued the day *before* the assassination, thereby enhancing the possibility of imperial involvement.[39] Yet another body of material insists that Shih Mi-yüan received personally from the throne secret directives to deploy the Palace Guard for the deadly mission.[40] Although not a party to the original conspiracy, the emperor was reportedly informed in advance of the intended slaying and gave his tacit approval. If this is correct, then Han T'o-chou was not assassinated, but legally executed.

The extent of imperial involvement can never be determined with any certainty, yet developments following Han T'o-chou's death clearly imply support for the action. First, immediately after the incident, the throne chose to advance the office or rank of all participants to the conspiracy. It elevated Assistant councillor Ch'ien Hsiang-tsu to chief councillor and Prince Jung to heir-apparent, conferred high official status upon the brother of Empress Yang, rewarded the commander of the Palace Guard with a prestigious assignment, and advanced Shih Mi-yüan from vice-president to chief executive at the Ministry of Rites.[41] Second, Han T'o-chou's political allies were summarily reprimanded. Another execution—this time unequivocally authorized by Ning-tsung—was ordered four days after the court assassination. The new victim was Han T'o-chou's close confidant, Su Shih-tan. Chief councillor Ch'en Tzu-ch'iang (n.d.) was banished for his role in furthering the ill-fated war policy. Even Li Pi, a former supporter of Han T'o-chou who subsequently joined the conspirators, held onto his post as assistant councillor only briefly before dismissal orders came.[42] By uniformly rewarding the conspirators while reprimanding associates of the special councillor, the emperor lent an element of legitimacy to the execution. His actions, made spontaneously and without the slightest hesitancy or reservation, suggest that the emperor, although perhaps disturbed by Han T'o-chou's death, was hardly surprised.

Finally, were the slaying an unauthorized act of a coterie of prominent palace figures and high officials, then the court would surely have been inundated with memorials attacking the group. This did not occur.[43] Although precedent-setting, the assassination generated surprisingly little reaction from scholar-official ranks.

Indeed, a statement made by Shih Mi-yüan months after the incident leaves little doubt that Ning-tsung indeed authorized the action. Upon uncovering a minor conspiracy in Ming-chou against his own life, Shih Mi-yüan requested to be relieved of official duties. This 1208 request was justified on the grounds that "Your Majesty executed the 'original evil' [Han T'o-chou] not long ago and I was *secretly* permitted to assist; [for this reason,] the remnants of his [one-time] faction harbor a strong hatred [for me]."[44]

It is, in all probability, the historical significance of the act that explains the confusion about imperial involvement. It was a tradition of the Sung dynasty, after all, that court officials be respected and given free expression of thought. Criticism of government policy was not only tolerated, but genuinely encouraged. Reflecting this spirit of tolerance, discredited chief councillors might be demoted or sent into exile, yet none were summarily executed. For Ning-tsung to break with so important and long-standing a tradition was tantamount to forsaking the ancestors, a serious violation of Confucian propriety. That the felonious act should be executed on palace grounds, no less, only added to its unsavoriness. Under the circumstances, it is understandable that many traditional historians, seeking to conceal the throne's complicity in the affair, attempted to place entire responsibility with Shih Mi-yüan and Empress Yang. His passive personality and dependency upon civil service advisors notwithstanding, it is inconceivable that Ning-tsung was totally unaware of events unfolding in his own backyard.

POLITICAL ENTRENCHMENT

That later historians identified Shih Mi-yüan as prime mover in the palace conspiracy may well be because, following the demise of Han T'o-chou, it was he who reaped the greatest political benefit. Immediately after the incident, the court advanced him to minister of rites (*Li-pu shang-shu*, 2b)[45] and concurrent superintendent over the household of the heir-apparent (*t'ai-tzu chan-shih*, 3b).[46] A promotion to coadministrator at the Bureau of Military Affairs (2a) and concurrent chief consultant to the heir-apparent (*t'ai-tzu pin-k'o*, 3b) followed only one month later. In 1208, he was further advanced to chief administrator of the military bureau (1b), assistant councillor (2a), and finally chief councillor of the right with joint authority over the military bureau. Honors included nomination as "secondary tutor to the heir-apparent" (*t'ai-tzu shao-fu*, 2b) and ennoblement as "duke."[47] Thus, within scarcely a year after Han T'o-chou's assassination, Shih Mi-yüan had replaced him as head of the bureaucracy. He was a relatively youthful forty-four.

Shih Mi-yüan served as chief councillor for only a month when the death of his mother necessitated a leave of absence for mourning. Although he returned to Ming-chou, the retirement was largely nominal. A mere twelve days following his departure from the capital, the chief councillor of the left, Ch'ien Hsiang-tsu, was dismissed from office.[48] By removing the one man who might overshadow Shih Mi-yüan in his absence, the throne, no doubt, intended to convey its complete confidence in the newly appointed councillor and its anticipation of his speedy return. No replacement councillor was ordered and for five months the bureaucracy had no chief. At the request, ostensibly, of the crown prince—who, at seventeen years old, was probably being goaded on by the empress—Ning-tsung suspended mourning obligations for Shih Mi-yüan. In June 1209 he presented the revived chief councillor with a mansion in the capital to facilitate "easy consultation."[49] This marked the beginning of what became the longest uninterrupted tenure of a chief minister in Sung history. Moreover, for the duration of the next quarter-century, Shih Mi-yüan was the *only* councillor; no one was appointed councillor of the left until Shih Mi-yüan himself moved to that post in 1233. This gave him, in effect, undisputed control over the court and its policies.

Shih Mi-yüan's early years in power drew generous praise and only modest censure, for he began by reversing the most reprehensible policies of his predecessor. Paramount among his initial concerns was the restoration of peace. The death of Han T'o-chou immediately triggered a flurry of diplomatic activity, reflecting a new determinism to break the longstanding impasse in negotiations and to secure a new pact with the Jurchen. Additional emissaries were commissioned to join those already up north in the hope of accelerating the peace process.[50] By late spring 1208, while Shih Mi-yüan was still chief of the military bureau, the two sides reached an agreement. The Sung conceded to an increase in its annual tribute, the modest surrender of territory in the lower Huai valley, and acceptance of a diplomatic status vis-à-vis the north roughly equal to that of the pre–Hsiao-tsung era. Even more demonstrative of Lin-an's shameless desperation is its assent to deliver the heads of Han T'o-chou and Su Shih-tan to the enemy.[51] The proviso, unprecedented in Sung-Chin relations, seemed to many in the south to be an affront to the empire's integrity, a challenge to its suzerainty and legitimacy. Minister of war Ni Ssu (1147–1220), for example, portrayed it as "an injury to the essence of the kingdom."[52] Imperial University Instructor Chen Te-hsiu (1178–1235) considered it "degrading."[53] In general, however, the concession generated only mild criticism. Even under humiliating conditions, peace was welcome. With the special councillor so universally despised, few were willing to speak out in defense of his corpse.

On the home front, Shih Mi-yüan moved to revive, politically or posthumously, *Tao-hsüeh* elements once disgraced under the Han T'o-chou regime. A partial restoration had begun as early as 1202, yet only under Shih Mi-yüan did the court announce a full recision of the former ban. Among those posthumously honored were Chu Hsi, Liu Cheng, Chao Ju-yü, and P'eng Kuei-nien.[54] Lou Yüeh and Lin Ta-chung (1131–1208), still alive at the time, were recalled to service in Lin-an.[55] This revival represents the first step in the long journey that ended in the official sanctioning of *Tao-hsüeh* as state orthodoxy.[56] Shih Mi-yüan's courtship with this influential group of philosophers readily earned for him a reputation as sponsor of talent and patron of philosophical inquiry, both important factors in his future consolidation of power.[57]

At the same time that he publicly embraced moralist thinkers by reversing the policies of his predecessor, Shih Mi-yüan also strengthened his own hand by quietly eliminating potential rivals in the capital. As previously noted, a coconspirator who later became councillor of the left, Ch'ien Hsiang-tsu, was dismissed for unknown reasons shortly after Shih Mi-yüan's elevation as councillor of the right, most probably at the new councillor's recommendation.[58] Another coconspirator whose political influence proved threatening, Chang Tzu (n.d.), was similarly removed from office.[59] This effectively left Shih Mi-yüan, in less than two years, undisputed chief of the bureaucracy and principal spokesman for the palace. It was a development in which not everyone could delight. Regarding the new councillor's close ties to the palace and special favor with the throne as all too reminiscent of the recent past, some officials did not hesitate to speak out disapprovingly.

Ni Ssu, for example, launched a broadside against Shih Mi-yüan as early as 1208, even before his installation as chief councillor. Pointing to the emperor's unique habit of "precipitately summoning him to court," Ni Ssu accused Shih Mi-yüan of scheming to become a second Han T'o-chou.[60] He also charged that Shih Mi-yüan, as coadministrator at the Bureau of Military Affairs, was so presumptuous as to commission low-ranking officials without consulting his colleagues. He even accused the favored Shih of flagrantly disregarding fundamental rules of etiquette by standing alongside superiors during imperial audiences, reflecting insuffer-able arrogance. The charges suggest that Shih Mi-yüan, immediately fol-lowing the demise of Han T'o-chou, had clearly surpassed all other con-tenders in becoming the special councillor's successor as power broker in the capital. For Ni Ssu, then minister of war and probably a serious candidate for the bureaucracy's top spot, this was an ominous sign, a personal as well as a public threat. Being among the first to recognize Shih Mi-yüan's political ambitiousness, Ni Ssu was first to suffer from it. Soon after Shih Mi-yüan became chief councillor, Ni Ssu was pressured to surrender his metropolitan post. Meanwhile, a former subordinate of Shih Mi-yüan at the Imperial Library, Wei Liao-weng (1178–1237), resigned in protest following the chief councillor's nomination. He accused Shih Mi-yüan of "monopolizing the affairs of the empire."[61] For similar reasons, Chen Te-hsiu also opted to leave the capital periodically. He complained that the chief councillor, by using ennoblements and salaries to manipulate officials, was demoralizing the entire civil service.[62]

From allegations such as these it may be inferred that Shih Mi-yüan's popularity in Lin-an began gradually to erode not long after he consoli-dated power, a development stemming largely from scholar-official appre-hension about the reemergence of one-man domination at court. At this early stage, however, his bureaucratic record was beyond reproach and the opposition had no single domestic issue around which to rally. This changed, quite radically, with the close of the Ning-tsung reign.

DEATH OF A PRINCE

From early on in his career, Shih Mi-yüan shared a special relationship with the heir-designate to Ning-tsung, Chao Hsün (elsewhere referred to as Prince Jung). He had served as tutor and advisor to the politically astute Chao Hsün during his formative years, subsequently allying with him and Empress Yang in 1207 to eliminate Han T'o-chou.[63] Thus, Shih Mi-yüan was probably no less shaken than the throne by the sudden death of the prince at twenty-eight. It was 1220 and the emperor nearly fifty-two. Although at least seven sons had been born to him prior to this, each one had died, curiously, within weeks of his birth.[64] Chao Hsün was initially adopted due to the emperor's failure to produce an heir. Now the tiresome and sensitive process of selecting a suitable substitute had to be repeated. In recognition of Shih Mi-yüan's close relationship with the former prince and his many years of loyal service at court, the emperor apparently turned to him for assistance in finding a replacement.

The selection must have been difficult, for nearly a year passed before a nephew of the emperor, Chao Hung (d. 1225), was finally adopted as imperial son.[65] Later known as Prince Chi, he was the only youth adopted by the throne at the time, which led many to consider him the inevitable heir. In fact, he was never officially designated as such.

Meanwhile, the elevation of Chao Hung to prince necessitated the selection of another member of the Chao clan to replace him as imperial nephew and adopted grandson of Chao K'ai (d. 1180), a one-time heir to the throne of Hsiao-tsung. Due to its proximity to the ruling family and the fact that the throne frequently took recourse to the line of Chao K'ai when in need of male heirs, the naming of a successor to that line was especially important. Rather surprisingly, the palace decided in favor of a distant cousin of the imperial clan residing at Shao-hsing, Chao Yün (b. 1205).[66]

For the next three years, the court took no further action and the bureaucracy, ordinarily given to fits and starts when an aging emperor fails to fix the succession, was uncharacteristically mute. Then, in mid-September 1224, as the emperor lay on his deathbed, a major upset occurred. An edict was revealed, apparently drafted by Shih Mi-yüan and approved by the emperor, elevating Chao Yün to imperial son. Ning-tsung died on the evening of the seventeenth. In the early hours of the next morning, under heavy guard, the chief councillor hastily summoned Chao Yün to the palace, read the imperial will naming him successor, and supervised his accession as the future Emperor Li-tsung. He then summoned Chao Hung. His bodyguards disarmed and without recourse, the prince was forced to pay obeisance by bowing before the new emperor. Subsequently, at instructions from the throne, the embittered prince took up residence in Hu-chou, just sixty or seventy kilometers north of the capital.[67]

In February of the next year, there came another shock. A small band of politically naive local men at Hu-chou staged an uprising that spelled doom for the prince.[68] Although Chao Hung appears not to have incited them to act, the group nonetheless rallied to his defense. Declaring him the only rightful heir to the throne of Ning-tsung and denouncing Shih Mi-yüan as a usurper, they demanded no less than the dismissal of the chief councillor and the surrender of the throne to the prince. To back up their demands, they boasted an army of some two hundred thousand men, claimed the support of a prominent rebel leader in Shantung, and threatened to use both in marching on the capital if demands were not met. In reality, they had managed to recruit only a few hundred untrained peasants and held no hope of attracting outside assistance. Even the prince reportedly withheld support for the rebel cause, despite what must have been an almost irresistible temptation to do otherwise. In fact, according to contemporary records, he personally led local forces in suppressing the uprising and had restored order long before the arrival at Hu-chou of government regulars. Innocent or not, his death warrant had been signed in Lin-an and Palace Guardsmen were obliged to implement it. He died by strangulation, the uprising having lasted a mere two weeks.

The role of Shih Mi-yüan in the dislodging and subsequent death of Chao Hung is, without a doubt, the thorniest issue of his quarter-century tenure—indeed, the most controversial succession of the entire Southern Sung period. Consequently, accounts provided by both contemporary statesmen and later historians are widely disparate. One body of material insists that the rescript naming Chao Yün imperial son was drafted at the emperor's instructions at least five days before his death, while Ning-tsung was still of sound mind and capable of making responsible decisions. It was merely "in accordance with the imperial will" that the chief councillor supervised the installation of Chao Yün as emperor. Thus, his conduct, totally in line with imperial wishes, was beyond reproach.[69]

Others contend that Shih Mi-yüan acted independently, even illicitly. They contend that tensions between the prince and the chief councillor began to mount soon after Chao Hung entered the palace, perhaps initially reflecting a clash of personalities. In time, the prince found Shih Mi-yüan's dominance at court unbearably constraining and offensive. In apparent temper tantrums, he repeatedly vowed to banish the councillor to the far fringes of the empire once in a position to act. Rumor has it that Shih Mi-yüan, through well-placed informants in the palace, was always aware of the prince's sentiments and began planning an alternative course well in advance. After identifying Chao Yün as a youth of considerable promise, Shih Mi-yüan allegedly sponsored his nomination as heir to the line of Chao K'ai. Fellow provincial Cheng Ch'ing-chih (1176–1251) then received private instructions from the councillor to begin grooming Chao Yün not for the role of royal nephew, but for emperor. Upon the death of Ning-tsung, so critics contend, Shih Mi-yüan willfully forged imperial documents to permit the throne to pass to Chao Yün. Even Empress Yang, an erstwhile ally of Shih Mi-yüan, strongly opposed the change and acquiesced only after receiving ominous threats from his office.[70] If such accounts are accurate, then the chief councillor stands guilty of some of the most flagrant abuses of bureaucratic authority in all of Sung history.

The renowned Ch'ing historian Chao Yi (1727–91) has argued in defense of the second body of material, placing responsibility for the action squarely on the shoulders of Shih Mi-yüan. He traces discrepancies in various historical accounts concerning the affair to the chief councillor's alleged tampering with court-compiled "Veritable Records."[71] Pointing to the fact that he remained in power for another nine years after the death of Ning-tsung and was consequently in a position to supervise the editing of these compilations, Chao Yi posits that Shih Mi-yüan systematically misrepresented historical fact to exculpate himself of any wrongdoing. As the "Basic Annals" of *Sung shih* were constructed largely upon the information drawn from the mendacious Veritable Records, Chao Yi dismisses them as totally unreliable. Rather, he considers accurate only accounts based on unofficial sources, such as the individual biographies of Empress Yang and Prince Chi. Indeed, the Basic Annals do tend to vindicate the chief councillor, while individual biographies contained in the same standard history, contradicting the Annals, accuse him of transgression of authority.[72]

Chao Yi's line of argument, while superficially appealing, is not well founded. Admittedly, Shih Mi-yüan could have supervised the daily collection and transcription of court records, the "records of rise and repose"; but Veritable Records for the Ning-tsung era were, in fact, compiled for the first time some five years *after* the chief councillor's death.[73] Furthermore, these were revised on five separate occasions thereafter,

with the final revision occurring during the reign of Tu-tsung (1264–74).[74]
It is inconceivable that Shih Mi-yüan, or any other Shih kinsman, could
influence the contents of these records over so long a time span. In addition,
compilation efforts were directed by reputable historians, not mere lackeys of the Shih house. Responsibility for compiling the 1238 draft of
Ning-tsung's Veritable Records, for example, was entrusted to Li Hsin-
ch'uan (1167–1244), one of the most respected and accomplished historians of the Southern Sung.[75] Chao Yi's argument, therefore, tends to
oversimplify a much more complex problem.

In the search to uncover the genuine role of Shih Mi-yüan in the succession controversy, an elaborate analysis of mounds of documents provides
few clues. With rumors rife and most of them unreliable, even contemporaries were poorly informed about events of 1224–25 and their confusion is mirrored in historical documents. Perhaps a little deductive
reasoning, in this case, would yield better results. First, there is the issue
of the popularity of Chao Hung after entering the palace. Most sources,
reflecting their unconcealed bias against Shih Mi-yüan, depict him as the
only major figure at court so dissatisfied with the prince's conduct as to
seek his removal. Even accounts that consider Ning-tsung personally
responsible for altering the succession, nonetheless attribute his disillusionment with Chao Hung to Shih Mi-yüan's constant aspersion of
the youth. Meanwhile, Empress Yang, who learned rather late of her
husband's death and the palace coup underway, allegedly opposed the
installation of Chao Yün on the grounds that the action was
unauthorized. She yielded, rumor has it, only under extreme pressure. On
the night of the succession, her brother, acting as a liaison between the
inner palace and the chief councillor's office, reportedly cautioned the
empress, "The armed forces and populace both in and away [from the
capital] have already submitted their minds [to this]. If [Chao Yün] is
not installed [as emperor], then calamity and revolt will surely arise and
the Yang house can hardly [expect] to remain among the living."[76]

In this way, it is suggested that Shih Mi-yüan, single-handedly, either
convinced or compelled Ning-tsung to abandon Chao Hung and elevate
his own personal favorite as heir to the throne, swiftly and effectively
countered any resistance from the influential Empress Yang, and coerced
both military and civilian officials into accepting his decision. Moreover,
we are to believe that such a complex series of maneuvers could be
executed without the slightest incident. This scenario is more than just a

bit farfetched. Regardless of Shih Mi-yüan's preponderant influence in the capital, there is little likelihood that he could demote a prince who enjoyed the favor of both emperor and empress. On the contrary, considerable evidence exists to suggest the exact opposite, that Chao Hung enjoyed no such favor and the royal couple was no less anxious than Shih Mi-yüan to be rid of him.

Sung anecdotist Chou Mi indicates that Empress Yang perhaps had more reason than the councillor to dislike Chao Hung.[77] This apparently stemmed from the selection by the empress of a grand-niece, née Wu, to be wife of the prince and future empress. As was common in the case of royal marriages, Chao Hung had little to say in the matter and found himself tied to a woman for whom he held no great affection. Seemingly out of spite, he doted on several favored concubines while entirely neglecting his wife. There were, no doubt, other tensions between the prince and princess that also got back to Empress Yang, prompting her to conclude that the self-indulgent Chao Hung was unfit to inherit the throne.

Other sources confirm the existence of tensions between Chao Hung and Empress Yang. In 1222, instructor Chen Te-hsiu admonished the prince, stating, "If [Your Highness], the emperor's son, can be filial to [Your] beneficent mother and reverent toward high officials, then heaven's mandate will be vested in You; *if not, then [Your Highness] can seriously imagine [the consequences]!*"[78] The implication here is quite clear: within scarcely one year of becoming imperial son, the prince had neglected palace decorum and utterly refused to humble himself before the empress and chief councillor, consequently alienating these two important decision makers. Furthermore, Chen Te-hsiu's warning of "serious consequences" should Chao Hung fail to modify his behavior suggests that tensions, already clearly visible to those outside the palace, posed an ominous threat to the prince's prospects for advancement to heir-apparent. In the end, Chao Hung did not heed the advice and his instructor soon resigned.

To be sure, Empress Yang represents, without parallel in the Southern Sung, the most aggressively influential yet tactfully manipulative empress of the era. Her own impressive political acumen more than offset Ning-tsung's glaring lack thereof and ensured her a place of importance in decision making. While Shih Mi-yüan was still rising in the bureaucracy and timid about involvement in the conspiracy against Han T'o-chou, Empress Yang, who was virtually the same age as Shih Mi-yüan, led the men in organizing the coup. For the remaining seventeen years of Ning-tsung's reign, she continued to maintain a strong presence both at court and within the palace. Mere oversight cannot explain Chen Te-hsiu's warning to Chao Hung to "be filial to [Your] beneficent mother," without mentioning his father the emperor. The omission represents an important comment on political reality. The freedom given Empress Yang to select a spouse for the newly installed prince, even to the extent of choosing her own niece, similarly attests to her unchallenged position as arbiter of palace matters. Small wonder that one perceptive historian portrays her as having "monopolized the empire's politics."[79]

Shih Mi-yüan and Empress Yang, meanwhile, had a long history of mutual consultation and cooperation, traceable to his early years as metropolitan official and interrupted only by her death in 1232. Rarely is there such conspicuous harmony between the palace and the chief councillor's office, especially when the two key personalities involved are both highly assertive. Proof that this relationship was not spoiled by the succession controversy of 1224 may be seen in Shih Mi-yüan's request that she temporarily hold court jointly with the new emperor from behind the "screen."[80] Having always enjoyed the empress's favor and aware of her preponderant interest and influence over palace matters, it is quite inconceivable that Shih Mi-yüan refused to consult her about the installation of Chao Yün and ludicrous that he would have used threats against her. Shih Mi-yüan may have been assertive, but reckless he was not, and threatening the empress would have been reckless. On the contrary, the empress's biographer is probably correct in asserting that she assisted, in some way, in drafting the imperial will that named Chao Yün successor to Ning-tsung.[81]

Yet another reason to question allegations that Shih Mi-yüan acted illicitly in elevating Chao Yün is the new emperor's subsequent treatment of him. Were the chief councillor free to place, quite capriciously, anyone of his choosing on the throne, Li-tsung would have slept very lightly at night. How could this be interpreted as anything but a direct threat to the imperial sway? The likely response, under such circumstances, would have been a move either to eliminate the chief councillor or at least substantially to diminish his influence at court. With Shih Mi-yüan already over sixty, Li-tsung could have easily granted him an early retirement or elevated him to an esteemed but nominal post such as councillor of the left. He chose not to do so. Until his very last days, Shih Mi-yüan remained the single most influential official in the capital and, after death, high honors and bureaucratic assignments were showered upon him and his kin on a scale unprecedented in Sung history.[82] Undeniably, Li-tsung owed a special political debt to Shih Mi-yüan, yet there were many ways of repaying him. Had the throne simply conferred upon him and his offspring titular honors, rather than high office and extravagant gifts, family fortunes, political and otherwise, might well have declined. On the contrary, other Shih kinsmen followed Shih Mi-yüan in holding influential metropolitan posts. What greater proof is there of imperial confidence and goodwill?

In conclusion, there is every reason to believe that Shih Mi-yüan did not act alone, or illicitly, in the ouster of Prince Chi. That he should be vulnerable to such charges is largely because of the unusually pervasive authority vested in him as chief councillor and the secretive manner in which court politics was conducted at the time. For most of the Sung, responsibility for drafting and executing an imperial will customarily fell upon the shoulders of the chief councillor. Imperial rescripts of any consequence passed through his office and he had access to the imperial seal. In this respect, Shih Mi-yüan was simply following standard procedure in assisting in the drafting of Ning-tsung's will and supervising the accession. During most periods, however, there were two councillors who handled such matters collectively, so outsiders rarely questioned the propriety of a given action. This did not hold for the Shih Mi-yüan era, when there was no secondary councillor. Permitting no other official to share his political power, he also had no one to share with him responsibility for controversial decisions.

The secretiveness with which the palace and the chief councillor chose to conduct court affairs also worked to Shih Mi-yüan's disadvantage. Like the assassination of Han T'o-chou, the dislodging of Chao Hung and enthronement of Li-tsung occurred behind closed doors, without open discussion or advance disclosure. In elevating Prince Chia to Emperor Ning-tsung some three decades earlier, Chao Ju-yü and Liu Cheng were careful not only to involve a wide political spectrum, but to keep the entire procedure public, thereby effectively forestalling any charges of impropriety on their part. Shih Mi-yüan failed to do either and consequently left himself vulnerable to countless accusations.

The propriety of the Li-tsung succession aside, it was Shih Mi-yüan's handling of the Hu-chou uprising that inspired the most heated debate and vehement denunciations. I have previously alluded to Chao Hung's death near his home of exile at Hu-chou in the aftermath of the ill-fated uprising. Virtually every account of the incident completely absolves Chao Hung of complicity in the affair. Having no intention of rebelling, he was reportedly taken captive by rebel fishermen and forced to accept the yellow robe reserved for emperors.[83] The exact circumstances surrounding the death of Chao Hung remained a mystery for much of the thirteenth century. Memorials submitted to the throne immediately after the incident merely allude to his "unfortunate" demise in the confusion of the rebellion, without providing details.[84] Even the one memorial that charges Shih Mi-yüan with personally arranging the death does not go on to divulge how death occurred.[85] Perhaps the facts of the case were kept secret, or maybe discussion was proscribed. (It is known that the court denied appeals for an open investigation.) Whatever the reason, only with the early Yüan dynasty did detailed reports surface about the Hu-chou affair.

The most important of these accounts, one that official historians quote extensively, is contained in *Ch'i-tung yeh-yü*, the memorabilia of the well-informed Chou Mi. According to this, Shih Mi-yüan dispatched to Hu-chou a contingent of Palace Guardsmen led by Hsia Chen—the same individual who commanded the guards commissioned by Empress Yang over seventeen years before to assassinate Han T'o-chou.[86] Accompanying them was allegedly one of Shih Mi-yüan's personal retainers, someone professing to be a doctor sent to provide Chao Hung with needed medical attention. His true mission, of course, was liquidation of the prince, a mission dutifully executed. Thus, according to Chou Mi, the death was no accident, but the premeditated act of one man, Shih Mi-yüan.[87]

Adding insult to injury, an angry court ordered Chao Hung to be buried on a straw mat, thereby denying him a suitable funeral. It also ordered his divestiture as prince.[88] These actions, quite understandable under the circumstances, created an inexplicable uproar in the capital that did not settle for many years. A flood of memorials urged the throne to redress this injustice by posthumously elevating his brother and dismissing the controversial chief councillor. Repeated in virtually all such documents is the moral plea that the emperor do this in expression of his magnanimity and "brotherly affection." In time, the posthumous status of Chao Hung was interpreted as an important measure of Li-tsung's respect for Confucian virtue. Focusing increasingly on the moral issue, questions about the legitimacy of his brother's ouster and subsequent death were eventually brushed aside.

The response of Li-tsung to the clamor was hardly constructive. He refused to alter the posthumous status of Chao Hung or to have him interred in a suitable coffin. Moreover, amidst a deluge of memorials demanding the dismissal of Shih Mi-yüan, he made a grand display of his continued support by honoring the councillor with titles of great esteem. In the summer of 1225, Shih Mi-yüan was named "grand preceptor" (T'ai-shih), the highest civil distinction offered by the Sung government, and ennobled "duke."[89] This further incensed critics, while adding fuel to the fire already consuming the court. Yet the emperor would not be swayed and, for the duration of Shih Mi-yüan's tenure, he remained steadfast in his decision. Not until the chief councillor was dead did he approve so much as a modest elevation in his late brother's status.[90]

In the aftermath of the political mishaps of 1224–25, the outer court became increasingly polarized giving rise to a level of political intolerance resembling, in certain respects, the desperate days of Ch'in Kuei and Han T'o-chou. Critics considered too vocal were gradually eliminated from metropolitan posts, a service rendered to Shih Mi-yuan by loyal supporters in the Censorate. The victims included such noted scholar-officials as Chen Te-hsiu, Wei Liao-weng, Hung Tzu-k'uei (n.d.), Teng Jo-shui, and Hu Meng-yü. Some were banished, others disenfranchised as officials, and at least one was punished with confiscation of family property.[91] No longer would the councillor overextend himself to accommodate the opposition, as he had done with a good measure of success in the past. As critics grew in number, Shih Mi-yüan became all the more intolerant. Before long, he even resorted to literary repression in an effort to silence the voices of protest.

From early on, Shih Mi-yüan reportedly banned the performance of "miscellaneous drama" (tsa-chü) in his official residence, ostensibly reacting to a satirical statement once made by a petty actor about the proliferation of Ming-chou natives at court.[92] Sometime after the death of Chao Hung, he was even accused of ordering a comprehensive ban on the writing of poetry by scholar-officials due to the political innuendo found in much of it.[93] While literary repression of this sort may be insignificant compared to the sweeping actions of Han T'o-chou against Tao-hsüeh partisans, the mere effort nonetheless permanently tarnished the chief councillor's former image as a reconciler, while further alienating once neutral elements in the bureaucracy. In this way, Shih Mi-yüan, and in turn the throne, were deprived of alternative policy views at precisely the time of greatest need.

FOREIGN POLICY

Under siege on the domestic front, the image of Shih Mi-yüan could have been salvaged by an effective foreign policy, but for him times were out of joint. The Shih of the early Southern Sung, in contrast with many politically mobile families, began with no history of involvement in the military. In fact, its first chief councillor, Shih Hao, was highly prejudiced against military men and a staunch opponent of military expansion. Shih Mi-yüan's views in this regard closely paralleled those of his father. Shortly after Han T'o-chou initiated the disastrous K'ai-hsi war, Shih Mi-yüan memorialized the throne expressing his vigorous opposition. His sentiments so resembled his father's that it could easily have been Shih Hao who wrote:

> Today there are those who posit that "he who acts first controls others, while he who acts later is controlled by others." . . . How can the lives of tens of millions [in South China] be taken lightly in a single venture [to capture the north]? The capital is our territorial base; [but] now many [troops] have been sent away to the border, while those remaining to guard [the capital] are few. Were bandits and rebels by chance to conspire and rise up, who would defend it against them?[94]

The memorial continued with a plea, again in the spirit of Shih Hao: improve the livelihood of the people, strengthen the empire's military, and wait for an opportune moment before attempting an invasion of the north. Understandably for a southerner, Shih Mi-yüan placed a high premium on the security of the south and wished to defer until the distant future, perhaps forever, any attempt at regaining lost territories to the north. The stunning failure of Han T'o-chou proved the wisdom of his counsel. By 1208, a policy of rapprochement had gained the upper hand and Shih Mi-yüan was its midwife. Appeasement, so acceptable then, suddenly lost its appeal again once the Mongols made their appearance in the Asian arena a few years later. As the war up north expanded, the perennially cautious chief councillor's strict adherence to a policy of self-containment seemed no less than irresponsible to many.

The armies of Chinggis Khan began their assault on the Chin empire in the year 1211 with invasions of Yün-chung and Chiu-yüan, in the northern portion of present-day Shansi.[95] From the far north they moved directly south, sinking their teeth ever deeper into the heart of the empire. The Jurchen were no match for them. By 1214, the Mongol threat loomed so large that the Chin capital was moved from the vicinity of modern Peking to K'ai-feng, site of the Sung capital prior to 1127. At this point, Chen Te-hsiu, who had just recently returned from the north as a Sung emissary, petitioned his government to sever diplomatic relations with the Chin. Predicting the imminent demise of that treacherous regime, he argued that Lin-an was only helping to prolong its fading life by making peace payments and should terminate these payments at once.[96] More important, he considered it a profound insult for his government to send envoys who must humble themselves before an alien court on the same ground where early Sung emperors once stood.[97]

In reality, Lin-an appears not to have tendered its annual tribute since 1211, chaotic conditions in and around the Jurchen capital of Chung-tu having made delivery nearly impossible.[98] Tribute items for 1212 and 1213 were consequently held in storage near the border, pending delivery at some future date. With the Jurchen capital now safely relocated in nearby K'ai-feng, the Sung had little excuse for further withholding the mounting treasure. Demands from the north in 1214 for a resumption of payments touched off heated debates in Lin-an, culminating in Chen Te-hsiu's demand to break relations altogether. Chief councillor Shih Mi-yüan did not concur. To him, the saving of face was hardly worth the risk of war—the very likely consequence of a severance of diplomatic ties. The only concession made to the opposition, and this a rather minor one, was to delay temporarily the payment of tribute. (In the end, payment was never resumed, although emissaries were exchanged.) As the Mongols persisted in gnawing away at the Jurchen empire, a growing body of officials in Lin-an became disillusioned with their government and its inability to develop a more farsighted and aggressive, if not militantly offensive, foreign policy. This inevitably meant for the architect of court policy, Shih Mi-yüan, progressively more severe criticism. While the providential Chen Te-hsiu could already see beyond the immediate Jurchen menace to the still larger Mongol threat, the chief councillor could scarcely decide what to do with stored tribute.[99]

Perhaps it was the memory of Han T'o-chou's miscalculation and the high price he paid for it or maybe his own long-standing pro-peace inclinations that prevented Shih Mi-yüan from embracing a more aggressive policy. Whatever his motives, he did little more than react to developments up north. Shortly after the Mongols began their initial thrust into North China, the chief councillor ordered border officials to fortify defenses in the event that Mongol-Jurchen hostilities created pressures along the Sung-Chin border.[100] He would go no further. When the Jurchen moved their capital to K'ai-feng in 1214 and the Hsi-hsia delcared war against them a year later, there was no perceptible reaction from Lin-an. Not only did it fail to formulate any coherent policy toward the Jurchen, but no policy emerged with reference to the Mongols or Hsi-hsia either. In the end, it was K'ai-feng that forced a change.

With the Mongols continuing their advance southward and the Hsi-hsia attacking from the west, the Jurchen were pressed from two sides. Their only escape was to the south, which made a reopening of hostilities with the Sung quite unavoidable. This finally occurred in the summer of 1217 with their assault on Hsiang-yang, in the north-central part of modern Hupei. On the advice of a subordinate, Shih Mi-yüan responded by ordering individual military leaders to arm for war and to exploit conditions in their various theaters in any way beneficial to the Sung government.[101] It was nonetheless clear that his office would support only defensive efforts and assumed no responsibility for the schemes of ambitious commanders that backfired. To his growing body of critics, political hedging of this sort was undermining the government's cause.

A source of further discontent was Shih Mi-yüan's policy, or nonpolicy, toward loyalist armies, the rebel bands up north who identified with Sung rule in the south. Although committed in peace to denying support to such groups, the eruption of war between K'ai-feng and Lin-an in 1217 freed the Sung from that commitment and many in the south hoped that a major change in policy would follow. Chaos in much of North China stemming from the Mongol invasion had driven many destitute peasants there to banditry, with a sizable number of these joining loyalist armies. Such armies were especially active in Shantung, where Jurchen authority had long been weak and proximity to the Sung border enabled easy access to supplies from a sympathetic south. Probably the most noted rebels in the area were Yang An-erh (d. 1214) and his protégé, Li Ch'üan (d. 1231).[102] Leaders of a group originally known as the "redcoat bandits," the two had been active as early as the Han T'o-chou era, when Lin-an extended generous aid in the hope of undermining the Chin government from within; yet fragmentation had prevented them from being especially effective. Ironically, their greatest expansion occurred after the peace of 1208, when government preoccupation with other domestic matters precluded a concentrated suppression effort. The Mongol invasion further preoccupied decision makers at K'ai-feng and the bandits, now in the guise of Sung loyalists, were free to line their pockets with unofficial subsidies from the south while consolidating their bases in Shantung.

Loyalist armies were frequently more bandit than loyalist in character. Li Ch'üan, for example, was initially a poor peasant who, upon losing his mother and eldest brother in a Mongol invasion of his hometown, joined a younger brother as recruits of Yang An-erh. Although a combination of anti-Mongol and anti-Jurchen sentiment may have partially influenced his decision and that of others like him to become rebels, human survival was probably a more overriding concern. For most loyalists, restoration of Sung rule in the north often represented little more than a slogan designed to lure Lin-an into providing material assistance. Despite serious questions about the genuineness of their loyalty, the growth of the former redcoat bandits from a few thousand to tens of thousands made them increasingly attractive to Sung border officials who saw them as an important check against further Jurchen movement south.

One such official was Ying Ch'un-chih (n.d.), prefect of the border city of Ch'u-chou, in the northern part of modern Kiangsu. At his request in 1217, Lin-an secretly agreed to extend limited assistance to various loyalist bands in Shantung.[103] While the Sung had little to lose and much to gain by supporting the rebels, Shih Mi-yüan remained ill at ease about the concession. Much like his father, he saw loyalist armies as largely self-serving and, if too strong, a potential border threat. After extending aid, therefore, he sought to manipulate loyalists through a carrot-and-stick approach. Armies successful on the battlefield were generously rewarded; the unsuccessful, like those whose loyalty had come into question, were subject to reprimands that included sharp reductions in aid and titular demotions. In the end, it was an arrangement that pleased no one. Officials who favored extensive aid regarded this modest gesture as inadequate, while those opposed to aid considered it too venturesome. Moreover, the policy as implemented by the chief councillor consisted of more carrot than stick, thereby giving the Sung the appearance of being weak—something both sides found offensive.

In time, Lin-an became more forthcoming with assistance. Li Ch'üan received his first in a series of Sung posts beginning in 1218, upon defeating Jurchen forces and capturing two major prefectures in central Shantung.[104] Once begun, the flow of material as well as moral support widened. By supplying provisions, the Sung sought to keep his troops well fed and thereby obviate their need to pillage border areas; by bestowing upon Li Ch'üan various official responsibilities and honors, it made a bid for his loyalty. There were those who found this expanded program of aid still too modest, the most influential of them being Chia She (d. 1223). As military commissioner for the eastern Huai region, he was charged with coordinating and supervising the activities of loyalist armies in Shantung. An ardent supporter of Li Ch'üan, he frequently criticized the court for providing inadequate aid to the loyalist leader. Furthermore, he complained about Lin-an's continued suspicion of Li Ch'üan as evinced by its refusal to allow him to participate in major military actions.[105] Chia She obviously did not share Shih Mi-yüan's fear that such participation might help whet the loyalist's appetite for power.

In time, the attitude of a good many Sung officials toward Li Ch'üan underwent dramatic change. Even Chia She, the once staunch supporter of the loyalist cause, completely reversed himself by the year 1222. Concluding that Li Ch'üan was not only self-serving, but a menace to the security of the south, he urged Lin-an to cut back on aid.[106] Chia She's replacement as military commissioner, Hsü Kuo (d. 1225), drew a similar conclusion,[107] as did prominent statesmen such as Chen Te-hsiu and Teng Jo-shui.[108] As Li Ch'üan amassed progressively greater wealth, weaponry, and political influence in Shantung, one Sung official after another warned of his impending treachery. However, they could not shake Shih Mi-yüan. Only with great difficulty had he finally acceded to an extension of aid and he was not inclined abruptly to break with this new policy. If nothing else, the chief councillor was compulsively consistent. Beyond simple consistency, there was also fear that withdrawal of support might induce the loyalist leader to pillage the border or, worse yet, attack the south out of indignation. Rather than risk this, titular honors from Lin-an continued to make their way to Shantung. Shih Mi-yüan also moved carefully in selecting military commissioners for the border region, for the most part avoiding appointees who might in any way offend or threaten Li Ch'üan.[109] Every effort was made to accommodate.

Despite the court's generosity—because of it, some might say—Li Ch'üan severed relations with Lin-an in 1227. Under a devastating Mongol siege at Yi-tu, he renounced loyalty to the Sung and surrendered to the enemy—the same armies responsible for the deaths of his mother and brother.[110] Upon accepting the Mongols' principally nominal appointment as chief administrator for Shantung and the southern Huai region, he began preparations to cross the Huai River and attack the Sung.[111] From this point on, there was no question that Li Ch'üan was a traitor, not a loyalist. Shih Mi-yüan, perhaps hoping that the defection represented more an act of desperation than genuine disillusionment with the south, made every effort to entice him into submission through additional offerings of titular appointments and provisions.[112] To the chief councillor, this was consistent with his carrot-and-stick policy, but to his many critics in and away from the capital, it reflected nothing short of submission to blackmail.

Ultimately, his immediate subordinate and close confidant, Cheng Ch'ing-chih, convinced Shih Mi-yüan to resort to arms against the rebel.[113] By the close of 1230, Lin-an had dispatched troops to suppress Li Ch'üan and he died at their hands less than two months later.[114] Following his defeat at Yang-chou, the remnants of his redcoat bandits dispersed, never again to pose a serious menace to the Sung.[115] The court had won the battle against Li Ch'üan, but Shih Mi-yüan had lost the war against his critics. The rapidity with which the rebel fell only confirmed that the councillor's excessive timidity, a virtue in his early career, had become a serious liability both for himself and the state. Indeed, his mismanagement of border affairs became a matter for censure, not only during his own era, but for centuries to come.

THE FINAL YEARS

After nearly five years of intense political strife, the court finally regained an element of calm during the early 1230s. This stems, in part, from Shih Mi-yüan's diminished role in political affairs. The Li Ch'üan incident had brought great pressure to bear upon the aging councillor and there were signs of fatigue.[116] At the throne's insistence, his appearances at court were reduced to one every ten days. In his absence, increased responsibility devolved on Assistant councillor Cheng Ch'ing-chih, protégé of Shih

Mi-yüan and tutor to Li-tsung prior to his accession.[117] This enabled the chief councillor to enjoy semiretirement while retaining a firm grip on the reins of government. It also ensured an element of continuity in court policy vis-à-vis the north.

As the Jurchen-Mongol war raged on with ever greater ferocity during Shih Mi-yüan's last years in power, Lin-an still tenaciously clung to its policy of nonintervention. Only in 1233 was this modified somewhat to allow for a joint Sung-Mongol military effort against the Jurchen; even so, Lin-an carefully avoided total immersion into the conflict.[118] Indeed, this policy became a part of Shih Mi-yüan's legacy, for no bureaucratic chief would again attempt an ambitious conquest of North China in a fashion resembling Han T'o-chou at the turn of the century.[119] To all intents and purposes, the Sung remained cautious, consequently accepting its fate as a *southern* empire in perpetuity.

Also contributing to the relative calm that set in at Lin-an during the chief councillor's last years were court endeavors to regain the support of one-time critics. Since the controversial death of Chao Hung, a good many prominent officials were denied metropolitan posts, others declined such appointments in protest against court policy. By the 1230s, the passage of time had helped to defuse succession-related controversies, while the suppression of Li Ch'üan relieved pressure on the foreign policy front. In a gesture of reconciliation, the throne ordered the restoration of rank and salary to outspoken critics such as Chen Te-hsiu and Wei Liao-weng in 1231; a year later, the two received additional promotions.[120] To avoid offending the chief councillor, however, they were not named to posts in the capital. In the hope, it seems, of facilitating the rapprochement now underway, the councillor subsequently requested permission to retire to his native Ming-chou.[121] The emperor adamantly refused but, apparently having recognized Shih Mi-yüan's deteriorating health, Li-tsung elevated him to chief councillor of the left, an esteemed but largely nominal post, and showered him with the highest honors his empire could offer.[122] Just eight days later, on November 28, 1233, Shih Mi-yüan died in his official residence at Lin-an. He was sixty-nine.

No less than his quarter-century tenure as chief councillor, the imperial honors and largess heaped upon Shih Mi-yüan had no precedent in Sung times. Ning-tsung began the process, following the fall of Han T'o-chou, with nominations as secondary tutor to the heir-apparent and "duke."[123] Upon waiving the standard mourning obligation and recalling him to the capital in 1209, the emperor made an unusually generous conferral of "fiefs of maintenance."[124] Shih Mi-yüan also received a mansion at the time but, unlike a similar gift from Hsiao-tsung to Shih Hao, this new residence was in the capital, not Ming-chou.[125] The flow from the palace broadened in subsequent years. Wishing to acknowledge the chief councillor's special merit, Ning-tsung ordered an ancestral temple erected in Lin-an in honor of the Shih household. An even greater tribute came when a memorial tablet for Shih Mi-yüan's deceased father was placed in the main sacrificial temple of Hsiao-tsung; this made Shih Hao only the second official of the Hsiao-tsung era to receive this honor.[126]

Under Li-tsung, imperial favor was extended to a growing body of kinsmen. Shortly before his death, Shih Mi-yüan's two living sons received *chin-shih* degrees through special conferral and immediate promotions to executive posts in the bureaucracy.[127] The emperor awarded official status or promotions to numerous grandsons, one son-in-law, and one grandson-in-law.[128] In the wake of the councillor's death, Li-tsung suspended court for three days, granted him the most prestigious of posthumous titles, and personally composed his tomb inscription.[129] Moreover, imperial concern extended to include the future wealth and status of Shih Mi-yüan's posterity. To prevent the councillor's controversial tenure from negatively affecting family fortunes years hence, his sons received a special "guaranty of security" (*pao-ch'üan*). In effect, the throne, with its many awesome powers, officially committed these to protecting Shih Chai-chih and Shih Yü-chih from both bureaucratic wrath and material want, expressly forbidding the outer court either to criticize the content or to propose recision of the guaranty order.[130] In life and death, imperial favor for Shih Mi-yüan seemed as boundless as it was immutable.[131]

It is appropriate, at this point, to ponder the reasons for Shih Mi-yüan's extraordinary success. How could he rise so rapidly within the civil service and retain the chief councillorship for so long? How did he escape the misfortune that befell most powerful ministers of the Southern Sung, with the court subsequently protecting, not confiscating, family wealth and property?

Compilers of a nineteenth-century gazetteer for Ming-chou wrote, "Although Mi-yüan was not a wise councillor, he nonetheless kept records of talented men, writing down [the names of] wise scholar-officials for use [in the bureaucracy]."[132] This statement, quite typical of assessments by most historians, is intriguing to say the least. To receive, at only seventeen years old, highest honors on the Ministry of Personnel's promotion examination and to obtain the coveted *chin-shih* degree by twenty-three clearly betrays exceptional talent and promise. This is not what one would expect of a mediocre man and Shih Mi-yüan's depiction as such relates, perhaps, not so much to native intelligence as to his narrow focus on politics. The chief councillor had no known ties to any specific community of intellectuals and held no sustained interest in philosophical inquiry. In contrast with Shih Hao, he wrote no poetry or scholarly essays; even his political memorabilia, letters and memorials, were never collected and printed. There is no evidence of personal identification with any prominent philosopher, academy, or school of thought. Although amateurishly curious about philosophy and the arts, he committed himself entirely to politics, and it was precisely this commitment that explains his astonishing success at court.

The period during which Shih Mi-yüan rose within the civil service, 1196–1207, represents an exceedingly trying time for the aspiring official. Deeply entrenched at court was Han T'o-chou, who could be as stubbornly intolerant as Ts'ai Ching without the idealistic sense of mission to justify his intolerance. Offending the special councillor meant coming under the scrutiny of censors or inclusion among the banished. That young Shih Mi-yüan should escape either fate and end up a bureaucratic executive implies a special capacity for maneuvering around or manipulating a political situation to his own advantage. Initially, by deemphasizing differences between himself and Han T'o-chou, he maintained a steady rise in the capital. Only after becoming a midlevel official did he dare publicly to criticize court policy, yet by wording his criticism with care, he managed to evade the special councillor's unpredictable wrath. At the same time, he fully exploited positions as tutor and advisor to the imperial prince to establish ties within the palace. Long before Han T'o-chou began to lose his grip over the court, Shih Mi-yüan had already come to be trusted by the influential Empress Yang and the impressionable Prince Jung, thereby ensuring him a place of importance following the special councillor's demise.

In the end, it was palace contacts of this sort that placed Shih Mi-yüan in the center of a daring assassination conspiracy. His exact level of involvement in the affair may never be known, but clearly he profited most from the elimination of Han T'o-chou. Shih Mi-yüan was not inclined to take political risks. His hesitancy to continue supporting fellow conspirators at the slightest hint of danger and, later, his timidity in acting against a petty rebel leader in Shantung both betray a pervasive cravenness. This is not to say that he was an outright coward; when the turn of events warranted decisive action, Shih Mi-yüan could take the appropriate leap.

Once in power, the passive and dependent character of Emperor Ning-tsung, combined with Shih Mi-yüan's favored position within the inner court, enabled him to remain on top. By the time of Li-tsung, the chief councillor's many years of service had left him a virtual institution. The emperor dared not remove him, nor was there any compelling reason to do so. Official criticism notwithstanding, Shih Mi-yüan was successfully navigating the empire through incredibly troubled waters. He delayed Sung involvement in North China's dangerously expanding conflict for as long as possible and, when involvement became imminent, he succeeded in confining hostilities to a few border regions. This afforded an empire perpetually threatened by war some measure of political and economic stability. It is a record that no other councillor in thirteenth-century Sung China could match.

The Southern Sung produced three other chief ministers who, like Shih Mi-yüan, wielded awesome powers during their day and held virtual lifelong tenures of office. At the outset there was Ch'in Kuei, after another half-century came Han T'o-chou, and toward the dynasty's close was Chia Ssu-tao (1213–75). When in power, they manipulated the emperor, dictated government policy, and intimidated critics by threatening banishment or, worse yet, death. Accompanying their preponderant influence was seemingly boundless imperial favor. Upon death, however, the throne completely reversed itself. In each case, the loyal opposition pressed and eventually convinced the emperor to rescind honorific titles, deny descendants access to high office, and even confiscate family possessions.[133] The three not only became targets of censure in their own time, but were vilified for centuries to come. Compilers of the official history for the dynasty, *Sung shih*, included each of their biographies in its section for "wicked officials."[134] Shih Mi-yüan and his kin, in sharp contrast, remained in the good graces of the throne for the duration of the dynasty. The former chief councillor's exalted posthumous status remained intact in perpetuity and the guaranty given his sons was never rescinded, contrary to the Ch'in Kuei precedent. Years after his death, the Shih continued to grow in political stature, amassing ever greater wealth along the way. Although a popular punching bag for contemporary officials and later historians alike, compilers of *Sung shih* consciously elected not to place Shih Mi-yüan's biography among those of the "wicked."

Such sustained favor may, in part, stem from Shih Mi-yüan's support for Li-tsung in the succession dispute of 1224. There are many historians who see the emperor as merely repaying a political debt.[135] In my view, such an interpretation perhaps oversimplifies historical fact and under-rates Shih Mi-yüan's extraordinary political perspicacity. It fails to explain, for example, the chief councillor's preponderant influence for the sixteen years prior to the installation of Li-tsung. The power he wielded and the favor he enjoyed, rather than beginning, merely expanded after 1224. Moreover, in repaying a political debt, titular honors and monetary awards would have sufficed; it was unnecessary to take the extreme step of ensuring the future standing of the entire family.

Shih Mi-yüan was not labeled a wicked official, it would appear, for the same reason that his influence at court remained strong both in life and death—the opposition had no single issue to exploit in uprooting him. In the case of Ch'in Kuei, unpopularity grew out of a controversial stand on the peace of 1138–41 and repressive tactics in dealing with court critics. By the time of his death, political foes far outnumbered allies and the majority easily prevailed. The vulnerability of Han T'o-chou is related to his ban on *Tao-hsüeh*, an inept foreign policy, and alienation of key palace figures. Chia Ssu-tao's unpopularity similarly stemmed from a combination of misguided foreign and domestic policies and the many enemies he created in the execution of these.[136] All three men, through high-handed and malicious treatment of critics, incurred the enmity of large segments of the scholar-official elite; the controversial policies identified with them could easily be exploited by the opposition in their subsequent vilification campaigns.

This was not true for Shih Mi-yüan. Although an autocrat of sorts, he made every effort to mollify critics through official advancement, titular honors, and salary increments; demotion or banishment represented a last resort. For the most part, he succeeded in this carrot-and-stick approach. He had his share of enemies, to be sure, but their numbers were initially slight. The succession controversy and bureaucratic reaction to this compelled the chief councillor, in later years, to be more firm with highly vocal critics; still, in using strong measures, he was both prudent and selective. While scathing indictments were often leveled against him, Shih Mi-yüan never responded with violence. At times he was unyielding and intolerant, perhaps, but he was never intimidating or malicious. At most, he was guilty of demoting critics and blocking transmission of their memorials. In this way, he kept the size of the opposition relatively small. Meanwhile, with Li-tsung personally involved in the Chao Hung affair and especially sensitive to it, critics could hardly question the legitimacy of the succession or the propriety of the councillor's handling of it without insulting the throne. They also could not find much fault with Shih Mi-yüan's foreign policy. Inept as it sometimes appeared, his cautious approach to both the Li Ch'üan affair and the border war ultimately ended in success. In effect, the chief councillor was beyond reproach.

Meanwhile, the court presence of key political allies, which continued for many years after his death, also mitigated against any abrupt change in the throne's attitude toward Shih Mi-yüan. No less than other powerful bureaucratic chiefs before and after him, the councillor staffed disciplinary agencies such as the Censorate with his own political minions and used them as a shield against official criticism. The most infamous of these were Li Chih-hsiao (n.d.), Liang Ch'eng-ta (n.d.), and Mo Tse (n.d.).[137] At the same time, recent history must have taught the chief councillor that such individuals, having created countless political enemies, would become the first targets of bureaucratic resistance after his departure.[138] Where Shih Mi-yüan differed from Ch'in Kuei and Han T'o-chou was in his ability to win strength from more than just subservient censors. With considerable foresight, he also raised up a coterie of highly reputable and experienced officials to take over in his absence. The most prominent of these were Cheng Ch'ing-chih, Ch'iao Hsing-chien (1156–1241), and Yü T'ien-hsi (d. 1241). Shih Mi-yüan shared power with his protégés without demanding that they sacrifice their own individual opinions. Thus, Cheng Ch'ing-chih felt free in 1230 to disagree with him over the Li Ch'üan affair without fear of falling from favor.[139] Ch'iao Hsing-chien did not worry about alienating the councillor when he raised objections to court policy toward the deceased Chao Hung.[140] Similarly, Yü T'ien-hsi is known to have maintained his own political independence, despite an intimate and abiding relationship with Shih Mi-yüan.[141]

Whereas Ch'in Kuei jealously guarded his relationship with the throne and systematically eliminated those whose influence threatened, in any way, to overshadow his own, Shih Mi-yüan intentionally assigned all three protégés to posts of political consequence, whereby they were permitted regular access to the palace. Having had prolonged exposure to the emperor when the chief councillor was alive, they held his absolute confidence by the time of Shih Mi-yüan's death, leaving them sufficiently entrenched in the bureaucracy to make removal by the opposition extremely difficult. Furthermore, their independence of action made them less vulnerable to charges of factional alliance with the chief councillor. It was a strategy that, in the end, proved highly effective. Cheng Ch'ing-chih and Ch'iao Hsing-chien were both destined themselves to become chief councillors, while Yü T'ien-hsi became assistant councillor and would have been named chief councillor but for his untimely death.[142] Through these men, Shih Mi-yüan continued to exert influence over the court, even in death. Their presence also helped moderate any political backlash against him that could have, in turn, adversely affected his politically active kin group. Thus Shih Mi-yüan, after twenty-five years on top of the civil service, was clearly unpopular in some quarters, yet the impact of this upon the bureaucratic promise of his kinsmen was initially quite negligible. So long as the procession of officials from Ming-chou continued, the Shih would remain its standard-bearer.

SUMMARY OF GENERATION SIX

Branch A. In addition to Shih Mi-yüan, Shih Hao sired three other sons who rose to positions of reasonable prominence.[143] The eldest of these, Shih Mi-ta, received his *chin-shih* degree in 1169 and entered the civil service when brother Shih Mi-yüan was a mere five years old.[144] Not much is known about his initial assignments in the bureaucracy, but his appointment in 1173 as correcting editor at the Imperial Library (*Pi-shu-sheng cheng-tzu*, 8b) is unlikely to have been his first. This was followed by several other minor assignments at the same library before his departure from the capital in 1177 to become fiscal intendant of Che-hsi (*t'i-chü*). Some five years later, Shih Mi-ta returned to Lin-an to serve as lesser lord at the Court of Imperial Family Affairs (*Tsung-cheng shao-ch'ing*, 5b). Other major assignments included those as drafting official at the Secretariat (*Chung-shu she-jen*, 4a), chief secretary of the heir-apparent (*t'ai-tzu tso shu-tzu*, 5b), and prefect of Ning-kuo commandary, in the southern part of modern Anhwei. In addition, he held several largely nominal posts as lecturer at the various imperially sponsored palaces and academic pavilions scattered throughout the imperial city.

With the exception of two regional assignments, the career of Shih

Mi-ta centered on the capital. Posts as lesser lord at the Court of Imperial Family Affairs and secretary to the heir-apparent also provided some access to the palace. There was the potential for even greater success, but opportunity did not avail itself. His rise to prominence coincided with the last years in the reign of Hsiao-tsung, when the aging emperor was more inclined to employ the talent of an earlier generation than to search for new talent. In the end, death came before opportunity, for Shih Mi-ta did not survive his longevous father.[145]

Much less is known about Shih Hao's second son, Shih Mi-cheng. He served for awhile as auxiliary official at the Imperial Archives (*chih pi-ko*, 8a), judicial intendant for Che-tung (*t'i-tien hsing-yü*), and prefect of T'ai-chou, along the coast of modern Chekiang.[146] Like his elder brother, he received an appointment as academician-in-waiting (*tai-chih*, 4b) at an imperial pavilion, but never became closely identified with the palace. His last years were spent in retirement before death came sometime during the first decade of the thirteenth century. A close friend, Lou Yüeh, eulogized Shih Mi-cheng as a renowned literator and the epitome of filial piety, suggesting that he was a respected member of the community.[147]

The youngest son of Shih Hao, Shih Mi-chien, evinced much more political promise than his two eldest brothers and there probably existed something of a rivalry between him and twin brother Shih Mi-yüan.[148] Lacking an official degree, he capitalized on the protection scheme to enter the civil service. With rank of 8a, he was given a secretarial post with the fiscal intendancy of Liang-che,[149] shortly before his father's death. The completion of mourning obligations saw Shih Mi-chien emerge once again, subsequently becoming vice-administrator (*t'ung-p'an*) for Ch'ü-chou, in the southwest of modern Chekiang. From early on, he was respected as an energetic, upright, and conscientious official who corrected the irregularities of subprefectural clerks, suppressed bands of local marauders, and improved public works projects in the various localities under his supervision.[150]

By the beginning of the thirteenth century, the career of Shih Mi-chien shifted away from the provinces, as he assumed metropolitan posts for the first time. From executive assistant at the Court of Imperial Treasury (*T'ai-fu ch'eng*, 8a), he moved on to become assistant at the Court of Agricultural Supervision (*Ssu-nung ch'eng*, 8a), chief at the High Office of Imperial Family Affairs (*Ta tsung cheng*), vice-director of construction (*chiang-tso shao-chien*, 6b), and transmitter of directives at the Bureau of

Military Affairs (*Shu-mi-yüan ch'eng-chih*, 6a). At the same time that brother Shih Mi-yüan was openly criticizing the court's war policy and establishing a liaison with the palace, Shih Mi-chien was also making significant advances in the capital. From 1206 through 1207, he served two brief terms as vice-prefect (6b) and then prefect (3b) of Lin-an.[151] Interestingly, he was named prefect less than two weeks before the slaying of Han T'o-chou; he retained the post for no more than two months. While his appointment at this critical juncture is highly curious, it appears to have been purely coincidental. There is no evidence to suggest that he too was involved in the murder conspiracy. Furthermore, the rivalry, and often tension, between the twins makes it highly unlikely that they would have cooperated on this or any other major venture. In fact, it may well be that the resignation of Shih Mi-chien after the assassination reflects tension between the two brothers centering on precisely this incident.

With Shih Mi-yüan's rise to a position of preeminence in the capital, Shih Mi-chien returned to service as a regional official. He held posts as civil and military commissioner for T'an-chou (*an-fu shih*), in the northeast of present-day Hunan, and then as prefect of Chen-chiang and Chienning, in modern Kiangsu and Fukien, respectively. Protesting Shih Mi-yüan's dominance at court, he chose to resign from government service altogether in 1218. Since leaving Lin-an over a decade before, his only metropolitan assignment had been as nominal academician-in-waiting (4b).[152]

The four sons of Shih Hao fared exceedingly well in the civil service: two obtained *chin-shih* degrees and all but one became high-ranking officials. Undoubtedly, such an extraordinary record owes something to Shih Hao's political standing in the capital. They all gained early access to the bureaucracy through the protection process and probably rose within it so rapidly in part due to their father's fine reputation and his many connections. At the same time, the importance of individual merit to bureaucratic success should not be underrated. The official degrees held by Shih Mi-ta and Shih Mi-yüan were certainly key factors in their advancement to metropolitan posts, just as the distinguished performance of Shih Mi-chien as a regional official was pivotal to his ascendancy. The two younger sons were also fortunate to have been rising in the civil service during the era of Han T'o-chou, when the vicissitudes of factional politics created an unusually high number of vacancies in the capital. This effectively enhanced bureaucratic fluidity and consequently increased opportunities for promotion. It is noteworthy that Shih Mi-yüan and Shih Mi-chien did not become especially promising until long after their father's death, which suggests that his influence was by no means a decisive factor in their ascendancy.

The offspring of Shih Hao dominate branch A of the Shih community, yet a bit is also known about the descendants of his four younger brothers. Shih P'u—as mentioned earlier, he received an official promotion due to the merit of his elder brother—had two sons, Shih Mi-tzu and Shih Mi-hsing, neither of whom held civil service status.[153]

The next brother, Shih Yüan, sired two male heirs, yet only one penetrated the civil service. This was Shih Mi-kao (n.d.). Lacking examination credentials, he entered the bureaucracy through protection, rising to become a prefect.[154] Shih Mi-kao never held a metropolitan post, but a sound record as a regional official and a reputation as a fine poet left him quite distinguished. Consequently, he sired an unusually prosperous line.

Shih Hao's third brother, Shih Yüan [II] had four sons; the most accomplished was Shih Mi-ning (n.d.).[155] Having served in modern Kansu as prefect of Ch'in-chou and fiscal intendant of Huai-an, there is little question that Shih Mi-ning was actively involved in the civil service. In addition, he also proved to be an accomplished poet whose works remain at least partially extant to this day. His literary attainments may indeed help explain how Shih Mi-ning became one of the first Shih kinsmen to marry a woman from the imperial Chao clan. As for his three brothers, all held bureaucratic rank, but no information exists on their careers and it may well be that they held rank without office.

In the case of Shih Chüan, the youngest brother of Shih Hao, two of his five sons entered the civil service. Shih Mi-lin (n.d.) was reportedly recommended for office by uncle Shih Hao, but declined.[156] In the end, he settled for a minor assignment as inspector at a wine warehouse. Accomplished as an official he was not, but his close association with prominent thinkers in Ming-chou, such as Yang Chien and Yüan Hsieh, suggests a strong academic orientation.[157] Brother Shih Mi-hou (fl. 1230–42), on the other hand, proved much more active in the bureaucracy. Toward the close of Shih Mi-yüan's tenure as chief councillor, he served as subprefect of modern Soochow.[158] Upon completing his assignment there, he retired with the rank of 6b. Over eight years later, in 1241, he temporarily returned to government service as vice-administrator of Chien-k'ang, modern Nanking. After only eight months at that post, he retired permanently.[159] Brother Shih Mi-lun held bureaucratic rank, but neither he nor the remaining sons of Shih Chüan appear to have held office.[160]

Branch B. As noted earlier, the first official of the Shih kin group and progenitor of branch B, Shih Ts'ai, had two male heirs: Shih Chün and Shih Jo-shui. The former, in turn, gave Shih Ts'ai five grandsons.[161] Eldest son Shih Mi-sun (n.d.) earned a *chin-shih* degree in 1196, making him the only grandson of Shih Ts'ai to do so. Despite his credentials, he appears never to have advanced beyond subprefectural registrar (9a).[162] Second son Shih Mi-hsiung (n.d.), without examination credentials, served in a variety of regional posts culminating in prefect with rank of 6b.[163] Of the remaining three sons of Shih Chün, two received bureaucratic rank and one, Shih Mi-tai, studied at the Imperial University, but in all probability none held office.[164] Shih Jo-shui was without heir.

In contrast with their cousins in branch A and branch C, heirs to the line of Shih Ts'ai failed to produce either statesmen or philosophers of any consequence; neither did the line yield even modestly prominent authors or poets. In the seventh generation, branch B produced three *chin-shih* degreeholders, yet only one of these went on to distinguish himself in the political arena. This was Shih Pen-chih (CS 1238), son of Shih Mi-tai, who served as prefectural vice-administrator with rank of 7a.[165] The other reasonably accomplished official was Shih Hua-chih, son of Shih Mi-hsiung. He rose to become prefect with rank of 5a.[166] Among their cousins in that generation, one studied at the Directorate of Education and another at the Military Academy, both in the capital, yet the majority either held rank without office or nothing at all. Fortunes took a turn for the worse in the eighth generation, when only one individual is known to have held a post and two-thirds could not even claim civil service rank. By the ninth generation, there were no officials at all and no individuals with bureaucratic rank.[167]

It is truly ironic that descendants of Shih Ts'ai—initially the most successful member of the Shih house—should decline with such ease while cousins in other branches were faring so well. Through protection, opportunities for education and official recruitment should have, in theory, been far greater for them than for their cousins. This simply illustrates that, in spite of bureaucratic privilege and family connections, official status could not be transmitted easily from one generation to the next independent of merit. This branch declined because its members were no longer competitive with their cousins and neighbors in Ming-chou. It is not that they were less studious or ambitious, but merely that they were outshone by the many stars around them.

Branch C. Unlike branch B, which was off to an early start in the race to gain official status, it was not until the sixth generation that branch C produced serious entries. The forefather of this branch, Shih Mu, was recognized by both his kinsmen and community to be exceptionally learned; still, he evinced little interest in government service. He had three sons, Shih Chan, Shih Chien [II], and Shih Jo-ch'ung. While the last two held civil service rank, they appear not to have held office, preferring instead to concentrate their energies on the training of their sons. With the sixth generation, the devotion of these men to scholarship and family finally yielded fruit. The line of youngest son Shih Chien [II] proved especially prosperous. Father of eight sons, a remarkable five of them earned *chin-shih* degrees. Beyond their accomplishments in the civil service, they also became well known for their scholastic attainments, no doubt reflecting the strong academic bent of their father and grandfather.

Eldest son Shih Mi-chung (d. 1244) received his degree in 1187 and entered the bureaucracy shortly afterward as subprefectural sheriff (9a) at E-chou, in the eastern part of modern Hupei.[168] Before long, he was named prefect of Chi-chou, in the heart of modern Kiangsi, and subsequently fiscal intendant for Fukien. His energetic leadership in the latter capacity is said to have attracted widespread attention, prompting Chen Te-hsiu to recommend him for high office despite his own long-standing feud with Shih Mi-yüan.[169]

In addition to being a conscientious official, Shih Mi-chung possessed a powerful intellect and this earned for him the admiration of many contemporaries. Philosopher Yang Chien stated, "Upright in disposition and humble about [his] talents, [Shih Mi-chung's] virtue is without parallel."[170] In the end, recommendations and praise of this sort did little to enhance his official advancement, for he never received an assignment in the capital. The principal reason for this was the reported friction between him and his cousin, the chief councillor.[171] After Shih Mi-yüan's death, the merit of a son led to Shih Mi-chung's honorary appointment in 1241 as palace academician (3a).[172] Already over eighty by this time, this was as close as he ever came to holding a metropolitan post.

Second son Shih Mi-kung (fl. 1193–1237), like his elder brother, was perhaps best known for his moral rectitude.[173] His first trip to the capital in an official capacity occurred in 1193 as a student at the Imperial University, where he eventually climbed to its highest level. Despite the academic exposure provided by his long affiliation with the university, it was not until 1217 that he finally earned *chin-shih* status—some thirty years after his eldest brother.[174] Upon securing the degree, Shih Mi-kung entered the civil service as an instructor (9b) at the local school at Hsia-chou, in the western part of modern Hupei. He also served as subprefect of Li-shui (8b) during the closing years of Shih Mi-yüan's tenure.[175] Immediately after the chief councillor's death, Shih Mi-kung received his first court appointment as director of the General Memorial Acceptance Bureau (*chien tu Chin-tsou yüan*), but he was not destined to remain there for long. A highly opinionated and insensitive individual, he often could be quite offensive. His vehement criticism of Shih Mi-yüan produced an enmity that followed the two men to the grave. Even after the chief councillor was long dead, Shih Mi-kung continued to deride him in particular and court policy in general as it pertained to Chao Hung's posthumous status. Ultimately, this abrasive character virtually guaranteed that his stay in the capital would be brief.[176] In 1237, he was named prefect of Wu-chou and later that of Ch'ü-chou (both in modern Chekiang), before finally retiring.[177]

In contrast with brother Shih Mi-chung, Shih Mi-kung could not claim an especially distinguished career. Rather, the respect that he later came to command among colleagues appears to have derived chiefly from his open criticism of cousin Shih Mi-yüan. The opposition undoubtedly took consolation in the fact that the councillor was unpopular even among his own kinsmen and exploited this to serve their partisan interests.[178] For Shih Mi-kung, such independence of spirit gained for him the style name "sole gentleman of virtue."

The other three sons of Shih Chien [II] with *chin-shih* credentials were Shih Mi-yü (n.d.), Shih Mi-min (n.d.), and Shih Mi-ying (n.d.). The first secured his degree in 1187, at the same time as his eldest brother, and soon became vice-administrator of Chiang-chou, in the northern portion of present-day Kiangsi.[179] He moved on, in 1223, to serve as prefect of southern Kiangsu's Ch'ang-chou, and ended his career with rank of 5a.[180] Although Shih Mi-yü held other regional posts,[181] there is no evidence of his receiving a metropolitan assignment. The same is true for the others. Shih Mi-min earned his degree in 1214 and, with rank of 6a, served as prefect of Jui-an (modern Wen-chou).[182] Shih Mi-ying, who also received his degree in 1214, served as prefect of Lien-chou and Ch'en-chou before retiring (ranked 5b).[183] Among the sons of Shih Chien [II] who held no degree, Shih Mi-shu (n.d.) is the only one known to have entered government service, at one point serving as vice-administrator of Chiang-chou (modern Kiangsi).[184] Brother Shih Mi-yüan [II], although a student at the Directorate of Education, appears not to have held office.[185]

As for the two older sons of Shih Mu, Shih Jo-ch'ung had four male heirs, none of which were identified with the civil service.[186] Curiously enough, a generation later, five out of six grandsons nonetheless did manage to secure minor bureaucratic rank, but this spirited revestment proved short-lived; only one out of five great-grandsons and no great-great-grandsons held bureaucratic status. To the extent that the line of Shih Jo-ch'ung never produced degreeholders and thereby found itself dependent upon the privileges of other kin to gain civil service status, it is understandable that it should fare so poorly relative to more industrious lines.

The final son of Shih Mu, Shih Chan, had five sons.[187] The eldest, Shih Mi-wen (n.d.), studied at the Imperial University and another, Shih Mi-chang, was identified with the Directorate of Education. Third son Shih Mi-chu held bureaucratic rank but, like his two younger brothers, appears never to have held office.

Branches D and E. The two junior branches of the Shih kin group grew only modestly from the fifth to sixth generations and little is known about the political activities of these rather obscure kinsmen. Shih Mi-chin (CS 1199), son of Shih Chi and grandson of Shih Ho, is among the most noted in the group. The only degreeholder within the two branches, he later became prefectural vice-administrator with rank of 7b.[188] Others within branch D, descendants of Shih Ho, all held civil service rank, but only Shih Mi-mao appears to have actually held office.[189] In the case of branch E, Shih Mi-ping (n.d.) distinguished himself as a student at the Directorate of Education and later as prefect of Wu-kang commandary with rank of 5b.[190] He was the only son of Shih Ch'eng [II] to hold office.

Some Observations

The strides made by Shih men from the fifth to sixth generations were no less than monumental. In so short a time span. the kin group grew to four times its previous size and almost instantaneously surfaced as politically the most influential house in the empire. In the fifth generation, only one of its thirteen males held a *chin-shih* degree and he was also its only high-level official. One became a midlevel and eight others low-level officials. During the subsequent generation, the Shih produced nine *chin-shih* degree-holders and four high-ranking officials. Another ten became midlevel officials, while twenty held lower ranks. Thus, some thirty-four out of forty-six males, or roughly 75 percent of this generation held civil service rank and/or office. Clearly, the sixth generation witnessed the kin group's total commitment to the race for bureaucratic appointment and kinsmen proved extraordinarily competitive.

At this point it seems appropriate to venture an explanation of their striking success. Did Shih kinsmen hold certain advantages over their neighbors in the competition for official degrees and appointments? To what extent did nepotism influence their success?

The educational training of the Shih appears to have differed little from that provided other prominent families in their native Ming-chou. For most Shih sons, rudimentary education began on the laps of their fathers and elders.[191] In time, the small size of the kin group and the absence of a strong classical tradition within it necessitated that most of its youth search beyond the confines of home for intellectual stimulation. Thus, many of those maturing toward the close of the twelfth century became disciples of local teachers such as Yang Chien and Yüan Hsieh.[192] This development marked the beginning of the kin group's identification with a school of thought, as family instruction came to be replaced by academy-oriented education. No doubt, the merit of Shih Ts'ai and Shih Hao entitled some kinsmen to study at the Directorate of Education in Lin-an, yet only a few chose to do so. With academic training derived chiefly from community contacts, Shih youth appear to have enjoyed few educational advantages over other provincials.

Nepotism also cannot explain the success of this generation. Shih Ts'ai and Shih Hao were never known to exploit their standing at court to obtain special favors for their kinsmen. To some extent, Shih Mi-yüan was guilty of nepotism. As will be seen in the next chapter, he did occasionally employ certain seventh-generation kinsmen, including his own son, in influential posts. However, these acts were not especially blatant and had a negligible effect upon the career prospects of peers in the sixth generation. For most aspirants to high office within his kin group, the impact of Shih Mi-yüan's prolonged stay at court was more negative than positive. So long as he remained, the Sung policy of "avoidance" made it extremely difficult for them similarly to receive major assignments there. Perhaps this helps account for the resentment that many kinsmen felt toward him.

Rather than aiding the advancement of kinsmen in the civil service, the increasingly controversial character of Shih Mi-yüan's tenure must have been viewed as posing a potential threat to their promise as scholar-officials. Historical experience had proven that the unpopularity of one political figure could easily devastate his entire kin group. The plummeting fortunes of the families of Ch'in Kuei and Han T'o-chou following their deaths were recent examples of this. With Shih Mi-yüan's record tainted by a messy succession issue and two assassinations, no doubt many kinsmen anticipated the effect of this record upon their own well-being; they begged him to step down.[193]

The only advantage held by members of the Shih community that is clearly tied to their political success was an inexplicable adeptness at the official examinations. Beginning with the sixth generation, this talent suddenly began to yield an unusually large number of degreeholders. Although not the most prolific producer of *chin-shih* in Ming-chou, the Shih certainly became one of the top three.[194] Upon obtaining the degree, there was a discernible preference for political involvement, especially for members of branch A. In this respect, they differed significantly from many degree-holding neighbors, whose devotion to scholarship and intellectual inquiry often prompted them to maintain a low profile as civil servants. Perhaps the influence of Shih Hao was responsible for this; there is no question that he personally placed a high premium on bureaucratic service. In the final analysis, it was the ability of sixth-generation youth to secure official degrees, combined with a special commitment to government service, that accounts for their unusual success.

To be sure, the Sung practice of recruitment through protection was instrumental in gaining early access to the civil service and a good many sixth-generation kinsmen took advantage of it. For each degreeholder, there were more than three individuals entering the bureaucracy through privilege. At the same time, this alone can hardly explain the kin group's extraordinary success. The most accomplished members of this generation generally owed their success to examination credentials and/or outstanding records as regional officials. While protection provided opportunity, it was ultimately individual merit that gave opportunity its real value.

The reign of Emperor Ning-tsung saw the Shih house reach the summit of its political climb, a place where it was destined to remain through much of the Li-tsung era as well. Ironically, implanted with success were also the seeds of decline. The controversy surrounding Shih Mi-yüan's quarter-century tenure as chief councillor left the Shih perilously divided. As kinsmen became increasingly alienated and began publicly to attack him and his record, tensions within the house swelled. Its moralists and politicos came to be separated by an ever widening gulf, gradually sapping the kin group of its former cohesion, replacing harmony with dissension, and accelerating its decline. For contemporaries living at the outset of Li-tsung's reign, however, this divisiveness was largely camouflaged by the brilliance of the Shih success. The flow of Shih youth to the capital, rather than narrowing, actually widened after the death of Shih Mi-yüan and it would take some time for this to change.

5

Eclipse

THE COURT OF LI-TSUNG

MOST SOUTHERN SUNG emperors enjoyed unusual political longevity. Kao-tsung reigned for thirty-five years, Hsiao-tsung for nearly twenty-seven, and Ning-tsung for thirty. Surpassing them all was Li-tsung, whose forty-year rule is matched in length by only one other Sung emperor, Jen-tsung (r. 1023–63). Unfortunately, the former shared little else in common with his illustrious Northern Sung predecessor. The relative prosperity and tranquility that characterized much of Jen-tsung's time was not to be found during the last decades of the Southern Sung. The political stability that had sprung from the assertive leadership of Kao-tsung and Hsiao-tsung did not continue into the era of Li-tsung. Even the consistency of court policy that accompanied the domination of Shih Mi-yüan, inept as it sometimes seemed, disappeared after the chief councillor's death. The empire went begging for a strong and decisive leader, but none was to be found, either in the person of the emperor or his chief ministers. As the fiscal and military standing of the Sung deteriorated, the court became all the more helpless at saving itself. It was, in large measure, utterly beyond human salvation.

The first two decades in the reign of Li-tsung were plagued with, it would seem, every natural calamity imaginable. Historical records sadly reveal that hardly a year passed without the occurrence of one or several serious earthquakes, droughts, floods, famine, and the like. At one point, the imperial capital of Lin-an was struck with such acute food shortages that men were snatched off the streets and sold, as butchers traded human flesh in its marketplaces. The populace, we are told, was so afraid of becoming victimized that no one dared go out after dusk.[1] Not only did these developments spark anxiety at court over the possible eruption of spontaneous rebellions, but they also ensured that tax revenues declined at precisely the time they were most desperately needed. Meanwhile, domestic worries prevented the throne from addressing an even more pressing problem: the growing Mongol threat.

Discussed in the preceding chapter is Shih Mi-yüan's foreign policy position, his insistence that the south not intervene in the expanding Mongol-Jurchen conflict to the north. For the most part, the court was not inclined to depart from this general principle. Not until his very last year in power—by which time Cheng Ch'ing-chih had already assumed many of Shih Mi-yüan's former responsibilities as chief councillor—did there occur the necessary adjustments to effect a Sung-Mongol alliance against the Jurchen. The temptation to form such a union proved irresistible for decision makers in Lin-an. The bait: Mongol promises to restore to the south a bit of border territory formerly under Jurchen control. The optimistic Cheng Ch'ing-chih also saw in this a unique opportunity to expand influence up north in general—the first step in a grand revival of Sung rule that, after 150 years of separation, would unite Chinese on both sides of the Huai River. With its long-time enemy already on the verge of defeat, Lin-an must have reasoned that a change in policy involved few risks while promising great returns. To some extent, it was correct.

Within six months after the alliance took effect, K'ai-feng collapsed and the Jurchen empire disintegrated. As anticipated, Lin-an did recover certain prefectures along its northwest border, but this merely whet the appetites of many. At this point, large contingents of Mongol armies had withdrawn in the aftermath of victory, leaving behind a political vacuum that attracted a good measure of attention in the Sung capital. Heated debate ensued, with officials weighing the pros and cons of aggressive intervention. Shih Mi-yüan had died several months earlier and successor Cheng Ch'ing-chih supported aggression, so troops were dispatched north in spring 1234. Their chief objective was to capture the Northern Sung capital of K'ai-feng and nearby Lo-yang, but there were problems. Sung forces had barely secured K'ai-feng before Mongol reinforcements arrived, forcing a hasty retreat. Angered by the greed of their onetime allies, the Mongols declared war on the Sung—a war destined to continue sporadi-

cally for the next several decades. Fortunately for Lin-an, the political
divisiveness and instability that had plagued the Mongol camp ever since
the death of Chinggis Khan some seven years earlier had prevented the
emergence of a leadership sufficient in strength to launch any full-scale
offensive against the distant south. Prolonged hostilities, rather than posing a serious threat to Sung suzerainty, simply turned the war-ravaged
border region into a wasteland, agriculturally unproductive and politically volatile.

Struck by both natural calamities and an untimely war, the Sung empire
was in dire straits by the second decade of Li-tsung's reign. Tu Fan
(1181–1244), the prefect of Ning-kuo commandary (some one hundred
kilometers west of the capital), described the situation with somber
vividness. Writing in 1240, he stated:

Droughts have occurred repeatedly and men have not [even] a kernel
of food; paper currency is grossly undervalued and commodity prices
soar; in the provisional capital [of Lin-an] the climate is gloomy,
while in nearby Che-hsi the roads are filled with starvation's dead;
refugees abound and pillaging is rampant—indeed [this indicates
that] domestic troubles are already pressing!

The newly risen northern armies are prone to victory and adept at
warfare; herds of bandits in the central plains, under [various]
pretexts, rise up; they attack our Pa and Shu (modern Szechwan),
overrun our Ching-hu [circuit] and Hsiang-yang [prefecture]; they
harass the banks of our Huai [River]; [meanwhile], officials of the
border region wantonly lie and conceal [about the situation there]
—indeed, [this indicates that] external threats are already serious!

Above, it is Heaven upon which a ruler relies; below, it is the
people. Of recent, cosmic phenomena have manifested abrupt changes:
unpropitious comets spurt out sharp rays; it thunders in the midst of
winter and snows when it is already spring; tides from the bay rush
toward the walls of the capital, while barren fields abound throughout the metropolitan district. Can this be anything but that [Your
Majesty] has not earned [the support of] Heaven and Heaven is
already angered?

Men die under spears and behind shields, they die from various
forms of starvation; father and son forsake each other, husband and
wife fail to protect one another; feelings of hatred swell in their

bosoms, while slanderous statements [against the court] fill the roadways. Can this be anything but that [Your Majesty] has not earned [the support of] the people and the people are already disaffected?

Is it possible for Your Majesty, in the company of two or three high officials, to live content above the rest of the world? Has not Your Majesty also contemplated the reason for things coming to this?

It is that, in the past, the powerful councillor [Shih Mi-yüan] superficially rendered the petty loyalty of a [mere] woman, while he surreptitiously encroached upon the great imperium of his ruler. He employed music, sensuality, and various pleasures to poison Your Majesty's mind from within, while [decisions of official] appointment or removal, life or death were all made solely at his will. Consequently, ethical norms underwent erosion, traditional customs declined, military governance went without renovation, and border preparations were neglected. The various domestic troubles and external worries of today are all the product of thirty years fomentation under the powerful councillor's [leadership]; and, like caring for an ulcer, [one must] await the proper time to remove it.

Adoption of the reign title Tuan-p'ing (in 1234) implied a transformation, but those [chosen] to fill the post of chief councillor have not been the appropriate persons [to inaugurate such change]; instead, [their own] failures and corruption have been actually greater [than before]! As a result, the sage [ruler] is perplexed and uncertain where to turn. Rather than consider those persons evil, [Your Majesty] regards them as virtuous; rather than criminal, [Your Majesty] holds them to be meritorious. Thus, the expectations of Heaven with regard to Your Majesty have turned to alienation, causing the appearance of abrupt changes and strange [cosmic phenomena]. The expectations of the people with regard to Your Majesty have turned to disappointment, causing the evolution of angry revolt.[2]

From this passage it is clear that Tu Fan regarded the empire's woes to stem largely from the emperor's amorous indulgences and his consequent neglect of political affairs. In fact, Tu Fan is not the only person to allude to this.[3] For much of his reign, Li-tsung is reported to have grossly neglected administration of the empire in his pursuit of lechery. That Tu Fan should insist upon blaming Shih Mi-yüan for the emperor's disgraceful behavior is probably more out of deference to the throne than to historical fact, for the pressures of leadership appear to have been the chief culprit.

Although his biographers in *Sung shih* argue that Li-tsung did not develop such habits until his "middle years,"[4] Tu Fan is more accurate in tracing them to the very beginning of his reign. Before becoming emperor, Li-tsung is described by historians to have been "exceptionally serious," "mild-mannered," "self-possessed," and even "wise."[5] Indeed, it was this upright conduct, in contrast with the unrestrained and temperamental character of Prince Chi, that allegedly inspired Ning-tsung to select him as heir to the throne. Shortly after his accession, however, the nineteen-year-old emperor began to evince signs of laxity. A memorial by Chen Te-hsiu submitted to the throne in the summer of 1225, merely a half-year after his reign officially commenced, is quite revealing in this regard.[6]

The memorial is principally one of remonstrance, reminiscent in certain respects of Chen Te-hsiu's reprobation of Prince Chi three years earlier. After praising the emperor for his moral rectitude and energetic leadership, Chen Te-hsiu went on to criticize him for opening court audiences noticeably later than his predecessors and warned that many officials had come to view this as indicative of imperial indolence. He also reminded the throne of the necessity to eat and dress simply, while avoiding entertainment and sexual indulgence, pursuant to the rules governing a son's mourning obligation for a deceased father. The implication throughout is that Li-tsung had already begun to lose his former discipline and was rapidly sinking into dissipation. Chen Te-hsiu then provided perceptive insight into the reason for this change of character by stating, "Your servant is aware that [Your Majesty] the Sage is pure in character and certainly not perturbed by external objects; but when one is single-minded [in ruling the empire] and [nonetheless] assailed by the multitude, it is only by being regal, determined, and unbeguiled that [the Sage Ruler] may avoid falling into profligacy and degeneration."[7]

The controversy stemming from the dislodging and subsequent death of Prince Chi has already been treated in the preceding chapter. Needless to say, both Shih Mi-yüan and Li-tsung found it to be an incurable sore-spot. The suggestion here by Chen Te-hsiu that this one incident was largely responsible for transforming a conscientious prince into a self-indulgent ruler provides some measure of the intensity of the controversy and the pressure it must have exerted on the throne. Few domestic issues generated such prolonged and heated debate as the affair of the ousted prince. With the passage of time, tensions gradually subsided, but Shih Mi-yüan's opponents refused to allow the matter to be forgotten. His death at the close of 1233 prompted critics to raise the issue once again, as they continued to do intermittently for the remainder of the Southern Sung.[8] For so young a ruler, new to the capital and inexperienced in palace politics, the strain proved disabling. Meanwhile, with an exceedingly able and domineering chief councillor like Shih Mi-yüan on hand to rule by virtual proxy, it is easy to understand why the "mild-mannered" Li-tsung simply chose to withdraw from the confusion of court squabbling to the calm of the inner palace; persistent critics created the need for escape and the presence of Shih Mi-yüan provided the means. As time wore on, other crises arose to produce new tensions, pressing the throne into still further seclusion.

Quite apart from partisan politics, the withdrawal of Li-tsung is also related to the various personalities and interest groups that surrounded him. The omnipresent Shih Mi-yüan not only permitted, but encouraged his political aloofness, preferring that the emperor never assert his independence. Similarly, Dowager Yang, despite her years, was as active as ever, always there to govern every aspect of the new ruler's personal life. Reminiscent of her intervention in selecting a wife for Chao Hung, historians note that she also took the liberty of choosing a spouse for her second son by adoption, Chao Yün. As in the earlier case, the recently installed emperor was forced to abandon his own favorite and accept a woman for whom he cared little.[9] Then there were students at the Imperial University who, after the death of Shih Mi-yüan, emerged as an important political force in the capital, frequently the throne's most annoyingly candid and persistent critics. The convergence at court of these various individuals and interest groups greatly dispirited, even emasculated, the insecure emperor. More than just emotionally desirable, retreat was politically expedient.

In the aftermath of Shih Mi-yüan's death, the court dismissed some of his most loyal supporters in the Censorate, while restoring to metropolitan posts such prominent onetime critics as Chen Te-hsiu and Wei Liao-weng.[10] An ever optimistic outer court suddenly took heart, viewing this as a sign of the emperor's new resolve to assert himself and prevent the rise of future autocrats; they were gravely mistaken. For the duration of his reign, Li-tsung continued to delegate sweeping authority to his chief councillors. Worse yet, there were times when he totally ignored ministerial advice and permitted petty favorites to overrule their bureaucratic superiors, thereby undermining the civil service hierarchy much as Han T'o-chou had done a generation earlier.[11] Factional strife, intense and vindictive, became the order of the day, far exceeding anything of the early thirteenth century. From Cheng Ch'ing-chih to Chia Ssu-tao, the vast majority of men selected as chief councillor were highly unpopular among their colleagues. For some, this stemmed from association with the late Shih Mi-yüan; for others, it was the predictable response to their own political intolerance. Whenever opposition to one autocratic council- lor threatened to create a crisis, the emperor—his predilection for aloof- ness matched only by his distaste for confrontation—merely replaced the controversial minister with another, no less arbitrary favorite. Bureau- cratic chiefs after Shih Mi-yüan, although at times awesomely powerful, did not hold onto power for long. They could not; none were as adept as he at the art of political manipulation. They antagonized, rather than humored colleagues, cashiered, rather than accommodated critics.

As bureaucrats wearied and the emperor aged, the civil service con- cerned itself progressively less with issues of substance and more with partisan politics. Thus, the Sung court never managed to prepare itself properly for its certain showdown with the Mongols, despite having over two decades of relative calm in which to do so; it also casually passed up numerous opportunities to explore peaceful coexistence, having decided, perhaps out of fear, to ignore Mongol overtures.[12] Lin-an took no action to impede Mongol pacifications of Korea, Yunnan, and Vietnam—moves brilliantly designed completely to encircle South China in preparation for a grand assault. In the late 1250s, when hostilities along the border began to intensify, even the most spirited of Sung armies could hardly withstand the enemy's intense barrage. Li-tsung died in 1264 and the Mongols, by this time, were making such deep inroads into the south that it was only a matter of time, anyone could see, before the Sung mandate would pass to alien hands.

DESCENDANTS OF SHIH HAO AT COURT

Despite the succession of economic and military crises that beset the Sung government in its last forty years, the effect of these upon the pros- perity of the Shih house was surprisingly negligible. Until the end of the dynasty, the Shih continued to grow in both size and political influence.

The seventh generation produced the kin group's third chief councillor, along with countless other high-ranking officials. Bureaucratic disesteem for Shih Mi-yüan notwithstanding, the Shih community enjoyed the steadfast favor, even patronage, of the emperor. Thus, Li-tsung was not only willing to appoint the former councillor's sons and nephews to the highest posts in the empire, but he came to their defense in times of political need. There is no question that unwavering imperial goodwill contributed much to the civil service achievements of Shih kinsmen in the aftermath of the chief councillor's death. Of Shih Hao's grandsons, fourteen in all, the offspring of Shih Mi-yüan were the most accomplished, so we will turn first to them.

A total of three sons were born to the chief councillor. The eldest of these, Shih K'uan-chih (fl. 1226), died by the age of twenty-four.[13] He held no bureaucratic posts of consequence, yet the merit of his father led to the assignment of rank 7a. Besides this, historical records say little else about him. They do, however, reveal much about brothers Shih Chai-chih (1205–49) and Shih Yü-chih (1215–93). As noted previously, both received honorary *chin-shih* degrees and appointments to high-ranking posts just days before their father's death. This alone gave them a distinct advantage over other aspirants for political office, whether within or outside of their kin group, but this was hardly their only advantage.

The sons of an influential statesman, quite apart from their own political ambition or bureaucratic experience, always had an edge over peers in the competition for civil service advancement. Through the personal and political connections of elders, they were commonly afforded the priceless opportunity to become intimately familiar with the bureaucratic process and the personalities charged with its management. In addition, they were often permitted regular access to the palace. This was true during the reign of Kao-tsung, when the lackluster son of Ch'in Kuei had so ingratiated himself in the throne that many considered him the inevitable heir to his father's post. The same can be said for later years. Shih Mi-yüan, for example, frequently accompanied Shih Hao when he attended important social gatherings;[14] in all probability, he also joined his father on occasional visits to Lin-an. Unfortunately, the younger Shih was a mere teenager when Shih Hao retired from the civil service, severely limiting his potential breadth of exposure to palace and court.

Unlike Shih Hao, Shih Mi-yüan spent most of his life in the capital; his sons, living with him in the official residence, were able to wet their feet in politics from early on. As it was, second son Shih Chai-chih readily took advantage of the opportunity. When only twenty years old, he reportedly became one of only two persons—the other was Cheng Ch'ing-chih —informed by the chief councillor in advance of the planned ouster of Prince Chi.[15] Later, in recognition of his expertise in classical literary styles and rules of etiquette, his father allegedly gave Shih Chai-chih special permission to edit imperial rescripts.[16] Free to move about the palace, he was one of the few individuals there about the same age as the new emperor. Indeed, Shih Chai-chih and Li-tsung became fast friends—an important factor, clearly, in the emperor's subsequent goodwill for the younger generation of Shih kinsmen. In all, the benefits that Shih Chai-chih personally accrued under the wings of his father had few parallels during his time and added much to his future promise as a civil servant.

The final years of Shih Mi-yüan at court saw his twenty-eight-year-old son receive appointments as lesser lord of the Imperial Treasury (*T'ai-fu shao-ch'ing*, 6b), vice-director of construction (6b), executive at the Ministry of Finance (*Hu-pu shih-lang*, 3b), and minor lecturer at an imperial palace (7b). These appointments, made while his father was still chief councillor, represented a flagrant violation of the long-standing policy of "avoidance," but Li-tsung was hardly fastidious about such technical issues. After his father's death, Shih Chai-chih offered to restore to the government the official mansion in Lin-an, as was custom, but the emperor insisted that it be retained by the family indefinitely.[17] Shih Chai-chih then left the capital and hastened to Ming-chou, where he spent the next two to three years in mourning. By maintaining an official residence in Lin-an, however, he was certain to return; more important, the emperor had personally intervened, symbolically, to demonstrate his abiding welcome.

Upon reentering the civil service in 1237, Shih Chai-chih initially received several regional assignments.[18] With rank of 4b, he served as prefect of Chia-hsing (1237), P'ing-chiang (1238–40, 1241–43), and Shao-hsing (1244–46), as well as civil and military commissioner for Che-tung circuit.[19] Interestingly, he was assigned to places within easy reach of the capital, an unmistakable sign of favor. Rumor has it that the emperor planned, as early as 1240, his restoration as court official, but relented under pressure from the Censorate.[20] When the emperor made a second attempt in 1248, the Censorate must have changed either in composition or attitude, for he encountered no noticeable resistance. After a fifteen-year absence, Shih Chai-chih finally returned to Lin-an as minister of personnel (*Li-pu shang-shu*, 3a), academician at the Tuan-ming Pavilion (3a), and then temporary cosignatory official at the Bureau of Military Affairs (*t'ung ch'ien-shu shu-mi-yüan-shih*, 2b).[21] Early the next year, he was named coadministrator for the military bureau (2a), a promotion that followed so closely upon the heels of the preceding one as to suggest that Shih Chai-chih was destined to claim, very soon, the top spot in the bureaucracy.[22] Unfortunately, fate intervened; he died before year's end at a relatively youthful forty-four.

Shih Mi-yüan's third son, Shih Yü-chih, also rose to the bureaucracy's executive level, despite his apparent lack of close personal ties to the emperor.[23] Initially entering the civil service through protection, he followed in his father's footsteps by successfully completing the all-important promotion examination while still a teenager. During the chief councillor's last years, Shih Yü-chih held several largely nominal assignments in the capital, culminating in his special appointment as vice-director of construction (6b) and assistant general transmitter of directives at the Bureau of Military Affairs (*Shu-mi-yüan fu tu ch'eng-chih*, 6a).

Shih Yü-chih was scarcely nineteen years old when his father died and, like his elder brother, he spent the 1234–37 period in mourning. Subsequently, he served for a short while in the capital as lesser lord (*shao-ch'ing*, 6a) of both Agricultural Supervision (*Ssu-nung*) and the Imperial Treasury (*T'ai-fu*); then came a long series of regional assignments. With rank of 4b, he became prefect of various large cities in modern Chekiang, including Ch'u-chou, Yen-chou, Wen-chou, Wu-chou, Shao-hsing, and Chien-ning. He held an array of other important provincial posts as well. In 1254, while prefect of Shao-hsing, Shih Yü-chih received his first executive-level metropolitan assignments as minister of war and concurrent minister of public works (*Ping-pu, Kung-pu shang-shu*, 3a), largely nominal posts that appear not to have demanded his return to the capital. The flow of honorary appointments as palace academician (most of which carried rank 3a), intermingled with regional assignments, continued until the last years of Li-tsung's reign. For the duration, Shih Yü-chih retained the emperor's goodwill. In expression of this, Li-tsung reportedly gave him a home in Ming-chou located "beyond the lake," to be distinguished from the residence in the heart of town given to Shih Hao some two generations earlier.[24] By the time of the Sung capitulation to the Mongols, Shih Yü-chih was already over sixty and had long retired from government service.[25] Under the Yüan, he voluntarily chose to live in isolation.

In their own right, Shih Chai-chih and Shih Yü-chih were highly successful civil servants. However, against the backdrop of their father's precedent-setting career and the advantages they held as his offspring, these accomplishments seem only modest. Their failure to go further is not difficult to explain. First, both received honorary *chin-shih* degrees and never went on to win examination credentials. In Sung times, careful distinction was made between the two and individuals who lacked the examination degree but aspired for the government's highest office could expect to meet stiff resistance. It could be done—there was the Han T'o-chou precedent—but not without challenging deeply imbedded bureaucratic prejudice. Further retarding the speed of their advancement was lingering bureaucratic ill-will toward Shih Mi-yüan. Regardless of the emperor's personal sentiments, he could hardly afford to ignore entirely the opinion of officialdom at large; a sizable portion of that group strongly opposed the rise of yet another Shih kinsman, and especially a son of Shih Mi-yüan, to the top of the bureaucracy. Added to these factors were the personal failures of the two men. For example, as prefect of P'ing-chiang, Shih Chai-chih came under pressure to resign because he allegedly "governed the prefecture in a rude fashion."[26] Later, colleagues denounced him for grossly mismanaging regional finances in the areas under his supervision, reportedly creating chaotic conditions.[27] Thus, while he may have been a talented writer, even a meritorious court official, his record of service away from Lin-an was blemished on several counts.

Shih Yü-chih, on the other hand, was known as an exceptionally conscientious and popular regional official with an impeccable civil service record. His problems were purely of a personal character. In particular, he had a lewd stepmother (his father's concubine) whose widely publicized promiscuity, in the aftermath of Shih Mi-yüan's death, was a source of constant embarrassment for the entire Shih community. When scandal culminated with the wife of Shih Yü-chih abandoning him, the young man's domestic affairs suddenly became one of the hottest pieces of gossip in the capital. Repeated admonishments that he "put his household in order" even reached the court.[28] Critics, of course, were not simply commenting on Shih Yü-chih's personal life. Any man impotent at ordering his own household is hardly fit to assist the emperor in governing the empire; the political message was unmistakable. Domestic affairs aside, colleagues also scoffed at Shih Yü-chih for being a notorious miser.[29] The early Ch'ing historian Ch'üan Tsu-wang wrote, "The two sons of

Mi-yüan were generally unconcerned about the comments of others."[30] In traditional China, an individual's moral conduct could have a pronounced effect upon official advancement. Just as the virtue of Shih Chao so enhanced his reputation that local officials enthusiastically nominated him "Mr. Eight Virtues of Conduct," the highly publicized improprieties of Shih Chai-chih and Shih Yü-chih could not but sully their reputations and dampen career prospects. As it was, the kin group's seventh generation produced men of both types and their fortunes were mixed.

Shih Hao had eleven grandsons in addition to the heirs of Shih Mi-yüan, all of whom held civil service rank. Shih Shou-chih (n.d.), son of Shih Mi-ta, was one of the most esteemed of these.[31] Portrayed as more a scholar than a statesman, he studied classical literature under Lou Yüeh (one of the few of his generation to do so) and was closely associated with prominent Ming-chou philosophers Yang Chien and Yüan Hsieh. After entering the civil service through protection, he rose in time to hold the rank of 6b. Although his career centered on the provinces, Shih Shou-chih apparently served for awhile in the capital, for Emperor Ning-tsung honored him with a sample of his own calligraphy. Yet he was not on good terms with Shih Mi-yüan—an uncle who was probably a few years his junior—and in the aftermath of publicly voicing disapproval of Shih Mi-yüan's record, Shih Shou-chih chose to retire while still quite young.

Half of Shih Hao's fourteen grandsons were the offspring of Shih Mi-cheng, a midlevel official. Four of the seven rose to midlevel posts and all held office in addition to rank. Shih Yi-chih (fl. 1194–1229) and Shih Ting-chih (fl. 1194–1207) both served as prefects.[32] Shih Tsung-chih (n.d.) and Shih An-chih (n.d.) are both identified as subprefects, yet the latter's high rank (5a) suggests a far more successful career than historical records divulge.[33] Shih Hsüan-chih, with rank of 6a, undoubtedly enjoyed a reasonably full career as well.[34] More obscure were the two remaining sons, Shih Shih-chih and Shih Hsien-chih, who served as minor inspectors.[35] None of the seven sons of Shih Mi-cheng became prominent, none are known to have held metropolitan posts; but being non-degreeholders, like their father, and relying on privilege to penetrate the bureaucracy, their political accomplishments can hardly be slighted.

The three remaining grandsons of Shih Hao to enter the civil service were the offspring of Shih Mi-chien. Shih Pin-chih (1190–1251) rose to become a high-ranking official. Embarking upon his career by holding a variety of regional posts, including six assignments as prefect, he was summoned to the capital in 1237 to serve as executive at the Ministry of Finance (*Hu-pu shih-lang*, 3b).[36] Shih Sui-chih (n.d.) also served briefly in a minor metropolitan post, but his career centered on the provinces; the same applies to Shih Ch'ung-chih.[37]

Turning to the brothers of Shih Hao, only one, Shih Yüan, produced an especially prosperous line, a function chiefly of the extraordinary fecundity of son Shih Mi-kao. As mentioned earlier, Shih Mi-kao was a prefect with midlevel rank. Two of his seven sons are also known to have served as prefects, Shih Yi-chih [III] (rank 6a) and Shih T'ing-chih (rank 5b).[38] Two other sons, Shih Sun-chih (n.d.) and Shih Ch'ih-chih (n.d.), are identified as students at the Directorate of Education—a privilege, no doubt, afforded them through the bureaucratic standing of their father. Little is known about the lives of Shih Hui-chih (ranked 5b) and Shih K'uei-chih (ranked 9b), but the civil service rank of the former suggests a rather successful career.

To the extent that all of Shih Hao's brothers and most of their sons, in turn, held civil service rank, it is understandable that a good many of their heirs in generation VII would manage to penetrate the bureaucracy as well. Shih Chüan, father of five boys (four of whom became officials), was grandfather of seven.[39] The most accomplished of these was Shih Shen-chih (n.d.), who served as prefectural vice-administrator (ranked 5a). Shih Chi-chih (CS 1229), one of only two *chin-shih* in the entire branch for this generation, nonetheless appears to have remained at the bureaucracy's lower level. Three other grandsons of Shih Chüan received civil service rank, without any indication of office-holding, and two were without status. In this seventh generation, another five officials are counted among descendants of Shih Hao's two remaining brothers, including two midlevel bureaucrats, Shih Wei-chih and Shih Wu-chih, and one degree-holder, Shih Ch'üan-chih.[40]

For branch A as a whole, generation VII was still one of reasonable prosperity, both economic and political, although qualitatively different from earlier times. Previously, socially aspiring Shih kinsmen focused on the examinations to penetrate and then succeed in the civil service. There existed a strong, and not altogether healthy, competitive spirit. The younger group, although nearly twice the size of the sixth generation, did not exceed them in *chin-shih* output and appears to have been more content to rest upon family privilege to succeed. This was certain to pose serious problems later on.

THE THIRD COUNCILLOR: SHIH SUNG-CHIH

It has already been shown that the greatest political strides for branch A were made during the fifth and sixth generations. Members of this branch tended to place a high premium on public service, even perhaps at the expense of intellectual pursuits. To be sure, Shih Hao came closer than anyone else in reconciling these two frequently divergent orientations, but most kinsmen proved unable to maintain so ideal a balance. With branch C, on the other hand, there existed a strong tradition of academic excellence that overshadowed politics, traceable to Shih Mu, its fourth-generation progenitor. More community-oriented than Assistant councillor Shih Ts'ai, Shih Mu held the community's respect as an erudite classicist.[41] Benefiting most from this erudition were Shih youth. Shih Hao, for example, had studied under uncle Shih Mu and probably owed some measure of his own literary attainments to that early training.[42] The most prosperous son of Shih Mu, Shih Chien [II], inherited both the academic bent and political aloofness of his father. He spent a good many years at the Imperial University without apparently attempting to make the short leap that separated it from the civil service.

Commencing with the sixth generation, members of branch C began to enter government service, yet without necessarily forsaking the legacy of scholarship that distinguished them from cousins in other branches. Shih Mi-chung, Shih Mi-kung, and Shih Mi-ying were principally scholars who dabbled in office-holding. Their political ambitions appear relatively modest and the greater part of their lives were spent at home, not on official assignment. Branch C produced the bulk of the kin group's philosophers and moralists — men who often looked upon power politics with disdain, not awe, and maintained a perceptible distance between themselves and the one kinsman who clearly did not share their idealism, Shih Mi-yüan. As the branch expanded in the seventh generation, however, diversification became inevitable. Despite a continued abundance of academics and moralists, professional bureaucrats in the mold of branch A also emerged. One member even embarked upon a military career.

In an essay on the early Southern Sung military hero Yüeh Fei (1103–41), Hellmut Wilhelm ventures to explain why a Sung official of such an accomplished civilian background should opt for a military career when its prestige value was so unfortunately low.[43] Despite the popular Sung idiom equating soldiers with cheap iron, Wilhelm suggests that the military still had its appealing side. The rigid controls that the Sung court had effectively imposed upon the civilian bureaucracy were, in good measure, not extended to the military establishment and this afforded military leaders greater opportunity for personal initiative. Moreover, most assignments were conveniently away from the capital, which enabled the politically less aggressive to avoid involvement in highly destructive factional conflicts. In essence, the military offered its leaders certain freedoms, including the freedom to implement their own policies without excessive outside interference and to do so in the environment least affected by the pettiness of partisan politics. The explanation, although quite sound, should be generalized for other periods of the Sung dynasty with great care; controls on the civilian and military bureaucracies could vary significantly even within a single reign and factional strife, while intense during certain periods, was not exactly the norm for Sung politics. Equally important to such a career change, it would seem, is the development of crisis situations and the patriotic response of civilians to these. Chang Chün, at the beginning of the Southern Sung, and Wen T'ien-hsiang (1239–82), at the end, are two prominent examples of civilians who later accepted military commands, not because they were frustrated civilians who longed for the freedoms of the military, but in response to the emergence of serious external threats to their empire.[44] As previously noted, Sung China's military security had declined to an all-time low during the 1220s: the Mongols continued to chisel away at the Jurchen empire, the K'ai-feng government was engaged in a war of aggression against Lin-an, and rebel Li Ch'üan was making ready for his own southern offensive. It is, by no coincidence, also at this time that the Shih produced their first and only military figure: Shih Sung-chih (1189–1257).

The eldest son of Shih Mi-chung, Shih Sung-chih first entered the civil service during the heyday of Shih Mi-yüan.[45] Shortly after receiving his *chin-shih* in 1220, it is reported that his uncle, the chief councillor, arranged for his appointment to the local Office of Finance (*Hu-ts'ao*) for the strategically vital prefecture of Hsiang-yang, in the north-central part of modern Hupei, near the Jurchen border.[46] While the appointment itself was not a military one, Shih Sung-chih focused on its military aspects from the outset. Soon after taking up responsibilities at Hsiang-yang, he once again presumed upon his influence in the chief councillor's office to compel a reluctant military commander to implement his own rather curious scheme for ordering the area's defense layout. To the commander's great surprise, the local government thereby saved sixty percent on military expenditures.

Upon being named prefectural vice-administrator (*t'ung-p'an*) for the same area in 1227, Shih Sung-chih led the way in transforming the unprofitable "military farm-colonies" (*t'un-t'ien*) of Hsiang-yang into a remunerative undertaking. This resulted in his concurrent assignment as subprefect and military consultant for Tsao-yang, another strategically important area due east of the prefectural seat at Hsiang-yang and a bit closer to the enemy's border. There, as well, Shih Sung-chih's reorganization of local *t'un-t'ien* enabled them to become solvent for the first time in recent history. In recognition of these astonishing achievements and the meritorious service of his ancestors, the court ennobled him "baron of Yin subprefecture" (*Yin-hsien-nan*, 5b) in 1230.[47]

Although his talents were recognized by Emperor Li-tsung from early on, only toward the close of 1232 did the forty-three-year-old Shih Sung-chih begin to receive metropolitan assignments. From lord assistant at the High Court of Justice (*Ta-li shao-ch'ing*, 6a), he jumped to lord chief justice (*Ta-li ch'ing*, 4b) and, concurrently, executive at the Ministry of Justice (*Hsing-pu shih-lang*, 3b). While important indicators of his rising status in the capital, the posts were largely nominal; at the same time that he received these commissions, Shih Sung-chih also served both as prefect of distant Hsiang-yang and as civil and military commissioner for Ching-hsi and Ching-hu circuits, comprising most of modern Hupei and Hunan, in the heart of the Sung domain. Within a short span of time, he had risen from virtual obscurity to empirewide prominence. That he should do so while Shih Mi-yüan still held onto the reins of power implies that Shih Sung-chih, unlike his father and uncles, maintained a reasonably positive relationship with the chief councillor. He also appears to have been on good terms with the emperor and his rising overseer at court, Cheng Ch'ing-chih.

Prior to this time, it had been an outstanding record as regional official, complemented by family connections, that had enabled Shih Sung-chih to rise so rapidly in the civilian bureaucracy. In the post–Shih Mi-yüan era, it was the role he played in helping to bring about the speedy collapse of the Jurchen empire that made further advancement possible and, in the process, confirmed his orientation toward the military. Biographical materials indicate that Shih Sung-chih had personally requested to serve at Hsiang-yang, having recognized its strategic importance and the opportunity it offered to prove his managerial talents even under less than ideal circumstances; if true, this decision is testimony to his considerable foresight. In the center of China and located along the Han River at a point where several northbound tributaries stretch deep into enemy territory, Hsiang-yang is among the most convenient bridges between north and south. In the words of one Sung official, it is the "fence" protecting the "gateway" to the entire south.[48] Few areas were more often the battleground of Sung-Chin wars, few changed hands so frequently. Only about four hundred kilometers southwest of the Jurchen capital at K'ai-feng, Hsiang-yang was positioned to play a decisive role in the enemy's demise. As military commissioner for most of south-central China, this also placed Shih Sung-chih in a most opportune position.

After two decades of warfare, the Mongol conquest of North China swiftly raced toward a climax during the last years of Shih Mi-yüan's tenure. By the end of 1232, invading hordes compelled the Jurchen emperor to abandon his capital of eighteen years at K'ai-feng and flee still farther south. He moved about for many months before finally taking refuge at Ts'ai-chou, a prefecture located in modern Honan province, halfway between K'ai-feng and Hsiang-yang and less than fifty kilometers from the Sung border. It was the summer of 1233, the Jurchen stood clearly on the verge of defeat, and the Mongols were anxious to clinch a rapid victory. With the enemy now in the deep south, the Mongols realized the necessity of enlisting Sung support. Their armies, drawn far from their own supply lines, could not be easily provisioned; maintaining their campaign at full strength thus required supplies from the south. Furthermore, the Mongols needed assurance from Lin-an that it would not act against their interests during the final stages of the assault, even though some fighting might spill over into Sung territory. Hence, the Mongol ruler sent emissaries to Hsiang-yang at the close of 1232 to open discussions for a joint military effort with the Sung against the Jurchen. As the chief councillor's nephew and prefect of Hsiang-yang, Shih Sung-chih proved to be the leading figure in these negotiations.[49]

Lin-an initially hesitated to accept the Mongol offer, delaying its consent until the Jurchen court had already taken up residence at Ts'ai-chou. With the backbone of the Jurchen army so near to its border, hostilities were certain to occur, regardless of Sung neutrality; and the opportunity to avenge the humiliation of Sung imperial clansmen once held prisoner by Jurchen captors had an irresistible appeal. The two sides thus reached an accord by the summer of 1233. Shih Sung-chih led troops north along a tributary of the Han River to attack T'ang-chou, located less than one hundred kilometers west of the enemy holdout. Meanwhile, he dispatched General Meng Kung (1195–1246) and others to the northeast to join the Mongols in their assault on Ts'ai-chou.[50] After little more than a half-year of combined effort, the allies utterly decimated enemy defenses and brought the Chin dynasty to an inglorious end. For his role in directing the Sung campaign, Shih Sung-chih received the honor of making the formal announcement of victory and forwarding to Lin-an the standard palace items to prove the enemy's defeat.[51] Although the military commissioner did not personally take part in the decisive battle at Ts'ai-chou, it was he who reaped the most politically. An appointment followed shortly as minister of war (*ping-pu shang-shu*, 2b).

No sooner did hostilities cease to the north than Shih Sung-chih found himself in the heat of a hazardous political battle in the south. Revanchist elements were on the rise at court and their call for a more aggressive foreign policy finally began to appeal to an emperor just begining to assert himself in the aftermath of Shih Mi-yüan's death. The new chief councillor, Cheng Ch'ing-chih, lacking the seasoned prudence of his predecessor, threw his weight behind the militants. With the support of Generals Chao K'uei (1186–1266) and Chao Fan (d. 1240), he convinced the emperor to order troops farther north in an attempt to regain the old capitals of K'ai-feng and nearby Lo-yang.[52] Shih Sung-chih clearly opposed the venture and the decision to act represented a serious political setback. Yet, even more sombering was the impact of aggression on the dynasty. Not only did the Sung fail to hold the area, as many had predicted, but the move provided the Mongols precisely the casus belli to justify aggression against the south. Faced with a resounding defeat, the revanchists blamed others for their own shortsightedness. Chao K'uei, striking out at Shih Sung-chih, insisted that his refusal to supply needed provisions at a critical stage had been responsible for the loss of K'ai-feng.[53] The veracity of the charge is unknown, although the pacifist inclination of Shih Sung-chih made it seem reasonable enough. Understandably, Cheng Ch'ing-chih was infuriated by the mere suggestion that his war minister, simply out of personal frustration, might have willfully sabotaged his first major undertaking as chief councillor. Tensions between the two men mounted, ending in Shih Sung-chih's decision to surrender his ministership. Remaining out west, he became prefect of E-chou, another strategically important area located southeast of Hsiang-yang on the southern bank of the Yangtze in northeastern Ching-hu circuit. The court also issued concurrent appointments as civil and military commissioner for the western Huai region.

Shih Sung-chih held one regional post after another for the next three years. The controversy surrounding his role in the aborted offensive of 1234 notwithstanding, he never fell from imperial favor. In addition to retaining high-level military posts and rank of 2b, his nobiliary status climbed to "earl" and then "marquis."[54] Reports have it that the throne also extended to him the privileges ordinarily afforded chief councillors.[55] All of this, no doubt, was related to the changing political climate in the capital. By the close of 1236, the court had come to prefer a more conciliatory approach to the Mongol problem. Chief councillor of the right Cheng Ch'ing-chih, who advocated a firm stand against the enemy, was replaced by the moderate Ch'iao Hsing-chien.[56] Meanwhile, Chief councillor of the left Ts'ui Yü-chih (1158–1239), a long-time supporter of Cheng Ch'ing-chih, found himself much more isolated in his largely nominal post and waning in his influence over the throne.[57] The swing of the pendulum, now in the direction of the moderates, greatly enhanced the prospects for Shih Sung-chih's revival in the capital and this was aided by his performance in the border war.

For the most part, the Sung was on the offensive in 1234, helping the Mongols to eliminate Jurchen rule in the north and then helping itself to an unwarranted share of the spoils. By the next year, there occurred a complete reversal. Along the border in Ching-hsi circuit, the Mongols struck against Tsao-yang, Sui-chou, and Ying-chou. In the interior, they attacked Mien-chou, in the heart of Ching-hu circuit, not far from its seat at Chiang-ling. After crossing the Huai in 1236, they continued their southern thrust, rapidly approaching the Yangtze River. Having mounted the spine of the Sung empire, they were positioned to launch a full-scale invasion. The level of tension in Lin-an, at that moment, can well be imagined.

Shih Sung-chih, as military commissioner for the western Huai and Ching-hu regions, had been entrusted with directing defense efforts for most of the empire's central and western flank.[58] His position as prefect of E-chou was also terribly important, for this placed him near the focus of the Mongol drive. Under his leadership, fighting was often hard and casualties heavy on both sides, yet Sung forces eventually managed to arrest the enemy offensive. Fortunately for Lin-an, the Mongols still experienced difficulty supplying distant cavalries and probably realized the futility of advancing any farther. Moreover, conquests of Korea and Russia must have placed considerable strain on enemy resources.[59] These factors, complemented by a strong Sung defense, led to a reduction in fighting and, before long, the initiation of peace overtures by the Mongols.[60] Shih Sung-chih had so impressed Li-tsung by early 1238 that a promotion followed as assistant councillor (2a). Not to waste his apparent martial talents in a civilian post, the emperor also turned over to him personal direction of virtually the entire Sung army.

Shih Sung-chih's advancement also marked a new determination on the part of Lin-an to restore peaceful relations with its new neighbor, the Mongols. Similar to Shih Hao and Shih Mi-yüan before him, Shih Sung-chih had always favored détente. Despite a highly accomplished career in the military, he consistently opposed military expansion of any sort. No less than Meng Kung, Chao K'uei, and Chao Fan, he led troops into battle and won glory from the victories claimed. However, his widely known pro-peace sentiments clearly distinguished him from the others.[61] The court certainly knew of Shih Sung-chih's views in this regard, so the decision to elevate him to assistant councillor may be seen as indicative of a major redirection of court policy away from revanchism. Reflecting this shift, Lin-an dispatched emissaries to the north almost immediately after announcing the promotion of Shih Sung-chih—the south's first peace gesture since hostilities had erupted four years earlier.[62] At the beginning of 1239, Li-tsung took an additional step in confirming his new commitment to peace by naming Shih Sung-chih chief councillor of the right. With Li Tsung-mien (d. 1239) then seated as councillor of the left, Ch'iao Hsing-chien as distinguished special councillor (*p'ing-chang chün-kuo chung-shih*), and Yü T'ien-hsi as assistant councillor, pro-peace elements were in complete command of the bureaucracy. Interestingly, all except Li Tsung-mien were former associates of Shih Mi-yüan.

Shih Sung-chih held onto power for nearly six years, during which he stood forth as the single most influential personality at court and the leading policymaker. In contrast with uncle Shih Mi-yüan, who for awhile enjoyed at least limited popularity, the younger Shih drew acrimonious censure from the outset. He tended to be arrogant in his display of power, uncompromising with the opposition, and intolerant of critics. He applied no carrot-and-stick approach to deal with the politically disaffected, only the stick. Having failed to learn from his uncle the skill of manipulating the opposition, he eventually fell victim to it.

On the positive side, the contributions of Shih Sung-chih to his beleaguered empire should not be slighted, the tendency among traditional historians who resent his perceived pacifism. There is no question that the Sung enjoyed, under him, much more political stability than under the leadership of predecessor Cheng Ch'ing-chih. Although never able to establish the dialogue with the Mongols that he hoped for, Shih Sung-chih had successfully denied the enemy a foothold in South China.[63] In fact, much of the territory in the central Huai valley once wrested from the Sung during the tenure of Cheng Ch'ing-chih was recaptured under the new administration—no small achievement in light of the chronic military and economic weaknesses of the empire and the formidable strength of Mongol armies.[64] On the other hand, the most serious problems besetting the declining Sung government were never resolved. First, despite a genuine interest on both sides to reach an agreement, peace remained elusive. Perhaps the Mongols felt that Lin-an was not negotiating in good faith, or maybe Lin-an regarded Mongol demands as excessive.[65] Whatever the reasons, Shih Sung-chih's inability to bring peace to the border ensured prolonged chaos and economic hardship there. A second and related issue was the empire's troubled economy. Government expenditures, most of which were military-related, continued to climb while tax revenues plummeted. As local official confronting grave fiscal and administrative problems, Shih Sung-chih exuded immense energy and imagination, yet as chief councillor he was hopeless at reversing the economic deterioration around him. Third, and most important, he failed to develop a working relationship with other high officials and intellectuals in the capital, a factor that inevitably weakened his effectiveness as bureaucratic chief.[66] As critics grew in number, they became more bold in their attacks. Among other things, they accused him of being unconscionably corrupt, self-serving, and autocratic.[67] They made many attempts to undermine his position, but there seemed to be no way of shaking the emperor's confidence in him. In the autumn of 1244, the opportunity they had long awaited finally came.

When Shih Sung-chih became chief councillor in 1239, father Shih Mi-chung was already over eighty years old. In consideration of his age and the chief councillor's filial duties, the emperor summoned the elder Shih and his wife to the capital to live in the official residence of their son and there to receive special care.[68] It is uncertain whether Shih Mi-chung ever accepted the offer, for when death came in 1244 he was at the family residence in Ming-chou. According to tradition, Shih Sung-chih should immediately have tendered his resignation and returned home to begin three years of mourning. This delighted the opposition, which anxiously awaited his departure from Lin-an. On the very next day, however, the throne ordered that mourning be suspended and that he remain in office. The uproar that this provoked in the capital far exceeded all expectations. Memorials of protest from a wide spectrum of scholar-officials flooded the court. Similar protests were endorsed by over 144 students at the Imperial University, 67 students at the National Military Academy, 94 students at the Lin-an Academy, and 34 at the Imperial-Clan Academy.[69] Certainly the most stirring and widely publicized memorial was that lodged by students of the Imperial University. It reveals so much about the attitude of contemporaries toward Shih Sung-chih at the time that a generous sampling seems appropriate.

> Your servants have been told that [the intimacy of the relationship between] ruler and parent parallels [that between] Heaven and Earth; loyalty [to the throne] and filial piety [to parents] have no [distinctions] between past and present. [Only] when one serves his parents with filial devotion can loyal devotion be transferred to his ruler. Since antiquity, [therefore,] it has been necessary to search for loyal officials among families with filial sons; it is impossible to expect loyalty of the unfilial. . . . We have never heard of [a son], who upon learning that a parent is critically ill, does not inquire [about his condition]; or, upon receiving notice that a parent has already died, does not consider hastening [home to begin mourning]. Could such [conduct] possibly represent that of one with a humane mind and [conscious of] Heaven's principles? . . .
>
> The concept of restoring [an official from mourning] does not exist in the classics of the sages, but the altering of ritual [merely] for expediency surely exists at the onset of a declining age. A high official of our dynasty such as Fu Pi (1003–83) was one who kept in mind the well-being of the state for the duration of his life and who advanced and withdrew [from public office] based upon the respect or disrespect [that this generated] throughout the realm—a so-called "important state official" whose daily presence was indispensable.

Messengers were sent a total of five times with edicts restoring him [to service], [but] Fu Pi regarded the altering of ritual, [like] metal and leather [instruments of war], as having no place during an age of peace. In the end, he did not heed the edict and the realm praises him [even] to this day.[70] Then, there are the likes of Cheng Chü-cheng (d. 1123) and Wang Fu (d. 1126), whose perversion and obstinacy made them oblivious to shame. They were firm in retaining their salary and rank, willingly [accepted] recalls, and [consequently] desecrated Heaven's principles. Ultimately, [such conduct] culminated in the disaster of the Ching-k'ang period (in 1126). [Let us not forget that] past incidents can be repeated![71]

Just what sort of person is this Sung-chih? He is devious in mind and deceitful in deportment. When previously serving as military commander, his pro-peace [stand] demoralized [both] commanders and troops. He used enormous wealth to gain the position of chief councillor, [whereupon] he gathered the [various] vile elements of the realm to become [members of] his exclusive faction. Meanwhile, he has snatched up the wealth and power of the realm, placing them at his personal disposal. As his relentless scheming multiplies, the danger [he poses to the empire] becomes unfathomable. Another day at court entails another day of catastrophe; another year there entails another year of distress. The utterances from a multitude of mouths are unanimous, their only fear is that his departure will be anything but speedy. When Sung-chih lost his father and a prompt dismissal [appeared imminent], [persons] both in and away [from the capital] were initially elated; but by then the throne had already issued the edict for his restoration. . . .

High officials assist the Son of Heaven by employing [the spirit of] filial piety to order the realm. If filial piety is not practiced by high officials [themselves], this will result in the entire realm becoming an empire [whose people] know no father. . . .

Is Your Majesty's decision to restore Sung-chih made because of his perceived talent for negotiating at distant places (that is, with the Mongols)? [In fact,] he originally lacked competence in border defense and is skilled merely at manipulating the court. Civil disorder in those empires and the murder [by aliens] of their own flesh and blood were brought about by Heaven. Sung-chih covets the accomplishments of Heaven so as to beguile the throne, convinced that the confusion and disruption along [our] three borders can be managed by him alone. Actually, he knows absolutely nothing about the intricacies of the enemy's [military] standing—which is[, at any rate,] beyond Sung-chih's ability to manage. Sung-chih simply wishes to exploit his reputation for managing the enemy so as to control the throne.

Or is Your Majesty's recall of Sung-chih made because he is considered to possess talent in administering [the empire's] finances? [In reality,] he originally lacked competence at making the empire plentiful and its people prosperous, as he merely has schemes [to secure] private fiefs and personal wealth. Among the sources of profit for the empire, the salt administration weighs heavy; [but] now, with the laws regulating paper currency having undergone numerous changes, the profit it yields to the empire is not [even] one- or two-tenths [its former size], while accumulations in [Shih Sung-chih's] private treasury are already beyond calculation. The empire's expanse diminishes daily, while Sung-chih's farmland and domiciles grow with each day; the empire's treasury is reduced daily, while Sung-chih's purse fattens with each day. Your Majesty's beneficent retention of him lies in his perceived benefit to Your empire; [Your Majesty] certainly does not realize that [he] will only bring Your empire immeasurable harm.

That Sung-chih can dare to orchestrate his own recall without vacillation is because he is familiar with Mi-yüan's precedent and is imitating, nay exceeding, him. Whereas it was a stepmother for whom Mi-yüan was to mourn, in the case of Sung-chih, mourning is for his father; whereas Mi-yüan hastened [home] for mourning and was restored [to office sometime] later, [only] after Sung-chih had been restored did he proceed to hasten for mourning. [Despite] Mi-yüan's obsession with securing his position, he nevertheless returned to his native place [following the death to fulfill his filial obligation] as bereaved son on the twenty-second day of the eleventh month of the first Chia-t'ai year (on January 4, 1209), being restored on the fourth day of the fifth month of the second Chia-t'ai year (on June 8, 1209). This is not at all like Sung-chih's [original] concealment of [his father's] death, deception of the throne, and desecration of Heaven's constant principles [as they relate to human relationships]. Such is the extent of his depravity!

Alas, the manner in which Sung-chih schemes is also wicked. Ever since his installation as chief councillor, he was certainly conscious of both parents being aged [and close to death]; [so] day and night he schemed, preparing in advance the documents [to justify] his recall. . . . [Even] the ignoble in the streets and alleys [of the capital] are aware of his wickedness. Can it be that Your Majesty alone is ignorant of it? Censors dare not speak out, for censors are Sung-chih's claws; policy review advisors dare not speak out, for policy advisors are Sung-chih's bosom [friends]; palace attendants dare not speak out, for palace attendants are [as intimate] to Sung-chih as hand and arm; secondary councillors dare not speak out, for secondary councillors [protect] Sung-chih as wings and feathers. . . .

Since antiquity, when high officials [from families] which, for as many as three [consecutive] generations, monopolized imperial favor and exploited the power [vested in them], they were inevitably [responsible for] the collapse of their empires. The Wang house of the Han dynasty and Ssu-ma house of the Wei are [examples] of this.[72] Alas, the Shih family [of our era] has held onto power now for three generations! Officers of the military know only that there exists a Shih house, scholar-officials of the realm know only that there exists a Shih house, even the [multitude of] attendants at every side of Your Majesty know only that there exists a Shih house. Your Majesty's power is so isolated on high that it is most frightening! Heaven wishes to remove them [and thereby brought about the death of Shih Sung-chih's father], but Your Majesty retains them. How could it be that in this vast Middle Kingdom there are no superior men [to lead it] and [Your Majesty must] place his faith in the inferior without realizing [that they are such]? By so doing, Your Majesty has willed that the three-hundred-year-old empire of T'ai-tsu should be destroyed at the hands of the Shih lineage!

The posted edict states, "Chao P'u (921–91)—during the Ch'ien-te era (963–67) when [the empire] had just been founded—and Chu Sheng-fei (1082–1144)—during the Shao-hsing era (1131–62) when [the empire] encountered adversity—both submitted to the alteration of ritual so that they might conclude their military missions."[73] Yet, the comparison of individuals requires some commonality. Can the grossly evil Sung-chih be mentioned in the same breath as a worthy such as Chao P'u? . . .

The posted edict also states, "Spies inform us of the [enemy's] formation of crack troops and there is news from the border that express messengers are [now] summoning [Mongol soldiers] to mount [their horses in preparation for war]. It is high autumn and horses are stalwart; once the cold of winter approaches, the earth will harden (thereby compelling the enemy either to attack at once or wait for another year)." [In fact,] during Sung-chih's occupancy of the vital post of chief councillor, he has avoided all mention of border affairs. The failure to defend T'ung-chou was not known until over a month later. The alarm at Shou-ch'un was not reported until the threat had [already] become serious.[74]

This trenchant indictment resembles in tone many memorials submitted to the court at the time, all of which took Li-tsung to task for insisting upon retaining the chief councillor. In essence, it accuses Shih Sung-chih of exploiting his post as bureaucratic chief to line his own pockets; misrepresenting to the throne developments along the border and thereby enhancing his personal reputation at the expense of the empire's security; and, perhaps most deplorable, being incapable of loyal service to the state to the extent that filial devotion to his own father is so demonstrably undernourished. Another salient point—and indeed the key to understanding the widespread unpopularity of the man—is the perceived threat of the Shih as a political force to the well-being of the Sung dynasty. The Wang family of the Han and the Ssu-ma of the Wei wielded such extraordinary power in their own day that they eventually toppled the Han and Wei to establish their own Hsin and Chin dynasties. It is noteworthy that university students should have suggested a parallel between the Shih of their time and political usurpers of the past, for this implies that many within the Sung political elite were greatly intimidated by the awesome influence represented by this kin group and considered it politically destabilizing.

Needless to say, such fears, assuming that they are genuine and not just rhetorical, were unjustified. Unlike the aristocratic houses of the early imperial period, the Shih were of scholar-official background. They rose to prominence and retained their newly won status through examination success and imperial favor. They had no regional, economic base to exploit in advancing their own interests. Political influence and wealth, having derived from court favor, could be withdrawn with the same ease that they were given. Surely thinkers of the time could appreciate the distinction between past and present. It may well be that the kin group's real threat was not directed so much against the ruling house as against the bureaucratic elite. By dominating some of the most esteemed posts in the civil service, Shih kinsmen must have been viewed as obstacles to the advancement of others aspiring for high office. By 1244, Shih Sung-chih had held onto the chief councillorship for almost six years and was astonishingly secure in his position. It was undoubtedly the nightmare of many that his tenure would follow a course similar to Shih Mi-yüan's, ending only with death. For politically aspiring scholar-officials and students at the Imperial University bound for the civil service, this must have been a dreaded prospect. Most allegations made in the student memorial were probably gross exaggerations or outright fabrications. That the opposition should nonetheless go to such extremes in their effort to unseat Shih Sung-chih serves to underscore the level of resentment that colleagues in the capital felt for him and his kin group.

For the next three months, the issue remained unsettled. Official and student groups were adamant in demanding the chief councillor's removal, while the throne refused to budge. In no time in Sung history does the mere waiver of mourning obligations for one official appear to have generated such an intense and drawn-out debate. Realizing the futility of it all, Shih Sung-chih requested to be relieved of his duties. He did so a total of six times before the emperor reluctantly accepted the resignation at the end of the year. The perseverance of the opposition had paid off and Li-tsung had lost a major confrontation with the forces of opinion in the capital.[75] When mourning duties were nearly over some two years later and the throne expressed an interest in reviving Shih Sung-chih, official resistance compelled the emperor to yield once more.[76] Shih Sung-chih formally retired shortly thereafter, never to surface again in the political arena.

Like earlier kinsmen Shih Hao and Shih Mi-yüan, Shih Sung-chih enjoyed the throne's complete confidence and generous favor. While serving as chief councillor and concurrent commissioner of military affairs, he was entrusted with direction of virtually the entire armed forces of the empire, from the valleys of the Huai and Yangtze rivers to the mountains of Hupei and Szechwan. These responsibilities made him one of few Sung statesmen to control the entire civil service and, at the same time, personally direct government armies. Even uncle Shih Mi-yüan—who, like most councillors of his era, served as chief of both the civilian and military bureaucracies—never commanded the armed forces. The distinct status of Shih Sung-chih at court is further revealed by the special permission granted him to leave the capital for prolonged periods in order to lead campaigns and to supervise military installations, even though this inevitably entailed some neglect of his many administrative duties as chief councillor.[77] Besides political power, the throne provided Shih Sung-chih with uncounted wealth through successive conferrals of fiefs of maintenance. It also honored him with titles of great esteem. He was ennobled "duke" upon his official retirement in 1246 and named "regional commandant" (chieh-tu-shih) following his death in 1257. Imperial goodwill could be generous and lasting, but fell short nonetheless of the princely treatment given Shih Mi-yüan. There is no indication that the court provided Shih Sung-chih a special residence in the capital or that it appointed his offspring to high office in the aftermath of his retirement and death. This may be related to the more straitened fiscal circumstances of the southern empire during its last years or the unending controversy surrounding his resignation in 1244; then again, perhaps this is because, unlike Shih Mi-yüan, he left behind few allies in the capital to protect him from the onslaught of critics—historical records allude to none.

In the final analysis, the political legacy of Shih Sung-chih was hardly a source of pride. The record of Shih Mi-yüan may have been uneven, but that of Shih Sung-chih is held up as uniformly wretched. In addition to the policy failures mentioned already, his reputation was also sullied by accusations that he used bribes to win high office and then exploited his office for personal financial gain; students at the Imperial University were not alone in making such charges. Worse yet, many considered him guilty of assassinating two outspoken critics; one was an executive at the Ministry of War, Hsü Yüan-chieh (d. 1245), and the other was his own nephew, Shih Ching-ch'ing (d. 1245).[78] Both died soon after Shih Sung-chih's resignation in 1244 and the mysterious circumstances surrounding the deaths led to charges of foul play. Although a special investigation failed to uncover evidence substantiating allegations of treachery on the part of Shih Sung-chih, mere suspicion was enough to damage irreparably his good name. Meanwhile, disparaging comments and innuendo directed against the former councillor could not but affect the standing of his kin group as a whole. It became necessary for the throne to weigh more carefully any future advancement of Shih kinsmen to executive posts against the possible reaction of the forces of opinion in and around the capital. While the confidence of Li-tsung in the merit of Shih men was surprisingly unshaken by the controversy surrounding Shih Sung-chih, he did not rule in a vacuum. During Sung times, the forces of opinion could be irrepressible and there is no question that they stood unalterably opposed to the advancement of another Shih to the top of the bureaucracy. It is thus not difficult to understand why the third chief councillor of the kin group was also its last.

OTHER KINSMEN IN BRANCH C

Besides Shih Sung-chih, Shih Mi-chung sired another son who similarly became a successful court official: Shih Yen-chih (fl. 1217–60).[79] Apparently quite precocious, the younger son received his *chin-shih* in 1217, three years before his elder brother and while still in his twenties. During the 1220s, Shih Yen-chih held several minor civilian posts prior to being appointed prefect of Chen-chou and, subsequently, Yang-chou, both in modern Kiangsu. He later served in various capacities at the History Bureau, in addition to assignments as directorate of military supplies (*chün-ch'i-chien*, 6a) and lord of the Imperial Treasury (*T'ai-fu ch'ing*, 4b). In the middle of the 1230s, he became prefect of Lin-an (3b), a post that he probably retained for four or five years.[80]

At the same time that Shih Sung-chih was rising to become assistant and then chief councillor, and possibly *because* of his growing influence, Shih Yen-chih received several executive-level appointments in the capital. In 1238 alone, he succeeded cousin Shih Pin-chih as executive at the Ministry of Justice (3b) and then moved on to become executive at the Ministry of Finance (3b), minister of war (2b), and minister of finance (2b).[81] This was a moment reminiscent of late 1207, when Shih Mi-yüan and brother Shih Mi-chien both held prominent posts in Lin-an; but this time, with Shih Sung-chih as assistant councillor and Shih Yen-chih his subordinate at the six ministries, there existed a much more conspicuous overlap of authority and greater opportunity for collusion between the two, should they be so inclined. Completely confident in them, the emperor found in this no reason for alarm. Following the appointment of Shih Sung-chih as chief councillor, however, the younger Shih finally submitted to the custom of avoidance and resigned from his metropolitan posts.

In 1242, Shih Yen-chih resurfaced as prefect of Shao-hsing and then Fu-chou, nominal academician at the Tuan-ming Palace (3a), and military commissioner for Fukien.[82] For the next eighteen years, he continued to receive high-ranking regional assignments; curiously, he was never recalled to the capital. The exact reasons for this are uncertain, although it may well be related to residual ill-will toward his brother within the civil service. Shih Yen-chih's final appointment came in 1259, when he became assistant military commissioner for the Yangtze valley.[83] It was in this capacity, during the summer of 1260, that he received orders to assist in breaking the Mongol blockade of E-chou. Tense about the outcome of a confrontation with so formidable an enemy, he allegedly chose to wait until Mongol armies had withdrawn before dispatching his own troops. Such cowardice reportedly infuriated Chief councillor Chia Ssu-tao, who ordered his immediate removal from the post and official demotion.[84] Retiring with the rank of 3a, he was never revived.[85]

Somewhat less eminent than Shih Sung-chih and Shih Yen-chih, two of the three remaining sons of Shih Mi-chung nonetheless made a mark for themselves as regional officials. Shih K'uei-chih [II] (n.d.) served as prefect with rank of 7a and Shih Yao-chih (n.d.) as prefect with rank of 5b.[86] Little is known about the development of their careers but in all probability the two owed some measure of their initial success to the political standing of their brothers.

While the sons of Shih Mi-chung were the only members of branch C to hold high-ranking posts in the civil service, some twenty-four others are known to have held mid- to low-level positions. Shih Mi-kung (who is later adopted as heir to branch E) reportedly fathered six sons, all of whom entered the bureaucracy. During the 1240s and 1250s, eldest son Shih K'en-chih (fl. 1241–53) received various regional assignments, including several as prefect, before retiring with rank of 5b.[87] Second son Shih Hsiao-chih (fl. 1253–58) once served as subprefect (ranked 7a),[88] and third son Shih Yü-chih [III] (n.d.), with rank 7b, served as prefectural vice-administrator (t'ung-p'an) of numerous areas, including the strategic E-chou.[89] Moreover, the three younger sons of Shih Mi-kung all received chin-shih degrees. Shih Neng-chih (fl. 1237–56) started out in the 1230s as sheriff of Ch'ang-chou (near modern Soochow) and eventually became prefect of the same (ranked 5a).[90] Shih Yu-chih (CS 1253) was advanced to the upper level of the Imperial University before being named inspector (ts'an-chün, 8b) for Yang-chou, retiring with rank of 6b.[91] Shih Chou-chih (CS 1241) is known to have served as prefect of Yen-chou (ranked 5b), southwest of the capital.[92] Thus, among the offspring of Shih Mi-kung alone, there were four midlevel and two low-level officials. In light of Shih

Mi-kung's personal frustration with government service, the obvious commitment and, indeed, success of his sons is quite remarkable. Fortunately, they served away from the capital, which enabled them to avoid the political controversies that permanently soiled the reputations of cousins Shih Chai-chih, Shih Yü-chih, and Shih Sung-chih.

One other *chin-shih* degreeholder is identified with branch C. This was Shih Wang-chih (CS 1229), son of Shih Mi-min—who, as was already noted, held *chin-shih* credentials as well.[93] He ended his career as lord assistant chief justice (*ta-li shao-ch'ing*, 6a), a metropolitan post, yet whether he served in the capital before or after Shih Sung-chih is not known. Shih Wang-chih had only one brother, Shih Sheng-chih (n.d.); he held civil service rank but, apparently, not office.[94] The line of Shih Mi-min thus did not prosper like some of the others, at least not in late Sung times.

Notably more successful in generation VII were the sons of Shih Mi-ying, younger brother of Shih Mi-min. Shih Yi-chih [II] (n.d.), as prefect of Lien-chou, in the northwest of modern Kwangtung, held rank 6a.[95] A second son of Shih Mi-ying, Shih Shih-chih [II] (n.d.), is identified as a former subprefect of Chien-k'ang; he ended his career with rank 6a.[96] Completing the family was Shih Pai-chih (n.d.), a onetime prefectural vice-administrator (7a).[97] With a *chin-shih* degree, Shih Mi-ying rose to a midlevel post while his sons, lacking examination credentials, achieved as much through bureaucratic privilege and family ties. Branch C produced a few other officials: the offspring of less prosperous lines who remained within the lower bureaucracy. Lacking information to suggest otherwise, they too must have owed their careers to privilege.

OBSERVATIONS

From a total of thirty-four civil servants in the sixth generation the Shih could claim sixty-three in the seventh, suggesting that the kin group was still very much on the rise; yet the number of persons with civil service status is but one measure of the waxing and waning of family fortunes, and often a misleading one. The Shih may have been unusually successful in channeling a growing number of kinsmen into the bureaucracy, but the experiences of those in the seventh generation also portended serious trouble on the horizon. The controversy surrounding Shih Mi-yüan and his unprecedented tenure as chief councillor had created for him many personal enemies. The unpopularity of Shih Sung-chih went a step further, creating enemies not only for him personally, but for his entire kin group. In the aftermath of his forced resignation, it became increasingly difficult for others to advance to top positions in the bureaucracy, regardless of their intellectual promise or political acumen. For this reason, Shih kinsmen gradually disappeared from the Sung court during the last years of the reign of Li-tsung. When the capital fell to the Mongols in 1276, there were no more kinsmen in positions of influence there. To a great extent, the Shih house was doomed even before the dynasty.

The seventh generation marked a major shift in the development of the kin group. Just as the political accomplishments of Shih Hao surpassed those of Shih Ts'ai and thereby enabled branch A to eclipse branch B in the fifth generation, so the death of Shih Mi-yüan and the emergence of Shih Sung-chih marked the beginning of a challenge to the preeminence of branch A by upstarts in branch C. This was not only reflected in the unusual political prominence of Shih Sung-chih and Shih Yen-chih, but also in the success of this branch in perpetuating itself in a fashion resembling the senior line. Thus, branch C managed to sustain a high level of growth from the sixth through the ninth generations, falling only slightly behind branch A, and its yield of scholar-officials is also impressive (see table 1). This contrasts sharply with the three other branches (B, D, E), which remain small in size and generate few officials. The distinctive prosperity of branch C can only be explained in terms of degree-holding. Of the kin group's nine chin-shih recipients in the sixth generation, five were the sons of Shih Chien [II]. A generation later, the two most politically accomplished kinsmen were grandsons of Shih Chien [II] who also held degrees. This is not to say that Shih Sung-chih and Shih Yen-chih refused to avail themselves of family contacts to rise within the bureaucracy; contacts were undoubtedly useful to bureaucratic advancement, but critical to such advancement was a combination of examination credentials and demonstrated professional competence. Although recruitment through protection may have been exploited by a growing body of kinsmen to penetrate the civil service—with some faring reasonably well despite the prejudice against non-degreeholders—the stature of a given branch, and indeed the entire kin group, rested largely upon the attainments of the degree-holding influential.

Branch A may have already entered its descent, yet the emperor's great esteem for Shih Mi-yüan and the boundless favor enjoyed by the councillor's descendants enabled this line to continue perpetuating itself through another generation or two. Only one of Shih Hao's fourteen known grandsons held the coveted *chin-shih* degree and none could boast exceptional performances as civil servants; still, three of them rose to become high officials and six made it to midlevel posts. In 1233, the eighteen-year-old Shih Chai-chih suddenly leaped from a post ranked 6b to one ranked 3b for no reason other than the influence of his father, thus proving that individual merit may have been the ideal but not always the reality of bureaucratic advancement. With twenty-seven civil servants in generation VII, branch A still surpassed branch C in total yield. Had the relationship between Shih Mi-yüan and the emperor been less intimate or had the emperor been more circumspect in his display of favor, there is every reason to believe that, by the seventh generation, fewer branch A kinsmen would have penetrated the civil service and none would have won high-level appointments. The seventh generation was undoubtedly the first and last in which the family name served as a decisive element in career success. By the close of the Southern Sung, the Shih name had so deteriorated that claiming it could more frequently close doors than open them. Soon after the Sung, starting with the twelfth generation, kinsmen began to avoid selecting for their children personal names that automatically identified them as members of the same kin group or branch.[98] What greater proof is there of the internal conflict and declining fortunes of a house than the rejection by its members of their blood heritage?

Most seventh-generation kinsmen died before the fall of the Sung dynasty; of those still alive, many had already retired. As a result, their careers as scholars and officials were little affected by the changing fortunes of the Sung house. This was not true for members of the next generation, many of whom were just beginning their political climb when their empire crumbled around them. To continue this study into the Yüan and Ming periods would be to go beyond its intended scope. It is nonetheless desirable at least to outline the kin group's fate in the post-Sung era so that the reader may better appreciate the true depths of its plunge and the shattering impact that dynastic change can easily have upon political elites, and especially the exceptionally privileged, in the middle period of Chinese history.

Table 1 Summary of Civil Service Attainments

Generation	Branch	Male kin	Males with civil service status	Bureaucratic rank		
				High-level	Midlevel[a]	Low-level
I		1	0			
II		1	0			
III		1	0			
IV		5	1	1		
V		13	10	1	1	8
VI	A	18	14	3	4	7
	B	5	4	0	1	3
	C	17	10	1	4	5
	D	4	4	0	0	4
	E	3	2	0	1	1
Total		47	34			
VII	A	34	27	3	11	13
	B	14	6	0	1	5
	C	30	26	2	9	15
	D	5	3	0	0	3
	E	3	1	0	0	1
Total		86	63			
VIII	A	79	52	0	13	39
	B	9	3	0	0	3
	C	45	36	0	4	32
	D	10	1	0	0	1
	E	6	2	0	0	2
Total		149	94			
IX	A	131	38	0	4	34[b]
	B	11	0	0	0	0
	C	102	11	0	0	11[c]
	D	10	0	0	0	0
	E	5	1	0	0	1
Total		259	50			
X	A	158	1	0	0	1[d]
	B	6	0	0	0	0
	C	83	0	0	0	0
	D	5	0	0	0	0
	E	6	0	0	0	0
Total		258				

Table 1 (continued)

a The rank for prefects varies depending upon the previous rank of an official. As high as
1b, it can also be as low as 7a. In the absence of specific information on the sinecure of a
given prefect, midlevel rank is assumed.
b Includes six Yüan officials.
c Includes three Yüan officials.
d Includes one Yüan official.

EPILOGUE

Genealogical records reveal that Shih Mi-yüan had a total of fourteen
grandsons, twelve of whom held civil service rank.[99] None of the fourteen rose to become high officials and just two are reported to have held
midlevel posts: Shih Chou-ch'ing (n.d.) and Shih Ch'ang-ch'ing, both
sons of Shih Chai-chih.[100] Another grandson, Shih Chi-ch'ing (son of
Shih Yü-chih), became prefect with rank of 7b.[101] The rest were
lesser, although not necessarily insignificant, officials. Of Shih Mi-yüan's
forty great-grandsons, only six held civil service status and most without
office. Others in branch A faced a similar fate. Excluding descendants of
Shih Mi-yüan, forty out of sixty-five kinsmen (61 percent) in generation
VIII are identified as civil servants; a generation later, this drops to
thirty-two out of ninety-one (35 percent).[102] Only one official is reported
in the tenth generation but this may simply reflect the inadequacy of
source materials.

Turning to branch C, the kin group's third chief councillor, Shih Sung-
chih, had three sons and twenty-two grandsons.[103] Eldest son Shih Chieh-
ch'ing is identified as prefect under the Sung (ranked 5a), Shih Tsao-ch'ing
was once an acting prefect (ranked 8b), and Shih Li-ch'ing held a minor
post. None served in the capital like their father. While five of Shih
Sung-chih's grandsons (23 percent) entered the civil service, they remained
at the entry level. These were largely the elder grandsons, individuals
maturing under Sung rule. There is no indication that heirs in the tenth
generation held bureaucratic status but, again, this may reflect inadequate
information. The pattern is similar for other lines in branch C. The
prosperous line of Shih Mi-kung, which produced three degreeholders
and six officials (all reasonably accomplished) in generation VII, doubled
in size by the next generation, but the younger group betrayed none of the
promise of their parents; although all twelve males claimed civil service
status, they remained at the entry level (even the one degreeholder) and

most appear never to have held office. Of the twenty-five great-grandsons of Shih Mi-kung in generation IX, only one is identified as an official: Shih Chiung-sun, who served the Yüan.[104] For the branch as a whole, it was not a time of optimism. While 36 out of 45 males in the eighth generation claimed civil service status, 32 of these were low-level initiates; by generation IX only 11 out of 102 held status at all (see table 1). The implication is clear: among both the highly prominent and the relatively obscure, decline had begun to set in by the eighth generation; by the ninth this had resulted in the exclusion of most Shih kinsmen from the civil service. Needless to say, the single most important factor in this develop-ment was the collapse of the Sung dynasty.

Many Shih kinsmen of the seventh and eighth generations lived through the trauma of dynastic change. Although the Mongol government may have welcomed their service, the vast majority chose seclusion instead.[105] For example, a grandson of Shih Yüan (Shih Hao's younger brother) in the eighth generation, Shih Shih-ch'ing (1213–86), was identified with the Imperial University and served the Sung government until the very end. When the Mongols finally conquered South China, he retired with the rank of 7a, refusing to so much as comment on the new government. He devoted himself instead to studies and farming.[106] The experience of branch C descendants was hardly different. A grand-nephew of Shih Sung-chih in the ninth generation, Shih Tsung-po (n.d.), similarly with-drew from public service, commenting, "Current affairs are such that it is preferable 'to cultivate one's self and order one's home' while awaiting [the resumption of] peace."[107] He was joined by cousin Shih Yen-po (n.d.). A grandson of Shih Mi-kung in branch C and the last chin-shih of the Shih community during the Sung dynasty, Shih Meng-ch'ing (1247–1306), also chose a life of seclusion after its collapse. In the absence of office-holding, he subsequently focused his energies on teach-ing the Chu Hsi brand of Neo-Confucianism, making him the first mem-ber of his kin group known to have entirely rejected the Lu Chiu-yüan school.[108] Other Yüan eremites included: Shih Fan-ch'ing (n.d.),[109] Shih Hsi-ch'ing (n.d.),[110] Shih Ming-sun (n.d.),[111] Shih Hui-sun (1234–1306),[112] Shih Sui-po (n.d.),[113] and Shih Kung-t'ing (1301–48),[114]—to name but a few. At least one kinsman, Shih Hsien-sun (fl. 1278), died in battle defending the Sung.[115] How many others were doomed to a similar fate can only be speculated.

Out of 149 males in the eighth generation and 259 in the ninth, a total of only twelve Shih men (2.5 percent) are known to have served the Yüan. Three of the twelve were of generation VIII. Shih Chü-ch'ing (fl. 1266–1307), grandson of Shih Mi-chien in branch A and originally a Sung official, remained in office after 1279, initially as local staff supervisor and then as subprefect for the alien regime.[116] A son of Shih Sung-chih, Shih Chieh-ch'ing (n.d.), having served the Sung as prefect with the high rank of 5a, later was identified with the Yüan in a minor official capacity.[117] Finally, there was Shih Fang-ch'ing (n.d.), son of Shih K'en-chih and grandson of Shih Mi-kung. A fiscal inspector with rank of 8b in Sung times, he became county sheriff under the Mongols.[118] Little is known about the careers of the nine individuals in the subsequent generation who served the Yüan; records simply reveal that they held minor posts. Four of the nine are identified as regional instructors: Shih Ching-sun, Shih Hsüan-sun, Shih Wei-sun, and Shih Fu-po [II].[119] The recent work of John Dardess suggests that education was a popular alternative to bureaucratic service in Yüan times—especially for descendants of prominent Sung families torn between community pressure to boycott the alien government and financial pressure to serve—as Confucian scholars involved in local education were only quasi officials.[120] Yet, with only 4 out of 259 Shih men in generation IX identified with regional schools during the Yüan, it is clear that this accommodation on the part of the Mongol government had little appeal, at least for the Shih. Meanwhile, the only reasonably successful civil servant in this generation was Shih Chiung-sun (CS 1324), great grandson of Shih Mi-kung. The kin group's single *chin-shih* recipient under the Mongol regime, he also was its only metropolitan official; he once served as associate instructor at the Directorate of Education (7a).[121]

For the Shih as a whole, inauguration of the Yüan dynasty not only brought economic and political hardship, but triggered the disintegration of the kin group as well. A total of ten kinsmen are known to have abandoned the ancestral home at Yin *hsien*, ostensibly for greener pastures. Eighth-generation Shih Shun-ch'ing [II], from a rather obscure line in branch A, was apparently among the first; he settled in Hu-chou, about 150 kilometers to the northwest.[122] Another eight men migrated in the ninth generation, precisely when official unemployment under the Yüan was starting to affect family finances. Some simply moved a few kilometers to counties not far from Yin; some traveled a few hundred kilometers to Hang-chou or Soochow; and at least one moved as far away as Fukien.

Although eight out of ten were of the once prosperous branch A, no other pattern seems to emerge.[123] One migrant, Shih Yü-sun [VII], was the great-grandson of Shih Mi-yüan; another descended from Shih Mi-cheng (the chief councillor's elder brother) and two from Shih Mi-chien (his younger brother). A grandson of Chief councillor Shih Sung-chih, Shih Yi-sun [III], is among the migrants in branch C. Some were the offspring of individuals who refused to serve the Yüan, others were not. Some came from large and formerly prosperous lines, others from the small and obscure. Although not well documented after generation IX, it is likely that this migration continued into the tenth and eleventh generations.[124] In large part, dispersal of kinsmen must have been fueled by hard times, for there are numerous reports of poverty among those who elected to remain in Ming-chou. Shih Mi-yüan's great-grandson, Shih Yi-sun (1297?–1375), was so poor that he allegedly "drank [only] water while composing treatises"—an allusion to the fact that he could no longer afford tea.[125] Some members of the kin group had forsaken government service even before the fall of Lin-an. In one case, an eighth-generation kinsman, for unknown reasons, assumed the occupation of printer.[126] Lacking the privileges of official status, many were reduced to the equivalent of commoners, preoccupying themselves principally with agriculture.[127] There is even a case of a kinsman taking withdrawal to the extreme and becoming a Taoist monk.[128] The many mansions, estates, gardens, and gifts of gold and jade that Sung emperors had so lavishly showered upon favored kinsmen all seem to have disappeared; just how this happened is, and will probably forever remain, a mystery.

The total powerlessness of the Shih in Yüan times is perhaps best depicted by the story of young Shih Mao-tsu (n.d.). A descendant of Shih Hao seven generations removed, great-grandson of Shih Ch'i-ch'ing (ranked 5b), grandson of Shih Ho-sun (ranked 9b), and second son of Shih Kung-lin (unranked), Shih Mao-tsu was orphaned at just over two years old.[129] His stepmother initially accepted the burden of raising the child and his two sisters, yet abject poverty left her little alternative but to sell them all into slavery sometime later. For the duration of his youth, Shih Mao-tsu lived as the slave of a wealthy family "north of the Yangtze." Although long separated from his kin in Ming-chou, the child continued to identify with them and never forgot their past glory. His melodramatic biographer wrote, "Whenever he thought of his kinfolk, he abruptly broke into sobbing and weeping; by nighttime, the stream of tears would drench his pillow—and so it went for seventeen years."[130] After reaching maturity but while still quite young, his masters were convicted of some crime, punishment for which resulted in their slaves being set free. An emancipated Shih Mao-tsu is then said to have hastened home in search of his lost family.

Originally, his grandfather owned some eight thousand *mou* of farmland in the vicinity of their home, but it was reportedly seized by "bullies" from the Hang-chou region. Out of an apparent fear of retaliation from the encroachers and a general lack of concern about the well-being of distant relatives, leading members of the Shih community refused to become involved in the legal battle over property rights. As a result, the land remained in the hands of its confiscators for two generations. After returning to Ming-chou, a persistent Shih Mao-tsu was eventually successful at convincing local authorities of the validity of his family's claim to the property, which resulted in its restoration. Historians say that he subsequently used it to support his aging grandmother and derelict uncles. Somewhat better off financially, he nonetheless appears to have remained uneducated and politically insignificant. Indeed, the historical importance of Shih Mao-tsu lies chiefly in the irony that he, a member of the once awe-inspiring Shih house, should have been humiliated by enslavement.

That the Shih were either unwilling or unable to prevent the enslavement of young Shih Mao-tsu and the confiscation of his grandfather's property by outsiders reflects their pervasive lack of kin group corporateness or cohesion. Perhaps cohesiveness dissipated in the aftermath of bitter political feuds during Sung times, or maybe it was absent from the very outset except at the superficial level of ordering the personal names of kinsmen. The story of Shih Mao-tsu also reveals that the Shih of post-Sung times lacked any significant political influence in the Ming-chou region. Once the most accomplished and prominent members of the local elite, the Shih of the late Yüan were weak and inconsequential. Bullies had no reason to fear offending the Shih and historians saw no reason to continue discussing them. Their power and glory were all a part of the distant past. No doubt, a certain level of wealth and influence continued to be held by a small group of kinsmen throughout the Yüan and Ming periods, and even into the Ch'ing, but the size of this group seems only to have shrunk over time.

There is no single, dramatic finale for the Shih. Some moved elsewhere out of choice, others out of necessity. A small fraction of the entire group served the alien Yüan dynasty, while most went into seclusion. A handful clung to minor official status, at least one became a slave. The kin group never entirely disappeared from Ming-chou. Centuries after the Sung had collapsed, the Shih still managed to produce an occasional degreeholder and bureaucrat, but never again a prominent statesman.[131] The Southern Sung was its heyday. Once gone, the Shih followed the dynasty into oblivion.

Conclusion

THE SUNG DYNASTY, for all its faults, was perhaps more successful than most dynasties in devising and maintaining a highly rational civil service—one that aspired to the ancient ideal of individual merit, even though reality often fell short of the ideal. What is clear is that civil service recruitment was based upon success at impartial examinations and even society's most privileged individuals found themselves enmeshed in the competition. And as the size of the educated pool of candidates grew—in part a function of a growing population, in part a function of expanding opportunities for education —competition for a fixed number of positions grew keen. In this context, bureaucratic privilege was not easy to maintain, for new talent could readily supplant the old. The Shih of the late twelfth century represented new talent, yet within a century they were eclipsed by others. Responsible for both developments was the examination system.

FACTORS AFFECTING BUREAUCRATIC FLUIDITY

This study of the Shih began with a discussion of civil service recruitment by examination: its enhanced importance during the T'ang, its centrality under the Sung, and the role it played in completely altering the composition of the ruling class. For those of nonofficial background, access to the civil service generally required examination success. Even the most socially privileged, in search of status and security, aspired to earn a degree. The highly competitive character of the examinations, combined with the imposition of progressively more stringent restrictions

on the inheritance of official privileges, mitigated against the entrenchment of a hereditary elite in the Sung comparable to the "great families"
of the early imperial period. Recruitment by merit cannot but undermine
hereditary privilege. The Shih experience tends to confirm this.

This study has also shown that the Shih thrust into politics was greatly
affected by regional developments. The increased economic importance
of the lower Yangtze region, the consequent proliferation of educational
institutions there, and the rise of local communities of intellectuals all
contributed to making the area and its natives unusually promising.
Enhancing this promise were reforms in the examination system under
Emperor Hui-tsung whereby the publicly funded prefectural school
emerged as the principal training ground for scholar-officials. Classical
training thus became accessible to those who otherwise held little hope of
obtaining it. Ultimately, the greatest boost to bureaucratic fluidity stemmed
from the Jurchen invasion of North China and the relocation of the Sung
capital in Lin-an, only about 150 kilometers from the Shih home at
Ming-chou. Proximity to the capital virtually guaranteed the area a prosperous economy and a strong voice in politics. Whereas government policy of the late Northern Sung provided the Shih an opportunity to *enter*
the bureaucracy, the Southern Sung brought the occasion to *dominate* it.
There is little question that the kin group's unusual success owes something to the special place and times in which it lived.

Degree-holding. Fortuitous circumstances notwithstanding, the Shih managed initially to penetrate and then to retain a prominent position within
the civil service through success at the examinations. Beginning in 1118
and continuing until 1265, they produced a total of twenty-six *chin-shih*
degreeholders, men with examination credentials, and the politically
influential among them were chiefly those with examination degrees. The
success of the Shih is made all the more startling in light of the relatively
small size of the kin group at the time of its ascendancy. Generation IV
consisted of only five males, yet one managed to win a degree, one of
thirteen did so in the fifth generation, and nine out of forty-seven (20
percent) in the sixth (see table 2).[1]

The reasons for so small a kin group generating such an abundance of
talent are not easy to discern. Shih success could be related to the
intensification of intellectual activity in and around Ming-chou following
the introduction there of the idealist school of Confucian thought; or

Table 2 Summary of Degreeholders

Generation	Degreeholders	Total number of male kinsmen
IV	1	5
V	1	13
VI	9	47
VII	12	86
VIII	3	149
IX	1 (Yüan)	259
X	0	258

maybe it is a reflection of the unique tendency among most Shih kinsmen to concentrate their intellectual energies on government service, even at the expense of scholarship and the arts. Curiously, while yielding far more officials than any other kin group in the area, no member of the Shih community became distinguished as a local teacher in the mold of Lou Yü or Yüan Hsieh.[2] I suspect that the Northern Sung ideal of scholar-official breadth, what some might call the "amateur ideal," was giving way in Southern Sung times to bureaucratic professionalism and specialization, especially at the highest levels of the civil service. The Shih succeeded in part because they were able to anticipate, or at least adjust quickly to, this trend.

Bureaucratic Privilege. With degrees, the Shih could fully exploit the privileges afforded them as civil servants, chiefly through protection, to draw undeserving kinsmen into the bureaucracy. As illustrated in figures 1 and 2, for every *chin-shih*, there could be as many as twenty or twenty-five non-degreeholders with bureaucratic status; although no more than 20 percent of any generation received examination degrees, as much as 75 percent of them held official rank. Meanwhile, it was also possible to receive quasi-*chin-shih* status through special conferrals which, if nothing else, served to enhance social status. At least five kinsmen received degrees as an act of "favor for the ancestors," while another eighteen received degrees from the Directorate of Education.[3] Admittedly, such degrees were not especially esteemed within the civil service and compilers of most local gazetteers would not include quasi-*chin-shih* on their lists of degreeholders; special degrees were also not very useful for rising to the

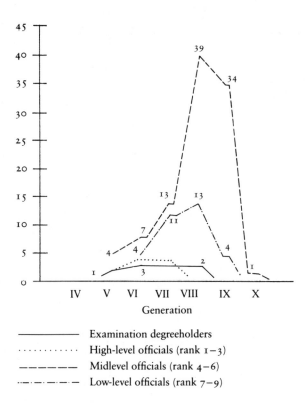

Figure 1   Office-holding for the Shih Branch A

top of the bureaucracy. Then again, such practices did give the Sung civil service an undeniable hereditary tint.

To be sure, there is a need to reassess the whole notion of the Sung civil service being a meritocracy founded upon examination success. Official rank could be distributed quite indiscriminately, even occasionally given to small children, and a majority of bureaucrats owed their status neither to special talent nor training. That the bureaucracy gave the appearance of being "open" stems in part from the character of earlier research, which generalized about the social composition of the entire bureaucracy based upon *chin-shih* examination lists.[4] This can be terribly misleading. Examination lists, I suspect, would generally contain an exceptionally large number of "newcomers," that is, men from families with no recent

Figure 2   Officeholding for the Shih Branch C

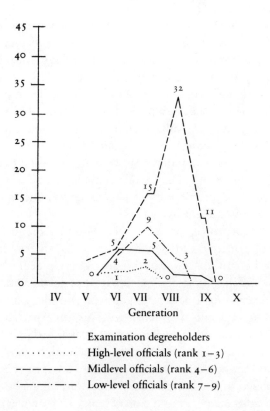

- ——————— Examination degreeholders
- · · · · · · · · · · High-level officials (rank 1–3)
- – – – – – – Midlevel officials (rank 4–6)
- ·—·—·—·— Low-level officials (rank 7–9)

history of civil service involvement. The Shih, for example, produced more *chin-shih*, relative to the size of the kin group, in the fourth through sixth generations, while still on the rise, than it did later on, upon reaching the pinnacle of success. In all likelihood, this is because, once established, the ease of gaining official status and honorary degrees through informal channels effectively discouraged many Shih youth from preparing for the highly rigorous examinations. Thus, examination lists may have consisted largely of bureaucratic upstarts while the bureaucracy itself was dominated by men from established families.

Having made this qualification, I still consider the Sung civil service to have *functioned* as a meritocracy, even though it may have consisted largely of the socially privileged. Shih kinsmen who, lacking *chin-shih* credentials, nonetheless managed to receive mid- to high-level assignments —individuals such as Shih Mi-chien, Shih Pin-chih, and Shih Yü-chih —had proven themselves as low-level regional officials before passing the necessary reviews and promotion examinations to move up the bureaucratic ladder. They may have penetrated the civil service through privilege, but they succeeded through individual merit. This is also true of degreeholders. Shih Mi-yüan rose to the chief councillorship, not because of Shih Hao's personal relationship with Emperor Hsiao-tsung, but because he won the confidence of Ning-tsung at a critical point in time. It was Shih Sung-chih's distinguished service along the Sung border, not the favor of uncle Shih Mi-yüan, that resulted in his elevation to bureaucratic chief. The list could go on. Thus, while enabling many to circumvent the examination system, privilege did not necessarily undermine the traditional ideal of appointment by merit.

We do know that protection and imperial favor had the effect of inflating the number of potential civil service recruits and thereby made official appointment difficult for all, degreeholders and non-degreeholders alike. The Shih community alone contained over 240 males with civil service status in Southern Sung times, yet a good many of these apparently held rank without office, status without salary. This was especially true for the eighth and ninth generations, when imperial favor for Shih Mi-yüan and Shih Sung-chih resulted in special conferrals of rank beyond normal protection quotas. Yet, to the extent that roughly 180 of these 240 individuals were confined to the bureaucracy's lower level (mostly 8b–9b), this placed severe limits on the transmission of rank to subsequent generations.[5] In the absence of demonstrated ability, either in examination halls or public office, their offspring were doomed to exclusion from the civil service. Bureaucratic status, therefore, was hereditary in the short but not the long run.

Biological Trends. Yet another component in the Shih success story—one so obvious that it is easily disregarded—is longevity. It is no coincidence that the most prominent and politically accomplished of its members were also the ones to enjoy exceptionally long life spans. Third-generation Shih Chao, "Mr. Eight Virtues of Conduct," lived until seventy-two; the kin group's first degreeholder, Shih Ts'ai, probably lived to be seventy or eighty;[6] its first chief councillor, Shih Hao, enjoyed a longevous eighty-eight years; its second councillor, Shih Mi-yüan, lived until sixty-nine; his son, Shih Yü-chih, came close to eighty. The progenitors of branches B and C, Shih Chün and Shih Chien [II], both lived beyond seventy years old; the latter's eldest son, Shih Mi-chung, was well over eighty when he died in 1244; grandson Shih Sung-chih, third chief councillor of the Shih house, lived until sixty-eight; and his brother, Shih Yen-chih, reached seventy-seven. It is widely recognized that a positive correlation exists between longevity and upward mobility, and it stands to reason: regardless of an individual's talent or the opportunities around him to improve his lot, an early death renders everything worthless. In the final analysis, it will never be known whether it was the wealth accompanying bureaucratic service that made for this unusual record of longevity or, conversely, longevity which facilitated career success and the subsequent accumulation of wealth. Perhaps the two are actually inseparable. What is known is that longevity tends to be hereditary, so the Shih certainly owe some element of their success to genetics.

Lawrence Stone, in his study of the British aristocracy during the sixteenth and seventeenth centuries, and P'an Kuang-tan, in his research on prominent families in Chekiang's Chia-hsing prefecture during the Ming-Ch'ing period, have both come to some interesting conclusions about longevity and declining family fortunes. Just as long lifespans are common among the upwardly mobile, the downwardly mobile tend to be plagued by short life spans.[7] In the case of the Shih, information on longevity is restricted to only a handful of kinsmen and this precludes our speculating along similar lines. The limited data that do exist for kinsmen of the sixth and seventh generations, when the kin group had reached the summit of its climb and was already beginning to decline, do not suggest shorter life spans, reflecting perhaps the kin group's sustained vitality.

As for the physical stamina of Shih kinsmen at the time of their political ascendancy, there is no better evidence than the size of individual families. Beginning with the fifth generation, there developed the almost universal tendency to sire as large a family as nature would permit. Shih Hao, for example, had four sons and five daughters. Of the four boys, Shih Mi-cheng was most prolific, with seven sons of his own and fourteen grandsons. Shih Mi-yüan had only three sons, but they made him grandfather of fourteen and great-grandfather of forty. The fifth-generation heir to branch B, Shih Chün, fathered five boys; in turn, they made him grandfather of fourteen. Branch C grew from three to seventeen males simply in the transition from fifth to sixth generations; Shih Mi-chung subsequently became father of five, grandfather of twelve, and great-grandfather of thirty-seven; brother Shih Mi-kung had five sons, twelve grandsons, and twenty-five great-grandsons. In this way, the kin group swelled from a mere 5 men in the fourth generation to 259 in the ninth. Furthermore, these figures hardly represent the true number of offspring. First, virtually nothing is known about the number of females, which probably tended to be greater than males.[8] Second, with infant mortality in traditional China quite high, children who died before five or ten years old were commonly excluded from the count, the Chinese regarding such premature deaths as inauspicious and best forgotten.

That the Shih should evince such unusual fecundity stems chiefly from its success in the civil service. High office and imperial favor brought wealth once beyond imagination.[9] This enabled kinsmen to support one or more concubines, in addition to their legal wives. When the kin group first embarked upon its civil service trek, families tended to be small. Shih Ts'ai apparently had no concubine and was survived by a single son. Only one generation later—with the ascendancy of its second high official, Shih Hao, and the entrance to the civil service of many more kinsmen— the Shih suddenly began to take on concubines and produce countless male heirs. Interestingly, those with the largest number of sons and grandsons also happen to be the most politically accomplished, thus confirming our assumption that family size relates closely to office-holding. Rapid growth of this sort appears quite prevalent among the socially mobile of the premodern period, when men reasoned that an abundance of sons served as insurance against political and biological extinction.[10] While this may have been true in the short run, it could be ruinous over the long haul. In a society where primogeniture was more the exception than the rule, sustained growth often led to impoverishment, as family property came to be divided among a progressively larger number of individuals.[11] Lacking concrete information on the distribution of wealth within the kin group, there is no way of knowing whether the Shih became impoverished for similar reasons; we do know that previously unbridled growth tapered off with the tenth generation. In the aftermath of prolonged official unemployment under the Yüan and increased migration to other areas, I suspect that the Shih community at Ming-chou shrank substantially in the fourteenth century, although, unfortunately, this cannot be documented.

Social Development. Ping-ti Ho has reviewed many of the social and economic developments of Ming and Ch'ing times that influenced bureaucratic fluidity.[12] Many of these changes actually have their roots in Sung China and had already begun to affect the composition and evolution of its political elite. For example, Ho notes that large-scale printing under the Ming contributed significantly to making education accessible to individuals outside the scholar-official elite.[13] Admittedly, the mass production of printed materials to which he refers did not exist during the Sung, yet great strides were nonetheless made in the art of printing and the volume of sales could be quite large. According to historian Jacques Gernet, printing methods were so advanced and the supply of material so plentiful that even commoners in the Sung could afford popular items.[14] Although the availability of printed matter to the population at large may be debated, there is no question that sizable book purchases were indeed within the means of certain individuals. Northern Sung literatus Sung Min-ch'iu (1019–79), for example, had a personal library of some 30,000 *chüan*; Ch'ao Kung-wu (n.d.), of the early Southern Sung, collected some 24,500 *chüan*; while Ch'en Chen-sun (n.d.), toward the end of the dynasty, boasted a library of over 51,000 *chüan*.[15] This suggests that a large body of material was available in print and, at least in certain circles, book collecting had become quite fashionable. The impact of such developments upon the diffusion of education in Sung China can well be imagined.

Ping-ti Ho also discusses the impact of publicly supported schools upon regional education and bureaucratic access. Basically, he concludes that their influence during Sung times must have been limited, chiefly due to government ineffectiveness at establishing an empirewide network and ensuring long-term funding.[16] This generalization is probably more true for the late than the early Sung and more applicable to China's interior than the wealthy Liang-che region. Moreover, it is important not to underestimate the role played by private academies in breaking down the barriers between urban and rural dwellers, the privileged and the unprivileged. Their proliferation during the thirteenth century provided an important alternative to publicly supported schools, while also helping to relieve those schools of overcrowding. At the same time, their frequent location in relatively isolated areas served to carry education far beyond the confines of the prefectural seat.[17] The experience of the Shih clearly demonstrates that the prefectural school, especially during the late Northern Sung, did have a profound impact upon educational access for those outside the bureaucratic elite.

While the social context from which the Shih emerged greatly affected its early rise within the civil service, there is little indication that personal wealth was crucial to kin group success. There is no known instance where a kinsman purchased an official degree or bribed an examiner —practices that, at any rate, were highly uncommon in Sung China. Neither did the Shih hold any financial advantages over other bureau-cratic aspirants in their community; in fact, they appear to have been among the poorest of Ming-chou's educated families. Shih Chien was, at best, a humble and landless clerk, while his son lived in rather straitened circumstances. Limited resources meant that early literary training had to be confined largely to the family; it only shifted to the local school after expansion during the Hui-tsung era made room for those less privileged. On the other hand, the Shih were not exactly penniless, as has been seen from reports that the widow Yeh became "well-to-do" in her late years. This modest income afforded them the luxury of whiling away uncounted hours in study, something poor peasants surely could not do. Neither can the Shih be considered completely handicapped in the competition for office. They possessed a tradition of education, albeit a rather weak one, that dated back to the widow Yeh. Perhaps less privileged than many around them, the Shih cannot be considered underprivileged relative to the population as a whole.

True affluence, however, did not come to the kin group until after its establishment within the bureaucratic elite; then its resources seem boundless. Chapters 3 and 4 contain discussions of the court's unusual generosity toward Shih Hao and Shih Mi-yüan, the bestowal upon them of innumerable gifts of property and wealth. Shih Sung-chih also appears to have accumulated conspicuous wealth while in office, shown by accusa-tions of students at the Imperial University that the empire's treasury was depleted while Shih Sung-chih's "purse fattens." If invested wisely, such wealth could have helped the Shih to reduce their dependence upon hand-outs from the court and to develop alternative sources of income in preparation for generations of official unemployment under the Yüan.

The concept of a kin group shielding itself from financial hardship by forming communally owned "charitable estates" was inspired by a promi-nent literatus of the eleventh century and gained currency during the Southern Sung.[18] The need to organize such estates, no doubt, stemmed from the realization by Sung officials that the capriciousness of the examination system and the practice of dividing land almost equally among male heirs both represented serious threats to the family's future security. Thus, land was set aside in the name of the kin group, rather than any one individual, and earnings from it were used to help train its youth for the examinations and to aid less fortunate kinsmen. The idea appealed to a growing body of scholar-officials, including those at Ming-chou. The Lou house, which had close ties to the Shih, had drawn upon the model of Fan Chung-yen to establish its own estate in the twelfth century.[19] The Shih, however, did not follow suit.[20] The ties binding them together were actually quite loose. There existed no cooperative or communal spirit. Wealth seemed to come easily and it was easily spent. By the fourteenth century, one of the most politically favored and well-endowed houses of the Sung era had fallen, quite irretrievably, upon hard times. If not all destitute, most kinsmen must have lived under highly straitened circumstances as they struggled, each in his own individual way, to find alternatives to bureaucratic service. Those few who retained an element of affluence exhibited little concern for less fortunate kinsmen; no one bothered, following the enslavement of Shih Mao-tsu, to attempt a ransom.

POLITICS AND ELITES

Man constantly searches for security and those in positions of power are always devising schemes to retain it, yet at few times in Chinese imperial history was this more difficult to do than its middle period. The decision by the Sung government to assume a highly active role in training men for its civil service represented a major break with the past. During the early imperial period, the great families were able to retain their dominance over Chinese society and government largely because they held a virtual monopoly on education. Schools were customarily private and often organized around the family, factors that inevitably restricted access to education and fostered a strong elitist spirit. Regardless of its own preferences, any government of that period seeking educated men to staff its bureaucracy had few alternatives to the great families. The Sung government, in contrast, by highly subsidizing private academies while simultaneously embarking upon a massive campaign to establish an empirewide network of publicly funded regional schools, effectively seized control of the one resource that had reduced all previous governments to dependency upon the old elite: education. With surprising speed, dependency was replaced by manipulation. Having fostered the development of prefectural schools and private academies, the Sung government then proceeded to strengthen its hand vis-à-vis the empire's politically influential by using these institutions to generate a larger and more diverse pool of potential recruits for the civil service. With an unprecedented number of educated men and a socially more heterogeneous group, scholar-official-dom was certain to be less cohesive and more loyal to its sponsor, the state. A larger pool of candidates for the civil service also enabled the court to be more selective in its recruitment efforts. On the positive side, this helped in professionalizing the bureaucracy. However, it could have negative consequences for potential recruits, who invested more time and effort to pass the competitive examinations and even with a degree could not be guaranteed an appointment.

Another factor that served to destabilize scholar-officialdom was political polarization at court. Beginning with the reign of Jen-tsung and continuing for the duration of the Northern Sung, differences among officials over political reform and court policy created intense factional strife. The ascendancy of one faction invariably occurred at the expense of its opposition and, as most factions tended to hold onto power for only a few years, this resulted in a high rate of bureaucratic turnover, especially at higher levels. During the Southern Sung, there emerged autocratic chief councillors, some of whom gave preference to close relatives or fellow provincials when selecting subordinates. Others proved thoroughly intolerant of critics. Individuals identified as a member of an opposing faction or those unpopular with the chief councillor were commonly demoted and sometimes subjected to confiscation of property and rescission of official privileges.

The Jurchen victory in the north and the relocation of the Sung capital at Lin-an represents yet another destabilizing factor. Officials of the Sung stranded in the north faced the difficult decision of whether to accommodate and serve the new rulers of the "central plains," to withdraw from politics altogether, and live as recluses in expression of their loyalty to the Sung, or to follow the court south of the Yangtze. Those who made the fateful decision permanently to abandon their ancestral homes in the north and flee south faced the awesome task of beginning anew as guests in an unfamiliar and sometimes hostile environment. That many such refugees came to the south in the company of few kinsmen and consequently were alone in confronting hardship did not make the adjustment any easier. Natives of the south were only slightly more secure. Those near the long Jurchen border constantly had to be on the alert against hostilities there, which tended to erupt on the average of once every thirty years and, once started, usually continued for some time; those beyond the enemy's striking range could nonetheless be affected by the economic repercussions of an invasion. Southerners as a whole were also negatively affected by the provincialization of the Southern Sung that is discussed in chapter 1, whereby the court came to draw heavily upon the Liang-che region in its selection of bureaucratic chiefs, neglecting in the process the remaining 90 percent of South China. For those from such neglected areas, this must have been a source of great professional and personal frustration.

Even more traumatic than the Jurchen sweep of North China was the total collapse of the Sung house in 1279. Inevitably, dynastic change has a profound effect upon the composition of national elites, as a new house in the process of consolidating power is prone to look suspiciously upon holdovers from the previous dynasty and prefer to trust more important posts to proven comrades.[21] Inauguration of the Yüan, however, was no ordinary dynastic change; it represented the first time in history that an alien house had unified all China and completely obliterated Han rule. The reaction of native scholar-officials was also out of the ordinary; they withdrew from government service on a massive scale. Such withdrawal apparently became almost fashionable and community pressure to conform must have been considerable. Some idea of the magnitude of this movement can be seen from the experience of the Shih. Whereas roughly 240 kinsmen are documented as having held official rank under the Southern Sung, only 10 did so during Yüan times—and they received only minor assignments. Meanwhile, the loss of political status entailed forfeiture of privileges such as tax and corvée exemption, not to mention the loss of bureaucratic income and community influence. Even the wealthiest of kin groups with impressive holdings in land and large capital reserves could hardly afford a century of official unemployment and, at the same time, hope to retain any semblance of regional influence.

In a study of T'ung-ch'eng county, Anhwei during the Ming and Ch'ing dynasties, Hilary Beattie has found that the locally prominent of this period resembled, in many respects, the great families of the early imperial period. They had a strong sense of self-identity, to the extent that a certain exclusiveness set in; they tended to organize as structured extended families and to form a highly complex, delicately contrived, and often politically motivated network of marriage alliances.[22] Also like the great families of the past, the subsequent elite was similarly able to persist for centuries without being significantly affected by the transition from Ming to Ch'ing; this stemmed chiefly from its strong foundation in landholding. Recent research by Robert Hartwell and Robert Hymes dealing with "local" or "gentry" elites during Sung times, paints a similar picture: the locally prominent formed a tightly knit, self-perpetuating group and, in the absence of substantial wealth and an elaborate network of social ties, the prospects for penetration of the bureaucracy by outsiders were exceedingly dismal.[23] Clearly, the Shih experience suggests the exact opposite. The Shih began with no base in landholding and a short and disesteemed history in their community; with office they obtained wealth and prominence but no strong sense of group consciousness, they formed no communal estate and more often fought than cooperated with one another. Beattie acknowledges a distinction between social and political elites—in her words, the "landed" as opposed to the "gentry" elite—and chooses the former as her focus. Such a distinction is implied in the Hymes study as well. It has long been recognized, however, that considerable overlap actually existed between the two. Landowners in China were never apolitical, just as political leaders were never entirely divorced from landowning. Moreover, those successful in the national political arena rarely severed ties with their native homes. Through political deals and marriage arrangements, they purposefully maintained a local presence. Shih Mi-yüan, for example, kept a large estate in Ming-chou, although he appears rarely to have occupied the place after becoming chief councillor; he is also known to have been surrounded at court by Ming-chou provincials, although the length and breadth of his political experience surely provided a much wider range of contacts. Continued close ties with home came only through effort and the Shih obviously considered the effort important. Thus, in premodern China (pre-Ch'ing society in particular) it is extremely difficult to speak of a social or regional elite as being separate and distinct from a political or national one.

The discrepancies between this book and other studies are not easily explained and any attempt at a thorough assessment would certainly require another volume. Several crucial points nonetheless should be raised here in the hope that they will be taken up by future scholars. First is the distinctive character of government and society in Sung times. In the early imperial period, education, regional finance, and social order were generally administered at the local level; authorities in the capital, while concerned about regional governance, lacked both the human and fiscal resources to become directly involved in everyday management. Only with the Sung did central government influence systematically extend beyond the prefectures to include subprefectures. Agents commissioned by the capital, beyond simply collecting taxes and keeping the peace, also organized a wide range of social relief programs, coordinated public works projects, supervised an expanding public school network, and even assisted in erecting temples to honor local notables. The Sung bureaucracy became massive over the course of time and this, in turn, gave the government an unusually pervasive presence, one that rested far less upon the influence of regional powers. This was not necessarily true for subsequent periods. Continued population growth, government revenues that did not keep pace with that growth, and the increasingly complex needs of local governance inevitably entailed more regional autonomy and greater dependence upon community leaders. Such dependency could only enhance the status of the locally prominent, effectively serving to entrench this group in a fashion far less commonplace in Sung times. A growing population, diminished central government supervision of local administration, and heightened regional influence also meant that the opportunities for bureaucratic advancement in Ming-Ch'ing times were, in all likelihood, significantly less than during the Sung.

Second, while the size of scholar-officialdom and the civil service grew enormously over the course of the Sung dynasty, the entire system retained a personal element, one making the emperor and his court appear less distant and removed. The Sung government was omnipresent in a manner once quite inconceivable. Efficient at bringing the wealth of the empire under its own control, the government also had final say in the allocation of that wealth. To meritorious subjects it could be overwhelmingly generous. Shih Hao, for example, regularly received from the emperor birthday gifts of gold, precious gems, and expensive teas; the throne often entertained him at state banquets and, at death, ordered a special tomb inscription to be drafted in his honor. Others were treated with imperial gifts ranging from large estates to pieces of calligraphy and rare books. The frequency of such practices suggests considerable intimacy in the ties between Sung emperors and their executives in the civil service, an intimacy shrewdly conceived to unite in spirit the emperor and his chief ministers. Officials serving away from the capital were not underrated either. Reflecting court confidence in their abilities, individual initiative was encouraged and they were afforded a good measure of discretionary authority.

Court-appointed officials were serving even at the subprefectural level, various social relief programs were administered directly by the central government through its appointed officials, state-supported and -supervised prefectural schools were training a growing number of local youth, local exemplars of morality were being singled out and given special honors by the court—the state had come to play a prominent role in the everyday life of its subjects. Beginning perhaps with the Mongol Yüan and continuing for the duration of the imperial period, increased regional autonomy must surely have made imperial leadership appear more impersonal, perhaps even irrelevant, to the larger population. Indeed, the unusual loyalty of officials to the Sung and the refusal of so many to serve the Yüan may, in part, be explained with reference to the highly personal character of government during this period. Certainly, withdrawal from the bureaucracy in the transition from Ming to Ch'ing, where again a native Chinese dynasty is replaced by an alien one, compares neither in scope nor duration to the earlier exodus.

A third distinctive characteristic of Sung China's political climate is the prevalent sense, among accomplished officials, of security—in good measure a false sense of security. The throne's great bounty toward meritorious officials—its generous gifts of homes, gardens, salary supplements, and wealth—fostered a sense of security that effectively discouraged the saving of existing wealth for an uncertain future. This was especially true for the highly successful, those with access to seemingly limitless wealth who spent it freely. In the case of the Shih, it was unnecessary to purchase mansions, as the government provided them free of charge; few seemed to concern themselves with the prospect that such homes might be among the first confiscated under a new regime. Indeed, for men living in the third century of Sung rule—when the dynasty, although plagued with a growing alien menace, still remained surprisingly immune to other symptoms of dynastic atrophy, namely large-scale peasant uprisings—a change in the mandate must have been unthinkable. Neither did Shih kinsmen invest substantially in private estates or communal property, for they had access to fiefs of maintenance and gifts of precious gems and metals; few apparently realized that these too could readily fall to new political leaders and local bullies or be thoughtlessly squandered by lackluster, unmotivated descendants. The estate-building activities of Fan Chung-yen, I would argue, was more the exception than the rule in Sung times. Meanwhile, the economic security accompanying great wealth also had an emotional side effect; with daily survival no longer a major concern, individual families could afford to indulge intragroup rivalries and personality conflicts. Perhaps less financial security in the sixth and seventh generations would have compelled the Shih to act more cooperatively, regardless of political and personal differences. Apart from petty rivalries, limitless wealth also enabled the Shih community to grow at an astonishing rate, with little apparent concern for the long-term impact upon the financial well-being of later generations.

Between generations four and nine, the kin group grew from 5 males to 13 to 47 to 86 to 149 to 259 (see table 2). The implications of this I have addressed elsewhere.[24] I will only say here that continued growth did not result in proportionate increases in degreeholders. On the contrary, the Shih were most successful at winning degrees in the sixth generation, when still not entrenched in the bureaucracy. The next generation, with nearly twice as many males, realized only a modest increase in degreeholders and this tapered off quickly. Thus, beyond a certain point, namely generation VII, kinship growth became a greater liability than asset, as alternatives to civil service careers needed to be found.

Thus, from beginning to end, it was largely developments in the capital or developments related to political success that brought both prosperity and doom to the Shih. With society so much more complex in later imperial times and the structure of government so different, the impact of court politics and policies upon the fortunes of the locally influential must have been significantly diminished. Consequently, the stability that Beattie finds in the Ming-Ch'ing era can hardly be generalized for the period preceding it. We must treat the Sung-Yüan epoch entirely on its own.

The Hymes study, which does focus on the Sung, nonetheless suggests an elite cohesiveness, a strategy for social climbing and retrenchment, that is indubitably alien to the Ming-chou Shih. Assertions that only reasonably large and well-organized kin groups would bother with civil service examinations, that success at the examinations was virtually impossible for those outside a small coterie of locally prominent kin groups, that political success merely *confirmed* social status (it did not itself *create* status), and that regional prominence, once attained, could easily be maintained over long periods of time[25]—these certainly are difficult to defend in light of the Shih experience. There exists at this point, simply too little empirical data to speak definitively about the broad issues raised by Hymes. What can be said, however, is that one kin group in Sung times *did* manage to reach the heights of bureaucratic success without the support of a well-organized kinship structure and without a long history of regional prominence; its regional status was clearly a reflection of attainments in the civil service and family privilege proved impossible to protect over an extended period. The Shih had no perceptible strategy for political success, they simply exploited the opportunities around them. Hymes's argument suggests that success breeds success, that the odds are against the upstart. This seems reasonable enough: we in America need hardly look to China to appreciate the persistency of privilege. I would only add that the upstart can often have the motivation that the privileged lack and, in Sung times, talent and motivation carried some families a long way indeed.

The Shih experience also presents problems in terms of Hartwell's assertion that the "professional elite" of Northern Sung times, with a focus on national politics, gives way, starting with the twelfth century, to a "multitude of local gentry lineages" with a distinct regional orientation.[26] The Shih clearly do not belong to Hartwell's "professional elite." They did not identify with old aristocratic traditions through the use of choronyms and they did not abandon residences at Ming-chou in favor of the capital; yet their total immersion in the civil service sets them apart from "local gentry lineages," which are portrayed as professionally diverse and inclined to engage in "non-governmental occupations—estate management, teaching, commerce, etc."[27] If the Shih must be classified, the term "professional" would probably be appropriate, but Hartwell's ideal is ill-suited to the Shih reality.

Also conflicting with the Shih experience is Hartwell's assertion: "Indeed in *every* instance of upward mobility supported by literary evidence, passage of the tests *followed* intermarriage with one of the already established elite gentry lineages."[28] There is no indication that early degree-holders of the Shih group, seeking nomination to take local civil service examinations, found it necessary first to form marriage alliances with elite families. The wife of Shih Ts'ai, née Sun, and that of Shih Hao, née P'ei, clearly did not come from the leading houses in the area, although we know little else about them.[29] Had the widow Yeh come from a comfortable home, she would probably have returned there following her husband's death, rather than attempt supporting a family on her own. The Shih represented too small a kin group in the early to mid-twelfth century to command the elaborate network of contacts that Hartwell and Hymes consider indispensable to examination success. I am in complete agreement with Hartwell about the trend toward regionalization in Southern Sung politics and the extent to which this development must have alienated many, forcing them to pursue other career options, but I do not believe this necessarily entailed a major or permanent shift away from politics and toward local teaching and commerce. The Shih, for example, found outlets in regional office-holding or military service. Withdrawal from government, for the Shih, occurred only with the advent of the Yüan dynasty.

As acknowledged earlier, the case of the Shih is anything but representative. The sudden rise of Shih Ts'ai from social and political obscurity to second spot in the bureaucracy, the special favor of Shih Hao at the court of Hsiao-tsung, the unprecedented tenure of Chief councillor Shih Mi-yüan, the fame and infamy of Shih Sung-chih, the saga of Shih Mao-tsu—they all serve to illustrate that the Shih experience, from start to finish, was largely an aberration. At the same time, it also demonstrates that Sung China's bureaucratic elite was anything but hereditary in character. Literary attainments and political acumen could land their masters at the top of the bureaucracy, while pressures from the forces of opinion—including the opinions of mere students—could destroy even the awesomely powerful. The shifting fortunes of the Shih house may not be typical of most families, but they reflect much of the society that nurtured that house.

Appendixes

190

1. *Chin-shih* Totals for Selected Prefectures in Liang-che Circuit

Year	Empirewide totals[a]	Ming-chou[b]	Ch'ang-chou[c]	Lin-an[d]	Soo-chow[e]	Shao-hsing[f]	Hu-chou[g]	Chia-hsing[h]
before 1056		34	97	46	77	52	41	11
1057		2	12	7	2	8	3	2
1059		3	5	3	7	2	1	0
1061		3	8	2	3	6	2	1
1063		4	8	4	4	4	1	2
1065		2	11	2	2	2	3	3
1067		0	14	2	4	3	1	0
1070		3	33	4	7	3	12	4
1073		2	38	2	8	11	16	3
1076		4	15	3	5	4	10	0
1079		2	22	5	4	1	12	5
1082		6	14	4	4	8	11	0
1085		1	12	8	6	5	13	3
1088		5	9	7	7	3	12	4
1091		3	14	4	8	6	3	3
1094		2	13	5	6	2	4	2
1097		4	20	3	4	4	12	1
1100	558	6	20	2	7	5	12	1
1103	538	2	20	2	8	9	9	2
1106	671	7	18	7	6	5	14	5
1109	685	4	32	6	8	10	11	11
1112	713	5	25	5	8	5	12	1
1115	670	1	16	7	12	10	18	5
1118	783	11	19	7	10	7	16	5
1121	630	5	13	5	5	9	9	3
1124	805	3	23	8	12	3	11	2
1128	451	2	14	4	12	6	15	4
1132	259	6	16	5	4	7	9	1
1135	220	7	8	7	4	10	4	8
1138	395	5	10	2	6	2	12	3
1142	254	6	17	2	8	9	13	4
1145	300	8	16	5	11	9	12	8
1148	330	2	16	5	7	9	11	6
1151	404	6	13	5	6	3	12	6
1154	356	0	21	8	11	10	13	8
1157	426	3	8	10	5	4	5	10
1160	412	13	22	12	5	5	10	15

Appendix 1. (continued)

Year	Empirewide totals[a]	Ming-chou[b]	Ch'ang-chou[c]	Lin-an[d]	Soo-chow[e]	Shao-hsing[f]	Hu-chou[g]	Chia-hsing[h]
1163	538	11	28	19	15	12	20	9
1166	493	4	20	26	8	11	13	12
1169	392	8	13	14	12	5	9	9
1172	389	8	13	10	11	10	12	8
1175	426	4	11	8	13	10	6	8
1178	417	5	7	14	5	7	15	5
1181	379	3	8	10	5	9	8	7
1184	394	5	11	11	8	12	14	6
1187	435	13	18	7	15	7	17	9
1190	537	12	11	10	20	6	15	14
1193	396	17	12	10	3	6	17	2
1196	499	23	14	13	10	15	16	8
1199	412	15	11	9	11	9	6	5
1202	497	6	11	12	15	6	5	3
1205	433	9	7	12	9	9	1	4
1208	426	13	15	11	11	5	1	10
1211	465	12	11	9	10	9	3	3
1214	504	23	5	9	7	9	2	4
1217	523	30	9	7	9	14	3	7
1220	475	18	8	11	13	11	0	9
1223	549	17	21	22	12	11	4	6
1226	989	45	24	15	12	1	6	29
1229	557	31	18	7	7	8	6	8
1232	493	48	7	14	4	25	3	11
1235	454	28	9	9	6	5	5	4
1238	422	38	10	8	10	15	2	8
1241	367	32	5	8	6	5	3	4
1244	424	16	10	4	6	10	2	2
1247	527	35	7	8	3	5	3	4
1250	513	25	3	4	8	10	0	9
1253	—	32	5	7	3	16	4	11
1256	601	30	9	6	5	10	1	7
1259	442	28	6	8	3	11	1	5
1262	637	12	6	13	5	13	3	4
1265	—	16	10	47	13	15	9	18
1268	664	3	12	16	6	8	3	4
1271	502	4	2	—	2	5	1	1
1274	—	4	2	—	6	5	1	5

Appendix 1. (continued)

Year	Empirewide totals[a]	Ming-chou[b]	Ch'ang-chou[c]	Lin-an[d]	Soo-chow[e]	Shao-hsing[f]	Hu-chou[g]	Chia-hsing[h]
Totals for the Northern Sung	124	531	160	234	187	269	79
Totals for the Southern Sung	741	570	493	406	434	356	359
Grand Totals	865	1101	653	640	621	625	434

a Empirewide *chin-shih* totals are available in an assortment of primary sources. That containing the most complete listing for the Southern Sung (the focus of this research) is the official Sung History, *Sung shih*. With this information scattered throughout its "Basic Annals" under entries for each examination year, it is a bit cumbersome to use. WHTK (*ch.* 32) and SHY (HC, 2) also contain *chin-shih* data, but their information for the Southern Sung does not appear to be either as complete or accurate as that in the official history. Consequently, *chin-shih* totals here are based upon SS.

Unfortunately, SS contains no accurate *chin-shih* data for the pre-1100 period, as these generally included *ming-ching* and *chu-k'o* totals. Moreover, the Sung government had no fixed examination date prior to 1057; instead, it arbitrarily ordered examinations in response to the demand created by bureaucratic vacancies. Beginning in 1057, this practice gave way to regular examinations every two years which, after 1067, was changed to once every three years. Due to the irregularity of examinations before 1057, this table contains only summarized totals for the earlier period.

b *Chin-shih* data for Ming-chou derives from the Yüan dynasty YYSMC (*ch.* 6). There exist some minor discrepancies between the totals in this gazetteer and those quoted in the Ming dynasty *(Chia-ching) Ning-po fu chih (ch.* 3), but they do not significantly affect the conclusions here. In fact, few gazetteers are in complete agreement with one another about these figures. *Chin-shih* lists for the Sung contained in gazetteers for the Ming and Ch'ing dynasties commonly include at least one or two dozen more names than Sung and Yüan works. This may very well be because earlier chroniclers had carelessly overlooked some individuals, omissions that were corrected by subsequent writers. On the other hand, this may also be related to regional expansion or migration, whereby the *chin-shih* of a once independent subprefecture or a migrant family came to be retroactively included among those of the old prefecture. As a rule, I have used the earliest available gazetteers containing complete *chin-shih* lists for the Sung. By virtue of their proximity in time to the period under study, they should be somewhat more reliable.

It should be noted that, in addition to the regular examination group, *chin-shih* figures here also include graduates from the Imperial University who secured their degrees through promotion. They do not include those who were conferred degrees either through decree examinations or a special act of imperial favor.

c In the absence of an earlier gazetteer with complete *chin-shih* data for the entire Sung period, figures here have been taken from *(Ch'ung-hsiu) Ch'ang-chou fu chih* (1618), *ch.* 17.

d   Data for Lin-an are from *(Hsien-ch'un) Lin-an chih* (1268), *ch.* 61. Unfortunately, it contains no information for the last decade of Sung rule, data that are also lacking in later gazetteers. Thus, *chin-shih* totals for Lin-an are slightly underrepresented here.

e   *Su-chou fu chih* (1368–98), *ch.* 13, is the source of *chin-shih* data for Soochow.

f   Data for Shao-hsing may be found in *Shao-hsing fu chih* (1573–1619), *ch.* 34.

g   Lacking an earlier gazetteer with a complete list of *chin-shih* from Hu-chou for the Southern Sung, the source used here is *Hu-chou fu chih* (1874), *ch.* 10.

h   Information on *chin-shih* from Chia-hsing may be found in *(Chih-yüan) Chia-ho chih* (1288), *ch.* 15.

2. Geographic Origins of Southern Sung Chief Councillors

Ch'eng-tu	Chang Chün (1097–1164), Han-chou, 2d/1135–9th/1137
E. Chiang-nan	Ch'in Kuei (1090–1155), Chiang-ning, 8th/1131–8th/1132, 3d/1138–10th/1155
	Wang Po-yen (1069–1141), Hui-chou, 12th/1128–2d/1129
Ching-chi	Wan-ssu Hsieh (1083–1157), K'ai-feng, 5th/1156–12th/1156
N. Ching-hsi	Chu Sheng-fei (1082–1144), Ts'ai-chou, 3d/1129–4th/1129, 9th/1132–4th/1133, 7th/1133–9th/1134
S. Ching-hsi	Fan Tsung-yin (1098–1136), Hsiang-yang, 5th/1130–7th/1131
E. Ching-tung	Lü Yi-hao (1071–1139), Chi-nan, 4th/1129–4th/1130, 9th/1131–9th/1133
Fukien	Ch'en K'ang-po (1097–1165), Ch'üan-chou, 9th/1159–6th/1162
	Chu Cho (1086–1163), Fu-chou, 3d/1161–6th/1162
	Huang Ch'ien-shan (d. 1129), Shao-wu, 8th/1127–2d/1129
	Li Kang (1083–1140), Shao-wu, 5th/1127–8th/1127
W. Hopei	Tu Ch'ung (n.d.), Hsiang-chou, intercalary (int.) 8th/1129–2d/1130
Liang-che	Shen Kai (n.d.), Hu-chou, 5th/1156–6th/1159
	T'ang Ssu-t'ui (d. 1164), Ch'u-chou, 6th/1157–12th/1160
Yung-hsing	Chao Ting (1085–1147), Chieh-chou, 9th/1134–12th/1136, 9th/1137–10th/1138

Ch'eng-tu:	Chang Chün (1097–1164), Han-chou, 12th/1163–4th/1164
S. Chiang-hsi	Chou Pi-ta (1126–1204), Chi-chou, 2d/1187–5th/1189
E. Chiang-nan	Hung Kua (1117–84), Jao-chou, 12th/1165–3d/1166
Fukien	Ch'en Chün-ch'ing (1113–86), Hsing-hua, 10th/1168–5th/1170
	Ch'en K'ang-po, Ch'üan-chou, 6th/1162–12th/1163, 11th/1164–2d/1165
	Liang K'o-chia (1128–87), Ch'üan-chou, 2d/1172–10th/1173, 9th/1182–11th/1186
	Tseng-Huai (1106–74), Chin-chiang, 10th/1173–6th/1174, 7th/1174–11th/1174
	Yeh Yung (1100–1167), Hsing-hua, 11th/1174–9th/1175
Liang-che	Chiang Ti (n.d.), Ch'ang-chou, 2d/1168–7th/1168
	Shih Hao (1106–94), Ming-chou, 1st/1163–5th/1163, 3d/1178–11th/1178
	T'ang Ssu-t'ui (n.d.), Ch'u-chou, 7th/1173–11th/1174
	Wang Huai (1126–89), Wu-chou, 8th/1181–5th/1188
	Wei Ch'i (d. 1184), Ming-chou, 12th/1166–11th/1167

Note: To avoid confusion and to enable consistency, this list contains only the names of prefectures (and not subprefectures) identified by *Sung shih* as the place of registry for individual councillors.

T'ung-ch'uan
Yeh Heng (1122–83), Wu-chou, 11th/1174–9th/1175
Chao Hsiung (1129–93), Tzu-chou, 11th/1178–8th/1181
Yü Yün-wen (1110–74), Tzu-chou, 8th/1169–9th/1172

KUANG-TSUNG ERA

Fukien   Liu Cheng (1129–1206), Ch'üan-chou, 1st/1189–8th/1194
Liang-che   Ko Pi (n.d.), Hu-chou, 3d/1193–1st/1194

NING-TSUNG ERA

S. Chiang-hsi   Ching T'ang (1138–1200), Lung-hsing, 1st/1196–8th/1200
E. Chiang-nan   Chao Ju-yü (1140–96), Jao-chou, 8th/1194–2d/1195
Fukien   Ch'en Tzu-ch'iang (n.d.), Fu-chou, 5th/1203–11th/1207
W. Hopei   Han T'o-chou (1152–1207), Hsiang-chou, 7th/1205–11th/1207
Liang-che   Ch'ien Hsiang-tsu (n.d.), Lin-an, 12th/1207–12th/1208
Hsieh Shen-fu (n.d.), T'ai-chou, int. 2d/1200–1st/1203
Shih Mi-yüan (1164–1233), Ming-chou, 10th/1208–11th/1208, 5th/1209–8th/1224
Yü Tuan-li (1135–1201), Ch'ü-chou, 4th/1195–4th/1196

LI-TSUNG ERA

Ch'eng-tu   Hsieh Fang-shu (d. 1272), Wei-chou, 11th/1251–8th/1255
E. Chiang-nan   Ch'eng Yüan-feng (1200–1269), Hui-chou, 7th/1256–4th/1258
Wu Ch'ien (1196–1262), Chiang-ning, 11th/1251–11th/1252
S. Ching-hu   Chao K'uei (1186–1266), Heng-shan, int. 2d/1249–3d/1250
W. Huai-nan   Tung Huai (n.d.), Hao-chou, 8th/1255–7th/1256
E. Kuang-nan   Ts'ui Yü-chih (1158–1239), Kuang-chou, 9th/1236–6th/1239
Liang-che   Cheng Ch'ing-chih (1176–1251), Ming-chou, 10th/1233–9th/1236, 4th/1247–11th/1251
Chia Ssu-tao (1213–75), T'ai-chou, 10th/1259–10th/1264
Ch'iao Hsing-chien (1156–1241), Wu-chou, 6th/1235–9th/1236, 11th/1236–2d/1241
Fan Chung (d. 1249), Wu-chou, 12th/1244–2d/1246
Li Tsung-mien (d. 1239), Lin-an, 1st/1239–int. 12th/1240
Shih Mi-yüan, Ming-chou, 8th/1224–10th/1233
Shih Sung-chih (1189–1256), Ming-chou, 1st/1239–12th/1244
Ting Ta-ch'üan (d. 1263), Chen-chiang, 4th/1258–10th/1259
Tu Fan (1182–1245), T'ai-chou, 12th/1244–4th/1245
T'ung-ch'uan   Yu Ssu (n.d.), Tzu-chou, 12th/1245–4th/1247

TU-TSUNG ERA

E. Chiang-nan   Ch'eng Yüan-feng (n.d.), Hui-chou, 3d/1267

Chiang Wan-li (1198–1274), Nan-k'ang, 3d/1269–1st/1270
Ma T'ing-luan (1222–89), Jao-chou, 3d/1269–11th/1272

Liang-che   Chia Ssu-tao (n.d.), T'ai-chou, 10th/1264–7th/1274
Yeh Meng-ting (n.d.), T'ai-chou, 8th/1267–1st/1269

3. Genealogy of the Shih

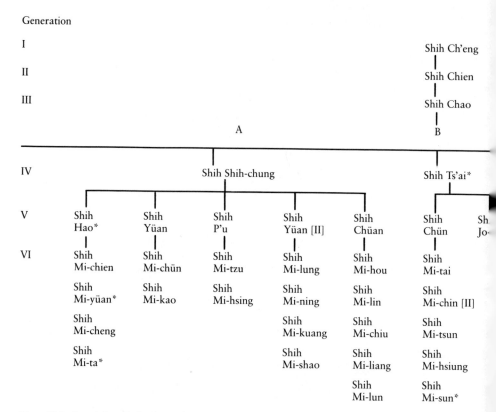

Generation

I

II

III

A

B

IV

V

VI

Note: This chart is based chiefly on the HSSSTP, with some modifications.
*Chin-shih recipients

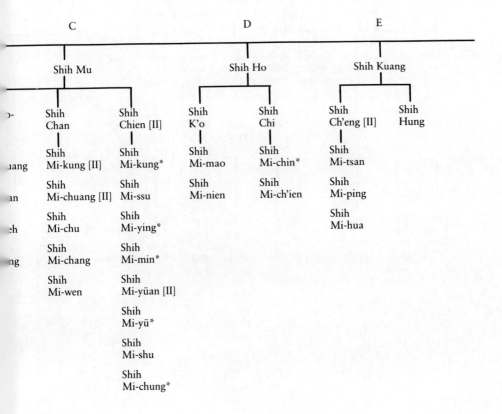

C   D   E

Shih Mu   Shih Ho   Shih Kuang

)-   Shih Chan   Shih Chien [II]   Shih K'o   Shih Chi   Shih Ch'eng [II]   Shih Hung

ıang   Shih Mi-kung [II]   Shih Mi-kung*   Shih Mi-mao   Shih Mi-chin*   Shih Mi-tsan

an   Shih Mi-chuang [II]   Shih Mi-ssu   Shih Mi-nien   Shih Mi-ch'ien   Shih Mi-ping

:h   Shih Mi-chu   Shih Mi-ying*   Shih Mi-hua

ng   Shih Mi-chang   Shih Mi-min*

Shih Mi-wen   Shih Mi-yüan [II]

Shih Mi-yü*

Shih Mi-shu

Shih Mi-chung*

Genealogy of the Shih (continued)

Branch A

Generation

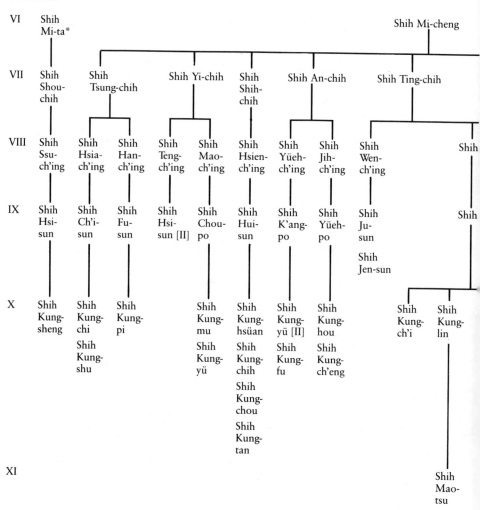

VI	Shih Mi-ta*								Shih Mi-cheng	
VII	Shih Shou-chih	Shih Tsung-chih		Shih Yi-chih		Shih Shih-chih	Shih An-chih		Shih Ting-chih	
VIII	Shih Ssu-ch'ing	Shih Hsia-ch'ing	Shih Han-ch'ing	Shih Teng-ch'ing	Shih Mao-ch'ing	Shih Hsien-ch'ing	Shih Yüeh-ch'ing	Shih Jih-ch'ing	Shih Wen-ch'ing	Shih
IX	Shih Hsi-sun	Shih Ch'i-sun	Shih Fu-sun	Shih Hsi-sun [II]	Shih Chou-po	Shih Hui-sun	Shih K'ang-po	Shih Yüeh-po	Shih Ju-sun Shih Jen-sun	Shih
X	Shih Kung-sheng	Shih Kung-chi Shih Kung-shu	Shih Kung-pi		Shih Kung-mu Shih Kung-yü	Shih Kung-hsüan Shih Kung-chih Shih Kung-chou Shih Kung-tan	Shih Kung-yü [II] Shih Kung-fu	Shih Kung-hou Shih Kung-ch'eng	Shih Kung-ch'i	Shih Kung-lin
XI										Shih Mao-tsu

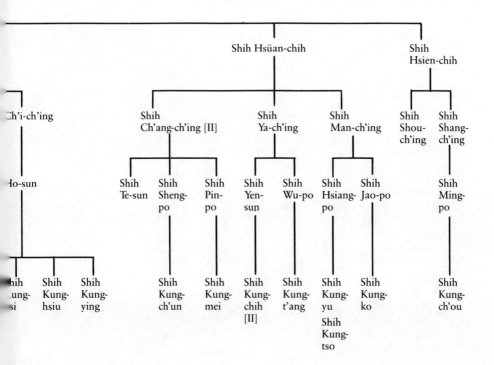

Genealogy of the Shih (continued)

Generation

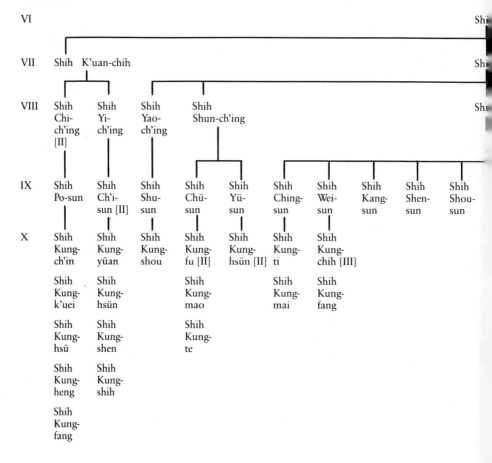

VI   Shi

VII   Shih K'uan-chih   Shi

VIII   Shih   Shih   Shih   Shih   Shi
         Chi-   Yi-   Yao-   Shun-ch'ing
         ch'ing   ch'ing   ch'ing
         [II]

IX   Shih   Shih   Shih   Shih   Shih   Shih   Shih   Shih   Shih   Shih
         Po-sun   Ch'i-   Shu-   Chü-   Yü-   Ching-   Wei-   Kang-   Shen-   Shou-
                         sun [II]   sun   sun   sun   sun   sun   sun   sun   sun

X   Shih   Shih   Shih   Shih   Shih   Shih   Shih
         Kung-   Kung-   Kung-   Kung-   Kung-   Kung-   Kung-
         ch'in   yüan   shou   fu [II]   hsün [II]   ti   chih [III]

         Shih   Shih   Shih   Shih   Shih
         Kung-   Kung-   Kung-   Kung-   Kung-
         k'uei   hsün   mao   mai   fang

         Shih   Shih   Shih
         Kung-   Kung-   Kung-
         hsü   shen   te

         Shih   Shih
         Kung-   Kung-
         heng   shih

         Shih
         Kung-
         fang

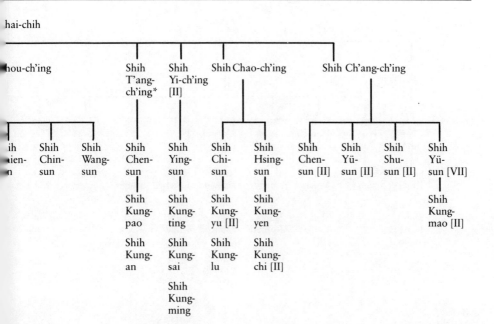

li-yüan

hai-chih

hou-ch'ing   Shih T'ang-ch'ing*   Shih Yi-ch'ing [II]   Shih Chao-ch'ing   Shih Ch'ang-ch'ing

ih ien- n   Shih Chin-sun   Shih Wang-sun   Shih Chen-sun   Shih Ying-sun   Shih Chi-sun   Shih Hsing-sun   Shih Chen-sun [II]   Shih Yü-sun [II]   Shih Shu-sun [II]   Shih Yü-sun [VII]

Shih Kung-pao   Shih Kung-ting   Shih Kung-yu [II]   Shih Kung-yen   Shih Kung-mao [II]

Shih Kung-an   Shih Kung-sai   Shih Kung-lu   Shih Kung-chi [II]

Shih Kung-ming

Genealogy of the Shih (continued)

Generation

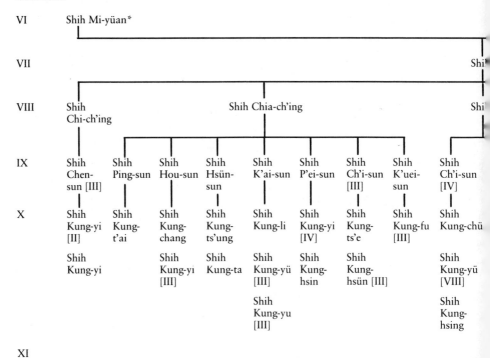

VI   Shih Mi-yüan*

VII   Shi*

VIII   Shih   Shih Chia-ch'ing   Shi
         Chi-ch'ing

IX   Shih   Shih   Shih   Shih   Shih   Shih   Shih   Shih   Shih
         Chen-   Ping-sun Hou-sun   Hsün-   K'ai-sun P'ei-sun Ch'i-sun K'uei-   Ch'i-sun
         sun [III]   sun   [III]   sun   [IV]

X   Shih   Shih   Shih   Shih   Shih   Shih   Shih   Shih   Shih
         Kung-yi   Kung-   Kung-   Kung-   Kung-li   Kung-yi   Kung-   Kung-fu   Kung-chü
         [II]   t'ai   chang   ts'ung   [IV]   ts'e   [III]

         Shih   Shih   Shih   Shih   Shih   Shih   Shih
         Kung-yi   Kung-yı   Kung-ta   Kung-yü   Kung-   Kung-   Kung-yü
                             [III]   [III]   hsin   hsün [III]   [VIII]

                                       Shih   Shih
                                       Kung-yu   Kung-
                                       [III]   hsing

XI

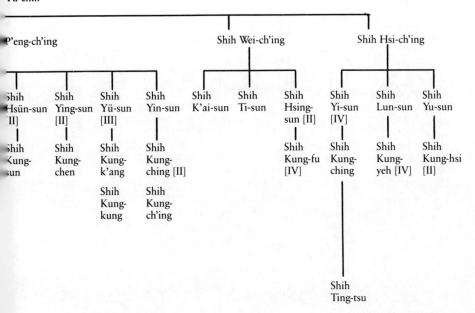

Yü-chih

P'eng-ch'ing   Shih Wei-ch'ing   Shih Hsi-ch'ing

Shih   Shih   Shih   Shih   Shih   Shih   Shih   Shih   Shih   Shih
Hsün-sun   Ying-sun   Yü-sun   Yin-sun   K'ai-sun   Ti-sun   Hsing-   Yi-sun   Lun-sun   Yu-sun
II]   [II]   [III]   sun [II]   [IV]

Shih   Shih   Shih   Shih   Shih   Shih   Shih   Shih
Kung-   Kung-   Kung-   Kung-   Kung-fu   Kung-   Kung-   Kung-hsi
sun   chen   k'ang   ching [II]   [IV]   ching   yeh [IV]   [II]

                            Shih   Shih
                            Kung-   Kung-
                            kung   ch'ing

                                                                                                 Shih
                                                                                                 Ting-tsu

Genealogy of the Shih (continued)

Generation

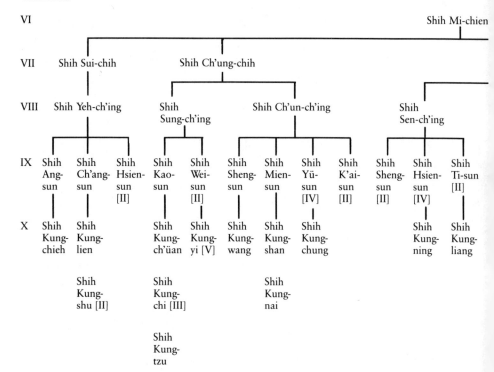

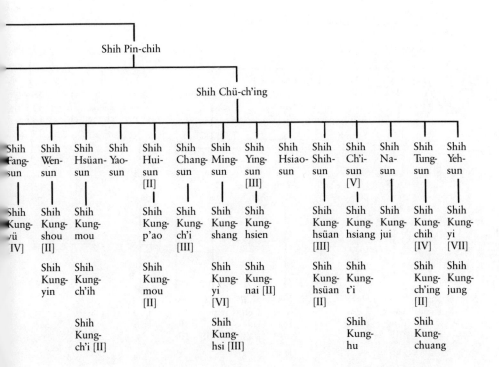

Genealogy of the Shih (continued)

Generation

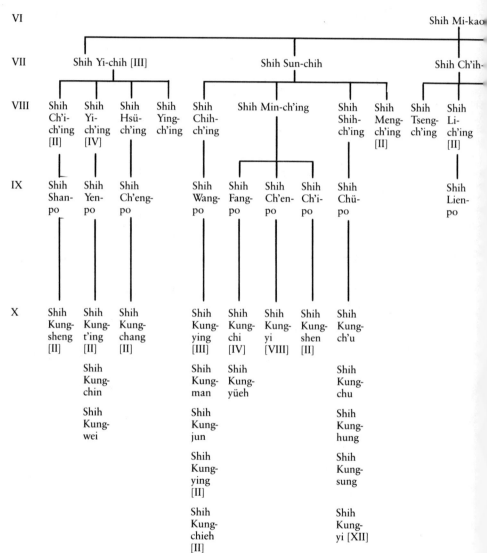

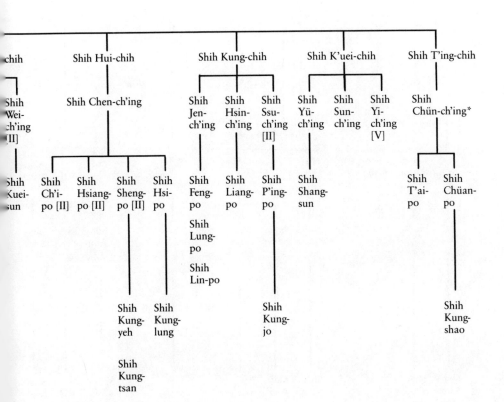

...chih
Shih Hui-chih
Shih Kung-chih
Shih K'uei-chih
Shih T'ing-chih

Shih
Wei-
ch'ing
[II]

Shih Chen-ch'ing

Shih
Jen-
ch'ing

Shih
Hsin-
ch'ing

Shih
Ssu-
ch'ing
[II]

Shih
Yü-
ch'ing

Shih
Sun-
ch'ing

Shih
Yi-
ch'ing
[V]

Shih
Chün-ch'ing*

Shih
K'uei-
sun

Shih
Ch'i-
po [II]

Shih
Hsiang-
po [II]

Shih
Sheng-
po [II]

Shih
Hsi-
po

Shih
Feng-
po

Shih
Liang-
po

Shih
P'ing-
po

Shih
Shang-
sun

Shih
T'ai-
po

Shih
Chüan-
po

Shih
Lung-
po

Shih
Lin-po

Shih
Kung-
yeh

Shih
Kung-
lung

Shih
Kung-
jo

Shih
Kung-
shao

Shih
Kung-
tsan

Genealogy of the Shih (continued)

Generation

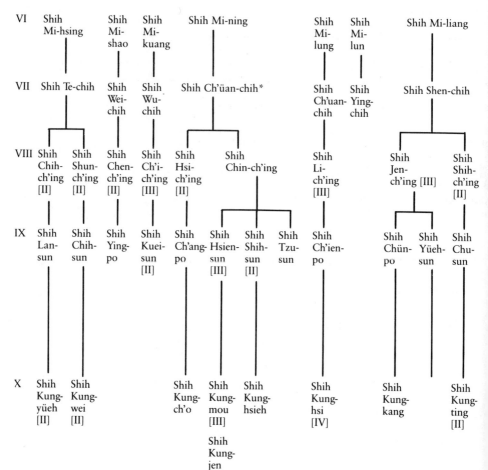

VI   Shih Mi-hsing   Shih Mi-shao   Shih Mi-kuang   Shih Mi-ning   Shih Mi-lung   Shih Mi-lun   Shih Mi-liang

VII   Shih Te-chih   Shih Wei-chih   Shih Wu-chih   Shih Ch'üan-chih*   Shih Ch'uan-chih   Shih Ying-chih   Shih Shen-chih

VIII   Shih Chih-ch'ing [II]   Shih Shun-ch'ing [II]   Shih Chen-ch'ing [II]   Shih Ch'i-ch'ing [III]   Shih Hsi-ch'ing [II]   Shih Chin-ch'ing   Shih Li-ch'ing [III]   Shih Jen-ch'ing [III]   Shih Shih-ch'ing [II]

IX   Shih Lan-sun   Shih Chih-sun   Shih Ying-po   Shih Kuei-sun [II]   Shih Ch'ang-po   Shih Hsien-sun [III]   Shih Shih-sun [II]   Shih Tzu-sun   Shih Ch'ien-po   Shih Chün-po   Shih Yüeh-sun   Shih Chu-sun

X   Shih Kung-yüeh [II]   Shih Kung-wei [II]   Shih Kung-ch'o   Shih Kung-mou [III]   Shih Kung-hsieh   Shih Kung-hsi [IV]   Shih Kung-kang   Shih Kung-ting [II]

Shih Kung-jen

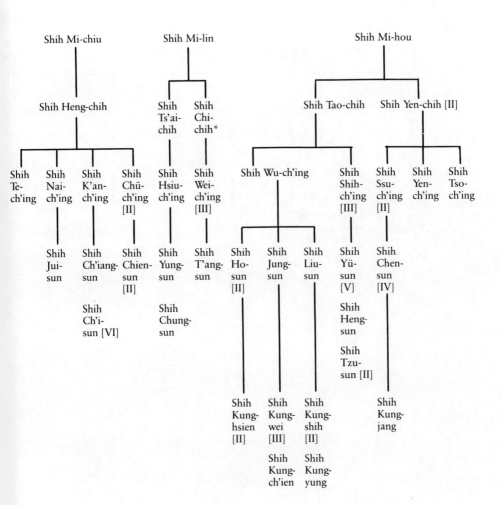

Genealogy of the Shih (continued)

Branch B

Generation

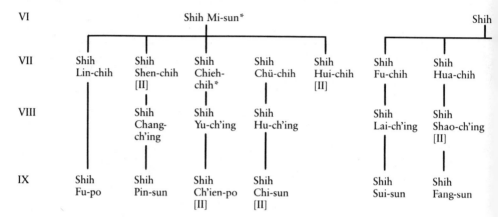

VI   Shih Mi-sun*   Shih

VII   Shih Lin-chih   Shih Shen-chih [II]   Shih Chieh-chih*   Shih Chü-chih   Shih Hui-chih [II]   Shih Fu-chih   Shih Hua-chih

VIII   Shih Chang-ch'ing   Shih Yu-ch'ing   Shih Hu-ch'ing   Shih Lai-ch'ing   Shih Shao-ch'ing [II]

IX   Shih Fu-po   Shih Pin-sun   Shih Ch'ien-po [II]   Shih Chi-sun [II]   Shih Sui-sun   Shih Fang-sun

X

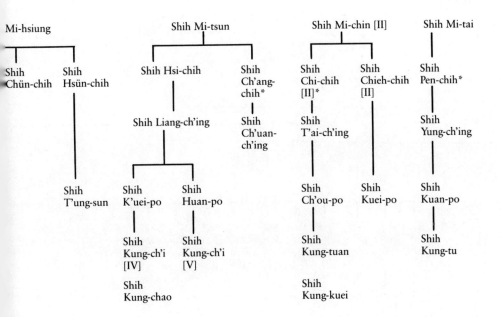

Genealogy of the Shih (continued)
Branch C

Generation

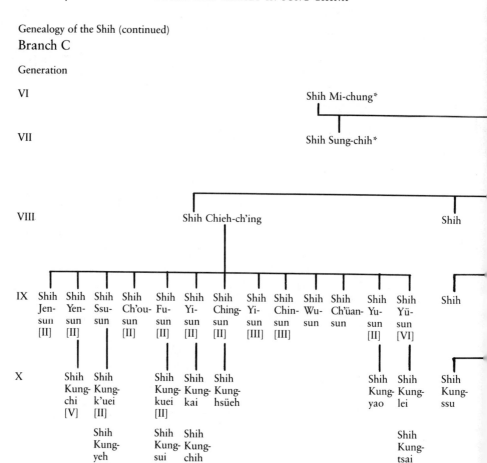

VI   Shih Mi-chung*

VII   Shih Sung-chih*

VIII   Shih Chieh-ch'ing   Shih

IX   Shih Shih Shih Shih Shih Shih Shih Shih Shih Shih Shih Shih Shih   Shih
     Jen- Yen- Ssu- Ch'ou- Fu- Yi- Ching- Yi- Chin- Wu- Ch'üan- Yu- Yü-
     sun   sun   sun   sun   sun   sun sun   sun sun   sun sun   sun   sun
     [II] [II]   [II] [II] [II] [II] [III] [III]   [II] [VI]

X   Shih Shih   Shih Shih Shih   Shih Shih   Shih
           Kung- Kung-   Kung- Kung- Kung-   Kung- Kung-   Kung-
           chi   k'uei   kuei kai   hsüeh   yao   lei   ssu
           [V]   [II]   [II]

                 Shih   Shih Shih   Shih
                 Kung-   Kung- Kung-   Kung-
                 yeh   sui   chih   tsai
                 [II]   [II] [V]   [II]

                 Shih
                 Kung-
                 hui

                 Shih
                 Kung-
                 hou
                 [II]

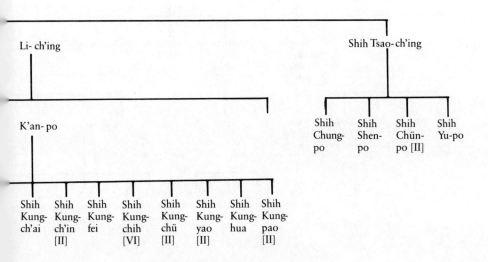

Li- ch'ing

K'an- po

Shih Tsao- ch'ing

Shih Chung- po

Shih Shen- po

Shih Chün- po [II]

Shih Yu-po

Shih Kung- ch'ai

Shih Kung- ch'in [II]

Shih Kung- fei

Shih Kung- chih [VI]

Shih Kung- chü [II]

Shih Kung- yao [II]

Shih Kung- hua

Shih Kung- pao [II]

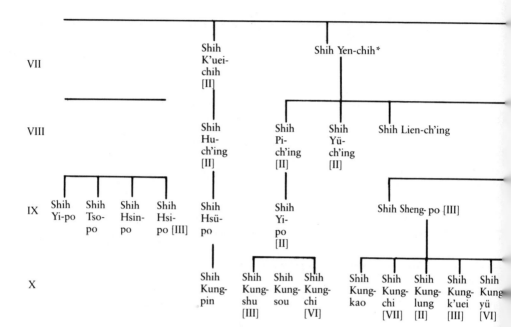

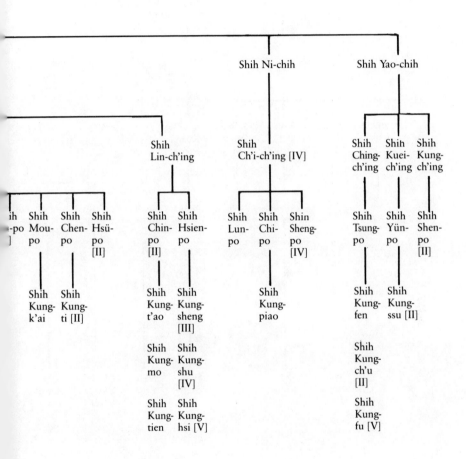

Genealogy of the Shih (continued)

Generation

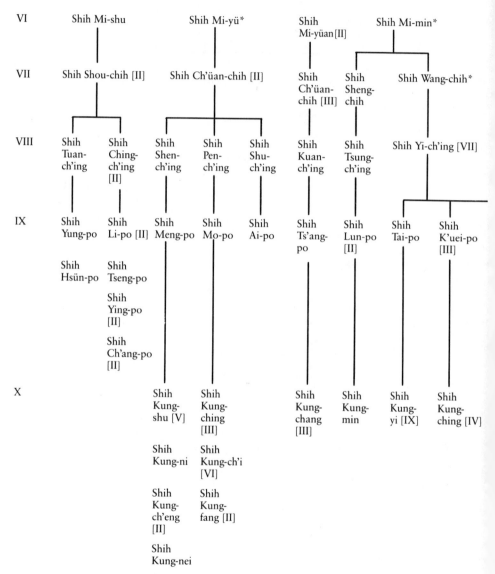

VI

Shih Mi-shu   Shih Mi-yü*   Shih Mi-yüan[II]   Shih Mi-min*

VII

Shih Shou-chih [II]   Shih Ch'üan-chih [II]   Shih Ch'üan-chih [III]   Shih Sheng-chih   Shih Wang-chih*

VIII

Shih Tuan-ch'ing   Shih Ching-ch'ing [II]   Shih Shen-ch'ing   Shih Pen-ch'ing   Shih Shu-ch'ing   Shih Kuan-ch'ing   Shih Tsung-ch'ing   Shih Yi-ch'ing [VII]

IX

Shih Yung-po   Shih Li-po [II]   Shih Meng-po   Shih Mo-po   Shih Ai-po   Shih Ts'ang-po   Shih Lun-po [II]   Shih Tai-po   Shih K'uei-po [III]

Shih Hsün-po   Shih Tseng-po

Shih Ying-po [II]

Shih Ch'ang-po [II]

X

Shih Kung-shu [V]   Shih Kung-ching [III]   Shih Kung-chang [III]   Shih Kung-min   Shih Kung-yi [IX]   Shih Kung-ching [IV]

Shih Kung-ni   Shih Kung-ch'i [VI]

Shih Kung-ch'eng [II]   Shih Kung-fang [II]

Shih Kung-nei

XI

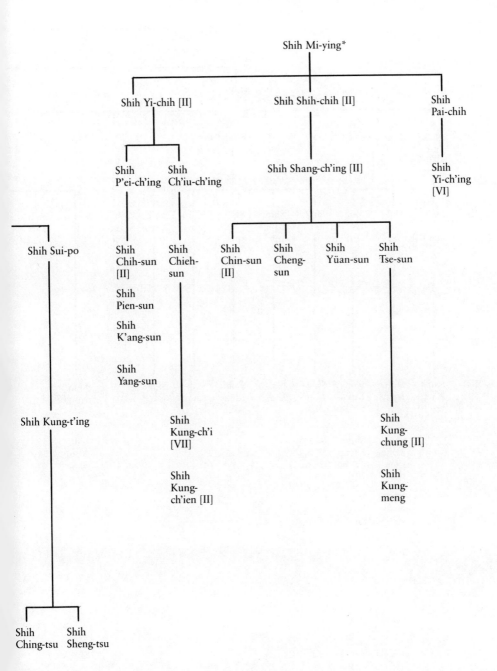

Genealogy of the Shih (continued)

Generation

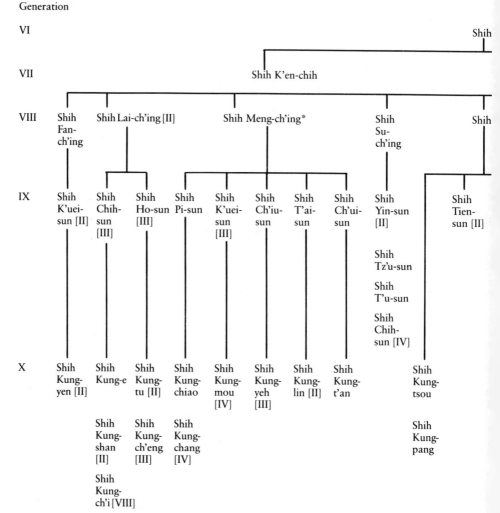

Generation										
VI										Shih
VII				Shih K'en-chih						
VIII	Shih Fan-ch'ing	Shih Lai-ch'ing [II]			Shih Meng-ch'ing*				Shih Su-ch'ing	Shih
IX	Shih K'uei-sun [II]	Shih Chih-sun [III]	Shih Ho-sun [III]	Shih Pi-sun	Shih K'uei-sun [III]	Shih Ch'iu-sun	Shih T'ai-sun	Shih Ch'ui-sun	Shih Yin-sun [II]	Shih Tien-sun [II]
									Shih Tz'u-sun	
									Shih T'u-sun	
									Shih Chih-sun [IV]	
X	Shih Kung-yen [II]	Shih Kung-e	Shih Kung-tu [II]	Shih Kung-chiao	Shih Kung-mou [IV]	Shih Kung-yeh [III]	Shih Kung-lin [II]	Shih Kung-t'an	Shih Kung-tsou	
		Shih Kung-shan [II]	Shih Kung-ch'eng [III]	Shih Kung-chang [IV]					Shih Kung-pang	
		Shih Kung-ch'i [VIII]								

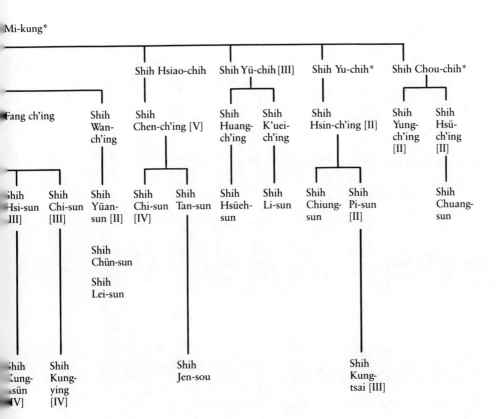

Mi-kung*

Shih Hsiao-chih   Shih Yü-chih [III]   Shih Yu-chih*   Shih Chou-chih*

Fang ch'ing

Shih Wan-ch'ing

Shih Chen-ch'ing [V]

Shih Huang-ch'ing

Shih K'uei-ch'ing

Shih Hsin-ch'ing [II]

Shih Yung-ch'ing [II]

Shih Hsü-ch'ing [II]

Shih Hsi-sun [III]

Shih Chi-sun [III]

Shih Yüan-sun [II]

Shih Chi-sun [IV]

Shih Tan-sun

Shih Hsüeh-sun

Shih Li-sun

Shih Chiung-sun

Shih Pi-sun [II]

Shih Chuang-sun

Shih Chün-sun

Shih Lei-sun

Shih Kung-sün [IV]

Shih Kung-ying [IV]

Shih Jen-sou

Shih Kung-tsai [III]

Genealogy of the Shih (continued)

Generation

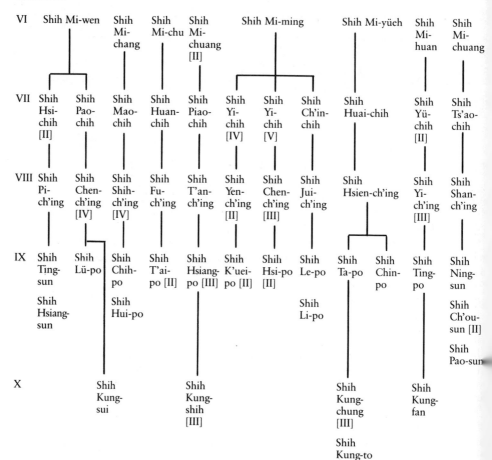

Branch D

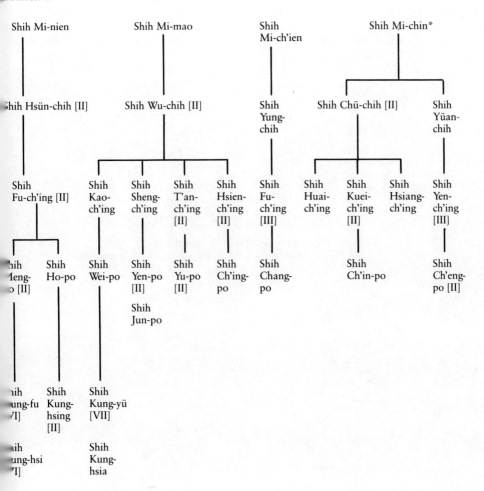

Genealogy of the Shih (continued)

Branch E

Generation

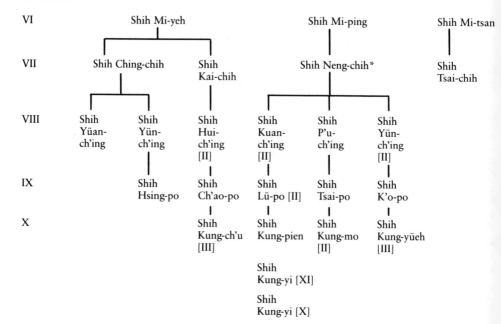

VI
    Shih Mi-yeh   Shih Mi-ping   Shih Mi-tsan

VII
  Shih Ching-chih Shih   Shih Neng-chih*   Shih
          Kai-chih   Tsai-chih

VIII
 Shih Shih Shih Shih Shih Shih
 Yüan- Yün- Hui- Kuan- P'u- Yün-
 ch'ing ch'ing ch'ing ch'ing ch'ing ch'ing
       [II] [II]   [II]

IX
    Shih Shih Shih Shih Shih
    Hsing-po Ch'ao-po Lü-po [II] Tsai-po K'o-po

X
       Shih Shih Shih Shih
       Kung-ch'u Kung-pien Kung-mo Kung-yüeh
       [III]   [II] [III]

          Shih
          Kung-yi [XI]

          Shih
          Kung-yi [X]

4. Bibliographic References for the Shih

GENERATION I

Shih Ch'eng, alleged son of Shih Wei-tse: YYWSC, 41.2a; HSSSTP, 8.10b.

GENERATION II

Shih Chien (1034?–58), son of Shih Ch'eng, husband of the widow Yeh (1033–1118):
PCSMC, 9.28a–29a; YYSMC, 5.33a–34a; HHYHC, 26.41b–42a; KKC, 74.12a–14b, 93.3a;
CCTC, 16.11a, 18.9a; HSSSTP, 8.10b–12b; *Ssu-ming jen-chien*, 3.2b.

GENERATION III

Shih Chao (1058–1130), son of Shih Chien, "Mr. Eight Virtues of Conduct": YYSMC,
9.33b; HHYHC, 26.42a; HSSSTP, 8.12b–14a; SYHA, 6.151.

GENERATION IV

Shih Ho, son of Shih Chao, prefectural examination candidate: HHYHC, 26.42b; HSSSTP,
5.13a–5.13b.
Shih Kuang, son of Shih Chao: KKC, 74.13b; HSSSTP, 5.13b.
Shih Mu, son of Shih Chao, prefectural examination candidate: PCSMC, 9.3a; SHHSC, 22.18b;
HHYHC, 26.49b–50a; MFCYML, 43.1a–2b; YYWSC, 43.12a; HSSSTP, 5.12a–13a.
Shih Shih-chung (1082–1124), son of Shih Chao, Imperial University student: KKC, 74.13b,
93.3a; HHYHC, 26.42b; HSSSTP, 8.14a–14b.
Shih Ts'ai (d. 1162), son of Shih Chao, CS (*chin-shih*) 1118, Tuan-ming-tien hsüeh-shih
(3a), assistant councillor (2a)[1]: PCSMC, 9.3b; YYMSC, 6.12a; HHYHC, 14.27a–27b,
28.42b; KKC, 105.1b; CCTC, 45.20a–22b; HSSSTP, 5.11a–12a.

GENERATION V

Shih Chan, son of Shih Mu, *hsiu-chih-lang* (8b): HSSSTP, 5.45a.
Shih Ch'eng [II], son of Shih Kuang, *teng-shih-lang* (9a): HSSSTP, 5.58b.
Shih Chi, son of Shih Ho, *hsüan-yi-lang* (8b): HSSSTP, 5.58a.
Shih Chien [II] (1124–94), son of Shih Mu, Imperial University student, *ch'eng-feng-lang*
(8b): SHHSC, 22.18b–20b; HHYHC, 26.50a; YYWSC, 43.12a; HSSSTP, 5.46a–46b.

Note: This list contains references to *major* sources of biographical information. For more
prominent individuals, also see references in notes. A list of abbreviations is on p. 251.

1   This represents the rank assigned to the office of assistant councillor, the highest post
held by Shih Ts'ai. I have tried to provide the highest sinecure rank whenever possible (it
is subject to less fluctuation than office rank). Unfortunately, as in this case, sinecure is
not always given in the original citation.

Shih Chüan, son of Shih Shih-chung, *ch'eng-yi-lang* (7b), assistant staff supervisor (8b): KKC, 74.13b; HHYHC, 26.42b; HSSSTP, 5.37a–37b.

Shih Chün (1129–1203), son Shih Ts'ai, *ch'ao-ch'ing tai-fu* (5b), prefectural vice-administrator: KKC, 105.1a–12b; HHYHC, 28.42b–45a; HSSSTP, 5.40b–41a.

Shih Hao (1106–94), son of Shih Shih-chung, CS 1145, chief councillor (1a): KKC, 93.1a–19b; PCSMC, 9.3a–17b; SS, 396.12065–69; YYSMC, 5.1a–2b, 6.13a; HHYHC, 27.29b–37b; CCTC, 18.8b–10a, 28.14a–15a; HSSSTP, 8.15a–17a; SYHA, 40.756–57; SSHP, 141, 141.24–25; *Mei-hsi wang hsien-sheng wen-chi*, 3.2b–6a.

Shih Hung, son of Shih Kuang, no record of official service: HSSSTP, 5.60a–60b.

Shih Jo-ch'ung, son of Shih Mu, no record of official service: HSSSTP, 5.43b.

Shih Jo-shui, son of Shih Ts'ai, no record of official service: HSSSTP, 5.40b–41a.

Shih K'o, son of Shih Ho, no record of official service: HSSSTP, 5.57a.

Shih P'u, son of Shih Shih-chung, *ch'eng-yi-lang* (7b), prefectural vice-administrator: KKC, 74.13b; HHYHC, 26.42b; *Ts'ui she-jen yü-t'ang lei-kao*, 7.5b.

Shih Yüan, son of Shih Shih-chung, *ch'ao-feng-lang* (7a), prefect: YYWSC, 43.16a; KKC, 74.13b; HHYHC, 26.42b; HSSSTP, 5.30b–31a.

Shih Yüan [II], son of Shih Shih-chung, minor inspector: KKC, 74.13b; HHYHC, 26.42b; HSSSTP, 5.35b–36a.

GENERATION VI

Branch A

Shih Mi-cheng, son of Shih Hao, *Fu-wen-ko tai-chih* (4b): KKC, 74.13b, 83.10a, 93.16a; HHYHC, 27.37b; HSSSTP 5.15a–15b; *Chia-ting Ch'ih-ch'eng chih*, 5.8a, 9.20a–20b.

Shih Mi-chien (1164–1232) , son of Shih Hao, *kuang-lu tai-fu* (2b), metropolitan prefect (3b): KKC, 74.13b; YYSMC, 5.22a–23a; HHYHC, 29.26b–30a; CCTC, 45.24b; SYHA, 74.1406–7; HSSSTP, 5.26a–27a; *Ho-lin chi*, 10.7b–8a; *Hsien-ch'un Lin-an chih*, 48.10b–11a, 50.9b; *Che-chiang t'ung-chih*, 113.22b, 114.14b.

Shih Mi-chiu, son of Shih Chüan, no record of official service: HSSSTP, 5.37b–38a.

Shih Mi-chün, son of Shih Yüan, no record of official service: HSSSTP, 5.35a.

Shih Mi-hou, son of Shih Chüan, *feng-chih tai-fu* (6a), prefectural vice-administrator: HHYHC, 29.9b–10a; HSSSTP, 5.39a; *Ching-ting Chien-k'ang chih*, 27.18b; *Ch'ung-hsiu Ch'in-ch'uan chih*, 3.17b.

Shih Mi-hsing, son of Shih P'u, no record of official service: HSSSTP, 5.35a–35b.

Shih Mi-kao, son of Shih Yüan, *feng-chih tai-fu* (6a), prefect: YYWSC, 43.16a; HSSSTP 5.30b–31a.

Shih Mi-kuang, son of Shih Yüan [II], *ping-yi-lang* (8b): HSSSTP, 5.36a.

Shih Mi-k'uo, nephew of Shih Hao, an official: KKC, 35.19b.

Shih Mi-liang, son of Shih Chüan, prefect: HSSSTP, 5.37b.

Shih Mi-lin, son of Shih Chüan, *hsiu-chih-lang* (8b), wine warehouse inspector: HHYHC, 29.9b–10a; SYHA, 74.1407; HSSSTP, 5.38b.

Shih Mi-lun, son of Shih Chüan, *ts'ung-yi-lang* (8b): HSSSTP, 5.37a.

Shih Mi-lung, son of Shih Yüan [II], *pao-yi-lang* (9a): HSSSTP, 5.37a.

Shih Mi-ning, son of Shih Yüan [II], *wu-kung tai-fu* (7a), prefect: CCTC, 31.8b–9b; SKTY, 31.52; HSSSTP, 5.36a.

Shih Mi-shao, son of Shih Yüan [II], *wu-yi tai-fu* (7a): HSSSTP, 5.35b–36a.

Shih Mi-ta (fl. 1169–85), son of Shih Hao, CS 1169, *Fu-wen-ko tai-chih* (4b), executive at Ministry of Rites (3b): KKC, 93.16a; YYSMC, 6.14b; HHYHC, 27.37b; CCTC, 31.7b–8a; HSSSTP, 5.14a.

Shih Mi-tzu, son of Shih P'u, no record of official service: HSSSTP, 5.35b.

Shih Mi-yüan (1164–1233), son of Shih Hao, CS 1187, *T'ai-shih* (1a), chief councillor (1a): SS, 414.12415–18; SSHP, 151.56; YYSMC, 5.10b–12a, 6.15b; HHYHC, 14.26b–34a; HSSSTP, 8.17a–18a; SB, 873–74.

Branch B

Shih Mi-chin [II], son of Shih Chün, *ch'eng-wu-lang* (9b): KKC, 105.11b; HSSSTP, 5.42b–43a.

Shih Mi-hsiung, son of Shih Chün, *ch'ao-san tai-fu* (6b), prefect: KKC, 105.11b; HHYHC 28.45a; HSSSTP, 5.41a–41b.

Shih Mi-sun, son of Shih Chün, CS 1196, *hsüan-yi-lang* (8b), subprefectural registrar (9a): KKC, 105.11b; HHYHC, 28.45a; YYSMC, 6.16b; HSSSTP, 5.41a.

Shih Mi-tai (var. Shih Mi-mai), son of Shih Chün, Imperial University student: KKC, 105.11b; HSSSTP, 5.43a.

Shih Mi-tsun, son of Shih Chün, *chiang-shih-lang* (9b): HSSSTP, 5.42a.

Branch C

Shih Mi-chang, son of Shih Chan, *ti-kung lang* (9b), student at Directorate of Education: HSSSTP, 5.45b.

Shih Mi-chu, son of Shih Chan, held minor official rank: HSSSTP, 5.45b.

Shih Mi-chuang, son of Shih Jo-ch'ung, no record of official service: HSSSTP, 5.45b.

Shih Mi-chuang [II], son of Shih Chan, no record of official service: HSSSTP, 5.46a.

Shih Mi-chung (d. 1244), son of Shih Chien [II], CS 1187, *Tuan-ming-tien hsüeh-shih* (3a), prefect: YYSMC, 5.21a–22a, 6.15b; HHYHC, 29.8b–9a; YYWSC, 38.12b; HSSSTP, 5.46a–46b; SYHA, 74.1406.

Shih Mi-huan, son of Shih Jo-ch'ung, *ch'eng-chieh-lang* (9b): HSSSTP, 5.44a–44b.

Shih Mi-kung (fl.1193–1237), son of Shih Chien [II], later adopted as heir to Shih Hung, CS 1217, *chung-feng tai-fu* (5b), prefect: SS, 423.12637–38; YYSMC, 6.19b; HHYHC, 30.14a–15b; HSSSTP, 5.60a–60b; SHHSC, 22.20b; CJCSC, 28.27a; SYHA, 74.1407; *Chih-cheng Ssu-ming hsü-chih*, 2.21b–23a; *Che-chiang t'ung-chih*, 115.11b, 115.33a, 190.22a; *Ching-ting Chien-k'ang chih* 27.24a.

Shih Mi-kung [II], son of Shih Chan, no record of official service: HSSSTP, 5.46a.

Shih Mi-min, son of Shih Chien [II], CS 1214, *ch'ao-yi tai-fu* (6a), prefect: SHHSC, 22.18b; YYSMC, 6.19a; YYWSC, 43.12a; HHYHC, 26.50b; HSSSTP, 5.55a; *Che-chiang t'ung-chih*, 115.21b.

Shih Mi-ming, son of Shih Jo-ch'ung, no record of official service: HSSSTP, 5.43b.

Shih Mi-shu, son of Shih Chien [II], *ch'eng-wu-lang*, (9b), prefectural vice-administrator: SHHSC, 22.18b; HSSSTP, 5.53a.

Shih Mi-wen, son of Shih Chan, Imperial University student, held minor official rank: HSSSTP, 5.45a.

Shih Mi-ying, son of Shih Chien [II], CS 1214, *ch'ao-ch'ing tai-fu* (5b), prefect: SHHSC, 22.18b; YYSMC, 6.18b; HHYHC, 30.5b–6a; YYWSC, 38.12b; HSSSTP, 5.55b–56a.

Shih Mi-yü (fl. 1187–1230), son of Shih Chien [II], CS 1187, *ch'ao-feng tai-fu* (5a), prefect: SHHSC, 22.18b; YYSMC, 6.15b; HSSSTP, 5.53b–54a; *Chih-shun Chen-chiang chih,* 17.30a; *Ch'ung-hsiu P'i-ling chih,* 8.12a.

Shih Mi-yüeh, son of Shih Jo-ch'ung, no record of official service: HSSSTP, 5.44a.

Branch D

Shih Mi-ch'ien, son of Shih Chi, *ch'eng-hsin-lang* (9b): HSSSTP, 5.58a.

Shih Mi-chin, son of Shih Chi, CS 1199, *ch'ao-feng-lang* (7b), prefectural vice-administrator: YYSMC, 6.17a; HHYHC, 20.18b–19a; HSSSTP, 5.58a–58b.

Shih Mi-mao, son of Shih K'o, *hsiu-chih-lang* (8b): HHYHC, 14.33b; HSSSTP, 5.57a.

Shih Mi-nien, son of Shih K'o, *ch'eng-chieh-lang* (9b): HSSSTP, 5.57a.

Branch E

Shih Mi-yeh, son of Shih Ch'eng [II], no record of official service: HSSSTP, 5.58b.

Shih Mi-ping, son of Shih Ch'eng [II], *ch'ao-feng tai-fu* (5a), prefect: HSSSTP, 5.59a–59b.

Shih Mi-tsan, son of Shih Ch'eng [II], *ts'ung-cheng-lang* (8b): HSSSTP, 5.59b.

GENERATION VII

Branch A

Shih An-chih, son of Shih Mi-cheng, *ch'ao-feng tai-fu* (5a), subprefect (8b): HHYHC, 30.28b–29a; HSSSTP, 5.16b–17a.

Shih Chai-chih (1205–49), son of Shih Mi-yüan, *Tuan-ming-tien hsüeh-shih* (3a), coadministrator of the Bureau of Military Affairs (2a), received special conferral of *chin-shih*: YYSMC, 5.11b; HHYHC, 14.39b–40b; CCTC, 45.22b–24a; SMWHC, 4.42b; *Che-chiang t'ung-chih,* 114.21a, 115.39a; *Wu-chün-chih,* 11.23.

Shih Chi-chih, son of Shih Mi-lin, CS 1229, *t'ung-yi-lang*(?), prefectural vice-administrator: YYSMC, 6.22a; HSSSTP, 5.38b–39a.

Shih Chih-chih, son of Shih Mi-kao, student at the Directorate of Education: HSSSTP, 5.32b.

Shih Ch'uan-chih, son of Shih Mi-lung, *ch'eng-chung-lang* (9a): HSSSTP, 5.27a.

Shih Ch'üan-chih, son of Shih Mi-ning, CS 1223, *ju-lin-lang* (8b): YYSMC, 6.20b; HSSSTP, 5.26b.

Shih Ch'ung-chih, son of Shih Mi-chien, *ch'ao-feng-lang* (7a), subprefect (8b): HSSSTP, 5.26b.

Shih Heng-chih, son of Shih Mi-chiu, prefectural examination candidate: HSSSTP, 5.37b–38a.

Shih Hsien-chih, son of Mi-cheng, *ch'eng-shih-lang* (9a), staff supervisor: HSSSTP, 5.18b–19a.

Shih Hsüan-chih, son of Shih Mi-cheng, *feng-chih tai-fu* (6a): HSSSTP, 5.17b–18a.

Shih Hui-chih, son of Shih Mi-kao, *chung-feng tai-fu* (5b): HSSSTP, 5.33a.

Shih K'uan-chih, son of Shih Mi-yüan, *ch'ao-feng-lang* (7a): HHYHC, 14.34a; HSSSTP, 8.18a; *Chen wen-chung-kung wen-chi,* 21.1b–2a.

Shih K'uei-chih, son of Shih Mi-kao, *ti-kung-lang* (9b): HSSSTP, 5.34b.

Shih Kung-chih, son of Shih Mi-kao, no record of official service: HSSSTP, 5.33b.

Shih Pin-chih (1190–1251), son of Shih Mi-chien, *Fu-wen-ko tai-chih* (4b), executive at Ministry of Finance (3b): HHYHC, 29.28b–30a; SYHA, 79.1494; CCTC, 45.25b;

HSSSTP, 5.27b–28a.

Shih Sa-chih, son of Shih Mi-kao, no record of official service: HSSSTP, 5.34a–34b.

Shih Shen-chih, son of Shih Mi-liang, *ch'ao-feng tai-fu* (5a), prefectural vice-administrator: HSSSTP, 5.37b.

Shih Shih-chih, son of Shih Mi-cheng, *hsiu-chih-lang* (8b), wine warehouse inspector: HSSSTP, 5.17a–17b; HHYHC, 30.18b; CJCSC, 30.25a.

Shih Shou-chih, son of Shih Mi-ta, *ch'ao-feng tai-fu* (5a): KKC, 93.16b; CCTC, 45.25a; HHYHC, 30.17a–17b; SYHA, 74.1409–10, 75.1435; HSSSTP, 5.14a–15a; *Nan-sung tsa-shih shih*, 1.40b.

Shih Sui-chih, son of Shih Mi-chien, *feng-chih tai-fu* (6a), prefect: HHYHC, 29.29b; HSSSTP, 5.26a.

Shih Sun-chih, son of Shih Mi-kao, student at Directorate of Education: HHYHC, 30.44b; YYWSC, 43.16a; HSSSTP, 5.31b.

Shih Tao-chih, son of Shih Mi-hou, *wen-lin-lang* (8b), student at Directorate of Education: HSSSTP, 5.39a.

Shih Te-chih, son of Shih Mi-hsing, *hsün-wu-lang* (8a), minor military official: HSSSTP, 5.35a–35b.

Shih Ting-chih (fl. 1191–1207), son of Shih Mi-cheng, *chung-feng tai-fu* (5b), prefect: KKC, 93.16b; HHYHC, 30.17b–18b; SYHA, 74.1410; HSSSTP, 5.16a–16b.

Shih T'ing-chih, son of Shih Mi-kao, no record of official service: HSSSTP, 5.34b–35a.

Shih Ts'ai-chih, son of Shih Mi-lin, *ch'ao-feng-lang* (7a): HSSSTP, 5.38b.

Shih Tsung-chih, eldest son of Shih Mi-cheng, *ch'ao-feng-lang*(7a), subprefect (8b): KKC, 93.16b; HHYHC, 30.18b; HSSSTP, 5.15a.

Shih Wei-chih, son of Shih Mi-shao, *ch'ao-feng tai-fu* (5a), prefect: HSSSTP, 5.25b–26a.

Shih Wu-chih, son of Shih Mi-kuang, *chung-hsün tai-fu* (5b): HSSSTP, 5.26a.

Shih Yen-chih [II], son of Shih Mi-hou, *ch'eng-chih-lang* (8b): HSSSTP, 5.40a.

Shih Yi-chih (fl. 1194–1229), son of Shih Mi-cheng, *ch'ao-san tai-fu* (6b), prefect: KKC, 93.16b; HHYHC, 30.18b; HSSSTP, 5.15b–16a; *Che-chiang t'ung-chih*, 114.21b, 115.21a; *Ch'ung-hsiu P'i-ling chih*, 8.12a.

Shih Yi-chih [III], son of Shih Mi-kao, *feng-chih tai-fu* (6a), prefect: HSSSTP, 5.30b–31a.

Shih Ying-chih, son of Shih Mi-lun, no record of official service: HSSSTP, 5.37a.

Shih Yü-chih, youngest son of Shih Mi-yüan, *Tzu-cheng-tien ta hsüeh-shih* (3a), minister of war (3a), received special conferral of *chin-shih*: YYSMC, 5.11b–12a; HHYHC, 30.26b–27b; HTHSC, 65.11a–11b; YVWSC, 37.19a–21a; CCTC, 45.22b–24a; SMWHC, 5.41b–46a; HSSSTP, 5.22b–23b.

Branch B

Shih Ch'ang-chih, son of Shih Mi-tsun, CS 1256, no record of official service: YYSMC, 6.28b; KKC, 105.11b; HSSSTP, 5.42b.

Shih Chi-chih [II], son of Shih Mi-chin [II], CS 1256, *wen-lin-lang* (8b): YYSMC, 6.28a; HSSSTP, 5.42b–43a.

Shih Chieh-chih, son of Shih Mi-sun, CS 1259, regional instructor: KKC, 105.11b; YYSMC, 6.28b; HSSSTP, 5.40b–41a.

Shih Chieh-chih [II], son of Shih Mi-chin [II], no record of official service: HSSSTP, 5.43a.

Shih Chü-chih, son of Shih Mi-sun, student at Directorate of Education: HSSSTP, 5.41a.

Shih Chün-chih, son Shih Mi-hsiung, no record of official service: HSSSTP, 5.41b–42a.

Shih Fu-chih, son of Shih Mi-hsiung, *hsün-wu-lang* (8a): HSSSTP, 5.41a–41b.

Shih Hsi-chih, son of Shih Mi-tsun, no record of official service: HSSSTP, 5.42a.

Shih Hsün-chih, son of Shih Mi-hsiung, *chiang-shih-lang* (9b), student at Military Academy: HSSSTP, 5.42a.

Shih Hua-chih, son of Shih Mi-hsiung, *ch'ao-feng tai-fu* (5a), prefect: HSSSTP, 5.41b.

Shih Hui-chih [II], son of Shih Mi-sun, no record of official service: HSSSTP, 5.41a.

Shih Lin-chih, son of Shih Mi-sun, no record of official service: HSSSTP, 5.40b.

Shih Pen-chih, son of Shih Mi-tai, CS 1238, *ch'ao-feng-lang* (7a), prefectural vice-administrator: YYSMC, 6.24b; HSSSTP, 5.43a.

Shih Shen-chih [II], son of Shih Mi-sun, no record of official service: HSSSTP, 5.40b.

Branch C

Shih Ch'in-chih, son of Shih Mi-ming, no record of official service: HSSSTP, 5.43b–44a.

Shih Chou-chih, son of Shih Mi-kung, CS 1241, *chung-feng tai-fu* (5b), prefect: YYSMC, 6.25a; HSSSTP, 5.64b –65a; *Che-chiang t'ung-chih*, 115.36b.

Shih Ch'üan-chih [II], son of Shih Mi-yü, *feng-yi-lang* (8a), prefectural vice-administrator: HSSSTP, 5.53b–54a

Shih Ch'üan-chih [III], son of Shih Mi-yüan [II], *ch'ao-san tai-fu* (6b): HSSSTP, 5.54b.

Shih Hsi-chih [II], son of Shih Mi-wen, student at Directorate of Education: HSSSTP, 5.45a.

Shih Hsiao-chih (fl. 1253–1258), son of Shih Mi-kung, *ch'ao-feng-lang* (7a): HHYHC, 30.15a; HSSSTP, 5, 63a–63b.

Shih Huai-chih, son of Shih Mi-yüeh, held minor official rank: HSSSTP, 5.44a.

Shih Huan-chih, son of Shih Mi-chu, *ch'eng-hsin-lang* (9b): HSSSTP, 5.45a.

Shih K'en-chih (fl. 1241–1253), son of Shih Mi-kung, *Yin-hsien k'ai-kuo-nan* (5b), prefect: HHYHC, 30.25a–25b; HSSSTP, 5.60a–60b.

Shih K'uei-chih [II], son of Shih Mi-chung, *ch'ao-feng-lang* (7a), prefect: HSSSTP, 5.49b–50a.

Shih Mao-chih, son of Shih Mi-chang, *ch'eng-hsin-lang* (9b): HSSSTP, 5.45b.

Shih Neng-chih (fl. 1237–1256), son of Shih Mi-kung, later adopted by Shih Mi-ping, CS 1241, *ch'ao-feng tai-fu* (5a), prefect: YYSMC, 6.25a; HHYHC, 30.25b; HTHSC, 67.14a; HSSSTP, 5.59a–59b; *Ch'ung-hsiu P'i-ling chih*, 8.14b.

Shih Ni-chih, son of Shih Mi-chung, no record of official service: HSSSTP, 5.51b.

Shih Pai-chih, son of Shih Mi-ying, *ch'ao-feng-lang* (7a), prefectural vice-administrator: HSSSTP, 5.56b.

Shih Pao-chih, son of Shih Mi-wen, *ch'eng-hsin-lang* (9b): HSSSTP, 5.45a.

Shih Piao-chih, son of Shih Mi-chuang [II], no record of official service: HSSSTP, 5.46a.

Shih Sheng-chih, son of Shih Mi-min, *ti-kung-lang* (9b): HSSSTP, 5.55a

Shih Shih-chih [II] (fl. 1259–1261), son of Shih Mi-ying, *ch'ao-yi tai-fu* (6a), subprefect (8b): HSSSTP, 5.56a; *Ching-ting Chien-k'ang chih*, 27.19a.

Shih Shou-chih [II], son of Shih Mi-shu, *ch'ao-ch'ing shih-lang* (7b), student at Directorate of Education: HSSSTP, 5.53a.

Shih Sung-chih (1189–1257), son of Shih Mi-chung, CS 1220, *Kuan-wen-tien ta hsüeh-shih* (2b), chief councillor (1a): SS, 414.12423–28; YYSMC, 5.23a–23b, 6.20a; HHYHC, 14.35b–39b; HSSSTP, 5.46a–46b; SSHP, 151.56–57; HTHSC, 80.3b–17a; *Kuei-hsin tsa-chih (pieh-chi)*, 6.16a–18b, 31a–32b; *Che-chiang t'ung-chih*, 110.24b; SB,876–79.

Shih Ts'ao-chih, son of Shih Mi-chuang, held minor official rank: HSSSTP, 5.44b.

Shih Wang-chih, son of Shih Mi-min, CS 1229, *ch'ao-ch'ing shih-lang* (7b), lord assistant chief justice (6b): YYWSC 43.12a–13a; YYSMC, 6.22a; HHYHC, 31.32b; HSSSTP, 5.55a.

Shih Yao-chih, son of Shih Mi-chung, *chung-feng tai-fu* (5b), prefect: HSSSTP, 5.52a–52b.

Shih Yen-chih (fl. 1217–60), son of Shih Mi-chung, CS 1217, *Tzu-cheng-tien ta hsüeh-shih* (3a), minister of finance (2b): HHYHC, 29.9a–29b; YYSMC, 6.19b; HSSSTP, 5.50a–51a; *Che-chiang t'ung-chih*, 114.15a, 114.21a; *Hsien-ch'un Lin-an chih*, 49.3b.

Shih Yi-chih [II], son of Shih Mi-ying, *feng-chih tai-fu* (6a), prefect: YYWSC, 38.12b; HSSSTP, 5.55b.

Shih Yi-chih [IV], son of Shih Mi-ming, held minor official rank: HSSSTP, 5.43b.

Shih Yi-chih [V], son of Shih Mi-ming, *chung-hsün-lang* (9a): HSSSTP, 5.43b.

Shih Yu-chih, son of Shih Mi-kung, CS 1253, Imperial University student, *ch'ao-san tai-fu* (6b), prefectural inspector (8b): YYSMC, 6.27b; HHYHC, 20.35a, 30.15b; HSSSTP, 5.64a.

Shih Yü-chih [II], son of Shih Mi-huan, *ch'eng-chieh-lang* (8b): HSSSTP, 5.44a–44b.

Shih Yu-chih [III], son of Shih Mi-kung, *ch'ao-san-lang* (7b), prefectural vice-administrator: HHYHC 30.15a–15b; SMWHC, 5.46b–47a; HSSSTP, 5.63b–64a.

Branch D

Shih Chü-chih [II], son of Shih Mi-chin, no record of official service: HSSSTP, 5.58a.

Shih Hsün-chih [II], son of Shih Mi-nien, no record of official service: HSSSTP, 5.57a.

Shih Wu-chih [II], son of Shih Mi-mao, student at Directorate of Education, regional instructor: HSSSTP, 5.57a–57b.

Shih Yüan-chih, son of Shih Mi-chin, *wen-lin-lang* (8b): HSSSTP, 5.58b.

Shih Yung-chih, son of Shih Mi-ch'ien *ch'eng-chih-lang* (8b): HSSSTP, 5.58a.

Branch E

Shih Ching-chih, son of Shih Mi-yeh, no record of official service: HSSSTP, 5.58b.

Shih Kai-chih, son of Shih Mi-yeh, held minor official rank: HSSSTP, 5.59a.

Shih Tsai-chih, son of Shih Mi-yeh, no record of official service: HSSSTP, 5.59b.

GENERATION VIII

Branch A

Shih Ch'ang-ch'ing, son of Shih Chai-chih, *ch'ao-san tai-fu* (6b): HSSSTP, 5.22a–22b.

Shih Ch'ang-ch'ing [II], son of Shih Hsüan-chih, *ch'ao-yi tai-fu* (6b), prefect: HSSSTP, 5.18b–19a.

Shih Ch'ang-ch'ing [III], "grandson" of Shih Mi-yüan, *ch'eng-feng-lang* (8b): HHYHC, 14.34a.

Shih Chao-ch'ing, son of Shih Chai-chih, *ch'eng-feng-lang* (8b): HHYHC, 14.34a; HSSSTP, 5.21b–22a.

Shih Chen-ch'ing, son of Shih Hui-chih, no record of official service: HSSSTP, 5.33a.

Shih Chen-ch'ing [II], son of Shih Wei-chih, no record of official service: HSSSTP, 5.35b.

Shih Chi-ch'ing, son of Shih Yü-chih, *ch'eng-yi-lang* (7b), prefect: HHYHC, 14.34a, 30.27a; SMWHC, 5.45b; HSSSTP, 5.22b–23a; *Chih-shun Chen-chiang chih*, 15.14b.

Shih Chi-ch'ing [II], son of Shih K'uan-chih, no record of official service: HSSSTP, 5.19a

Shih Chi-ch'ing, son of Shih Ting-chih, *ch'ao-ch'ing-lang* (7b), prefect: HSSSTP, 5.16a; *Yi-pai-chai kao*, 34.2b–4a; *Chih-shun Chen-chiang chih*, 16.4a.

Shih Chi-ch'ing [II], son of Shih Yi-chih [II], held official rank: HSSSTP, 5.30b.

Shih Chi-ch'ing [III], son of Shih Wu-chih, no record of official service: HSSSTP, 5.36a.

Shih Chia-ch'ing, son of Shih Yü-chih, *ch'eng-shih-lang* (9a): HHYHC, 30.27a; SMWHC, 5.45b.

Shih Chih-ch'ing, son of Shih Sun-chih, *ti-kung-lang* (9b): HSSSTP, 5.31b.

Shih Chih-ch'ing [II], son of Shih Te-chih, minor official: HSSSTP, 5.35a–35b.

Shih Chih-ch'ing, son of Shih Ch'üan-chih, *ch'eng-shih-lang* (9a): SS, 41.798; HHYHC, 14.34a; HSSSTP, 5.36b.

Shih Ching-ch'ing [II], son of Shih Shou-chih [II], *chiang-shih-lang* (9b): HSSSTP, 5.53a–53b.

Shih Chou-ch'ing, son of Shih Chai-chih, *feng-chih tai-fu* (6a), received special conferral of *chin-shih*: HHYHC, 14.34a; HSSSTP, 5.20a–20b.

Shih Chü-ch'ing (fl. 1266–1313), son of Shih Pin-chih, *ch'eng-wu-lang* (9b), subprefect (8b) under the Sung, later served the Yüan as subprefect: HHYHC, 29.29b–30a; HSSSTP, 5.28a–28b.

Shih Ch'un-ch'ing, son of Shih Ch'ung-chih, *ch'ao-feng tai-fu* (5a), prefect: HTHSC, 65.10b; HSSSTP, 5.27a.

Shih Chün-ch'ing, son of Shih T'ing-chih, CS 1250, *chung-feng tai-fu* (5b), prefectural vice-administrator for Lin-an: YYSMC, 6.27a; HHYHC, 30.19a; HSSSTP, 5.34b–35a; *Hsien-ch'un Lin-an chih*, 50.21a.

Shih Han-ch'ing, son of Shih Tsung-chih, *ch'eng-shih-lang* (8b): HSSSTP, 5.15a–15b.

Shih Hsi-ch'ing, son of Shih Yü-chih, *ch'eng-shih-lang* (9a), Yüan eremite: HSSSTP 5.25b; *Sung wen-hsien-kung ch'üan-chi*, 23.11a.

Shih Hsi-ch'ing [II], son of Shih Ch'üan-chih, no record of official service: HSSSTP, 5.36b.

Shih Hsia-ch'ing, son of Shih Tsung-chih, *ch'ao-feng tai-fu* (5a), prefect: HSSSTP, 5.15a.

Shih Hsien-ch'ing, son of Shih Shih-chih, *ch'ao-ch'ing tai-fu* (5b), prefectural vice-administrator: CJCSC, 30.25a; HHYHC, 30.49a; HSSSTP, 5.17a–17b.

Shih Hsin-ch'ing, son of Shih Kung-chih, no record of official service: HSSSTP, 5.34a.

Shih Hsiu-ch'ing, son of Shih Ts'ai-chih, *chiang-shih-lang* (9b): HSSSTP, 5.38b.

Shih Hsü-ch'ing, son of Shih Yi-chih [II], *ts'ung-shih-lang* (8b): HSSSTP, 5.31a.

Shih Hui-ch'ing, son of Shih Chai-chih, *ch'eng-shih-lang* (9a): SS, 41.798; YYWSC, 38.14a; HHYHC, 14.34a.

Shih Jen-ch'ing, son of Shih Kung-chih, held minor official rank: HSSSTP, 5.33b.

Shih Jen-ch'ing [II], son of Shih Shen-chih, *chiang-shih-lang* (9b): HSSSTP, 5.37b.

Shih Jih-ch'ing, son of Shih An-chih, *ti-kung-lang* (9b), sheriff (9b): HSSSTP 5.17a.

Shih K'an-ch'ing, son of Shih Heng-chih, no record of official service: HSSSTP, 5.38a.

Shih Li-ch'ing [II], son of Shih Ch'uan-chih, *ch'eng-hsin-lang* (9b): HSSSTP, 5.37a.

Shih Li-ch'ing [III], son of Shih Ch'ih-chih, *hsiu-wu-lang* (8b), military officer: HSSSTP, 5.32b–33a.

Shih Lu-ch'ing, "grandson" of Shih Mi-yüan, *ch'eng-feng-lang* (8b): HHYHC, 14.34a.

Shih Man-ch'ing, son of Shih Hsüan-chih, *ch'ao-yi tai-fu* (6a): HSSSTP, 5.18b.

Shih Mao-ch'ing, son of Shih Yi-chih, *ch'eng-yi-lang* (7b), prefectural vice-administrator: HSSSTP, 5.15b–16a.

Shih Meng-ch'ing [II], son of Shih Sun-chih, no record of official service: HSSSTP, 5.32b.

Shih Min-ch'ing, son of Shih Sun-chih, no record of official service: HSSSTP, 5.31b–32a.

Shih Ming-ch'ing, "grandson" of Shih Mi-yüan, *ch'eng-feng-lang* (8b): HHYHC, 14.34a.

Shih Nai-ch'ing, son of Shih Heng-chih, no record of official service: HSSSTP, 5.38a.

Shih P'eng-ch'ing, son of Shih Yü-chih, *ch'ao-shih-lang* (9a): HHYHC, 14.34a, 30.27a; SMWHC, 5.45b; HSSSTP, 5.24b.

Shih Sen-ch'ing, son of Shih Pin-chih, *ch'ao-feng tai-fu* (5a), prefectural vice-administrator of Lin-an: HTHSC, 67.8a–8b; HHYHC, 29.29b; HSSSTP, 5.27b; *Hsien-ch'un Lin-an chih*, 50.20b.

Shih Shang-ch'ing, son of Shih Hsien-chih, *ti-kung-lang* (9b): HSSSTP, 5.19a.

Shih Shao-ch'ing, "grandson" of Shih Mi-yüan, *ch'eng-shih-lang* (9a): SS 41.798; HHYHC, 14.34a.

Shih Shih-ch'ing (1213–86), son of Shih Sun-chih, Imperial University student, *ch'ao-feng-lang* (7a), fiscal inspector (8b), Yüan eremite: YYWSC, 38.13a, 43.15b–18a; CCTC, 45.25b; HHYHC, 14.40b; HSSSTP, 5.32a–32b.

Shih Shih-ch'ing [II], son of Shih Shen-chih, *chiang-shih-lang* (9b): HSSSTP, 4.37b.

Shih Shih-ch'ing [III], son of Shih Tao-chih, no record of offical service: HSSSTP, 5.39b.

Shih Shou-ch'ing, son of Shih Hsien-chih, no record of official service: HSSSTP, 5.18b.

Shih Shun-ch'ing, son of Shih Chai-chih, *ch'eng-feng-lang* (8b): HHYHC, 14.34a; HSSSTP, 5.19b–20a.

Shih Shun-ch'ing [II], son of Shih Te-chih, *ts'ung-yi-lang* (8b), later migrated to Hu-chou: HSSSTP, 5.35b.

Shih Ssu-ch'ing, also known as Shih Ya-ch'ien, son of Shih Shou-chih, *feng-yi-lang* (8a), subprefect (8b):HSSSTP, 5.14a; *Chih-shun Chen-chiang chih*, 16.7a.

Shih Ssu-ch'ing [II], son of Shih Yen-chih [II], no record of official service: HSSSTP, 5.40a.

Shih Ssu-ch'ing [III], son of Shih Kung-chih, no record of official service: HSSSTP, 5.34a.

Shih Sun-ch'ing, son of Shih K'uei-chih, no record of official service: HSSSTP, 5.34b.

Shih Sung-ch'ing, son of Shih Ch'ung-chih, *feng-chih tai-fu* (6a), prefect: HSSSTP, 5.26b.

Shih T'ang-ch'ing, son of Shih Chai-chih, CS 1265, *ch'eng-feng-lang* (8b), prefectural vice-administrator: YYSMC, 6.29b; HHYHC, 14.34a, 20.38b, 30.19a; HSSSTP, 5.21a–21b.

Shih Te-ch'ing, son of Shih Heng-chih, no record of official service, migrated to Yü-yao *hsien*: HSSSTP, 5.37b–38a.

Shih Teng-ch'ing, son of Shih Yi-chih, died early: HSSSTP, 5.15b.

Shih Tseng-ch'ing, son of Shih Ch'ih-chih, student at Directorate of Education: HSSSTP, 5.32b.

Shih Tso-ch'ing, son of Shih Yen-chih [II], no record of official service: HSSSTP, 5.40a.

Shih T'ung-ch'ing, "grandson" of Shih Mi-yüan, auxiliary lecturer: SS, 41.798; HHYHC, 14.34a.

Shih Wei-ch'ing (1276–1323), son of Shih Yü-chih, Yüan eremite: CJCSC, 30.9a–12b; HHYHC, 30.27a; HSSSTP, 5.25a.

Shih Wei-ch'ing [II], son of Shih Ch'ih-chih, no record of official service: HSSSTP, 5.33a.

Shih Wei-ch'ing [III], son of Shih Chi-chih, student at Directorate of Education: HSSSTP, 5.38b–39a.

Shih Wen-ch'ing, son of Shih Ting-chih, *ch'ao-feng tai-fu* (5a), prefect: HHYHC, 30.18b;

HSSSTP, 5.16a.

Shih Wu-ch'ing, son of Shih Tao-chih, student at Directorate of Education: HSSSTP, 5.39a.

Shih Ya-ch'ing, son of Shih Hsüan-chih, *ch'ao-feng tai fu* (5a), prefect: HSSTP, 5.19a.

Shih Yao-ch'ing, son of Shih Chai-chih, *ch'eng-feng-lang* (8b): HHYHC, 14.34a; HSSSTP, 5.19b.

Shih Yeh-ch'ing, son of Shih Sui-chih, *feng-yi-lang* (8a), staff supervisor (8b): HSSSTP, 5.26a.

Shih Yen-ch'ing, son of Shih Yen-chih [II], no record of official service: HSSSTP, 5.40a.

Shih Yi-ch'ing, son of Shih K'uan-chih, *ch'eng-shih-lang* (9a): SMWHC, 5.45b; HHYHC, 30.27a; HSSSTP, 5.19b.

Shih Yi-ch'ing [II], son of Shih Chai-chih, *ch'eng-feng-lang* (8b), prefectural vice-administrator: HHYHC, 14.34a; HSSSTP, 5.21b.

Shih Yi-ch'ing [IV], son of Shih Yi-chih [II], *ch'ao-ch'ing tai-fu* (5b), prefectural vice-administrator: HSSSTP, 5.31a.

Shih Yi-ch'ing [V], son of Shih K'uei-chih, no record of official service: HSSSTP, 5.34b.

Shih Ying-ch'ing, son of Shih Yi-chih [II], no record of official service: HSSSTP, 5.31b.

Shih Yü-ch'ing, son of Shih K'uei-chih, no record of official service: HSSSTP, 5.34b.

Shih Yüeh-ch'ing, son of Shih An-chih, *chiang-shih-lang* (9b): HSSSTP, 5.16b–17a.

Branch B

Shih Chang-ch'ing, son of Shih Shen-chih [II], no record of official service: HSSSTP, 5.40b.

Shih Ch'uan-ch'ing, son of Shih Ch'ang-chih, no record of official service: HSSSTP, 5.42b.

Shih Hu-ch'ing, son of Shih Chü-chih, no record of official service: HSSSTP, 5.41a.

Shih Lai-ch'ing, son of Shih Fu-chih, no record of official service: HSSSTP, 5.41a–41b.

Shih Liang-ch'ing, son of Shih Hsi-chih, *ch'eng-shih-lang* (9a): SS, 41.798; HHYHC, 14.34a; HSSSTP, 5.42a.

Shih Shao-ch'ing [II], son of Shih Hua-chih, *chiang-shih-lang* (9b): HSSSTP, 5.41b.

Shih T'ai-ch'ing, son of Shih Chi-chih [II], no record of official service: HSSSTP, 5.42b.

Shih Yu-ch'ing, son of Shih Chieh-chih, student at Directorate of Education: HSSSTP, 5.40b–41a.

Shih Yung-ch'ing, son of Shih Pen-chih, *ti-kung-lang* (9b), sheriff (9b): HSSSTP, 5.43a.

Branch C

Shih Chen-ch'ing [III], son of Shih Yi-chih [V], no record of official service: HSSSTP, 5.43b.

Shih Chen-ch'ing [IV], son of Shih Pao-chih, no record of official service: HSSSTP, 5.45a.

Shih Chen-ch'ing [V], son of Shih Hsiao-chih, *hsiu-chih-lang* (8b), sheriff (9b): HSSSTP, 5.63a–63b.

Shih Ch'i-ch'ing [IV], son of Shih Ni-chih, *ch'ao-feng tai-fu* (5a): HSSSTP, 5.51b.

Shih Chieh-ch'ing, son of Shih Sung-chih, *ch'ao-feng tai-fu* (5a), prefect, served as minor official under the Yüan: HHYHC, 14.39b; HSSSTP, 5.46a–46b.

Shih Ching-ch'ing (1228–45), son of Shih Yao-chih, *chiang-shih-lang* (9b), prominent critic of uncle Shih Sung-chih: SS, 414.12426–27; CCTC, 45.25b; HHYHC, 30.27b–29a; HSSSTP, 5.52a–52b.

Shih Ch'iu-ch'ing, son of Shih Yi-chih [II], *t'ung-chih-lang* (8a): HSSSTP, 5.56a.

Shih Fan-ch'ing, son of Shih K'en-chih, *t'ung-shih-lang* (8a), subprefect (8b): HSSSTP, 5.60a.

Shih Fang-ch'ing, son of Shih K'en-chih, *wen-lin-lang* (8b), fiscal inspector (9b), served as county sheriff under the Yüan: HHYHC, 30.45b; CCTC, 45.25b; SYHAPY, 87.3; HSSSTP, 5.62a–62b; *Sung-shih yi*, 34.15b.

Shih Fu-ch'ing, son of Shih Huan-chih, no record of official service: HSSSTP, 5.45b.

Shih Hsin-ch'ing [II], son of Shih Yu-chih, *ch'eng-shih-lang* (9a): HSSSTP, 5.64a.

Shih Hsü-ch'ing [II], son of Shih Chou-chih, *t'ung-shih-lang* (8a): HSSSTP, 5.64b.

Shih Hu-ch'ing [II], son of Shih K'uei-chih [II], *ch'eng-feng-lang* (8b), prefectural vice-administrator: HSSSTP, 5.49b.

Shih Huang-ch'ing, son of Shih Yu-chih [III], *hsiu-chih-lang* (8b): HSSSTP, 5.63b.

Shih Jui-ch'ing, son of Shih Ch'in-chih, no record of official service: HSSSTP, 5.43b–44a.

Shih Kuan-ch'ing, son of Shih Ch'üan-chih [III], *t'ung-chih-lang* (8a), subprefect: HSSSTP, 5.54b.

Shih Kuei-ch'ing, son of Shih Yao-chih, *hsüan-chiao-lang* (8b), subprefect (8b): HSSSTP, 5.52b.

Shih K'uei-ch'ing, son of Shih Yü-chih [III], no record of official service: HSSSTP, 5.63b–64a.

Shih Kung-ch'ing, son of Shih Yao-chih, *hsiu-chih-lang* (8b): HSSSTP, 552b–53a.

Shih Lai-ch'ing [II], son of Shih K'en-chih, *ju-lin-lang* (8b): HSSSTP, 5.60a.

Shih Li-ch'ing, son of Shih Sung-chih, *ch'eng-feng-lang* (7a): HHYHC, 14.39b; HSSSTP, 5.48a.

Shih Lien-ch'ing, son of Shih Yen-chih, *hsüan-chiao-lang* (8b), prefect: HSSSTP, 5.51a.

Shih Lin-ch'ing, son of Shih Yen-chih, *hsüan-chiao-lang* (8b), prefect: HSSSTP, 5.51a–51b.

Shih Meng-ch'ing (1247–1306), son of Shih K'en-chih, CS 1265, subprefectural registrar (9b): YYSMC, 6.29b; CCTC, 45.25b; SYHA, 87.1645–47; CJCSC, 28.25b–28b; KCSMHC 2.33a; HHYHC, 30.44b–45b; HSSSTP, 5.60b–61b; *Sung-shih yi*, 34.14a–15b; *Hsin yüan shih*, 235.6b–7a.

Shih P'ei-ch'ing, son of Shih Yi-chih [II], *hsiu-chih-lang* (8b), subprefect (8b): HSSSTP, 5.55b.

Shih Pen-ch'ing, son of Shih Ch'üan-chih [II], *ti-kung-lang*, (9b), subprefectural registrar (9b): HSSSTP, 5.54a.

Shih Pi-ch'ing, son of Shih Hsi-chih [II], no record of official service: HSSSTP, 5.45a.

Shih Pi-ch'ing [II], son of Shih Yen-chih, *hsüan-yi-lang* (8b): HSSSTP, 5.50a.

Shih Shan-ch'ing, son of Shih Ts'ao-chih, no record of official service: HSSSTP, 5.44b.

Shih Shang-ch'ing [II], son of Shih Shih-chih [II], *ti-kung-lang* (9b): HSSSTP, 5.56a.

Shih Shen-ch'ing, son of Shih Ch'üan-chih [II], *ch'ao-feng tai-fu* (5a): HSSSTP, 5.53b–54a.

Shih Shih-ch'ing [IV], son of Shih Mao-chih, *ch'eng-hsin-lang* (9b): HSSSTP, 5.45b.

Shih Shu-ch'ing, son of Shih Ch'üan-chih [II], *feng-yi-lang* (8a): HSSSTP, 5.54a–54b.

Shih Su-ch'ing, son of Shih K'en-chih, *hsiu-chih-lang* (8b): HSSSTP, 5.61b.

Shih T'an-ch'ing, son of Shih Piao-chih, no record of official service: HSSSTP, 5.46a.

Shih Tsao-ch'ing, son of Shih Sung-chih, *ch'eng-feng-lang* (8b): HSSSTP, 5.48b.

Shih Tsung-ch'ing, son of Shih Sheng-chih, *feng-yi-lang* (8a), sheriff (9b): HSSSTP, 5.55a.

Shih Tuan-ch'ing, son of Shih Shou-chih [II], *ch'ao-feng tai-fu* (5a): HSSSTP, 5.53a.

Shih Wan-ch'ing, son of Shih K'en-chih, *t'ung-shih-lang* (8a): HSSSTP, 5.63a.

Shih Yen-ch'ing [II], son of Shih Yi-chih [IV], no record of official service: HSSSTP, 5.43b.

Shih Yi-ch'ing [III], son of Shih Yü-chih [II], *ch'eng-chieh-lang* (9b): HSSSTP, 5.44a–44b.

Shih Yi-ch'ing [VI], son of Shih Pai-chih, *ch'ao-feng-lang* (7a), prefectural vice-administrator: HSSSTP, 5.56b.

Shih Yi-ch'ing [VII], son of Shih Wang-chih, *ts'ung-shih-lang* (8b), inspector for salt monopoly: YYWSC, 43.12a; HHYHC, 31.23b; HSSSTP, 5.55a.

Shih Yü-ch'ing [II], son of Shih Yen-chih, *ch'eng-wu-lang* (9b): HSSSTP, 5.50a.

Shih Yung-ch'ing [II], son of Shih Chou-chih, *ts'ung-shih-lang* (8b): HSSSTP, 5.64b.

Branch D

Shih Fu-ch'ing [II], son of Shih Hsün-chih [II], *ch'eng-hsin-lang* (9b): HSSSTP, 5.57a.

Shih Fu-ch'ing [III], son of Shih Yung-chih, no record of official service: HSSSTP, 5.58a.

Shih Hsiang-ch'ing, son of Shih Chü-chih [II], no record of official service: HSSSTP, 5.58a–58b.

Shih Hsien-ch'ing [II], son of Shih Wu-chih [II], no record of official service: HSSSTP, 5.57b.

Shih Huai-ch'ing, son of Shih Chü-chih [II], no record of official service: HSSSTP, 5.58a.

Shih Kao-ch'ing, son of Shih Wu-chih [II], no record of official service: HSSSTP, 5.57a.

Shih Kuei-ch'ing [II], son of Shih Chü-chih [II], no record of official service: HSSSTP, 5.58a.

Shih Sheng-ch'ing, son of Shih Wu-chih [II], no record of official service: HSSSTP, 5.57a–57b.

Shih T'an-ch'ing [II], son of Shih Wu-chih [II], no record of official service: HSSSTP, 5.57b.

Shih Yen-ch'ing [III], son of Shih Yüan-chih, no record of official service: HSSSTP, 5.58b.

Branch E

Shih Hui-ch'ing [II], son of Shih Kai-chih, student at Directorate of Education: HSSSTP, 5.59a.

Shih Kuan-ch'ing [II], son of Shih Neng-chih, no record of offical service: HSSSTP, 5.59a.

Shih P'u-ch'ing, son of Shih Neng-chih, *ts'ung-shih-lang* (8b), subprefect (8b): HSSSTP, 5.59a–59b.

Shih Yüan-ch'ing, son of Shih Ching-chih, no record of official service: HSSSTP, 5.58b.

Shih Yün-ch'ing, son of Shih Ching-chih, no record of official service: HSSSTP, 5.58b.

Shih Yün-ch'ing [II], son of Shih Neng-chih, *chiang-shih-lang* (9b): HSSSTP, 5.59b.

GENERATION IX

Branch A

Shih Ang-sun, son of Shih Yeh-ch'ing, *hsiu-chih-lang* (8b), regional military advisor: HSSSTP, 5.26a.

Shih Ch'ang-po, son of Shih Hsi-ch'ing [II], *ti-kung-lang* (9b), sheriff: HSSSTP, 5.36b.

Shih Chang-sun, son of Shih Chü-ch'ing, minor Yüan official: HSSSTP, 5.29a.

Shih Ch'ang-sun, son of Shih Yeh-ch'ing, *chung-feng tai-fu* (5b): HSSSTP, 5.26a.

Shih Ch'en-po, son of Shih Min-ch'ing, no record of official service: HSSSTP, 5.32a.

Shih Chen-sun, son of Shih T'ang-ch'ing, *t'ung-shih-lang* (8a): HSSSTP, 5.21a–21b.

Shih Chen-sun [II], son of Shih Ch'ang-ch'ing, no record of official service: HSSSTP, 5.22a.

Shih Chen-sun [III], son of Shih Chi-ch'ing, *ch'eng-feng-lang* (8b): HSSSTP, 5.22b–23a.

Shih Chen-sun [IV], son of Shih Shih-ch'ing [III], no record of official service: HSSSTP, 5.40a.

Shih Ch'eng-po, son of Shih Hsü-ch'ing, no record of official service: HSSSTP, 5.31b.

Shih Ch'i-po, son of Shih Min-ch'ing, no record of official service: HSSSTP, 5.32a.

Shih Ch'i-po [II], son of Shih Chen-ch'ing, no record of official service: HSSSTP, 5.33a.

Shih Chi-sun, son of Shih Chao-ch'ing, prefect: HSSSTP, 5.21b–22a.

Shih Ch'i-sun, son of Shih Hsia-ch'ing, *ts'ung-shih-lang* (8b): HSSSTP, 5.15a.

Shih Ch'i-sun [II], son of Shih Yi-ch'ing, no record of official service: HSSSTP, 5.19b.

Shih Ch'i-sun [III], son of Shih Chia-ch'ing, no record of official service: HSSSTP, 5.24a.

Shih Ch'i-sun [IV], son of Shih P'eng-ch'ing, no record of official service: HSSSTP, 5.24b.

Shih Ch'i-sun [V], son of Shih Chü-ch'ing, minor Yüan official: HSSSTP, 5.29b–30a.

Shih Ch'i-sun [VI], son of Shih K'an-ch'ing, no record of official service: HSSSTP, 5.38a.

Shih Ch'iang-sun, son of Shih K'an-ch'ing, no record of official service: HSSSTP, 5.38a.

Shih Chien-sun, son of Shih Chou-ch'ing, no record of official service: HSSSTP, 5.21a.

Shih Chien-sun [II], son of Shih Chü-ch'ing [II], no record of official service: HSSSTP, 5.38a–38b.

Shih Ch'ien-po, son of Shih Li-ch'ing [II], no record of official service: HSSSTP, 5.37a.

Shih Chih-sun, son of Shih Shun-ch'ing [II], no record of official service, later migrated to Soochow area: HSSSTP, 5.35b.

Shih Chin-sun, son of Shih Chou-ch'ing, no record of official service: HSSSTP, 5.21a.

Shih Ching-sun, son of Shih Chou-ch'ing, minor Yüan official: HSSSTP, 5.20a.

Shih Chou-po, son of Shih Mao-ch'ing, held official rank: HSSSTP, 5.15b.

Shih Chu-sun, son of Shih Shih-ch'ing [II], no record of official service: HSSSTP, 5.37b.

Shih Chü-po, son of Shih Shih-ch'ing, no record of official service: HSSSTP, 5.32a.

Shih Chü-sun, son of Shih Shun-ch'ing, no record of official service: HSSSTP, 5.19b.

Shih Ch'üan-po, son of Shih Chün-ch'ing, no record of official service: HSSSTP, 5.35a.

Shih Chün-po, son of Shih Jen-ch'ing [II], no record of official service: HSSSTP, 5.37b.

Shih Chung-sun, son of Shih Hsiu-ch'ing, no record of official service: HSSSTP, 5.38b.

Shih Fang-po, son of Shih Min-ch'ing, no record of official service: HSSSTP, 5.31b–32a.

Shih Fang-sun, son of Shih Chü-ch'ing, no record of official service: HSSSTP, 5.28a.

Shih Feng-po, son of Shih Jen-ch'ing, no record of official service: HSSSTP, 5.34a.

Shih Fu-sun, son of Shih Han-ch'ing, military commissioner: HSSSTP, 5.15a–15b.

Shih Heng-sun, son of Shih Shih-ch'ing [III], no record of official service: HSSSTP, 5.39b.

Shih Ho-sun, son of Shih Ch'i-ch'ing, *hsiu-chih-lang*, (8b), subprefectural registrar (9b): HSSSTP, 5.16a; HHYHC, 31.30b; *Yi-pai-chai kao*, 34.2b–4a.

Shih Ho-sun [II], son of Shih Wu-ch'ing, no record of official service: HSSSTP, 5.39a.

Shih Hou-sun, son of Shih Chia-ch'ing, no record of official service: HSSSTP, 5.16b–17a.

Shih Hsi-po, son of Shih Chen-ch'ing, no record of official service: HSSSTP, 5.33b.

Shih Hsi-sun, son of Shih Ssu-ch'ing, *wen-lin-lang* (8b): HSSSTP, 5.14a–14b.

Shih Hsi-sun [II], son of Shih Teng-ch'ing, *ti-kung-lang* (9b): HSSSTP, 5.15b.

Shih Hsiang-po, son of Shih Man-ch'ing, *chiang-shih-lang* (9b): HSSSTP, 5.18b.

Shih Hsiang-po [II], son of Shih Chen-ch'ing, no record of official service: HSSSTP, 5.33a.

Shih Hsiao-sun, son of Shih Chü-ch'ing, no record of official service: HSSSTP, 5.29b.

Shih Hsien-sun, parentage uncertain, prefect, Sung martyr: *Chao-chung-lu*, 7a.

Shih Hsien-sun [II], son of Shih Yeh-ch'ing, no record of official service: HSSSTP, 5.26b.

Shih Hsien-sun [III], son of Shih Chin-ch'ing, prefectural examination candidate: HSSSTP, 5.36b.

Shih Hsien-sun [IV], son of Shih Sen-ch'ing, minor Yüan official: HSSSTP, 5.27b.

Shih Hsing-sun, son of Shih Chao-ch'ing, no record of official service: HSSSTP, 5.22a.

Shih Hsing-sun [II], son of Shih Wei-ch'ing, no record of official service: HSSSTP, 5.25b.

Shih Hsüan-sun, son of Shih Chü-ch'ing, regional instructor under the Yüan: HSSSTP, 5.28a–28b.

Shih Hsün-sun, son of Shih Chia-ch'ing, no record of official service: HSSSTP, 5.23b.

Shih Hsün-sun [II], son of Shih P'eng-ch'ing, no record of official service: HSSSTP, 5.24b.

Shih Hui-sun (1234–1306), son of Shih Hsien-ch'ing, *ch'eng-chih-lang* (8b), police inspector (9b): CJCSC, 30.24a–25a; HHYHC, 30.49a–49b; HSSSTP, 5.17a–17b.

Shih Hui-sun [II], son of Shih Chü-ch'ing, no record of official service: HSSSTP, 5.28b.

Shih Jao-po, son of Shih Man-ch'ing, no record of official service: HSSSTP, 5.18b.

Shih Jen-sun, son of Shih Wen-ch'ing, *wen-lin-lang* (8b): HSSSTP, 5.16a.

Shih Ju-sun, son of Shih Wen-ch'ing, *t'ung-chih-lang* (8a), staff supervisor (8b), migrated to Fukien: HSSSTP, 5.16a–16b.

Shih Jui-sun, son of Shih Nai-ch'ing, no record of official service: HSSSTP, 5.38a.

Shih Jung-sun, son of Shih Wu-ch'ing, no record of official service: HSSSTP, 5.39a.

Shih K'ai-sun, son of Shih Wei-ch'ing, no record of official service: HSSSTP, 5.25a.

Shih K'ai-sun [II], son of Shih Ch'un-ch'ing, no record of official service: HSSSTP, 5.27b.

Shih K'ai-sun [III], son of Shih Chia-ch'ing, no record of official service: HSSSTP, 5.23b–24a.

Shih K'ang-po, son of Shih Yüeh-ch'ing, *ch'ao-feng tai-fu* (5a), prefectural vice-administrator: HSSSTP, 5.16b–17a.

Shih Kang-sun, son of Shih Chou-ch'ing, no record of official service: HSSSTP, 5.20b.

Shih Kao-sun, son of Shih Sung-ch'ing, *hsiu-chih-lang* (8b): HSSSTP, 5.26b.

Shih Kuci-sun, son of Shih Wei-ch'ing [II], no record of official service: HSSSTP, 5.33a.

Shih Kuei-sun [II], son of Shih Ch'i-ch'ing [III], no record of official service: HSSSTP, 5.36a.

Shih K'uei-sun, son of Shih Chia-ch'ing, no record of official service: HSSSTP, 5.24a.

Shih Lan-sun, son of Shih Chih-ch'ing [II], no record of official service: HSSSTP, 5.35a.

Shih Liang-po, son of Shih Hsin-ch'ing, no record of official service: HSSSTP, 5.34a.

Shih Lien-po, son of Shih Li-ch'ing, no record of official service: HSSSTP, 5.32b.

Shih Lin-po, son of Shih Jen-ch'ing, no record of official service: HSSSTP, 5.33b.

Shih Liu-sun, son of Shih Wu-ch'ing, no record of official service, migrated to Ting-hai *hsien*: HSSSTP, 5.39b.

Shih Lun-sun, son of Shih Hsi-ch'ing, no record of official service: HSSSTP, 5.25b.

Shih Lung-po, son of Shih Jen-ch'ing, no record of official service: HSSSTP, 5.33b.

Shih Mien-sun, son of Shih Ch'un-ch'ing, *chiang-shih-lang* (9b): HSSSTP, 5.27a.

Shih Ming-po, son of Shih Shang-ch'ing, *hsiu-chih-lang* (8b): HSSSTP, 5.19a.

Shih Ming-sun, son of Shih Chü-ch'ing, no record of official service, fled to Ming-chou during Yüan: HSSSTP, 5.29a; HHYHC, 31.9a.

Shih Na-sun, son of Shih Chü-ch'ing, no record of official service, migrated to Yü-yao *hsien*: HSSSTP, 5.30a.

Shih P'ei-sun, son of Shih Chia-ch'ing, no record of official service: HSSSTP, 5.24a.

Shih Pin-po, son of Shih Chang-ch'ing, no record of official service: HSSSTP, 5.18a.

Shih P'ing-po, son of Shih Ssu-ch'ing [II], no record of official service: HSSSTP, 5.34a.

Shih Ping-sun, son of Shih Chia-ch'ing, no record of official service: HSSSTP, 5.23a–23b.

Shih Po-sun, son of Shih Chi-ch'ing [II], no record of official service: HSSSTP, 5.19a.

Shih Shan-po, son of Shih Ch'i-ch'ing [II], no record of official service: HSSSTP, 5.30b.

Shih Shen-sun, son of Shih Chou-ch'ing, no record of official service: HSSSTP, 5.20b.

Shih Sheng-po, son of Shih Ch'ang-ch'ing, no record of official service: HSSSTP, 5.17b.

Shih Sheng-po [II], son of Shih Chen-ch'ing, no record of official service: HSSSTP, 5.33b.

Shih Sheng-sun, son of Shih Ch'un-ch'ing, *hsiu-chih-lang* (8b), sheriff (9b): HSSSTP, 5.27a.

Shih Sheng-sun [II], son of Shih Sen-ch'ing, *ts'ung-cheng-lang* (8b), subprefectural registrar (8b): HSSSTP, 5.27b.

Shih Shih-sun, son of Shih Chü-ch'ing, no record of official service: HSSSTP, 5.29b.

Shih Shih-sun [II], son of Shih Chin-ch'ing, no record of official service: HSSSTP, 5.36b.

Shih Shou-sun, son of Shih Chou-ch'ing, no record of official service: HSSSTP, 5.20b.

Shih Shu-sun, son of Shih Yao-ch'ing, *chiang-shih-lang* (9b): HSSSTP, 5.19b.

Shih Shu-sun [II], son of Shih Ch'ang-ch'ing, no record of official service: HSSSTP, 5.22b.

Shih T'ai-po, son of Shih Chün-ch'ing, *ti-kung-lang* (9b): HSSSTP, 5.34b–35a.

Shih T'ang-sun, son of Shih Wei-ch'ing [III], no record of official service: HSSSTP, 5.38b.

Shih Te-sun, son of Shih Ch'ang-ch'ing, no record of official service: HSSSTP, 5.17b.

Shih Ti-sun, son of Shih Wei-ch'ing, no record of official service: HSSSTP, 5.25a.

Shih Ti-sun [II], son of Shih Sen-ch'ing, *chiang-shih-lang* (9b): HSSSTP, 5.28a.

Shih Tung-sun, son of Shih Chü-ch'ing, no record of official service: HSSSTP, 5.30a–30b.

Shih Tzu-sun, son of Shih Chin-ch'ing, no record of official service: HSSSTP, 5.37a.

Shih Tzu-sun [II], son of Shih Shih-ch'ing [II], no record of official service: HSSSTP, 5.39b.

Shih Wang-po, son of Shih Chih-ch'ing, no record of official service: HSSSTP, 5.31b.

Shih Wang-sun, son of Shih Chou-ch'ing, no record of official service: HSSSTP, 5.21a.

Shih Wei-sun, son of Shih Chou-ch'ing, regional instructor under Yüan: HSSSTP, 5.20a.

Shih Wei-sun [II], son of Shih Sung-ch'ing, *chiang-shih-lang* (9b): HSSSTP, 5.26b.

Shih Wen-sun, son of Shih Chü-ch'ing, no record of official service: HSSSTP, 5.28a.

Shih Wu-po, son of Shih Ya-ch'ing, *chiang-shih-lang* (9b): HSSSTP, 5.18a.

Shih Yao-sun, son of Shih Chü-ch'ing, no record of official service, Taoist monk: HSSSTP, 5.28b.

Shih Yeh-sun, son of Shih Chü-ch'ing, no record of official service: HSSSTP, 5.30b.

Shih Yen-po, son of Shih Yi-ch'ing [IV], *chiang-shih-lang* (9b), Yüan eremite: CCTC, 45.25b; HHYHC, 30.29a; HSSSTP, 5.52a–52b.

Shih Yen-sun, son of Shih Ya-ch'ing, *chiang-shih-lang* (9b): HSSSTP, 5.18a.

Shih Yi-sun [IV] (1298–1375), son of Shih Hsi-ch'ing, *ch'eng-shih-lang* (9a), Yüan eremite: HSSSTP, 5.25b; *Sung wen-hsien-kung ch'üan-chi*, 23.11a–12a.

Shih Yin-sun, son of Shih P'eng-ch'ing, no record of official service: HSSSTP, 5.25a.

Shih Ying-po, son of Shih Chen-ch'ing, *chiang-shih-lang* (9b): HSSSTP, 5.35b–36a.

Shih Ying-sun, son of Shih Yi-ch'ing [II], no record of official service: HSSSTP, 5.21b.

Shih Ying-sun [II], son of Shih P'eng-ch'ing, no record of official service: HSSSTP, 5.24b.

Shih Ying-sun [III], son of Shih Chü-ch'ing, no record of official service, migrated to Yü-yao *hsien*: HSSSTP, 5.29a–29b.

Shih Yu-sun, son of Shih Hsi-ch'ing, no record of official service: HSSSTP, 5.25b.

Shih Yü-sun, son of Shih Shun-ch'ing, no record of official service: HSSSTP, 5.20a.

Shih Yü-sun [II], son of Shih Ch'ang-ch'ing, no record of official service: HSSSTP, 5.22a–22b.

Shih Yü-sun [III], son of Shih P'eng-ch'ing, no record of official service: HSSSTP, 5.24b–25a.

Shih Yü-sun [IV], son of Shih Ch'un-ch'ing, no record of official service: HSSSTP, 5.27a.

Shih Yü-sun [V], son of Shih Shih-ch'ing [III], no record of official service: HSSSTP, 5.39b–40a.

Shih Yü-sun [VII], son of Shih Ch'ang-ch'ing, migrated to Chen-chiang: HSSSTP, 5.22b.

Shih Yüeh-po, son of Shih Jih-ch'ing, no record of official service: HSSSTP, 5.17a.
Shih Yüeh-sun, son of Shih Jen-ch'ing [II], no record of official service: HSSSTP, 5.37b.
Shih Yung-sun, son of Shih Hsiu-ch'ing, no record of official service: HSSSTP, 5.38b.

Branch B

Shih Chi-sun [II], son of Shih Hu-ch'ing, no record of official service: HSSSTP, 5.41a.
Shih Ch'ien-po [II], son of Shih Yu-ch'ing, no record of official service: HSSSTP, 5.40b.
Shih Ch'ou-po, son of Shih T'ai-ch'ing, prefectural examination candidate: HSSSTP, 5.42b–43a.
Shih Fu-po, grandson of Shih Lin-chih, no record of official service: HSSSTP, 5.40b.
Shih Huan-po, son of Shih Liang-ch'ing, no record of official service: HSSSTP, 5.42a–42b.
Shih Hui-po, son of Shih Shih-ch'ing [IV], no record of official service: HSSSTP, 5.45b.
Shih Kuan-po, son of Shih Yung-ch'ing, no record of official service: HSSSTP, 5.43a.
Shih Kuei-po, grandson of Shih Chieh-chih [II], no record of official service: HSSSTP, 5.43a.
Shih K'uei-po, son of Shih Liang-ch'ing, no record of official service: HSSSTP, 5.42a.
Shih Pin-sun, son of Shih Chang-ch'ing, no record of official service: HSSSTP, 5.40b.
Shih Sui-sun, son of Shih Lai-ch'ing, no record of official service: HSSSTP, 5.41a–41b.
Shih T'ung-sun, grandson of Shih Hsün-chih, no record of official service: HSSSTP, 5.42a.

Branch C

Shih Ai-po, son of Shih Shu-ch'ing, no record of official service: HSSSTP, 5.54a.
Shih Ch'ang-po [II], son of Shih Ching-ch'ing [II], no record of official service: HSSSTP, 5.53a.
Shih Chen-po, son of Shih Lien-ch'ing, no record of official service: HSSSTP, 5.51a.
Shih Cheng-sun, son of Shih Shang-ch'ing [II], no record of official service: HSSSTP, 5.56a.
Shih Chi-po, son of Shih Ch'i-ch'ing [IV], *chiang-shih-lang* (9b): HSSSTP, 5.51b–52a.
Shih Chi-sun [III], son of Fang-ch'ing, no record of official service: HSSSTP, 5.62b.
Shih Chi-sun [IV], son of Shih Chen-ch'ing [V], no record of official service: HSSSTP, 5.63a.
Shih Chieh-sun, son of Shih Ch'iu-ch'ing, no record of official service: HSSSTP, 5.56a.
Shih Chih-po, son of Shih Shih-ch'ing [IV], no record of official service: HSSSTP, 5.45b.
Shih Chih-sun [II], son of Shih P'ei-ch'ing, no record of official service: HSSSTP, 5.55b.
Shih Chih-sun [III], son of Shih Lai-ch'ing [II], no record of official service: HSSSTP, 5.60a.
Shih Chih-sun [IV], son of Shih Su-ch'ing, no record of official service: HSSSTP, 5.61b.
Shih Chin-po, son of Shih Hsien-ch'ing, no record of official service: HSSSTP, 5.44a.
Shih Chin-po [II], son of Shih Lin-ch'ing, no record of official service: HSSSTP, 5.51a–51b.
Shih Chin-sun [II], son of Shih Shang-ch'ing [II], no record of official service: HSSSTP, 5.56a.
Shih Chin-sun [III], son of Shih Chieh-ch'ing, no record of official service: HSSSTP, 5.47b.
Shih Ching-sun [II], son of Shih Chieh-ch'ing, no record of official service: HSSSTP, 5.47a.
Shih Ch'iu-sun, son of Shih Meng-ch'ing, no record of official service: HSSSTP, 5.60b–61a.
Shih Chiung-sun, son of Shih Hsing-ch'ing [II], CS 1324 (Yüan), ranked 7a (Yüan): KCSMHC, 2.27a; HHYHC, 30.15b; HSSSTP, 5.64a.
Shih Ch'ou-sun, son of Shih Chieh-ch'ing, *chiang-shih-lang* (9b): HSSSTP, 5.46b.
Shih Ch'ou-sun [II], son of Shih Shan-ch'ing, no record of official service: HSSSTP, 5.44b.
Shih Ch'üan-sun, son of Shih Chieh-ch'ing, no record of official service: HSSSTP, 5.47b.
Shih Chuang-sun, son of Shih Hsü-ch'ing [II], no record of official service: HSSSTP, 5.64a.

Shih Ch'ui-sun, son of Shih Meng-ch'ing, no record of official service: HSSSTP, 5.61a.

Shih Chün-po [II], son of Shih Tsao-ch'ing, no record of official service: HSSSTP, 5.49a.

Shih Chün-sun, son of Shih Wan-ch'ing, no record of official service: HSSSTP, 5.63a.

Shih Chung-po, son of Shih Tsao-ch'ing, no record of official service: HSSSTP, 5.49a.

Shih Fu-po [II], son of Shih Yü-ch'ing [II], *t'ung-chih-lang* (8a), regional instructor under the
    Yüan: HSSSTP, 5.50b.

Shih Fu-sun [II], son of Shih Chieh-ch'ing, no record of official service: HSSSTP, 5.47a.

Shih Ho-sun [III], son of Shih Lai-ch'ing [II], no record of official service: HSSSTP, 5.60a.

Shih Hsi-po [II], son of Shih Chen-ch'ing [III], no record of official service: HSSSTP,
    5.43b.

Shih Hsi-po [III], son of Shih Tsao-ch'ing, no record of official service: HSSSTP, 5.48b.

Shih Hsi-sun [III], son of Shih Fang-ch'ing, no record of official service: HSSSTP, 5.62b.

Shih Hsiang-po [III], son of Shih T'an-ch'ing, no record of official service: HSSSTP, 5.46a.

Shih Hsiang-sun, son of Shih Pi-ch'ing, no record of official service: HSSSTP, 5.45a.

Shih Hsien-po, son of Shih Lin-ch'ing, no record of official service: HSSSTP, 5.51b.

Shih Hsin-po, son of Shih Tsao-ch'ing, no record of official service: HSSSTP, 5.48b.

Shih Hsü-po, son of Shih Hu-ch'ing [II], no record of official service: HSSSTP, 5.49b.

Shih Hsü-po [II], son of Shih Lien-ch'ing, no record of official service: HSSSTP, 5.51a.

Shih Hsüeh-sun, son of Shih Huang-ch'ing, no record of official service: HSSSTP, 5.63b.

Shih Hsün-po, son of Shih Tuan-ch'ing, no record of official service: HSSSTP, 5.53a.

Shih Jen-sun [II], son of Shih Chieh-ch'ing, *ch'eng-feng-lang* (8b): HSSSTP, 5.46a.

Shih K'an-po, son of Shih Li-ch'ing, *ch'eng-shih-lang* (9a), county magistrate under the Yüan:
    HSSSTP, 5.48a–48b.

Shih K'ang-sun, son of Shih P'ei-ch'ing, no record of official service: HSSSTP, 5.55b.

Shih K'uei-po [II], son of Shih Yen-ch'ing [II], no record of official service: HSSSTP, 5.43b.

Shih K'uei-po [III], son of Shih Yi-ch'ing [VII], no record of official service: HSSSTP, 5.55a.

Shih K'uei-sun [II], son of Shih Fan-ch'ing, no record of official service: HSSSTP, 5.60a.

Shih K'uei-sun [III], son of Shih Meng-ch'ing, no record of official service: HSSSTP, 5.60b.

Shih Le-po, son of Shih Jui-ch'ing, no record of official service: HSSSTP, 5.44a.

Shih Lei-sun, son of Shih Wan-ch'ing, no record of official service: HSSSTP, 5.63a.

Shih Li-po, son of Shih Jui-ch'ing, no record of official service: HSSSTP, 5.43b–44a.

Shih Li-po [II], son of Shih Ching-ch'ing [II], no record of official service: HSSSTP, 5.53b.

Shih Li-sun, son of Shih K'uei-ch'ing, no record of official service: HSSSTP, 5.63b–64a.

Shih Lü-po, son of Shih Chen-ch'ing [IV], no record of official service: HSSSTP, 5.45a.

Shih Lun-po, son of Shih Ch'i-ch'ing [IV], no record of official service: HSSSTP, 5.51b.

Shih Lun-po [II], son of Shih Tsung-ch'ing [II], no record of official service: HSSSTP, 5.55a.

Shih Meng-po, son of Shih Shen-ch'ing, no record of official service: HSSSTP, 5.53b–54a.

Shih Mo-po, son of Shih Pen-ch'ing, no record of official service: HSSSTP, 5.54a.

Shih Mou-po, son of Shih Yü-ch'ing [II], *ch'eng-wu-lang* (9b): HSSSTP, 5.50b–51a.

Shih Ning-sun, son of Shih Shan-ch'ing, no record of official service: HSSSTP, 5.44b.

Shih Pao-sun, son of Shih Shan-ch'ing, no record of official service: HSSSTP, 5.44b.

Shih Pi-sun, son of Shih Meng-ch'ing, Yüan eremite: CJCSC, 28.28a; HSSSTP, 5.60b.

Shih Pi-sun [II], son of Shih Hsin-ch'ing [II], no record of official service: HSSSTP, 5.64a.

Shih Pien-sun, son of Shih P'ei-ch'ing, no record of official service: HSSSTP, 5.55b.

Shih Shen-po, son of Shih Tsao-ch'ing, no record of official service: HSSSTP, 5.49a.

Shih Shen-po [II], son of Shih Hung-ch'ing, no record of official service: HSSSTP, 5.52b–53a.

Shih Sheng-po [III], son of Shih Yü-ch'ing [II], no record of official service: HSSSTP, 5.50a–50b.

Shih Sheng-po [IV], son of Shih Ch'i-ch'ing [IV], *chiang-shih-lang* (9b): HSSSTP, 5.52a.

Shih Ssu-sun, son of Shih Chieh-ch'ing, *chiang-shih-lang* (9b): HSSSTP, 5.46b.

Shih Sui-po, son of Shih Yi-ch'ing [VII], Yüan eremite: YYWSC, 43.12a; HHYHC, 31.23b; HSSSTP, 5.55a–55b.

Shih Ta-po, son of Shih Hsien-ch'ing, no record of official service: HSSSTP, 5.44a.

Shih Tai-po, son of Shih Yi-ch'ing [VII], no record of official service: HSSSTP, 5.55a.

Shih T'ai-po [II], son of Shih Fu-ch'ing, no record of official service: HSSSTP, 5.45b.

Shih T'ai-sun, son of Shih Meng-ch'ing, no record of official service: HSSSTP, 5.61a.

Shih Tan-sun, son of Shih Chen-ch'ing [II], no record of official service: HSSSTP, 5.63a–63b.

Shih Tien-sun [II], son of Shih Fang-ch'ing, no record of official service: HSSSTP, 5.62a–62b.

Shih Ting-po, son of Shih Yi-ch'ing [VI], no record of official service: HSSSTP, 5.44a–44b.

Shih Ting-sun, son of Shih Pi-ch'ing, no record of official service: HSSSTP, 5.45a.

Shih Ts'ang-po, son of Shih Kuan-ch'ing, no record of official service: HSSSTP, 5.54b.

Shih Tse-sun, son of Shih Shang-ch'ing [II], no record of official service: HSSSTP, 5.56b.

Shih Tseng-po, son of Shih Ching-ch'ing [II], no record of official service: HSSSTP, 5.53b.

Shih Tso-po, son of Shih Tsao-ch'ing, no record of official service: HSSSTP, 5.48b.

Shih Tsung-po, adopted son of Shih Ching-ch'ing, *chiang-shih-lang* (9a), Yüan eremite: HSSSTP, 5.25b; *Sung wen-hsien-kung ch'üan-chi*, 23.11a–12a.

Shih T'u-sun, son of Shih Su-ch'ing, no record of official service: HSSSTP, 5.61b.

Shih Tz'u-sun, son of Shih Su-ch'ing, no record of official service: HSSSTP, 5.61b.

Shih Wu-sun, son of Shih Chieh-ch'ing, no record of official service: HSSSTP, 5.47b.

Shih Yang-sun, son of Shih P'ei-ch'ing, no record of official service: HSSSTP, 5.55b.

Shih Yen-sun [II], son of Shih Chieh-ch'ing, *chiang-shih-lang* (9b): HSSSTP, 5.46b.

Shih Yi-po, son of Shih Tsao-ch'ing, no record of official service: HSSSTP, 5.48b–49a.

Shih Yi-po [II], son of Shih Pi-ch'ing [II], no record of official service: HSSSTP, 5.50a.

Shih Yi-sun [II], son of Shih Chieh-ch'ing, no record of official service: HSSSTP, 5.47a.

Shih Yi-sun [III], son of Shih Chieh-ch'ing, no record of official service: HSSSTP, 5.47a–47b.

Shih Yin-sun [II], son of Shih Su-ch'ing, no record of official service: HSSSTP, 5.61b.

Shih Ying-po [II], son of Shih Ching-ch'ing [II], no record of official service: HSSSTP, 5.53b.

Shih Yu-po, son of Shih Tsao-ch'ing, no record of official service: HSSSTP, 5.49a.

Shih Yu-sun [II], son of Shih Chieh-ch'ing, no record of official service: HSSSTP, 5.47b–48a.

Shih Yü-sun [VI], son of Shih Chieh-ch'ing, no record of official service: HSSSTP, 5.48a.

Shih Yüan-sun, son of Shih Shang-ch'ing [II], no record of official service: HSSSTP, 5.56a.

Shih Yüan-sun [II], son of Shih Wan-ch'ing, no record of official service, migrated to Hang-chou: HSSSTP, 5.63a.

Shih Yün-po, son of Shih Kuei-ch'ing, no record of official service: HSSSTP, 5.52b.

Shih Yung-po, son of Shih Tuan-ch'ing, no record of official service: HSSSTP, 5.53a.

Branch D

Shih Chang-po, son of Shih Fu-ch'ing [III], no record of official service: HSSSTP, 5.58a.

Shih Ch'eng-po [II], son of Shih Yen-ch'ing [III], no record of official service: HSSSTP, 5.58b.

Shih Ch'in-po, son of Shih Kuei-ch'ing [II], no record of official service: HSSSTP, 5.58a.

Shih Ch'ing-po, son of Shih Hsien-ch'ing [II], no record of official service: HSSSTP, 5.57b.

Shih Ho-po, son of Shih Fu-ch'ing [II], no record of official service: HSSSTP, 5.57a.

Shih Jun-po, son of Shih Sheng-ch'ing, no record of official service: HSSSTP, 5.57a–57b.

Shih Meng-po [II], son of Shih Fu-ch'ing [II], no record of official service: HSSSTP, 5.57a.

Shih Wei-po, son of Shih Kao-ch'ing, no record of official service: HSSSTP, 5.57a.

Shih Yen-po [II], son of Shih Sheng-ch'ing, no record of official service: HSSSTP, 5.57b.

Shih Yu-po [II], son of Shih T'an-ch'ing, no record of official service: HSSSTP, 5.57b.

Branch E

Shih Ch'ao-po, son of Shih Hui-ch'ing [II], no record of official service: HSSSTP, 5.59a.

Shih Hsing-po, son of Shih Yün-ch'ing, no record of official service: HSSSTP, 5.58b.

Shih K'o-po, son of Shih Yün-ch'ing [II], no record of official service: HSSSTP, 5.59b.

Shih Lü-po [II], son of Shih Kuan-ch'ing [II], *chiang-shih-lang* (9b): HSSSTP, 5.59a.

Shih Tsai-po, son of Shih P'u-ch'ing, no record of official service: HSSSTP, 5.59a–59b.

GENERATION X

Branch A

Shih Kung-an, son of Shih Chen-sun, no record of official service: HSSSTP, 5.21a–5.21b.

Shih Kung-chang, son of Shih Hou-sun, no record of official service: HSSSTP, 5.23b.

Shih Kung-chang [II], son of Shih Ch'eng-po, no record of official service: HSSSTP, 5.31a.

Shih Kung-chen, son of Shih Ying-sun, no record of official service: HSSSTP, 5.24b.

Shih Kung-ch'eng, son of Shih Yüeh-po, no record of official service: HSSSTP, 5.17a.

Shih Kung-chi, son of Shih Ch'i-sun, no record of official service: HSSSTP, 5.15a.

Shih Kung-chi [II], son of Shih Hsing-sun, no record of official service: HSSSTP, 5.22a.

Shih Kung-chi [III], son of Shih Kao-sun, no record of official service: HSSSTP, 5.26b.

Shih Kung-chi [IV], son of Shih Fang-po, no record of official service: HSSSTP, 5.32a.

Shih Kung-ch'i, son of Shih Ho-sun, no record of official service: HSSSTP, 5.16a.

Shih Kung-ch'i [II], son of Shih Hsüan-sun, no record of official service: HSSSTP, 5.28b.

Shih Kung-ch'i [III], son of Shih Chang-sun, no record of official service: HSSSTP, 5.29a.

Shih Kung-chieh, son of Shih Ang-sun, no record of official service: HSSSTP, 5.26a.

Shih Kung-chieh [II], son of Shih Wang-po, no record of official service: HSSSTP, 5.31b.

Shih Kung-ch'ien, son of Shih Jung-sun, no record of official service: HSSSTP, 5.39a.

Shih Kung-chih, son of Shih Hui-sun, no record of official service: HSSSTP, 5.17b.

Shih Kung-chih [II], son of Shih Yen-sun, no record of official service: HSSSTP, 5.18a.

Shih Kung-chih [III], son of Shih Wei-sun, no record of official service: HSSSTP, 5.20b.

Shih Kung-chih [IV], son of Shih Tung-sun, no record of official service: HSSSTP, 5.30a.

Shih Kung-ch'ih, son of Shih Hsüan-sun, no record of official service: HSSSTP, 5.28b.

Shih Kung-chin, son of Shih Yen-po, no record of official service: HSSSTP, 5.31a.

Shih Kung-ch'in, son of Shih Po-sun, no record of official service: HSSSTP, 5.19a.

Shih Kung-ching, son of Shih Yi-sun [IV], Yüan eremite: HSSSTP, 5.25b; *Sung wen-hsien-kung ch'üan-chi*, 23.11b–12a.

Shih Kung-ching [II], son of Shih Yin-sun, no record of official service: HSSSTP, 5.25a.

Shih Kung-ch'ing, son of Shih Yin-sun, no record of official service: HSSSTP, 5.25a.

Shih Kung-ch'ing [II], son of Shih Tung-sun, no record of official service: HSSSTP, 5.30a.

Shih Kung-ch'o, son of Shih Ch'ang-po, no record of official service: HSSSTP, 5.36b.

Shih Kung-chou, son of Shih Hui-sun, no record of official service: HSSSTP, 5.17b.

Shih Kung-ch'ou, son of Shih Ming-po, no record of official service: HSSSTP, 5.19a.

Shih Kung-chu, son of Shih Chü-po, no record of official service: HSSSTP, 5.32a.

Shih Kung-ch'u, son of Shih Chü-po, no record of official service: HSSSTP, 5.32b.

Shih Kung-chü, son of Shih Ch'i-sun [IV], no record of official service: HSSSTP, 5.24b.

Shih Kung-ch'üan, son of Shih Kao-sun, no record of official service: HSSSTP, 5.26b.

Shih Kung-chuang, son of Shih Tung-sun, no record of official service: HSSSTP, 5.30a.

Shih Kung-ch'un, son of Shih Sheng-po, no record of official service: HSSSTP, 5.17a.

Shih Kung-chung, son of Shih Yü-sun[III], no record of official service: HSSSTP, 5.27a.

Shih Kung-fang, son of Shih Wei-sun, no record of official service: HSSSTP, 5.20b.

Shih Kung-fu, son of Shih K'ang-po, no record of official service: HSSSTP, 5.18b.

Shih Kung fu [II], son of Shih Chü-sun, no record of official service: HSSSTP, 5.19b.

Shih Kung-fu [III], son of Shih K'uei-sun, no record of official service: HSSSTP, 5.24a.

Shih Kung-fu [IV], son of Shih Hsing-sun [II], no record of official service: HSSSTP, 5.25b.

Shih Kung-heng, son of Shih Po-sun [II], no record of official service: HSSSTP, 5.19a.

Shih Kung-hou, son of Shih Yüeh-po, no record of official service: HSSSTP, 5.17a.

Shih Kung-hsi, son of Shih Ho-sun, no record of official service: HSSSTP, 5.16a.

Shih Kung-hsi [II], son of Shih Yu-sun, no record of official service: HSSSTP, 5.25b–26a.

Shih Kung-hsi [III], son of Shih Ming-sun, no record of official service: HSSSTP, 5.29a.

Shih Kung-hsi [IV], son of Shih Ch'ien-po, no record of official service: HSSSTP, 5.37a.

Shih Kung-hsiang, son of Shih Ch'i-sun [V], no record of official service: HSSSTP, 5.30a.

Shih Kung-hsieh, son of Shih Shih-sun [II], no record of official service: HSSSTP, 5.36b.

Shih Kung-hsien, son of Shih Ying-sun [III], no record of official service: HSSSTP, 5.29b.

Shih Kung-hsien [II], son of Shih Ho-sun, no record of official service, migrated to Hsiang-shan *hsien*: HSSSTP, 5.39a.

Shih Kung-hsin, son of Shih P'ei-sun, no record of official service, HSSSTP, 5.24a.

Shih Kung-hsing, son of Shih Ch'i-sun, no record of official service: HSSSTP, 5.24b.

Shih Kung-hsiu, son of Shih Ho-sun, no record of official service: HSSSTP, 5.16a.

Shih Kung-hsü, son of Shih Po-sun, no record of official service: HSSSTP, 5.19a.

Shih Kung-hsüan, son of Shih Hui-sun, no record of official service: HSSSTP, 5.17b.

Shih Kung-hsüan [II], son of Shih Shih-sun, no record of official service: HSSSTP, 5.29b.

Shih Kung-hsüan [III], son of Shih Shih-sun, no record of official service: HSSSTP, 5.29b.

Shih Kung hsün, son of Shih Ch'i-sun [II], no record of official service: HSSSTP, 5.19b.

Shih Kung-hsün [II], son of Shih Yü-sun, no record of official service: HSSSTP, 5.20a.

Shih Kung-hsün [III], son of Shih Ch'i-sun [III], no record of official service: HSSSTP, 5.24a.

Shih Kung-hu, son of Shih Ch'i-sun [II], no record of official service: HSSSTP, 5.30a.

Shih Kung-hung, son of Shih Chü-po, no record of official service: HSSSTP, 5.32a.

Shih Kung-jang, son of Shih Chen-sun [IV], no record of official service: HSSSTP, 5.40a.

Shih Kung-jen, son of Shih Hsien-sun [III], no record of official service: HSSSTP, 5.36b.

Shih Kung-jo, son of Shih P'ing-po [II], no record of official service: HSSSTP, 5.34a.

Shih Kung-jui, son of Shih Na-sun, no record of official service: HSSSTP, 5.30a.

Shih Kung-jun, son of Shih Wang-po, no record of official service: HSSSTP, 5.31b.

Shih Kung-jung, son of Shih Yeh-sun, no record of official service: HSSSTP, 5.30b.

Shih Kung-kang, son of Shih Chün-po, no record of official service: HSSSTP, 5.37b.

Shih Kung-k'ang, son of Shih Yü-sun [III], no record of official service: HSSSTP, 5.25a.

Shih Kung-ko, son of Shih Jao-po, no record of official service: HSSSTP, 5.18b.

Shih Kung-k'uei, son of Shih Po-sun, no record of official service: HSSSTP, 5.19a.

Shih Kung-kung, son of Shih Yü-sun [III], no record of official service: HSSSTP, 5.25a.

Shih Kung-li, son of Shih K'ai-sun, no record of official service: HSSSTP, 5.24a.

Shih Kung-liang, son of Shih Ti-sun [II], no record of official service: HSSSTP, 5.28a.

Shih Kung-lien, son of Shih Ch'ang-sun, no record of official service: HSSSTP, 5.26a.

Shih Kung-lin, son of Shih Ho-sun, no record of official service: *Yi-pai-chai kao*, 34.2b–4a.

Shih Kung-lu, son of Shih Chi-sun, no record of official service: HSSSTP, 5.22a.

Shih Kung-lung, son of Shih Hsi-po, no record of official service: HSSSTP, 5.33b.

Shih Kung-mai, son of Shih Ching-sun, no record of official service: HSSSTP, 5.20a.

Shih Kung-man, son of Shih Wang-po, no record of official service: HSSSTP, 5.31b.

Shih Kung-mao, son of Shih Chü-sun, no record of official service: HSSSTP, 5.19b.

Shih Kung-mao [II], son of Shih Yü-sun [VII], no record of official service: HSSSTP, 5.22b.

Shih Kung-mei, son of Shih Pin-po, no record of official service: HSSSTP, 5.18a.

Shih Kung-ming, son of Shih Ying-sun, no record of official service: HSSSTP, 5.21b.

Shih Kung-mou, son of Shih Hsüan-sun, no record of official service: HSSSTP, 5.28b.

Shih Kung-mou [II], son of Shih Hui-sun [II], no record of official service: HSSSTP, 5.28b.

Shih Kung-mou [III], son of Shih Hsien-sun [III], no record of official service: HSSSTP, 5.36b.

Shih Kung-mu, son of Shih Chou-po, no record of official service: HSSSTP, 5.15b.

Shih Kung-nai, son of Shih Mien-sun, no record of official service: HSSSTP, 5.27a.

Shih Kung-nai [II], son of Shih Ying-sun [III], no record of official service: HSSSTP, 5.29b.

Shih Kung-ning, son of Shih Hsien-sun [II], no record of official service: HSSSTP, 5.27b.

Shih Kung-pao, son of Shih Chen-sun, no record of official service: HSSSTP, 5.21a–21b.

Shih Kung-p'ao, son of Shih Hui-sun [II], no record of official service: HSSSTP, 5.28b.

Shih Kung-pi, son of Shih Fu-sun, no record of official service: HSSSTP, 5.15b.

Shih Kung-sai, son of Shih Ying-sun, no record of official service: HSSSTP, 5.21b.

Shih Kung-shan, son of Shih Mien-sun, no record of official service: HSSSTP, 5.27a.

Shih Kung-shang, son of Shih Ming-sun, no record of official service: HSSSTP, 5.29a.

Shih Kung-shao, son of Shih Ch'üan-po, no record of official service: HSSSTP, 5.35a.

Shih Kung-shen, son of Shih Ch'i-sun [II], no record of official service: HSSSTP, 5.19b.

Shih Kung-shen [II], son of Shih Ch'i-po, no record of official service: HSSSTP, 5.32a.

Shih Kung-sheng, son of Shih Hsi-sun, no record of official service: HSSSTP, 5.14b.

Shih Kung-sheng [II], son of Shih Shan-po, no record of official service: HSSSTP, 5.30b.

Shih Kung-shih, son of Shih Ch'i-sun [II], no record of official service: HSSSTP, 5.19b.

Shih Kung-shih [II], son of Shih Liu-sun, no record of official service: HSSSTP, 5.39b.

Shih Kung-shou, son of Shih Shu-sun, no record of official service: HSSSTP, 5.19a.

Shih Kung-shou [II], son of Shih Wen-sun, no record of official service: HSSSTP, 5.28a.

Shih Kung-shu, son of Shih Ch'i-sun, no record of official service: HSSSTP, 5.15a.

Shih Kung-shu [II], son of Shih Ch'ang-sun, no record of official service: HSSSTP, 5.26a.

Shih Kung-sun, son of Shih Hsün-sun [II], no record of official service: HSSSTP, 5.24b.

Shih Kung-sung, son of Shih Chü-po, no record of official service: HSSSTP, 5.32a.

Shih Kung-ta, son of Shih Hsün-sun, no record of official service: HSSSTP, 5.23b.

Shih Kung-t'ai, son of Shih Ping-sun, no record of official service: HSSSTP, 5.23a.

Shih Kung-tan, son of Shih Hui-sun, no record of official service: HSSSTP, 5.17b.

Shih Kung-t'ang, son of Shih Wu-po, no record of official service: HSSSTP, 5.18a.

Shih Kung-te, son of Shih Chü-sun, no record of official service: HSSSTP, 5.19b.

Shih Kung-ti, son of Shih Ching-sun, no record of official service: HSSSTP, 5.20a.

Shih Kung-t'i, son of Shih Ch'i-sun [V], no record of official service: HSSSTP, 5.30a.

Shih Kung-ting, son of Shih Ying-sun, no record of official service: HSSSTP, 5.21b.

Shih Kung-ting [II], son of Shih Chu-sun, no record of official service: HSSSTP, 5.37b.

Shih Kung-t'ing [II], son of Shih Yen-po, no record of official service: HSSSTP, 5.31a.

Shih Kung-tsan, son of Shih Sheng-po, no record of official service: HSSSTP, 5.33b.

Shih Kung-ts'e, son of Shih Ch'i-sun [III], no record of official service: HSSSTP, 5.24a.

Shih Kung-tso, son of Shih Hsiang-po, no record of official service: HSSSTP, 5.18b.

Shih Kung-ts'ung, son of Shih Hsün-sun, no record of official service: HSSSTP, 5.23b.

Shih Kung-tzu, son of Shih Kao-sun, no record of official service: HSSSTP, 5.26b.

Shih Kung-wang, son of Shih Sheng-sun, no record of official service: HSSSTP, 5.27a.

Shih Kung-wei, son of Shih Yen-po, no record of official service: HSSSTP, 5.31a.

Shih Kung-wei [II], son of Shih Chih-sun, no record of official service: HSSSTP, 5.35b.

Shih Kung-yeh, son of Shih Sheng-po, no record of official service: HSSSTP, 5.33b.

Shih Kung-yeh [IV], son of Shih Lun-sun, no record of official service: HSSSTP, 5.25b.

Shih Kung-yen, son of Shih Hsing-sun, no record of official service: HSSSTP, 5.22a.

Shih Kung-yi, son of Shih Chen-sun [III], regional instructor under the Yüan: SMWHC, 5.45a; HSSSTP, 5.23a; *Shao-hsing fu-chih* (1586), 29.3b.

Shih Kung-yi [II], son of Shih Chen-sun [III], no record of official service: HSSSTP, 5.23a.

Shih Kung-yi [III], son of Shih Hou-sun, no record of official service: HSSSTP, 5.23b.

Shih Kung-yi [IV], son of Shih P'ei-sun, no record of official service: HSSSTP, 5.24a.

Shih Kung-yi [V], son of Shih Wei-sun, no record of official service: HSSSTP, 5.26b.

Shih Kung-yi [VI], son of Shih Ming-sun, no record of official service: HSSSTP, 5.29a.

Shih Kung-yi [VII], son of Shih Yeh-sun, no record of official service: HSSSTP, 5.30b.

Shih Kung-yi [VIII], son of Shih Ch'en-po, no record of official service: HSSSTP, 5.32a.

Shih Kung-yi [XII], son of Shih Chü-po, no record of official service: HSSSTP, 5.32a.

Shih Kung-yin, son of Shih Wen-sun, no record of official service: HSSSTP, 5.28a.

Shih Kung-ying, son of Shih Ho-sun, no record of official service: HSSSTP, 5.16a.

Shih Kung-ying [II], son of Shih Wang-po, no record of official service: HSSSTP, 5.31b.

Shih Kung-ying [III], son of Shih Wang-po, no record of official service: HSSSTP, 5.31b.

Shih Kung-yu, son of Shih Hsiang-po, no record of official service: HSSSTP, 5.18b.

Shih Kung-yu [II], son of Shih Chi-sun, no record of official service: HSSSTP, 5.22a.

Shih Kung-yu [III], son of Shih K'ai-sun, no record of official service: HSSSTP, 5.23b–24b.

Shih Kung-yü, son of Shih Chou-po, no record of official service: HSSSTP, 5.15b.

Shih Kung yü [II], son of Shih K'ang-po, no record of official service: HSSSTP, 5.17a.

Shih Kung-yü [III], son of Shih K'ai-sun, no record of official service: HSSSTP, 5.24a.

Shih Kung-yü [IV], son of Shih Fang-sun, no record of official service: HSSSTP, 5.29a.

Shih Kung-yü [VII], son of Shih Ch'i-sun [IV], no record of official service: HSSSTP, 5.24b.

Shih Kung-yüan, son of Shih Ch'i-sun [II], no record of official service: HSSSTP, 5.19b.

Shih Kung-yüeh, son of Shih Fang-po, no record of official service: HSSSTP, 5.31b.

Shih Kung-yüeh [II], son of Shih Lan-sun, no record of official service: HSSSTP, 5.35a.

Shih Kung-yung, son of Shih Liu-sun, no record of official service: HSSSTP, 5.39b.

Branch B

Shih Kung-chao, son of Shih K'uei-po, no record of official service: HSSSTP, 5.42a.
Shih Kung-ch'i [IV], son of Shih K'uei-po, no record of official service: HSSSTP, 5.42a.
Shih Kung-ch'i [V], son of Shih Huan-po, no record of official service: HSSSTP, 5.42a–42b.
Shih Kung-kuei, son of Shih Ch'ou-po, no record of official service: HSSSTP, 5.42b.
Shih Kung-tu, son of Shih Kuan-po, no record of official service: HSSSTP, 5.43a.
Shih Kung-tuan, son of Shih Ch'ou-po, no record of official service: HSSSTP, 5.43a.

Branch C

Shih Jen-sou, son of Shih Tan-sun, no record of official service: HSSSTP, 5.63b.
Shih Kung-ch'ai, son of Shih K'an-po, no record of official service: HSSSTP, 5.48a.
Shih Kung-chang [III], son of Shih Kuan-ch'ing, no record of official service: HSSSTP, 5.54b.
Shih Kung-chang [IV], son of Shih Pi-sun, no record of official service: HSSSTP, 5.60b.
Shih Kung-ch'eng [II], son of Shih Meng-po, no record of official service: HSSSTP, 5.53b.
Shih Kung-ch'eng [III], son of Shih Ho-sun [II], no record of official service: HSSSTP, 5.60b.
Shih Kung-chi [V], son of Shih Yen-sun [II], no record of official service: HSSSTP, 5.46b.
Shih Kung-chi [VI], son of Shih Yi-po [II], no record of official service: HSSSTP, 5.50a.
Shih Kung-chi [VII], son of Shih Sheng-po [III], no record of official service: HSSSTP, 5.50b.
Shih Kung-ch'i [VI], son of Shih Mo-po, no record of official service: HSSSTP, 5.54a.
Shih Kung-ch'i [VII], son of Shih Chieh-sun, no record of official service: HSSSTP, 5.56a.
Shih Kung-ch'i [VIII], son of Shih Chih-sun [III], no record of official service: HSSSTP, 5.60a.
Shih Kung-chiao, son of Shih Pi-sun, no record of official service: HSSSTP, 5.60b.
Shih Kung-ch'ien [II], son of Shih Chieh-sun, no record of official service: HSSSTP, 5.56a.
Shih Kung-chih [V], son of Shih Yi-sun [II], no record of official service: HSSSTP, 5.47a.
Shih Kung-chih [VI], son of Shih K'an-po, no record of official service: HSSSTP, 5.48b.
Shih Kung-ch'in [II], son of Shih K'an-po, no record of official service: HSSSTP, 5.48a.
Shih Kung-ching [III], son of Shih Mo-po, no record of official service: HSSSTP, 5.54a.
Shih Kung-ching [IV], son of Shih K'uei-po [III], no record of official service: HSSSTP, 5.55a.
Shih Kung-ch'u [II], son of Shih Tsung-po, no record of official service: HSSSTP, 5.52b.
Shih Kung-chü [II], son of Shih K'an-po, no record of official service: HSSSTP, 5.48b.
Shih Kung-chung [II], son of Shih Tse-sun, no record of official service: HSSSTP, 5.56b.
Shih Kung-chung [III], son of Shih Ta-po, no record of official service: HSSSTP, 5.44a.
Shih Kung-e, son of Shih Chih-sun [III], no record of official service: HSSSTP, 5.60a.
Shih Kung-fan, son of Shih Ting-po, no record of official service: HSSSTP, 5.44b.
Shih Kung-fang [II], son of Shih Mo-po, no record of official service: HSSSTP, 5.54a.
Shih Kung-fei, son of Shih K'an-po, no record of official service: HSSSTP, 5.48a.
Shih Kung fen, son of Shih Tsung-po, no record of official service: HSSSTP, 5.52b.
Shih Kung-fu [V], son of Shih Tsung-po, no record of official service: HSSSTP, 5.52b.
Shih Kung-hou [II], son of Shih Ssu-sun, no record of official service: HSSSTP, 5.46b.
Shih Kung-hsi [V], son of Shih Hsien-po, no record of official service: HSSSTP, 5.51b.
Shih Kung-hsüeh, son of Shih Ching-sun [II], no record of official service: HSSSTP, 5.47a.
Shih Kung-hsün [IV], son of Shih Hsi-sun [III], no record of official service: HSSSTP, 5.62b.
Shih Kung-hua, son of Shih K'an-po, no record of official service: HSSSTP, 5.48b.
Shih Kung-hui, son of Shih Ssu-sun, no record of official service: HSSSTP, 5.46b.

Shih Kung-kai, son of Shih Yi-sun [II], no record of official service: HSSSTP, 5.47a.

Shih Kung-k'ai, son of Shih Mou-po, no record of official service: HSSSTP, 5.51a.

Shih Kung-kao, son of Shih Sheng-po [III], no record of official service: HSSSTP, 5.50b.

Shih Kung-kuei [II], son of Shih Fu-sun [II], no record of official service: HSSSTP, 5.47a.

Shih Kung-k'uei [II], son of Shih Ssu-sun, no record of official service: HSSSTP, 5.46b.

Shih Kung-k'uei [III], son of Shih Sheng-po [III], no record of official service: HSSSTP, 5.50a.

Shih Kung-lei, son of Shih Yü-sun [VI], no record of official service: HSSSTP, 5.48a.

Shih Kung-lin [II], son of Shih T'ai-sun, no record of official service: HSSSTP, 5.61a.

Shih Kung-lung [II], son of Shih Sheng-po [III], no record of official service: HSSSTP, 5.50b.

Shih Kung-meng, son of Shih Tse-sun, no record of official service: HSSSTP, 5.56b.

Shih Kung-min, son of Shih Lun-po [II], no record of official service: HSSSTP, 5.55a

Shih Kung-mo, son of Shih Chin-po [II], no record of official service: HSSSTP, 5.51b.

Shih Kung-mou [IV], son of Shih K'uei-sun, no record of official service: HSSSTP, 5.60b.

Shih Kung-nei, son of Shih Meng-po, no record of official service: HSSSTP, 5.53b.

Shih Kung-ni, son of Shih Meng-po, no record of official service: HSSSTP, 5.53b.

Shih Kung-pang, grandson of Shih Fang-ch'ing, no record of official service: HSSSTP, 5.61a.

Shih Kung-pao [II], son of Shih K'an-po, no record of official service: HSSSTP, 5.48b.

Shih Kung-piao, son of Shih Chi-po, no record of official service: HSSSTP, 5.52a.

Shih Kung-pin, son of Shih Hsü-po, no record of official service: HSSSTP, 5.49b.

Shih Kung-shan [II], son of Shih Chih-sun [III], no record of official service: HSSSTP, 5.60a.

Shih Kung-sheng [III], son of Shih Hsien-po, no record of official service: HSSSTP, 5.51b.

Shih Kung-shih [III], son of Shih Hsiang-po [III], no record of official service: HSSSTP, 5.46a.

Shih Kung-shu [III], son of Shih Yi-po [II], no record of official service: HSSSTP, 5.50a.

Shih Kung-shu [IV], son of Shih Hsien-po, no record of official service: HSSSTP, 5.51b.

Shih Kung-shu [V], son of Shih Meng-po, no record of official service: HSSSTP, 5.53b.

Shih Kung-sou, son of Shih Yi-po [II], no record of official service: HSSSTP, 5.50a.

Shih Kung-ssu, son of Shih K'an-po, no record of official service: HSSSTP, 5.48a.

Shih Kung-ssu [II], son of Shih Yün-po, no record of official service: HSSSTP, 5.52b.

Shih Kung-sui, grandson of Shih Chen-ch'ing [IV], no record of official service: HSSSTP, 5.45a.

Shih Kung-sui [II], son of Shih Fu-sun [II], no record of official service: HSSSTP, 5.47a.

Shih Kung-t'an, son of Shih Ch'ui-sun, no record of official service: HSSSTP, 5.61a.

Shih Kung-t'ao, son of Shih Chin-po [II], no record of official service: HSSSTP, 5.51b.

Shih Kung-ti [II], son of Shih Chen-po [II], no record of official service: HSSSTP, 5.51a.

Shih Kung-tien, son of Shih Chin-po [II], no record of official service: HSSSTP, 5.51a.

Shih Kung-t'ing (1302–48), son of Shih Sui-po, Yüan eremite: YYWSC, 43.11b–15b; HHYHC, 31.23b–24b; HSSSTP, 5.55a–55b; Hsin yüan shih, 238.3b; Che-chiang t'ung-chih, 192.14b.

Shih Kung-to, son of Shih Ta-po, no record of official service: HSSSTP, 5.44a.

Shih Kung-tsai [II], son of Shih Yü-sun [VI], no record of official service: HSSSTP, 5.48a.

Shih Kung-tsai [III], son of Shih Pi-sun, no record of official service: HSSSTP, 5.64a.

Shih Kung-tsou, grandson of Shih Fang-ch'ing, no record of official service: HSSSTP, 5.61a.

Shih Kung-tu [II], son of Shih Ho-sun [II], no record of official service: HSSSTP, 5.60b.

Shih Kung-yao, son of Shih Yu-sun [II], no record of official service: HSSSTP, 5.48a.

Shih Kung-yao [II], son of Shih K'an-po, no record of official service: HSSSTP, 5.48b.

Shih Kung-yeh [II], son of Shih Ssu-sun, no record of official service: HSSSTP, 5.46b.

Shih Kung-yeh [III], son of Shih Ch'iu-sun, no record of official service: HSSSTP, 5.61a.

Shih Kung-yen [II], son of Shih K'uei-sun, no record of official service: HSSSTP, 5.60a.

Shih Kung-yi [IX], son of Shih Tai-pai, no record of official service: HSSSTP, 5.55a.

Shih Kung-ying [IV], son of Shih Chi-sun [III], no record of official service: HSSSTP, 5.62b.

Shih Kung-yü [V], son of Shih Sheng-po [III], no record of official service: HSSSTP, 5.50a.

Branch D

Shih Kung-fu [VI], son of Shih Meng-po [II], no record of official service: HSSSTP, 5.57a.

Shih Kung-hsi [VI], son of Shih Meng-po [II], no record of official service: HSSSTP, 5.57a.

Shih Kung-hsia, son of Shih Wei-po, no record of official service: HSSSTP, 5.57a.

Shih Kung-hsing [II], son of Shih Ho-po, no record of official service: HSSSTP, 5.57a.

Shih Kung-yü [VI], son of Shih Wei-po, no record of official service: HSSSTP, 5.57a.

Branch E

Shih Kung-ch'u [III], son of Shih Ch'ao-po, no record of official service: HSSSTP, 5.59a.

Shih Kung-mo [II], son of Shih Tsai-po, no record of official service: HSSSTP, 5.59a–59b.

Shih Kung-pien, son of Shih Lü-po [II], no record of official service: HSSSTP, 5.59a.

Shih Kung-yi [X], son of Shih Lü-po [II], no record of official service: HSSSTP, 5.59a.

Shih Kung-yi [XI], son of Shih Lü-po [II], no record of official service: HSSSTP, 5.59a.

Shih Kung-yüeh [III], son of Shih K'o-po, no record of official service: HSSSTP, 5.59b.

GENERATION XI

Branch A

Shih Ch'un-tsu, parentage unknown, Yüan-Ming official: HTHSC, 64.15a–15b.

Shih Mao-tsu, grandson of Shih Ho-sun, son of Shih Kung-lin, a slave: HHYHC, 31.30b–31b; *Yi-pai-chai kao*, 34.2b–4a; *Che-chiang t'ung-chih*, 184.10b–11a.

Shih Ting-tsu, son of Shih Kung-ching, grandson of Shih Yi-sun [IV], midlevel official during early Ming; son Shih Sui held same rank: *Sung wei-hsien-kung ch'üan-chi*, 23.11b–12a.

Branch C

Shih Ching-tsu, son of Shih Kung-t'ing, Ming official, ranked 4a: HHYHC, 21.2b, 31.24a; YYWSC, 43.11a, 43.14b.

Shih Sheng-tsu, son of Shih Kung-t'ing, *ming-ching* degree-holder, low-level Ming official: HHYHC, 31.24a; YYWSC, 43.14a.

Abbreviations

Notes

INTRODUCTION

1 For more on this, see T'ung-tsu Ch'ü, *Han Social Structure*, ed. Jack Dull (Seattle: University of Washington Press, 1972), pp. 164–65; Pan Ku, *The History of the Former Han Dynasty*, trans. Homer H. Dubs (Baltimore: Waverly, 1935), 1:109, 122; idem, *Han shu* (Peking: Chung-hua, 1962), *ch.* 1b, pp. 58, 66; Ssu-ma Ch'ien, *Records of the Grand Historian*, trans. Burton Watson (New York: Columbia University Press, 1961), 1:111; idem, *Shih chi* (Peking: Chung-hua, 1959), *ch.* 8, pp. 380, 386; Ssu-ma Kuang, *Tzu-chih t'ung-chien* (Peking: Chung-hua, 1956), *ch.* 12, p. 383.

2 Ch'ü, *Han Social Structure*, pp. 165–67.

3 For more on the emergence of this new elite, see Yang Lien-sheng, "Tung-han ti hao-tsu," *Ch'ing-hua hsüeh-pao* 11, no. 4 (Oct. 1936), pp. 1007–31; Ch'ü, *Han Social Structure*, chap. 5.

4 Ch'ü, *Han Social Structure*, p. 202; Hans Bielenstein, "The Restoration of the Han Dynasty," *The Museum of Far Eastern Antiquities Bulletin*, no. 26 (1954).

5 Yang, "Tung-han ti hao-tsu," p. 1031. One prominent exception to this is the Wang house of T'ai-yüan, which reportedly owed its initial rise to prominence during the Later Han to bureaucratic service. See Moriya Mitsuo, *Riku-chō mombatsu no ichi kenkyū* (Tokyo: Tōyō Daigaku, 1951), p. 139.

6 T'ang Ch'ang-ju convincingly argues that the arbiter system was initially introduced by the Wei ruling house to make official recruitment based more upon personal qualifications than pedigree. To this extent, it was designed to curb the political influence of the hereditary families, a group to which the Wei founder Ts'ao Ts'ao did not belong. Unfortunately, hereditary families soon learned to manipulate the system to their own advantage. See T'ang Ch'ang-ju, *Wei chin nan-pei ch'ao shih lun-ts'ung* (Peking: San-lien, 1955), pp. 85–126.

7 Wang Yi-t'ung, *Wu-ch'ao men-ti* (Nanking: 1943), p. 109.

8 Ch'ü, *Han Social Structure*, pp. 207–9; David G. Johnson, *The Medieval Chinese Oligarchy* (Boulder, Colo.: Westview, 1977), p. 117; Moriya, *Riku-chō mombatsu*, pp. 35–37.

9   Johnson, *Medieval Chinese Oligarchy*, pp. 26–41; T'ang, *Wei-chin nan-pei ch'ao*, pp. 115, 122–23.

10 Yang Shu-fan, *Chung-kuo wen-kuan chih-tu shih* (Taipei: San-min, 1976), pp. 63–71, 191–222; Howard J. Wechsler, *The Cambridge History of China* 3 (Cambridge: Cambridge University Press, 1979), pt. 1, pp. 179, 212–15.

11 Howard J. Wechsler, Denis Twitchett, and Richard W. L. Guisso, *Cambridge History* 3, pt. 1, pp. 212–15, 274–77; Denis Twitchett, "The Composition of the T'ang Ruling Class: New Evidence from Tunhuang," in Arthur F. Wright and Denis Twitchett, eds., *Perspectives on the T'ang* (New Haven: Yale University Press, 1973), pp. 47–85 (esp. 64); Patricia B. Ebrey, *The Aristocratic Families of Early Imperial China: A Case Study of the Po-ling Ts'ui Family* (Cambridge: Cambridge University Press, 1978), pp. 29–33; Ch'en Yin-k'o, "T'ang-tai cheng-chih-shih shu-lun kao," in *Ch'en yin-k'o hsien-sheng ch'üan-chi* (repr., Taipei: Chiu-ssu, 1978), pp. 151–305 (esp. 151–200).

12 Twitchett, "Composition of the T'ang Ruling Class"; Wechsler and Twitchett, *Cambridge History* 3, pt. 1, pp. 212–13, 261, 382–83.

13 Mao Han-kuang has some interesting observations pertaining to this development. In his research on the T'ang court's selection of chief councillors, he has found that there was clearly a tendency to place progressively more emphasis upon an individual's credentials as a degree-holder; as a result the chief councillorship became increasingly the exclusive domain of degreeholders. Thus, in the first century of T'ang rule, only 12.6 percent of its chief councillors held the *chin-shih* degree. This increased to 33.3 percent during its second century and 82.2 percent during its third. Members of the great families who aspired for high office were consequently compelled to secure a degree, leaving them much more vulnerable to the whims of the court and the capriciousness of the examinations. See Mao Han-kuang, "T'ang-tai ta shih-tsu ti chin-shih ti," *(Kuo-li) Chung-yang yen-chiu-yüan, Ch'eng-li wu-shih chou-nien chi-nien lun-wen chi* (June 1977), pp. 593–614 (esp. p. 613).

14 Johnson, *Medieval Chinese Oligarchy*, pp. 45–46, 121–52; Twitchett, "Composition of the T'ang Ruling Class," p. 83; Edwin G. Pulleyblank, *The Background of the Rebellion of An Lu-shan* (London: Oxford University Press, 1955), app. 5.

15 Mao Han-kuang, "Chung-kuo chung-ku she-hui-shih lüeh-lun kao," *(Kuo-li) Chung-yang yen-chiu-yüan, Li-shih yü-yen yen-chiu-so chi-k'an* 47, pt. 3 (1976), pp. 341–431 (esp. 362); Ch'en Yin-k'o, "T'ang-tai cheng-chih-shih"; Twitchett, "Composition of the T'ang Ruling Class."

16 Johnson, *Medieval Chinese Oligarchy*; idem, "The Last Years of a Great Clan: The Li Family of Chao Chün in Late T'ang and Early Sung," *Harvard Journal of Asiatic Studies* 37, no. 1 (June 1977), pp. 5–102; Sun Kuo-tung, "T'ang-sung chih chi she-hui men-ti chih hsiao-jung," *Hsin-ya hsüeh-pao* 4, no. 1 (1959), pp. 211–304.

17 Ebrey, *Aristocratic Families*, pp. 112–15.

18 Johnson notes that over 62 percent of the chief councillors during the latter half of the T'ang were from hereditary families; this actually represented something of an increase over the first half of the dynasty. See Johnson, *Medieval Chinese Oligarchy*, p. 132.

19 Much has been written on the rise of regional commanders and the tension between them and the central government during the latter half of the T'ang. For some discus-

sion of this problem in English, see C. A. Peterson, "The Restoration Completed: Hsien-tsung and the Provinces," in Wright and Twitchett, eds., *Perspectives on the T'ang* (New Haven: Yale University Press, 1973), pp. 151–91; Michael T. Dalby, *Cambridge History* 3, pt. 1, pp. 611–35.

20 Nishikawa Masao, "Kahoku godai ōchō no bunshin kanryō," *Tōyō bunka kenkyūjo kiyō* 27, pt. 3 (March 1962), pp. 211–61.

21 Ibid., p. 226. Also see Wang Gungwu, *The Structure of Power in North China during the Five Dynasties* (Kuala Lumpur: University of Malaya Press, 1963); and Edmund H. Worthy, "The Founding of Sung China, 950–1000: Integrative Changes in Military and Political Institutions," Ph.D. diss., Princeton University, 1976.

22 Nishikawa notes that, by the middle of the Northern Sung, the civil service in North China had already been taken over by civilian officials. See "Bunshin kanryō," p. 216.

23 Johnson, *Medieval Chinese Oligarchy*, pp. 141–48; Johnson, "Last Years of a Great Clan," pp. 75–81; Aoyama Sadao, "The Newly-Risen Bureaucrats in Fukien at the Five-Dynasties–Sung Period, with Special Reference to Their Genealogies," *The Memoirs of the Toyo Bunka* 21 (1962), pp. 1–48.

24 For some discussion of this social substratum, see Twitchett, "Composition of the T'ang Ruling Class," pp. 56–57; Nishikawa, "Bunshin kanryō," p. 222.

25 Mao Han-kuang, "Wo-kuo chung-ku ta shih-tsu chih ko-an yen-chiu: Lang-ya wang-shih," *Li-shih yü-yen yen-chiu-so chi-k'an* 37, pt. 2 (1967), pp. 577–610 (esp. 607–9); Ebrey, *Aristocratic Families*, p. 171. It is important to note that this was not the case during the Former Han dynasty, when society appears to have been much more fluid. See Martin C. Wilbur, *Slavery in China during the Former Han Dynasty, 206 B.C.–A.D. 25* (Chicago: Field Museum of Natural History, 1943), pp. 41–46; Ch'ü, *Han Social Structure*, pp. 229–31.

26 Ebrey, *Aristocratic Families*, pp. 103–12; Mao, "Wo-kuo chung-ku ta shih-tsu," pp. 581–83.

27 Aoyama, "The Newly-Risen Bureaucrats"; Kinugawa Tsuyoshi, "Sōdai no meizoku; kanan roshi no baai," *Chūgoku kankei ronsetsu shiryo* 15, pt. 3a (1973), pp. 37–53.

28 Ping-ti Ho, *The Ladder of Success in Imperial China; Aspects of Social Mobility, 1368–1911* (New York: Columbia University Press, 1962), pp. 137–67; P'an Kuang-tan, *Ming-ch'ing liang-tai chia-hsing ti wang-tsu* (Shanghai: Shang-wu, 1947), pp. 94–96.

29 The Lü house of Honan was the only other to hold this distinction. See Kinugawa, "Sōdai no meizoku"; Chao Yi, *Nien-erh-shih cha-chi*, rev. ed. (Taipei: Ting-wen, 1978), p. 551.

30 Ebrey, *Aristocratic Families*; Mao, "T'ang-tai ta shih-tsu ti chin-shih-ti"; idem, "Wo-kuo chung-ku ta shih-tsu chih ko-an yen-chiu"; idem, "Liang-chin *nan-pei-ch'ao shih-tsu cheng-chih chih yen-chiu*," M.A. thesis, National Cheng-chih University, 1966; Ch'en Yi-yen, "Pei-sung t'ung-chih chieh-ts'eng she-hui liu-tung chih yen-chiu," M.A. thesis, National Cheng-chih University, 1971.

31 Official ranks are based upon those provided in: Chang Fu-jui, *Les Fonctionnaires des Song: Index des titres* (Paris: Ecole Pratique des Hautes Etudes, 1962) and WHTK, *ch.* 66–67.

32 I have used a Ch'ing dynasty genealogy for information on obscure members of the

Shih group, the *Hsiao-shan shih-shih tsung-p'u* (HSSSTP). Yet it is hardly the ideal source. Not only is it removed in time from the Sung, but was compiled by an alleged branch of the Ming-chou house which had long abandoned the ancestral home. Then again, the detail of this genealogy betrays a high level of documentation and suggests that the HSSSTP drew heavily upon reasonably reliable Ming-chou sources, sources apparently no longer extant. As with historical documents, information here on Shih women is dismally scant.

There has been some effort by Japanese scholars to address the affinal ties of Shih kinsmen based largely upon historical works, but information can be gathered for scarcely 5 percent of the entire Shih community. See Ihara Hiroshi, "Sōdai minshū ni okeru kanko no kon-in kankei," *Chūo daigaku daigakuin kenkyū nenpō* 1 (March 1972), pp. 157–68.

33 Aoyama, in "The Newly-Risen Bureaucrats," argues that the Sung bureaucratic elite became increasingly more entrenched during the eleventh century and suggests that the opportunities for social mobility gradually diminished toward the close of that century. While this may have been true to a limited degree, it is difficult to generalize that this occurred on an empirewide scale. As will be seen in the case of the Shih, opportunities for official recruitment during the late eleventh and early twelfth centuries could hardly have been better.

34 From the Han through the T'ang dynasties, probably the most accessible route to the civil service for the socially obscure was through military service. See Wilbur, *Slavery in China*, pp. 36–38; Ch'ü, *Han Social Structure*, pp. 83–84; Mao, "Liang-chin nan-pei-ch'ao," pp. 48–53; and Johnson, *Medieval Chinese Oligarchy*, p. 31. In contrast, Ch'en Yi-yen finds that less than 10 percent of the Northern Sung "ruling class" were of military background. See "Pei-sung t'ung-chih chieh-ts'eng," pp. 13–24.

35 Kinugawa's study of the Lü, "Sōdai no meizoku," is the first of its kind, but is regrettably brief and not much more than a summary of the development of the Lü house. The only known study of elite mobility during the Sung is a Master's thesis by Ch'en Yi-yen (see n. 30) which analyzes the data contained in the "Collected Biographies" section of *Sung shih* and, in a quantitative fashion, discusses the social composition of the Sung ruling class. The study unfortunately suffers from the failure of its author to draw upon other sources, but it remains useful as a general commentary on bureaucracy and society.

36 See chap. 1, n. 1.

1. The Setting

1 Undoubtedly the finest English-language study of the Sung bureaucracy is E. A. Kracke, Jr., *Civil Service in Early Sung China, 960–1067* (Cambridge, Mass.: Harvard University Press, 1953). For more on the topic of the Sung civil service and social mobility, see Kracke, "Family vs. Merit in Chinese Civil Service Examinations under the Empire," *Harvard Journal of Asiatic Studies* 10, no. 2 (Sept. 1947), pp. 103–23; Aoyama, "The Newly-Risen Bureaucrats"; Li Cheng-fu, *Sung-tai k'o-chü chih-tu chih yen-chiu* (Taipei: Cheng-chih University, 1963); Teng Ssu-yü, *Chung-kuo k'ao-shih chih-tu shih* (Taipei: Hsüeh-sheng, 1967), pp. 135–75; Yang Shu-fan, *Chung-kuo*

wen-kuan, pp. 294–408; idem, "Sung-tai kung-chü chih-tu," in *Sung-shih yen-chiu chi* 4 (Taipei: Chung-hua t'sung-shu, 1969), pp. 239–73.

2 Kracke translates *chin-shih* as "doctorate in letters," while Ping-ti Ho provides a literal translation of "advanced scholar" (Kracke, *Civil Service*, p. 61; Ho, *Ladder of Success*, p. 12). For discussion of the various competitive examinations, see Li, *Sung-tai k'o-chü chih-tu*, sec. 2; Teng, *Chung-kuo wen-kuan*, sec. 2, pt. 2; Yang, *Chung-kuo wen-kuan*, pp. 314–23.

3 Kracke, *Civil Service*, p. 65.

4 ss, *ch.* 156, pp. 3625–29.

5 Kracke, *Civil Service*, pp. 65–66; Yang, *Chung-kuo wen-kuan*, pp. 322–23.

6 I have dealt with *yin-pu* more extensively elsewhere; see "Political Success and the Growth of Kin Groups: The Shih of Ming-chou during the Sung," in P. Ebrey and J. Watson, eds., *Kinship Organization in Late Imperial China* (Berkeley: University of California Press, 1986). Also see Kracke, *Civil Service*, pp. 73–75; Umehara Kaoru, "Sōdai no onin seido," *Tōhō gakuhō* (Kyoto) 52, pp. 501–36; Yang, *Chung-kuo wen-kuan*, pp. 370–77.

7 Davis, "Political Success and the Growth of Kin Groups," esp. fn. 3.

8 ss, *ch.* 159, pp. 3724–35.

9 John W. Chaffee, "Education and Examinations in Sung Society (960–1279)," Ph.D. diss., Univ. of Chicago, 1979, p. 40.

10 ss, *ch.* 159; Chang Chin-chien, *Chung-kuo wen-kuan chih-tu shih* (Taipei: Hua-kang, 1977), p. 113.

11 Chang, *Chung-kuo wen-kuan*, pp. 166–69.

12 ss, *ch.* 159.

13 ss, *ch.* 158–59; Umehara Kaoru, "Sōdai sensen no hitokomo," *Tōyōshi kenkyū* 39, no. 4 (March 1981), pp. 79–114; Yang, *Chung-kuo wen-kuan*, pp. 370–77; idem, "Sung-tai kung-chü," p. 268; Chang, *Chung-kuo wen-kuan*, pp. 186–89; Jui Ho-cheng, "Lun sung t'ai-tsu chih ch'uang-yeh k'ai-kuo," in *Sung-shih yen-chiu chi* 5 (1970), pp. 460–61.

14 WHTK, *ch.* 34, p. 327.

15 This is what Kracke refers to as "recruitment through transfer" (*Civil Service*, pp. 72–73). Rather than a vehicle for entrenching the bureaucratic elite, Kracke considers it an important program designed to enhance the fluidity of the system, pointing to the fact that members of the sub-bureaucracy could use it to be promoted to the regular civil service. No doubt, there do exist some cases of this. On the other hand, the incidence of such occurrences was never very high, even during the early Sung. As will be shown in this study of the Shih, the process was not accessible until the house had already established itself as a member of the bureaucratic elite, whereupon it was used as a means of entrenchment.

16 Kracke, *Civil Service*, pp. 91–93; Chaffee, "Education and Examinations," p. 34.

17 Ho, *Ladder of Success*, chap. 1; Mao, "Liang-chin nan-pei-ch'ao," pp. 77–78.

18 Yang, *Chung-kuo wen-kuan*, pp. 329–35; Teng, *Chung-kuo k'ao-shih*, p. 148. It has been suggested that decree examinations offered essentially honorary degrees for a select few and highly talented individuals, many of whom already held regular degrees. See Chaffee, "Education and Examinations," chap. 5.

19   SSCW, *ch.* 14, pp. 12a–12b; HTC, *ch.* 90, p. 2303; Yang, *Chung-kuo wen-kuan*, pp. 326–27; Li, *Sung-tai k'o-chü chih-tu*, pp. 120–21.

20   Yang, *Chung-kuo wen-kuan*, p. 305.

21   Ibid., p. 328; Teng, *Chung-kuo k'ao-shih*, pp. 144–45; Chao T'ieh-han, "Sung-tai ti chou-hsüeh," in *Sung-shih yen-chiu chi* 2 (1964), pp. 343–62 (esp. 355–58); H. R. Williamson, *Wang An-shih; A Chinese statesman and educationalist of the Sung Dynasty* 2 (London: Probsthain, 1935), p. 322.

22   It is important to note that the Imperial University was divided into two parts, *Kuo-tzu chien* and *T'ai-hsüeh.* Entrance to the former was restricted to the sons and grandsons of officials with rank of seven or above, representing a lingering element of the more rigidly stratified T'ang period. For most of the Sung, it contained no more than two hundred students. The latter consisted principally of the offspring of officials with rank of seven or below, although some persons of nonofficial background were also permitted to enter. With full implementation of the "three-levels measure," the *T'ai-hsüeh* was completely altered. First, in addition to the offspring of bureaucrats, the school also came to admit graduates of the prefectural school. Second, it grew to many times its former size. Whereas it was probably quite small in the early Northern Sung, it later expanded to accommodate over three thousand students. This growth, coupled with the higher quality of its student body, eventually enabled it to over-shadow the *Kuo-tzu chien,* despite the latter's more elevated status. For more, see Wang Chien-ch'iu, "Sung-tai t'ai-hsüeh yü t'ai-hsüeh-sheng," M.A. thesis, Fu-jen University (Taipei), 1965; and SS, *ch.* 157, pp. 3657–72.

23   We know, for example, that at least one member of the Shih lineage had been so recommended during the Southern Sung. See HHYHC, *ch.* 30, p. 44b; YYWSC, *ch.* 43, p. 16a. Examination of *chin-shih* lists in local gazetteers also reveals that the practice continued throughout the Southern Sung. For examples, see *(Hsien-ch'un) Lin-an chih,* *ch.* 61; YYSMC, *ch.* 6.

24   Yoshinobu Shiba, "Ningpo and Its Hinterland," in G. William Skinner, ed., *The City in Late Imperial China* (Stanford: Stanford University Press, 1977), pp. 391–439; Shiba Yoshinobu, "Sōdai minshū no toshika to chiiki kaihatsu," *Machikaneyama ronsō,* no. 3 (Dec. 1969), pp. 127–48; Linda Walton-Vargo, "Education, Social Change, and Neo-Confucianism in Sung-Yüan China: Academies and the Local Elite in Ming Prefecture (Ningpo)," Ph.D. diss., University of Pennsylvania, 1978, chap. 1.

25   Additional information on the historical evolution of Ming-chou can be found in PCSMC, *ch.* 1; HHYHC, *ch.* 1. According to Shiba, it was immediately after being moved further inland from its previous location near the coast that Ming-chou was given prefectural status. Apparently, the T'ang court had big plans for the region, but most of them were economic and not political in character. See Shiba, "Ningpo and Its Hinterland," p. 392.

26   For more on this economic shift, see Yoshinobu Shiba, "Urbanization and the Devel-opment of Markets in the Lower Yangtze Valley," in John W. Haeger, ed., *Crisis and Prosperity in Sung China* (Tucson: University of Arizona Press, 1975), pp. 13–48.

27   Walton-Vargo, "Education, Social Change, and Neo-Confucianism," p. 37.

28   Ibid.; Shiba, "Sōdai minshū," pp. 139–40; *Chiu t'ang shu* (Peking: Chung-hua, 1975), *ch.* 41, pp. 1061–62.

29 PCSMC, *ch*. 5, pp. 1b–2b.

30 The above source places the population of Ming-chou during the reign of Sung T'ai-tsung (r. 975–97) at a mere 27,681 households, while giving a figure of 136,072 households for the T'ien-hsi period (1017–21). Under normal circumstances, it is impossible for a population to increase fourfold in just thirty or forty years. Although the 27,700 figure is given as the population of the entire prefecture, I suspect that it merely represents that for the prefectural seat of Yin *hsien*. This would put the entire prefectural population at about 45,000 to 50,000 households. Still, this does not alter the assumption here that the mid-T'ang and early Sung populations for Ming-chou were very similar.

Ultimately, there are many problems involved in comparing population figures for the two periods. It was common, for example, that prefectures grew in size from the T'ang to Sung and eventually came to include subprefectures that were previously a part of other administrative districts. So the Sung population may be larger, in part, because of changes in the size of the administrative unit. Indeed, Ming-chou is one case in point. Whereas it only included four prefectures in T'ang times, two more were added during the Sung. Without question, part of its population growth in the eleventh century can be explained by geographic expansion. For more on this topic, see Aoyama Sadao, "Zui-Tō-Sō san-dai ni okeru kosū no chiiki teki kōsatsu," *Rekishigaku kenkyū* 6, no. 5 (1936), pp. 411–46; and no. 6, pp. 529–54 (esp. 540).

31 Cf. n. 28.

32 This and subsequent information about the Jurchen invasion of Lin-an and Ming-chou is based upon accounts contained in SS, *ch*. 25–26; PCSMC, *ch*. 11, pp. 14b–21a; HHYHC, *ch*. 14, pp. 13b–22a; CYHNYL, *ch*. 31, pp. 1a–13a.

33 PCSMC, *ch*. 11, pp. 19b–20a.

34 A Jurchen invasion of Yang-chou a year earlier resulted in destruction of a similar magnitude. See SSCW, *ch*. 17, p. 3b.

35 A member of the Shih family, for example, is reported to have led some two thousand persons to safety in this way. No doubt, the heads of other prominent families organized similar rescue efforts. See SHHSC, *ch*. 22, pp. 18b–19a.

36 Fukuda Ritsuko, "Sōdai gishō shōkō, Minshū rōshi o chūshin to shite," *Chūgoku kankei ronsetsu shiryo*, no. 14, pt. 3b, pp. 188–206 (esp. 193).

37 cf. n. 28.

38 The flow of migrants from North China to the south continued almost without interruption during the first decade of the Southern Sung; the impact upon the lower Yangtze was considerable. One author indicates that, from 1102 to 1162, such migrations had contributed to a population increase for Liang-che circuit of nearly 30 percent. I suspect this estimate to be quite modest, with 30 percent representing the increase for the first ten years of the Southern Sung alone. See Chang Chia-chü, *Liang-sung ching-chi chung-hsin ti nan-yi* (Wuhan: Jen-min, 1957), pp. 41–66 (esp. 50).

39 Shiba, "Sōdai minshū," pp. 146–47.

40 *Yüan shih* (Peking: Chung-hua, 1976), *ch*. 62, p. 1496.

41 Court officials often referred to the area's strategic importance. One such example may be found in SSCW, *ch*. 18, pp. 24a–24b.

42 Some indication of this can be seen in the special relief given Ming-chou in the aftermath of the Jurchen invasion. See HHYHC, *ch.* 14, pp. 22a–23b.

43 *Hang-chou fu chih* (1784), *ch.* 44.

44 For more on the immigration of imperial clansmen to Ming-chou, see SS, *ch.* 413, p. 12400; WHTK, *ch.* 259, p. 2057.

45 PCSMC, *ch.* 2, pp. 3b–5b, and *ch.* 11, pp. 6a–14b; Walton-Vargo, "Education, Social Change, and Neo-Confucianism," pp. 108–20.

46 Ibid.; Yeh Hung-sa, "Lun sung-tai shu-yüan chih-tu chih ch'an-sheng chi ch'i ying-hsiang," in *Sung-shih yen-chiu chi* 9 (1977), pp. 417–73.

47 For more on the topic of prefectural schools in Sung China, see Walton-Vargo, "Education, Social Change, and Neo-Confucianism," pp. 58–61, 129–36; Chao T'ieh-han, "Sung-tai ti chou-hsüeh"; idem, "Sung-tai ti hsüeh-hsiao chiao-yü," *Hsüeh-shu chi-k'an* 3, no. 2 (Dec. 31, 1954), pp. 36–47; Lin Tzu-hsü, "Sung-tai ti-fang chiao-yü ti fa-chan," *Hua-kang hsüeh-pao* 2 (Dec. 1965), pp. 155–76; Liu Tzu-chien, "Lüeh-lun sung-tai ti-fang kuan-hsüeh ho ssu-hsüeh ti hsiao-chang," *(Kuo-li) Chung-yang yen-chiu-yüan, Li-shih yü-yen yen-chiu-so chi-k'an* 36, pt. 1 (1965), pp. 237–48; SHY: CJ, 2; WHTK, *ch.* 46.

48 In addition to ordering the establishment of local schools, the court also required that they be endowed with a minimum of 1,000 *mou* (approximately 150 acres) of arable land (SHY: CK, 2, 3b–5b). Meanwhile, the Sung government was also quite generous with its support of monasteries and private academies in the region. For more information on the endowment of private educational institutions, see PCSMC, *ch.* 13, pp. 16a–23a (esp. 16a–18a).

49 Walton-Vargo, "Education, Social Change, and Neo-Confucianism," pp. 58–61; Williamson, *Wang An-shih*, 1: 18–23.

50 For more on the backgrounds of Ming-chou's most famous lineages, see Walton-Vargo, "Education, Social Change, and Neo-Confucianism," chaps. 2, 3; Fukuda, "Sōdai gishō shōkō"; Chang Ch'i-yün, "Sung-tai ssu-ming chih hsüeh-feng," in *Sung-shih yen-chiu chi* 3 (1966), pp. 33–71.

51 PCSMC, *ch.* 2, pp. 3b–5b, and *ch.* 12, pp. 7b–9a; *(Ch'ien-tao) Ssu-ming t'u-ching, ch.* 9, pp. 8b–10a.

52 An inscription commemorating the rebuilding of the prefectural school and its acquisition of a new plot of land alludes to its impoverishment and implies that former property had been lost. See *Ssu-ming t'u-ching, ch.* 9, pp. 8b–10a.
   These arable lands generally represented small plots scattered throughout the countryside. Destruction of school records, which contained leases for the land as well as detailed information about their location, could easily prevent the school from ever relocating and recovering its property.

53 SYHA (*ch.* 6) persistently attempts to identify locally prominent intellectuals of Ming-chou during the eleventh century with major schools of thought. At best, such identifications were weak. One of the special characteristics of scholarly associations in the area (especially during this early period) was that kinship ties and personal friendships were at the core of intellectual identifications. For the vast majority, family instruction was the focus of educational training and friendships the source of intellectual stimulation. An allusion by Wang An-shih to this phenomenon is especially

interesting. See Wang An-shih, *Lin-ch'uan chi, ch.* 83, pp. 3b–5a. It was only after family members had reached a certain level of literary attainment that they turned to the local school and locally prominent teachers for further education. Once academies began to flourish during the Southern Sung, then we find that kinship-based associations came to be replaced by personal identifications with a particular academy or school of thought, but this was a rather late development.

54 Walton-Vargo, "Education, Social Change, and Neo-Confucianism," chap. 3.

55 For more on the early history of Neo-Confucianism, see Fung Yu-lan, *A History of Chinese Philosophy* 2, trans. Derk Bodde (Princeton, N.J.: Princeton University Press, 1952), chaps. 11–12.

56 Fung, *Chinese Philosophy*, chaps. 13–14.

57 Lu Chiu-yüan lived in Hsiang-shan for about five years during the latter half of the 1180s. For more, see SS, *ch.* 434, pp. 12879–82; SYHA, *ch.* 58, pp. 1066–68.

58 For more information about them and their activities, see SS, *ch.* 407, pp. 12289–92; SYHA, *ch.* 74. As will be discussed in chap. 3, a prominent member of the Shih community also had a close relationship with Lu Chiu-yüan and, like Yang Chien and Yüan Hsieh, may have played some role in drawing him to the area as well.

59 *Chin-shih* lists have been used by a variety of researchers in this way, including Ho, *Ladder of Success*; and Chung-li Chang, *The Chinese Gentry: Studies on Their Role in Nineteenth-Century Chinese Society* (Seattle: University of Washington Press, 1955).

60 Walton-Vargo, "Education, Social Change, and Neo-Confucianism" (p. 180) has a chart that simply lists the number of *chin-shih* from Ming-chou for the Southern Sung, but, unfortunately, it contains many errors.

61 For statistics on the geographic distribution of *chin-shih* during Ming and Ch'ing times, see Ho, *Ladder of Success*, pp. 226–37.

62 During the 1232 examination, for example, 48 of a total of 493 *chin-shih* were natives of Ming-chou. It may very well be that this highly unusual occurrence is related to power politics. At this particular time, two natives of Ming-chou, Shih Mi-yüan and Cheng Ch'ing-chih, were serving as chief councillor and assistant councillor, respectively. There is always the possibility that the examiners sought to ingratiate themselves with the powers that be by recommending an exceptionally large number of their fellow provincials for conferral of *chin-shih* degrees. (Although the government had devised a variety of methods to keep the identities of the examinees secret, it was not always successful.) On the other hand, if this were the case, then we should expect a sudden decline in Ming-chou's *chin-shih* output after Shih Mi-yüan's death in 1233 and Cheng Ch'ing-chih's dismissal in 1236, but this did not occur.

63 Ho places the Sung population in 1223 at 12,670,910 households. Even if we were to estimate Ming-chou's population to stand at about 200,000 households at that time, this nonetheless represents only 1.58 percent of the total population. See Ping-ti Ho, "An Estimate of the Total Population of Sung-Chin China," in Françoise Aubin, ed., *Études Song: In mémoriam Étienne Balazs* (Paris: Mouton, 1970), p. 48.

64 The most complete list of Ming-chou natives who went on to become high officials during the Sung is contained in HHYHC, *ch.* 14.

65 Wang Tz'u-weng is the only bureaucratic chief from the region who did not

hold a *chin-shih* degree.

66 Migration to the south was sizable during the early years of the Southern Sung, but was reduced to a virtual trickle after 1140, when peace agreements between the Sung and Chin made such migrations illegal. For more on the refugee problem, see chap. 3 of this book.

67 This was Han T'o-chou, who will be discussed in chap. 4.

68 While many Southern Sung emperors appointed only one chief councillor, some appointed two, with councillorship of the left representing an honorary post. For more on this development, see chap. 3, n. 14.

69 Two well-known Southern Sung chief councillors who reputedly wielded such influence were Shih Mi-yüan and Chia Ssu-tao, both of whom will be discussed in later chapters.

70 For *chin-shih* lists, see YYSMC, *ch.* 6. The principal reason why so many imperial clansmen held *chin-shih* degrees is that they were permitted to take a special examination through the Court of Imperial Family Affairs (*Tsung-cheng-ssu*) rather than be subjected to the rigors of the prefectural examinations. On the other hand, a *chin-shih* degree obtained through the ordinary process was still more valued and, no doubt, there were a good many clansmen who chose to take the ordinary route; the exact breakdown of regular and irregular degreeholders is uncertain. For more on this special examination, see Yang, *Chung-kuo wen-kuan*, p. 326.

71 Additional information on this Sung policy of denying imperial clansmen access to high office may be found in HTC, *ch.* 153, pp. 4094, 4112, and *ch.* 154, p. 4125.

72 For biographical information on the Lou, see Walton-Vargo, "Education, Social Change, and Neo-Confucianism," pp. 46–49; Fukuda, "Sōdai gishō"; SYHA, *ch.* 6, p. 145, and *ch.* 79, pp. 1489–91; PCSMC, *ch.* 8, pp. 9a–11b; YYSMC, *ch.* 5, pp. 7a–8b; SS, *ch.* 354, pp. 11163–64, and *ch.* 395, pp. 12045–48.

73 YYSMC, *ch.* 6.

74 Assertions by Walton-Vargo, "Education, Social Change, and Neo-Confucianism" (p. 46) that the Shih represent a "hereditary local clan" are untenable, but further discussion of this will be left for chap. 2.

2. DREDGING THE STREAM

1 Johnson, "Last Years of a Great Clan," pp. 55–56.

2 Shiba, for example, indicates that the economic and demographic development of Ming-chou continued unabated throughout this period of division. This was apparently the case for most of the lower Yangtze. See Shiba, "Ningpo and its Hinterland," pp. 391–96.

3 This and subsequent information on the early history of the Shih is based upon accounts in YYWSC, *ch.* 41, pp. 1a–4a; and HSSSTP, *ch.* 8, pp. 10a–10b. I have been unable to locate any genealogy for the Ming-chou Shih. A *Shih-shih chia-chuan* [Family History of the Shih] is mentioned in various sources as late as the nineteenth century and is clearly regarded by Ch'ing writers as *the* most authoritative genealogy, its compilation having been sponsored by descendants of the Shih house in Ming-chou. However, attempts to locate it have not been successful. Genealogies of other Shih kin groups in the lower Yangtze region which claim to be branches of the Ming-chou

house do exist in the United States. The most informative of these is the *Hsiao-shan shih-shih tsung-p'u*, a work of the late Ch'ing period available at Columbia University; however, such a source must be used with great care. In most cases, I have used this genealogy merely to supplement information contained in more reliable sources, such as contemporary gazetteers and collected writings.

A fifth-generation member of the kin group writing in the twelfth century, Shih Hao, similarly alleges that his family descended from the famous Li-yang house, although he fails to provide specific information about the nature of their link. See MFCYML, *ch.* 41, pp. 1a–10b.

4   Ou-yang Hsiu, *Chi ku-lu pa-wei*, *ch.* 6, pp. 9b, 16a, 17a, 17b.

5   YYWSC, *ch.* 41, p. 2a.

6   For more on this topic, see Maurice Freedman, *Chinese Lineage and Society: Fukien and Kuangtung* (London: Athlone, 1966), p. 37.

7   The only mention of him outside genealogies is in YYWSC, *ch.* 41, p. 2a.

8   HSSSTP, *ch.* 5, p. 11a–13b.

9   Biographical information on Shih Chien may be found in PCSMC, *ch.* 9, pp. 28a–29a; YYSMC, *ch.* 5, pp. 33a–34a; HHYHC, *ch.* 26, pp. 41b–42a; KKC, *ch.* 74, pp. 12a–14b, and *ch.* 93, p. 3a; CCTC, *ch.* 16, p. 11a, and *ch.* 18, p. 9a; Liu Tz'u-fu, *Ssu-ming jen-chien*, *ch.* 3, p. 2b; and HSSSTP, *ch.* 8, pp. 10b–12b.

10   KKC, *ch.* 93, p. 3a; and PCSMC, *ch.* 9, p. 28a, respectively.

11   KKC, *ch.* 74, pp. 12a–14b. Although the colophon is itself undated, mention of the offices currently held by her great-great-grandsons reveals that it was written either in 1206 or 1207.

12   YYSMC, *ch.* 5, p. 33a.

13   The chief agents of law enforcement in Sung China were "stalwart men." Little is known about them other than that they were generally unsalaried and clearly of low social status. For more on their role in the village service system, see Brian E. McKnight, *Village and Bureaucracy in Southern Sung China* (Chicago: University of Chicago Press, 1971), chap. 3.

It was apparently commonplace that local administrators of justice, whether sheriffs or clerks, accepted bribes to flog personal enemies. Even more widespread was the practice of accepting bribes *not* to punish a convicted criminal. An interesting case that closely parallels this one may be found in James T. C. Liu, "The Sung Views on the Control of Government Clerks," *Journal of Economic and Social History of the Orient* (Leiden) 10, pt. 2/3 (1967), pp. 317–44 (esp. 324).

14   CCTC, *ch.* 16, p. 11a, and *ch.* 18, p. 9a; SYHA, *ch.* 6, p. 149.

15   CCTC, *ch.* 18, p. 9a.

16   Similar accounts can be found in HHYHC, *ch.* 26, pp. 41b–42a; HSSSTP, *ch.* 8, p. 11a.

17   Scattered throughout his collected writings (CCTC) are letters and essays that betray an active correspondence with Ch'ing-dynasty descendants of the Shih in Ming-chou. There is one such person, in fact, with whom Ch'üan Tsu-wang maintained a lively intellectual exchange spanning many years. His frequent discussion of Sung members of the Shih and numerous references to its genealogy leave little doubt that he knew much about the oral as well as written traditions of the kin group.

18   SKTY, pt. B, *ch.* 14, p. 1471.

19 KKC, *ch.* 74, pp. 12a–14b.

20 PCSMC, *ch.* 9, pp. 28a–29a; YYSMC, *ch.* 5, pp. 33a–34a.

21 PCSMC, *ch.* 9, p. 28b.

22 Ibid. Also see KKC, *ch.* 93, p. 3a.

23 YYSMC, *ch.* 9, p. 33b.

24 Cf. n. 13 above.

25 E. A. Kracke (*Civil Service*, pp. 72–73) has briefly discussed the relative ease with which clerks could rise from the subbureaucracy to the ranks of officials. The Sung government, in fact, instituted regular examinations for recruiting men from the subbureaucracy.

In contrast with Kracke, James T. C. Liu indicates that the prospects for social mobility among clerks were rather bleak, especially after the early years of the Sung dynasty. See Liu, "Sung Views on the Control of Government Clerks," pp. 321–23.

26 For biographical information on Shih Chao, see YYSMC, *ch.* 9, p. 33b; SYHA, *ch.* 6, p. 151; HHYHC, *ch.* 26, p. 42; HSSSTP, *ch.* 8, pp. 12b–14a.

27 YYSMC, *ch.* 9, p. 33b; SYHA, *ch.* 6, p. 151.

28 PCSMC, *ch.* 9, p. 29a; YYSMC, *ch.* 5, p. 33b.

29 Ibid.

30 Ting Ch'uan-ching, *Sung-jen yi-shih hui-pien* (repr., Taipei: Shang-wu, 1966), *ch.* 18, p. 898.

31 See chap. 1 of this book.

32 Whereas earlier accounts simply indicate that Shih Chao declined the appointment, sources of the Ch'ing dynasty offer a much more dramatic record of his declination. Two such sources state that, upon hearing of his selection, Shih Chao fled with his mother to a nearby mountain, apparently out of fear that he might be compelled to go to the capital against his will. Even a special messenger of the local government could not persuade him to leave his hideout and return home (SYHA, *ch.* 6, p. 151; HHYHC, *ch.* 26, p. 42b). Although no more than a tale, the fact that legends should develop around Shih Chao reveals much about his continued position of reverence in the community, even centuries after his death.

33 KKC, *ch.* 74, p. 13a.

34 Most accounts attribute only four sons to Shih Chao, but Lou Yüeh's colophon gives five, as do more recent genealogical sources. Apparently, Shih Kuang did not live to reach maturity. See KKC, *ch.* 74, p. 13b; HSSSTP, *ch.* 5, p. 13b.

35 See chap. 1 of this book.

36 There is no complete biography of Shih Shih-chung but, due to the subsequent prominence of his eldest son, there do exist many scattered references to him. See KKC, *ch.* 74, p. 13b, and *ch.* 93, p. 3a; HHYHC, *ch.* 26, p. 42b; HSSSTP, *ch.* 8, pp. 14a–14b.

37 For biographical information on Shih Ts'ai, see KKC, *ch.* 105, p. 1b; CCTC, *ch.* 45, pp. 20a–22b; HHYHC, *ch.* 14, pp. 27a–27b, and *ch.* 28, p. 42b.

38 SHHSC, *ch.* 22, p. 18b; HHYHC, *ch.* 26, pp. 49b–50a.

39 Nephew Shih Hao, for example, indicates that only a hundred, or perhaps several hundred, lives were spared through his efforts (MFCYML, *ch.* 43, p. 2a).

40 SHHSC, *ch.* 22, p. 18b; HHYHC, *ch.* 26, p. 42b.

41 HHYHC, *ch.* 26, p. 50a.

42 Also see *(Hsien-ch'un) Lin-an chih, ch.* 51, p. 9a.

43 The exact date of his appointment as subprefect of Yung-chia is uncertain but it was probably during the mid- to late 1130s; it was at this time that Li Kuang was serving as prefect of Wen-chou. See ss, *ch.* 363, p. 11341.

44 The practice of "sponsorship" is discussed at length by Kracke in *Civil Service* (chaps. 6–11). Basically, the court required, as a matter of policy, that an official solicit letters of recommendation *(chien-chü)*, or sponsorship, from executive- or administrative-level officials and submit these to the bureaucracy before he himself could be considered for an administrative assignment. Its objective was to eliminate the corrupt while advancing the diligent and morally upright official. With the exception of posts at the very top and very bottom of the civil service, most appointments required such recommendations.

That Shih Ts'ai received the recommendation of Li Kuang does not imply that the two shared any special relationship or that Shih Ts'ai was from a privileged or well-connected background. Rather, low-level officials needed recommendations as a matter of routine, while administrative-level officials were required to recommend a given number of persons during their tenure of office. This was not an action of special favor in most cases. Meanwhile, unlike the promotion examination, sponsorship did not necessarily help accelerate an individual's advancement in the civil service. Officials with recommendations in hand still had to wait until they had accumulated the requisite experience and seniority before they were considered for promotion. Thus, the effect of this policy upon bureaucratic fluidity was probably minimal.

45 SHY: HC, 20, 10a.

46 For more on Ch'in Kuei's role in the peace process, see ss, *ch.* 26–29, and *ch.* 473, pp. 13747–65; SSCW, *ch.* 20; *Sung-shih chi-shih pen-mo* (Taipei: Ting-wen, 1978), *ch.* 72.

47 The emperor stated on more than one occasion that the court's peace policy was his own, not merely that of his chief councillor; once peace had been fixed, he supported it unconditionally. See ss, *ch.* 31, p. 584; Ch'en Teng-yüan, "Ch'in Kuei p'ing," *Chin-ling hsüeh-pao* 1, no. 1 (May 1931), pp. 27–46 (esp. 40–41).

48 Not only did this result in the ultimate destruction of Li Kuang's career, but his son also came under attack years later for "personally compiling the empire's history" (ss, *ch.* 363, p. 11342).

49 CYHNYL, *ch.* 163, p. 7b.

50 Ibid., p. 18a.

51 Ibid., *ch.* 164, p. 2a.

52 SHY: SH, 44, 4b; CYHNYL, *ch.* 164, p. 10b.

53 CYHNYL, *ch.* 165, p. 1a.

54 SHY: SH, 7, 49a; SSCW, *ch.* 22, pp. 7a–7b; CYHNYL, *ch.* 165, p. 3b.

55 CYHNYL, *ch.* 165, p. 8a.

56 Translated by Kracke as "assistant-executive of the Secretariat-Chancellery," I have chosen to translate *ts'an-chih cheng-shih* as simply "assistant councillor." The post was second from the top in the bureaucracy after that of chief councillor. See Kracke, *Translation of Civil Service Titles*, p. 41.

Several sources indicate that Shih Ts'ai merely served as signatory official at the

Bureau of Military Affairs and not concurrent assistant councillor (PCSMC, *ch*. 9, pp. 3b, 29a; CYHNYL, *ch*. 165, p. 11a; SSCW, *ch*. 22, p. 8a; HTC, *ch*. 130, p. 3439). A letter of acceptance composed by a nephew of Shih Ts'ai on his behalf, however, clearly reveals that he was also named assistant councillor (MFCYML, *ch*. 14, pp. 4a–4b). Thus, there is little question that such an appointment was made, although it may have occurred sometime after his assignment to the military bureau. Meanwhile, both the individual who Shih Ts'ai replaced in 1153 and the man who replaced him in 1154 were assigned the two posts concurrently—a common practice in Southern Sung times. It is unlikely that the pattern was broken in the case of Shih Ts'ai.

57 CYHNYL, *ch*. 166, p. 10b; SSCW, *ch*. 22, p. 10a; HTC, *ch*. 130, p. 3444.

58 Ibid.

59 CCTC, *ch*. 45, pp. 20a–22b.

60 PCSMC, *ch*. 9, p. 3a.

61 Ch'üan Tsu-wang points to the case of Lin Ta-nai, a man who had fallen from favor with Ch'in Kuei and subsequently came under attack by Shih Ts'ai, as further proof of an alliance between Shih Ts'ai and Ch'in Kuei (CCTC, *ch*. 45, p. 21b).

62 PCSMC, *ch*. 9.

3. SETTING ROOTS IN THE CAPITAL

1 A variety of sources provide biographical information on Shih Hao. The earliest full-length biography was written immediately after his death in 1194 by Lou Yüeh, a noted scholar and fellow provincial. Being a tomb inscription commissioned by no less than the emperor himself and written by a reputable contemporary, it is highly reliable. See KKC, *ch*. 93, pp. 1a–19b.

   Another detailed and well-written biography is contained in PCSMC (*ch*. 9, pp. 2a–17b). Written in 1228 on the occasion of his son's twentieth year as chief councillor, there exists a greater possibility of biased reporting; however, as it is based largely upon the tomb inscription of Lou Yüeh, bias is minimal. Fortunately, there is an abundance of information on Shih Hao in a variety of other sources, including a recent Master's thesis. See Chiang Yi-pin, "Shih hao yen-chiu," M.A. thesis, Chung-kuo Wen-hua University (Taipei) 1980; SS, *ch*. 396, pp. 12065–69; YYSMC, *ch*. 5, pp. 1a–2b; CCTC, *ch*. 18, pp. 8b–10a, and *ch*. 28, pp. 14a–15a; HHYHC, *ch*. 27, pp. 29b–37b; HSSSTP, *ch*. 8, pp. 15a–17a.

2 PCSMC, *ch*. 9, p. 3a. Also see chap. 2 of this book.

3 SYHA (*ch*. 40, pp. 756–57) fails clearly to identify Shih Hao with any specific teacher or school of thought, although an attempt is made.

4 PCSMC, *ch*. 9, p. 3b; YYSMC, *ch*.6, p. 13a. The biography of Shih Hao in SS (*ch*. 396, p. 12065) is in error when it gives 1144 as the date of his *chin-shih* conferral.

5 Yü-yao is located slightly to the north and west of Yin *hsien*. Although common that new bureaucratic recruits should serve as subprefectural sheriffs, it was uncommon (especially in Northern Sung times) for officials to be assigned posts so near to home.

6 In 1148 Shih Hao reportedly served as a minor official with the salt administration in Ming-chou's Ch'ang-kuo subprefecture. His tenure there must have been quite brief,

for only one source bothers to mention it. See *(Ta-te) Ch'ang-kuo-chou t'u-chih, ch. 6,* pp. 7a–8b.

7   KKC, *ch.* 93, p. 3a; SYHA, *ch.* 40, pp. 756–57. Chang Chiu-ch'eng represents an important link between Northern Sung and Southern Sung adherents of Neo-Confucianism. He was a disciple of Yang Shih (1053–1135), who was himself a disciple of Ch'eng Hao. Through his identification with Chang Chiu-ch'eng, Shih Hao came to be linked to the transmission of the Ch'eng brothers. For more on Chang Chiu-ch'eng, see SYHA, *ch.* 40, pp. 741–50; SS, *ch.* 374, pp. 11577–79. Also see Fung Yu-lan, *History of Chinese Philosophy* 2, p. 533.

8   For more information on Wu Ping-hsin, see YYSMC, *ch.* 4, pp. 41b–42a; SYHAPY, *ch.* 44, pp. 17b–18a.

9   Although it was the recommendation of Wu Ping-hsin that directly preceded Shih Hao's appointment to the Imperial University, there were other prominent officials who also sponsored him. One of them was Chu Cho (d. 1163), a censor during the late 1150s who subsequently became chief councillor (SS, *ch.* 372, p. 11534). Li Hsin-ch'uan suggests that Shih Hao was able to secure such important posts in the capital because he formed alliances with unnamed "influentials" (CYHNYL, *ch.* 174, p. 10a).

10 SS, *ch.* 396, p. 12065; CYHNYL, *ch.* 182, p. 8a. Kao-tsung actually failed to sire any sons of his own, causing him to install two male members of the imperial family as adopted sons in 1160. For some time, however, he apparently had difficulty deciding which of the two to select as heir-apparent; this caused many court officials, including Shih Hao, considerable anxiety.

11 CYHNYL, *ch.* 185, p. 1b.

12 CYHNYL, *ch.* 200, p. 2b; SS, *ch.* 396, pp. 12065–66; SSCW, *ch.* 23, p. 37b.

13 PCSMC, *ch.* 9, p. 5b; SS, *ch.* 33, pp. 619–20.

14 The term *yu ch'eng-hsiang* is an abbreviated form of the chief councillor's formal title that, for most of the Southern Sung, was *shang-shu yu p'u-yeh t'ung chung-shu men-hsia p'ing-chang shih.* For the first two hundred years of Sung history, the chief councillor was commonly referred to as simply *tsai-hsiang,* but this was changed to *ch'eng-hsiang* during the dynasty's final one hundred years (the middle of Hsiao-tsung's reign) to reflect the increased importance attached to the post.

     Throughout the Northern Sung, it was uncommon for the head of the civilian bureaucracy concurrently to be entrusted with leadership of the military bureaucracy. Indeed, the Sung founders intentionally established the Bureau of Military Affairs (*Shu-mi-yüan*)—usually headed by civilian officials, but independent of the regular bureaucracy—to ensure that no single individual was in control of both political and military machines. As the Sung became plagued with progressively more serious border threats, this system proved not only cumbersome, but militarily disabling. The persistent Hsi-hsia menace to the west during the last three decades of the eleventh century prompted the government to revive the Ministry of War (*Ping-pu*), which for most of the early Northern Sung was virtually powerless. Whereas the Bureau of Military Affairs was directly responsible to the throne, the Ministry of War reported to the chief councillor's office. This was but the first step in the expansion of the chief councillor's authority. Even though the military bureau was revived during the Southern Sung, the chief councillor retained his influence over the military, for it then became common practice to delegate to him concurrent authority over the Bureau of Military Affairs.

The political influence of Southern Sung bureaucratic chiefs was also expanded by their monopoly over the chief councillor's seat. For most of the Northern Sung, there were at least two councillors, that of the "left" and the "right," who shared responsibility for administration of the bureaucracy. The two posts were preserved during the Southern Sung, but councillorship of the left was frequently unfilled; on those occasions when it was filled, the position tended to be little more than honorary. In this way, the councillor of the right came completely to control the bureaucratic machine.

It was during the reign of Hsiao-tsung that the term *ch'eng-hsiang* developed currency. This occurred in the aftermath of bureaucratic reforms in 1172 that led to elimination of the chief administrative spots in the "three ministries" *(san-sheng)* and the delegation of their former responsibilities to the chief councillor. At least in theory, this served further to enhance his authority. For more information on these various bureaucratic changes and their significance, see Chou Tao-chi, "Sung-tai tsai-hsiang ming-ch'eng yü ch'i shih-ch'üan chih yen-chiu," in *Sung-shih yen-chiu chi* 3 (1966), pp. 245−63; Lin T'ien-wei, "Sung-tai ch'üan-hsiang hsing-ch'eng chih fen-hsi," in *Sung-shih yen-chiu chi* 8 (1976), pp. 141−70; ss, *ch.* 161; WHTK, *ch.* 49.

15 KKC, *ch.* 93, p. 3b.

16 ss, *ch.* 35, p. 692.

17 Wang Teh-yi "Sung hsiao-tsung chi ch'i shih-tai," in *Sung-shih yen-chiu chi* 10 (1978), pp. 245−302.

18 The extent of Hsiao-tsung's filial devotion was most apparent after the death of Kao-tsung in 1187. Reportedly so overcome with grief that he became totally incapacitated, he refused to hold court with any regularity and delegated most of his duties to the heir-apparent. It was undoubtedly due to his extreme response to the loss of his father that he was posthumously named "the filial emperor." See ss, *ch.* 35, pp. 687−91.

19 For details on this and other peace agreements, see Herbert Franke, "Treaties between Sung and Chin," in Francoise Aubin, ed., *Études Song; in mémórian Étienne Balazs,* pp. 55−82.

20 For more on the prince and his war, see Tao Jing-shen, *The Jurchen in Twelfth-Century China: A Study of Sinicization* (Seattle: University of Washington Press, 1976), pp. 68−70; idem, *Chin hai-ling-ti ti fa sung yü ts'ai-shih chan-yi ti k'ao-shih* (Taipei: National Taiwan University, 1963); *Chin shih, ch.* 5; *Sung-shih chi-shih pen-mo, ch.* 73−74.

21 *Chin shih, ch.* 87, p. 1937.

22 CYHNYL, *ch.* 200, p. 15b; SSCW, *ch.* 23, pp. 42b−43a; HTC, *ch.* 137, pp. 3651−52.

23 *Chin shih, ch.* 6, p. 130; HTC, *ch.* 137, p. 3654.

24 For more on Ch'in Kuei's policy of "leaving the south to southerners and the north to northerners," see ss, *ch.* 473, p. 13751; *Sung-shih chi-shih pen-mo, ch.* 72, p. 737.

25 Shih Hao is the only member of the Ming-chou kin group of Sung times whose collected writings are extant. For more on his position on this issue, see MFCYML, *ch.* 7, pp. 4a−6a, 13a−14b, *ch.* 8, pp. 2b−3b; *ch.* 36, pp. 2a−3b. Also see PCSMC, *ch.* 9,

pp. 3a–17b; ss, *ch.* 393, pp. 12065–69; sscw, *ch.* 23, p. 42b; htc, *ch.* 138, pp. 3664–66.

26 mfcyml, *ch.* 8, p. 3b

27 Ibid., *ch.* 7, pp. 4a–6a.

28 Ibid., *ch.* 36, p. 2b.

29 Ibid., *ch.* 7, pp. 4a–6a.

30 His distrust of, even disdain for, the military became more apparent some fifteen years later. See pp. 69–70.

31 *Kuei-cheng-jen* or *hui-cheng-jen* were refugees from the north who flowed into the south at a relatively steady pace for much of the Southern Sung. Originally Lin-an welcomed these compatriots, providing them with special monetary awards and social privileges. As their numbers grew, however, their welcome wore thin. Besides adding to population pressures (which were especailly acute in the Liang-che region), they were also a drain on government resources. Throughout the Southern Sung, debate raged on as to whether the court should accept or reject them. For more on this topic, see Huang K'uan-ch'ung, "Lüeh-lun nan-sung shih-tai ti kuei-cheng-jen," *Shih-huo yüeh-k'an* 7, no. 3 (June 1977), pp. 111–20; and vol. 7, no. 4 (July 1977), pp. 172–83.

32 Franke, "Treaties between Sung and Chin," pp. 78–79; cyhnyl, *ch.* 142, pp. 14a–14b.

33 mfcyml, *ch.* 7, p. 11a.

34 Ibid., pp. 12a–12b. Other Southern Sung officials held similar suspicions. See Huang K'uan-ch'ung, "Lüeh-lun nan-sung shih-tai ti kuei-cheng-jen," pt. 2, pp. 174–75; idem, "Wan-sung ch'ao-ch'en tui kuo-shih ti cheng-yi; Li-tsung shih-tai ti ho-chan, pien-fang, yü liu-min," M.A. thesis, National Taiwan University, 1974, pp. 134–48.

35 mfcyml, *ch.* 7, pp. 9a–9b; kkc, *ch.* 93, p. 26a, and *ch.* 94, p. 13a.

36 "Remittances" is apparently a reference to personal taxes collected by the Sung government that were commonly applied toward social relief programs. mfcyml, *ch.* 7, pp. 9a–9b.

37 Ibid., p. 12b.

38 See his biography in ss, *ch.* 361, pp. 11297–311.

39 Ibid., p. 11307.

40 htc, *ch.* 137, p. 3642.

41 ss, *ch.* 361, p. 11307.

42 "Loyalist armies" should be distinguished from "loyalist refugees." The latter were merely migrants who individually fled south in search of a new home. The able-bodied among them might become military conscripts, but they were not necessarily soldiers by profession. Loyalist armies, on the other hand, were relatively large rebel bands that rose up against Jurchen rule in North China, proclaiming their loyalty to the Sung and seeking aid from it. Rather than migrate south, the vast majority remained in the north, menacing the government there. The Sung did not openly provide assistance to them during times of peace, for to do so would represent a violation of the terms of its treaty with the Jurchen. In war, however, aid from Lin-an was often quite generous. The antigovernment activities of such groups was certain to distract the enemy, thereby diminishing the effectiveness of its campaigns against the south. Meanwhile, the Sung did not have to worry about loyalist armies getting out of

control because they never operated within Sung territory. The Sung consequently had much to gain and little to lose by supporting them.

43   SS, *ch.* 361, p. 11309; HTC, *ch.* 138, pp. 3664–65; Li Yu-wu, *Ssu-ch'ao ming-ch'en yen-hsing lu,* in *Sung-shih tzu-liao ts'ui-pien,* pt. 2, *ch.* 3, pp. 7b, 10a ff.

44   HTC, *ch.* 138, pp. 3664–66.

45   KKC, *ch.* 93, p. 9b; PCSMC, *ch.* 9, pp. 12b–14b.

46   For Wang Shih-p'eng's biography, see SS, *ch.* 387, pp. 11882–87.

47   The entire text of the indictment by Wang Shih-p'eng is contained in Wang Shih-p'eng, *Mei-hsi wang hsien-sheng wen-chi, ch.* 3, pp. 2b–6a. Also see Tung Meng-lan, *Nan-sung wen-lu, ch.* 5, pp. 14b–16b; HTC, *ch.* 138, p. 3666.

48   A native of modern Szechwan whose family had a long history of military service, Wu Lin was himself a highly accomplished general. He had fought long and hard against the Jurchen and Hsi-hsia for control over an area where their two borders converged with that of the Sung, focusing on the southern part of present-day Kansu.
     In early 1162, he captured for the Sung a strategic area located inside the Jurchen empire, Te-shun commandary, and expanded his operations in the region. Although the court did not openly support the venture, it nonetheless refused to discourage him. Not until the end of 1162 did it decide, for reasons that are not certain, to order his recall. In the process of withdrawing, Wu Lin lost some 33,000 troops and abandoned the thirteen prefectures plus three commandaries previously wrested away from the Jurchen.
     It cannot be said with any certainty that Shih Hao was singularly responsible for the recall, but in light of his political views, this remains a possibility. With the territory in question so far removed from the heart of the Sung empire, he is likely to have considered it to be not worth the risk of an escalation in the war. There were also reasons to question the reliability of the general. Wu Lin operated on the edge of the empire; Lin-an could never be certain of his loyalty. Were he to become personally ambitious, any effort at suppression would be extremely difficult to execute. (The grandson of Wu Lin, Wu Hsi, with the support of revanchist Han T'o-chou, did rebel many years later.) More important, Shih Hao still entertained hopes for a peaceful settlement to the larger conflict and the activities of Wu Lin could only impede the peace process. For more on this topic, see Ihara Hiroshi, "Nan sō shisen no okeru goshi no seiryoko; go sei no ran zenshi," in *Aoyama hakushi koki kinen: Sōdai shi ronsō* (Tokyo: 1974), pp. 1–33; SS, *ch.* 32–33, and *ch.* 366, pp. 11414–24; HTC, *ch.* 136–38.

49   In particular, Wang Shih-p'eng is referring to Shih Cheng-chih (no relation to Shih Hao), who reportedly served the chief councillor as "father" (HTC, *ch.* 138, p. 3666).

50   Shih Hao was originally named prefect of Shao-hsing following his resignation as chief councillor, but official criticism led to the assignment's rescinder shortly thereafter. See KKC, *ch.* 93, p. 10a; HTC, *ch.* 138, p. 3666.

51   HTC, *ch.* 138, pp. 3666–69. "To capture the armor" of combatants generally means to take them captive, although this figure often includes deserters who abandoned their armor on the battlefield and fled.

52   HTC, *ch.* 138, pp. 3670, 3673.

53   These were Shih Mi-yüan and Shih Mi-chien. See chap. 4.

54 KKC, *ch.* 93, p. 10b; PCSMC, *ch.* 9, p. 14a; *(Chia-t'ai) K'uai-chi chih, ch.* 2, p. 47a; HTC, *ch.* 140, p. 3742.

55 KKC, *ch.* 93, p. 11a; PCSMC, *ch.* 9, p. 14a. SS, *ch.* 34, p. 654, is apparently in error at referring to him as prefect of Fu-chou.

56 HHYHC, *ch.* 27, p. 35a. "Charitable estates" established by local governments for social relief should be distinguished from those established by individuals or lineages. For discussion of the latter type, see Denis Twitchett, "The Fan Clan's Charitable Estates," in David Nivison and Arthur Wright, eds. *Confucianism in Action* (Stanford: Stanford University Press, 1959), pp. 97–133. For more on other aspects of social relief institutions during the Sung, see Wang Teh-yi, *Sung-tai tsai-huang ti chiu-chi cheng-ts'e* (Taipei: Chung-kuo hsüeh-shu, 1970).

57 HHYHC, *ch.* 27, p. 35a.

58 Ibid. Also see Shih Hao's memorial on the topic in MFCYML, *ch.* 8, pp. 5b–8a.

59 KKC, *ch.* 93, p. 11b.

60 PCSMC, *ch.* 9, p. 15b; SS, *ch.* 35, p. 667.

61 PCSMC, *ch.* 9, p. 15a.

62 The most complete account of the incident is contained in SS, *ch.* 396, pp. 12067–68. Also see KKC, *ch.* 93, p. 13a; PCSMC, *ch.* 9, p. 15b; SS, *ch.* 35, p. 669.

63 This is in reference to two peasants of the Ch'in dynasty (221–207 B.C.) who rebelled because they were unable to report on time for conscript labor service, an offense punishable by death under Ch'in law. See *Shih chi* (Peking: Chung-hua, 1975), *ch.* 48, pp. 1949–50.

64 KKC, *ch.* 93, p. 11a.

65 PCSMC, *ch.* 9, p. 17a.

66 SS, *ch.* 396, p. 12068; *ch.* 35, pp. 675, 680, 684; *ch.* 36, p. 695.

67 KKC, *ch.* 93, p. 14b; PCSMC, *ch.* 9, pp. 17a–17b.

68 A late Southern Sung literatus, Liu K'o-chuang, suggested that Shih Hao was one of only two officials of his era to be so honored. The second was Cheng Ch'ing-chih (see chap. 4). See HTHSC, *ch.* 170, pp. 7b–8a.

69 SHY: L, 62, 80b; MFCYML, *ch.* 30, pp. 1a–1b. The original Sung edition of the PCSMC contains maps of Ming-chou's Yin subprefecture which point out the Shih mansion and its adjoining garden (see illus. 2). Located on apparently level land in the center of Ming-chou's prefectural seat at Yin *hsien*, it was the area's largest private estate. The PCSMC was compiled a half-century after the gift was originally made and, at that time, the mansion was still in the hands of the Shih community.

70 Chang Hao, *Yün-ku tsa-chi*, in *Sung-jen cha-chi pa chung, ch.* 4, p. 66.

71 In addition to their regular salary, high-level Sung officials (that is, those with rank of three or above) were also entitled to "fiefs of maintenance." This was originally a practice of the T'ang dynasty whereby members of the imperial clan and an occasional high official, upon being enfeoffed by the central government, were allowed to collect directly from a designated number of taxpayers their tax obligation to the local government. In reality, the individual recipient of such a fief had no rights to the land, merely to the tax generated by it. The fiefs of maintenance themselves tended to be nominal; but accompanying them were "actual fiefs of maintenance" (*shih shih-feng*), usually just one-tenth the size of the nominal fief. It was ultimately the

latter that represented the true income supplement of the enfeoffed individual.

The practice during Sung times was similar to that of the T'ang, except that fiefs became more widely accessible to scholar-officials and more restricted for imperial clansmen. It was slightly modified during the Southern Sung, however, to reflect the empire's more limited resources. Subsequently, the court was more economical in distributing fiefs and limited inheritance to one or two generations. (There were previously few restrictions on inheritance.) For more on this topic, see Denis Twitchett, *Financial Administration under the T'ang Dynasty* (Cambridge: Cambridge University Press, 1963), p. 213, fn. 76; Niida Noboru, "Tōdai no hōshaku oyobi shoku hōsei," *Tōhō gakuho* (Tokyo), no. 10, pt. 1 (1939), pp. 1–64; ss, *ch.* 170, pp. 4075–76.

The total number of fiefs of maintenance given to Shih Hao is uncertain, but it appears to have been especially high in light of the many extant edicts of conferral. See Chou Pi-ta, *Wen-chung chi, ch.* 102, 103, 107; Ts'ui Tun-shih, *Ts'ui she-jen yü-t'ang lei-kao, ch.* 3, 5.

72 For more on this, see Ts'ui, *Ts'ui she-jen yü-t'ang lei-kao, ch.* 7, pp. 5b–6a.

73 Chang Hao, *Yün-ku tsa-chi, ch.* 4, p. 66.

74 MFCYML, *ch.* 8, pp. 4b–5b, and *ch.* 30, p. 1b.

75 PCSMC (*ch.* 9, pp. 3a–17b) contains several stories about conflicts between Shih Hao and his student, both before and after the accession.

76 Wang Teh-yi, "Sung hsiao-tsung chi ch'i shih-tai," pp. 245–302.

77 Ibid., pp. 271–83.

78 The four were: Yü Yün-wen (1110–74), Ch'en K'ang-po (1097–1165), Liang K'o-chia (1128–87), and Wang Huai (1127–90). They all tended to be passive individuals who rarely differed with the throne over policy. With the exception of Liang K'o-chia, they all served as councillor of the left for some time, another reason for their unusual political longevity at the court of Hsiao-tsung. For their biographies, see ss, *ch.* 383, pp. 11791–800; *ch.* 384, pp. 11807–13; *ch.* 396, pp. 12069–72.

79 The others were Ch'en K'ang-po and Liang K'o-chia.

80 Wang Teh-yi, "Sung hsiao-tsung chi ch'i shih-tai," p. 268.

81 See n. 14 above.

82 ss, *ch.* 34, pp. 660–64, and *ch.* 213, pp. 5580–82.

83 ss, *ch.* 434, p. 12880. Also see chap. 1 of this book.

84 YYSMC, *ch.* 5, p. 2b. Chu Hsi, in fact, appears to have held him in high regard. See Chu Hsi, *Hui-an hsien-sheng wen-kung wen-chi, ch.* 27, pp. 12b–13b.

85 MFCYML, *ch.* 9, pp. 1a–3a; ss, *ch.* 396, pp. 12068–69.

86 ss, *ch.* 35, p. 675, and *ch.* 434, p. 12889.

87 HTC, *ch.* 153, p. 4105.

88 For a complete listing, see CCTC, *ch.* 31, p. 8a.

89 The exact number who obtained office through the merit of Shih Hao is unknown, but the general rule during the Southern Sung was that as many as ten individuals could be admitted to the bureaucracy due to the merit of one chief councillor. See ss, *ch.* 159, p. 3734.

90 KKC, *ch.* 74, p. 13b; YYWSC, *ch.* 43, p. 16a; HHYHC, *ch.* 26, p. 42b; HSSSTP, *ch.* 5, pp. 30b–31a.

91 KKC, *ch.* 74, p. 13b; HHYHC, *ch.* 26, p. 42b; HSSSTP, *ch.* 5, pp. 35a–35b.

92 Ts'ui Tun-shih, *Ts'ui she-jen yü-t'ang lei-kao, ch.* 7, p. 5b.

93 Only brief mention of them is made in historical sources. See KKC, *ch.* 74, p. 13b; HHYHC, *ch.* 26, p. 42b; HSSSTP, *ch.* 5, pp. 35b–36a, 37a–37b.

94 KKC, *ch.* 105, pp. 1a–12b; HHYHC, *ch.* 28, pp. 42b–45a; HSSSTP, *ch.* 5, pp. 40b–41a.

95 For biographical information on the sons of Shih Mu, see SHHSC, *ch.* 22, pp. 18b–20b; YYWSC, *ch.* 43, p. 12a; HHYHC, *ch.* 26, p. 50a; CJCSC, *ch.* 28, p. 27a; HSSSTP, *ch.* 5, pp. 43b–56b.

96 SHHSC, *ch.* 22, pp. 18b–20b.

97 HSSSTP, *ch.* 5, pp. 57a–60b.

98 Most writings of Shih kinsmen are no longer extant, but there does exist a relatively complete list of titles for all of their known works. See CCTC, *ch.* 31, pp. 8a–9a; HHYHC, *ch.* 52–58. According to these lists, the only member of the fifth generation, excluding Shih Hao, who wrote anything is Shih Yüan [II], whose composition on medicine is no longer available.

99 Shih Hao frequently referred to himself as poor. In light of the fact that his father never held an official post and died quite young, this may very well be true. See MFCYML, *ch.* 17, pp. 8b–9b, and *ch.* 42, pp. 7a–7b.

100 HHYHC, *ch.* 26, p. 50a.

101 The first person from Ming-chou to become assistant councillor was Wang Tz'u-weng in 1140. See PCSMC, *ch.* 8, pp. 28a–30a; HHYHC, *ch.* 14, pp. 24a–26a.

102 See chap. 1 of this book.

4. BLOSSOMING IN AUTUMN

1 HSSSTP, *ch.* 8, pp. 16a–16b; CCTC, *ch.* 45, p. 24b.

2 KKC, *ch.* 93, pp. 16a–17b.

3 CCTC (*ch.* 45, p. 24b) insists that Shih Mi-yüan and Shih Mi-chien were twins, whereas HSSSTP (*ch.* 8, p. 16b) argues that the two were born to different concubines.

4 For biographical information on Shih Mi-yüan, see SB, pp. 873–74; SS, *ch.* 414, pp. 12415–18; YYSMC, *ch.* 5, pp. 10b–12a; SSHP, *ch.* 151, p. 56; HHYHC, *ch.* 14, pp. 26b–34a. Although Shih Mi-yüan eventually became the most powerful bureaucratic chief of the Southern Sung, he has been largely neglected by historians. Most primary materials contain only brief biographies that tend to be strongly biased against him. One of the few relatively impartial accounts is contained in HHYHC.

5 That Shih Mi-yüan was especially close to his father is revealed by reports that he was frequently in Shih Hao's company, joining him in his travels and at his side during formal banquets. For more, see YYSMC, *ch.* 5, p. 10a; HHYHC, *ch.* 14, pp. 29b–30a.

6 Whereas most individuals entering the civil service began with rank 9b, the sons of former chief councillors were permitted to enter at the elevated 8b level.

7 SHY: SH, 28, 49b; SS, *ch.* 414, p. 12415; HHYHC, *ch.* 14, p. 30a. YYSMC (*ch.* 5, p. 10b) erroneously places Shih Mi-yüan as intendant for "eastern Che."

8 SS, *ch.* 35, pp. 687–91; HTC, *ch.* 151, pp. 4029–32.

9 SS, *ch.* 243, p. 8654.

10 Ibid., *ch.* 36, p. 696.

11   Ibid., p. 701, and *ch.* 243, pp. 8653–55.

12   For more on this incident, see SB, pp. 59–63, 802–4; SS, *ch.* 36, p. 710; *ch.* 37, pp. 714–15; *ch.* 243, pp. 8646–48, 8653–55, 8656–58; *ch.* 392, pp. 11984–87; HTC, *ch.* 153, pp. 4108–11.

13   HTC, *ch.* 153, p. 4108.

14   Chou Mi, *Kuei-hsin tsa-chih (hsü-chi)*, B, p. 24b.

15   There is a phrase in the Confucian *Analects* that reads, "The superior man wishes to be *slow in his speech* and earnest in his conduct" (emphasis mine). Although the phrase used by Chou Mi closely resembles this, it is clear from the context that the two have different meanings. See James Legge, trans., *Confucian Analects*, in *The Chinese Classics* I (Shanghai: 1935), p. 172.

16   For biographical information on Han T'o-chou, see SB, pp. 376–84; Ch'en Teng-yüan, "Han p'ing-yüan p'ing," *Chin-ling hsüeh-pao* 4, no. 1, (Nov. 1934), pp. 89–142; SS, *ch.* 474, pp. 13771–78.

17   SS, *ch.* 474, p. 13771.

18   Ibid., *ch.* 243, p. 8656.

19   Chao Ju-yü, a member of the imperial Chao clan, was named chief councillor by Emperor Ning-tsung principally out of gratitude for his role in orchestrating the 1194 succession. Although initially an ally of Han T'o-chou, the two were destined to come into conflict as they represented opposite sides of the imperial family: Chao represented paternal and Han maternal interests. In the end, the court was reminded of the unwritten Sung rule of avoiding employment of paternal clansmen in high office, whereupon Chao Ju-yü was dismissed. For more on this dismissal, see SS, *ch.* 392, pp. 11987–88; HTC, *ch.* 154, p. 4125.

20   P'eng Kuei-nien (1142–1206), for example, called for the dismissal of Han T'o-chou just months after the accession of Ning-tsung, complaining that he was an evil and manipulative man who would bring disaster to the empire *(Chih-t'ang chi, ch.* 5, pp. 16b–20b).

21   For more on the *Tao-hsüeh* ban, see Conrad Schirokauer, "Neo-Confucians under Attack: The Condemnation of Wei-hsüeh," in John W. Haeger, ed., *Crisis and Prosperity in Sung China* (Tucson: University of Arizona Press, 1975), pp. 163–98; Ch'en Teng-yüan, "Han p'ing-yüan p'ing," pp. 123–32; SS, *ch.* 429, pp. 12767–68, and *ch.* 474, pp. 13772–73; HTC, *ch.* 154, pp. 4153–54; *Sung-shih chi-shih pen-mo, ch.* 80, pp. 967–86.

22   For a further listing, see *Sung-shih chi-shih pen-mo, ch.* 80, p. 876; HTC, *ch.* 154, pp. 4153–54.

23   HTC, *ch.* 156, p. 4198.

24   Han T'o-chou was the great-grandson of the Northern Sung statesman Han Ch'i (1008–75), a native of Hsiang-chou, in the northeastern corner of modern Honan (SS, *ch.* 312, p. 10021). It is uncertain just when his family migrated to the south, but it appears to have occurred long before Han T'o-chou's birth. While a northerner by ancestry, he was a southerner by birth.

25   As early as 1189, the Jurchen consented to a 20 percent reduction in the Sung "tribute." The reason for this action is unknown, but it must have been interpreted by some in the south as a sign of weakness (SS, *ch.* 36, p. 697; HTC, *ch.* 151, p. 4057). A

decade later, the Mongols began to build up their strength along the Jurchen border. Although it was not until the 1210–11 period that hostilities finally broke out between the two, no doubt the Sung considered the Mongol presence alone to be a sufficient distraction to make the Jurchen vulnerable.

26 *P'ing-chang chün-kuo-shih* was a special title given only to seven bureaucratic chiefs in the entire Sung period. Generally revived during times of military conflict, the post was more elevated than that of chief councillor and the individual occupying it had sweeping authority over both the military and civilian bureaucracies. For more on this post and its significance, see Lin T'ien-wei, "Sung-tai ch'üan-hsiang hsing-ch'eng chih fen-hsi," pp. 141–70 (esp. 154–59).

27 The best discussion of this war is contained in *Sung-shih chi-shih pen-mo*, ch. 83, pp. 925–34.

28 For discussion of Wu Hsi and his rebellion, see SS, *ch*. 475, pp. 13811–14; *Sung-shih chi-shih pen-mo*, ch. 84, pp. 935–42.

29 SS, *ch*. 38, p. 741, and *ch*. 474, pp. 13775–76; HTC, *ch*. 157, pp. 4243–44.

30 Teng Yu-lung (n.d.) and Ch'iu Ch'ung (n.d.) are but two examples of this. See SS, *ch*. 38, pp. 740–43, and *ch*. 474, pp. 13775–76; HTC, *ch*. 158, p. 4256.

31 SS, *ch*. 395, pp. 12059–62, and *ch*. 474, p. 13776; HTC, *ch*. 158, pp. 4266–68.

32 SS, *ch*. 398, p. 12108, and *ch*. 474, p. 13776; HTC, *ch*. 158, p. 4268.

33 Official accounts of the incident may be found in SS, *ch*. 243, pp. 8656–57, and *ch*. 246, pp. 8734–35.

34 The most detailed account presenting this view is Chou Mi, *Ch'i-tung yeh-yü*, ch. 3, pp. 7a–11b. Other accounts that support it include SS, *ch*. 243, pp. 8656–57; HHYHC, *ch*. 14, p. 31a.

35 SS, *ch*. 398, p. 12108; *ch*. 394, p. 12035; *ch*. 474, pp. 13776–77; *Liang-ch'ao kang-mu pei-yao*, *ch*. 10, p. 28b; YYSMC, *ch*. 5, pp. 10b–11a; *Nan sung shu*, *ch*. 49, p. 4a; SSHP, *ch*. 151, p. 56. Surprisingly, Shih Mi-yüan's biography in SS (*ch*. 414) does not discuss his role in the conspiracy.

36 For excerpts of Shih Mi-yüan's memorial criticizing the court's war policy, see SS, *ch*. 414, p. 12416; Yang Shih-ch'i, *Li-tai ming-ch'en tsou-yi*, *ch*. 235, p. 6a.

37 Chou Mi, *Ch'i-tung yeh-yü*, ch. 3, p. 8b.

38 *Liang-ch'ao kang-mu pei-yao*, *ch*. 10, pp. 26b–32a; SS, *ch*. 243, p. 8657.

39 Chou Mi, *Ch'i-tung yeh-yü*, ch. 3, pp. 8b–9a; SS, *ch*. 414, p. 12416, and *ch*. 474, pp. 13776–77.

40 SS, *ch*. 38, p. 746; SSCW, *ch*. 29, pp. 38b–39b; SSHP, *ch*. 151, p. 56, and *ch*. 187, p. 8; HTC, *ch*. 158, p. 4269.

41 Chou Mi, *Ch'i-tung yeh-yü*, ch. 3, p. 9b; SS, *ch*. 38, p. 746; HTC, *ch*. 158, pp. 4269–71.

42 SS, *ch*. 38, p. 746, and *ch*. 398, pp. 12107–9; HTC, *ch*. 158, p. 4271.

43 Critics of Shih Mi-yüan during his early years as chief councillor complained about his political standing, personality, etc., but never was he blamed for the death of Han T'o-chou. It was only after his implication in the forced suicide of an imperial prince some eighteen years later that contemporaries began referring to him as an assassin and placing upon him responsibility for the slaying of Han T'o-chou.

44 HTC, *ch*. 158, p. 4288. Emphasis mine.

45 The emperor reportedly wished to appoint him to be top seat at the military bureau, but Shih Mi-yüan declined, accepting the inferior minister of rites post. See *Liang-ch'ao kang-mu pei-yao, ch.* 10, p. 31a.

46 SHY: CK, 7, 44a; SS, *ch.* 414, p. 12417.

47 SS, *ch.* 38, pp. 746–47; *ch.* 39, pp. 749–51; *ch.* 414, p. 12417.

48 Ibid., *ch.* 39, p. 751.

49 SHY: L, 62, 85a–85b; CK, 77, 1a–1b; HTC, *ch.* 158, p. 4288.

50 SS, *ch.* 395, pp. 12062–63; HTC, *ch.* 158, pp. 4272, 4274.

51 HTC, *ch.* 158, p. 4275.

52 SS, *ch.* 398, p. 12115; HTC, *ch.* 158, pp. 4275–76.

53 SS, *ch.* 437, p. 12957; HTC, *ch.* 158, p. 4281.

54 SS, *ch.* 391, pp. 11972–77; *ch.* 392, pp. 11981–90; *ch.* 393, pp. 11995–99; *ch.* 429, pp. 12751–70.

55 Ibid., *ch.* 393, pp. 12012–16, and *ch.* 395, pp. 12045–48.

56 For more on this development, see James T. C. Liu, "How Did a Neo-Confucian School Become the State Orthodoxy?" *Philosophy East and West* 23, no. 4 (Oct. 1973), pp. 483–505.

57 HHYHC, *ch.* 14, p. 33a.

58 HTC, *ch.* 158, p. 4284.

59 Ibid., *ch.* 159, p. 4308.

60 For more on Ni Ssu's criticism of Shih Mi-yüan, see SS, *ch.* 398, pp. 12113–16; HTC, *ch.* 158, pp. 4274–75, 4281; Wei Liao-weng, *Ho-shan hsien-sheng ta ch'üan-chi, ch.* 85, pp. 1a–12b.

61 SS, *ch.* 437, pp. 12965–66.

62 Ibid., p. 12959.

63 Ibid., *ch.* 243, pp. 8656–57, and *ch.* 246, pp. 8734–35; *Sung-shih chi-shih pen-mo, ch.* 88, p. 989; HTC, *ch.* 158, p. 4269.

64 SS, *ch.* 37–40. The "Basic Annals" for Ning-tsung's reign contain scattered entries that record the births, and deaths of his numerous sons. It is extremely curious that they all died so very young. Unfortunately, official records do not identify their individual mothers, so there is no way of determining the extent to which palace jealousies and foul play may have been responsible for this phenomenon.

65 SB, pp. 57–58; SS, *ch.* 40, p. 777, and *ch.* 246, pp. 8735–38.

66 SS, *ch.* 40, p. 777, and *ch.* 41, pp. 783–84.

67 Ibid., *ch.* 41, p. 784, and *ch.* 246, pp. 8735–38; SSCW, *ch.* 30, p. 29b, and *ch.* 31, pp. 1a–2a; HTC, *ch.* 162, pp. 4422–23, and *ch.* 169, p. 4599.

68 For more on this incident, see SB, p. 58; Chou Mi, *Ch'i-tung yeh-yü, ch.* 14, pp. 3a–8a; SS, *ch.* 41, p. 785; *ch.* 246, pp. 8735–38; *ch.* 476, pp. 13826–29; SSCW, *ch.* 31, pp. 4a–4b; HTC, *ch.* 163, pp. 4226–27; *Sung-chi san-ch'ao cheng-yao* (PPTSCC), *ch.* 1, pp. 1a–1b. I have dealt elsewhere with some of the historiographical issues related to the succession controversy. See "Shih Mi-yüan at the Hands of Traditional Historians: The Succession of 1224," Paper presented at the 1985 International Symposium on Song History (May 1985), Hangzhou University.

69 There are a variety of contemporary Sung and post-Sung sources that support this position, including HTHSC, *ch.* 170, p. 2b; *Liang-ch'ao kang-mu pei-yao, ch.* 16, pp.

32a–32b; ss, *ch.* 40, p. 781, and *ch.* 41, p. 784; sscw, *ch.* 31, pp. 1a–2a; yysmc, *ch.* 5, pp. 11a–11b; htc, *ch.* 162, pp. 4422–25, and *ch.* 163, pp. 4426–29.

70 ss, *ch.* 243, pp. 8656–58; *ch.* 246, pp. 8735–38; *ch.* 465, pp. 13596–97; sshp, *ch.* 62, p. 7; htc, *ch.* 163, pp. 4435–36.

71 Chao Yi, *Nien-erh-shih cha-chi* (Taipei: Ting-wen, 1978), *ch.* 23, pp. 496–97.

72 ss, *ch.* 243, pp. 8656–58, and *ch.* 246, pp. 8735–38.

73 Veritable Records for Ning-tsung's reign were first compiled in 1238 (ss, *ch.* 42, p. 816).

74 These records were rewritten in 1242, 1245, 1261, 1263, and 1268. See ss, *ch.* 42, p. 823; *ch.* 43, p. 832; *ch.* 45, pp. 877, 885; *ch.* 46, p. 901.

75 Among other things, he authored the monumental chronicle for the reign of Sung Kao-tsung entitled *Chien-yen yi-lai hsi-nien yao-lu.*

76 ss, *ch.* 243, p. 8657.

77 Chou Mi, *Kuei-hsin tsa-chih,* pt. C, pp. 28b–29a.

78 htc, *ch.* 162, p. 4406. Emphasis mine.

79 Ibid.

80 ss, *ch.* 243, p. 8658; sscw, *ch.* 31, p. 2a; htc, *ch* 162, p. 4423.

81 ss, *ch.* 246, p. 8737.

82 Ch'in Kuei and Han T'o-chou, on the other hand, were stripped of all former privileges after their deaths. See ss, *ch.* 473, pp. 13764–65, and *ch.* 474, p. 13778; *Sung-shih chi-shih pen-mo, ch.* 72, pp. 762–63, and *ch.* 82, pp. 922–23.

83 In addition to the sources listed in n. 68 above, some discussion of the affair also appears in the memorials of contemporary scholar-officials critical of the chief councillor. See Chen Te-hsiu, *Chen wen-chung-kung wen-chi, ch.* 4, pp. 11a–16a; Hu Meng-yü, *Hsiang-t'ai shou-mo, ch.* 1, pp. 1a–8a; Wei Liao-weng, *Ho-shan hsien-sheng ta ch'üan-chi, ch.* 19, pp. 1a–6a; ss, *ch,* 437, p. 12961; htc, *ch.* 163, pp. 4426–28, 4434–36.

84 Ibid.

85 See memorial by Teng Jo-shui (n.d.) in htc, *ch.* 163, pp. 4435–36.

86 Chou Mi, *Ch'i-tung yeh-yü, ch.* 14, pp. 3a–8a.

87 There are a variety of Yüan and post-Yüan works that give credence to Chou Mi's account. See ss, *ch.* 41, p. 785, and *ch.* 246, p. 8737; sscw, *ch.* 31, p. 4b; htc, *ch.* 163, pp. 4426–27.

88 ss, *ch.* 246, p. 8737; htc, *ch.* 163, pp. 4451–52.

89 ss, *ch.* 41, p. 786. Actually, Shih Mi-yüan declined the honorary title of "grand preceptor" in 1225, but the conferral was made once again just before his death in 1233.

90 The first such elevation occurred in the summer of 1234, about eight months after Shih Mi-yüan's death. Further posthumous elevations followed the death of Li-tsung in 1264. See ss, *ch.* 41, p. 802; *ch.* 46, p. 892; *ch.* 246, pp. 8737–38.

91 For their biographies, see ss, *ch.* 437, pp. 12957–65, 12965–71; *ch.* 406, pp. 12264–67; *ch.* 455, pp. 13378–81; *Sung shih yi, ch.* 16, pp. 2a–5a, respectively.

92 Chang Tuan-yi, *Kuei-erh chi,* pt. C, p. 33a.

93 Fu Ts'eng, *Nan sung tsa-shih shih, ch.* 6, pp. 26a–26b. In reality, it would have been virtually impossible to enforce a comprehensive ban on the writing of poetry, although

the chief councillor may have attempted to place limits on its use at court or its political content.

94 Yang Shih-ch'i, *Li-tai ming-ch'en tsou-yi, ch.* 235, p. 6a; ss, *ch.* 414, p. 12416.

95 *Chin shih, ch.* 13, pp. 293–94; HTC, *ch.* 159, pp. 4300–4301, 4303, 4310. For more on the Mongol invasion and Sung policy during this formative period, see Charles A. Peterson, "First Sung Reactions to the Mongol Invasion of the North, 1211–17," in John W. Haeger, ed., *Crisis and Prosperity in Sung China* (Tucson: University of Arizona Press, 1975), pp. 215–52.

96 ss, *ch.* 437, p. 12959; HTC, *ch.* 160, pp. 4338–39.

97 Similar positions were also held by a host of contemporaries. For their views, see Huang K'uan-ch'ung, "Wan-sung ch'ao-ch'en," pp. 14–19.

98 sscw, *ch.* 30, pp. 14a–15a. Peterson notes that an exchange of ambassadors *did* occur in 1212 and the annual tribute may have been paid at that time. See "First Sung Reactions to the Mongol Invasion," p. 226.

99 For more on Chen Te-hsiu's position on this vital issue, see Chen Te-hsiu, *Chen wen-chung-kung wen-chi, ch.* 3, pp. 17b–18b.

100 HTC, *ch.* 159, p. 4305.

101 ss, *ch.* 403, pp. 12203–7; HTC, *ch.* 160, pp. 4361–62.

102 For additional information on their backgrounds and activities, see Sun K'o-k'uan, "Nan-sung-chin-yüan chien ti shan-tung chung-yi-chün yü li ch'üan," in *Meng-ku han-chün yü han wen-hua yen-chiu* (Taipei: Wen-hsing, 1958), pp. 11–43; ss, *ch.* 476–77; HTC, *ch.* 160, p. 4336. I have addressed more fully the issue of Sung support for loyalists in my chapters covering the reigns of Sung Kuang-tsung, Ning-tsung, and Li-tsung in *The Cambridge History of China*, Sung volume (forthcoming).

103 ss, *ch.* 403, pp. 12207–8, and *ch.* 476, pp. 13818–19; HTC, *ch.* 161, pp. 4363–64.

104 ss, *ch.* 476, pp. 13818–19; HTC, *ch.* 161, pp. 4367–68.

105 For more on Chia She's criticism of court policy, see ss, *ch.* 403, pp. 12207–10.

106 HTC, *ch.* 162, pp. 4412, 4416.

107 Ibid., p. 4418.

108 ss, *ch.* 437, p. 12959; HTC, *ch.* 163, pp. 4435–36.

109 During his brief tenure as military commissioner for the border region, Hsü Kuo was constantly at odds with Li Ch'üan. Following his death in the summer of 1225, the chief councillor chose to replace him with the more yielding Hsü Hsi-chi (n.d.). About sixteen months later, Hsü Hsi-chi was replaced by Liu Cho (d. 1227), but friction between him and Li Ch'üan led to his dismissal some four months later. Liu Cho was then replaced by Yao Ch'ung (d. 1227) and Yang Shao-yün (n.d.), both considered to be more accommodating toward Li Ch'üan. There is little question that, in selecting military commissioners, Shih Mi-yüan was especially sensitive to the reaction of the Shantung rebel. Evidence to support this may be found in HTC, *ch.* 163, pp. 4432, 4453, and *ch.* 164, pp. 4457, 4462.

110 ss, *ch.* 477, p. 13836; HTC, *ch.* 164, p. 4460.

111 Shantung was still considered Jurchen territory, despite their declining authority in the region. Lacking either real or nominal control over the area, the Mongols were in no position to name Li Ch'üan chief administrator there. Similarly, they were not in control over the southern Huai region, which remained in Sung hands. Mongol

assignments to Li Ch'üan, therefore, were merely intended to represent a nominal expression of support.

112 SS, *ch.* 477, p. 13842; HTC, *ch.* 165, p. 4489.

113 Shih Mi-yüan was already in his midsixties by this time and the emperor came to rely increasingly more upon Cheng Ch'ing-chih to dispose of routine matters on the chief councillor's behalf. In fact, the Li Ch'üan fiasco marks the beginning of Shih Mi-yüan's semiretirement, for it was then that he was permitted to reduce his attendance at court. There is little question that the decision to dispatch troops was made largely by the assistant councillor, although Shih Mi-yüan undoubtedly endorsed it. For more on the role of Cheng Ch'ing-chih in this incident, see HTHSC, *ch.* 170, pp. 3b–4b; SS, *ch.* 477, pp. 13842–44; HTC, *ch.* 165, pp. 4492–4496.

114 SSCW, *ch.* 31, pp. 25b–26a, and *ch.* 32, p. 1a.

115 The invincible wife of Li Ch'üan, accompanied by the remnants of his army, returned to Shantung following his death and reaffirmed their loyalty to the Mongols. The son of the rebel leader was eventually assigned an official post, emerging in the 1260s as a major political threat to the Mongols. See SS, *ch.* 477, p. 13851; *Yüan shih, ch.* 206, pp. 4591–94; HTC, *ch.* 165, p. 4501, and *ch.* 166, p. 4524.

116 One account indicates that Shih Mi-yüan was so distraught about the outcome of the campaign against Li Ch'üan that he attempted suicide by plunging into a pool, only to be saved by a concubine. See HTC, *ch.* 165, p. 4496.

117 For biographical information on Cheng Ch'ing-chih, see SB, pp. 156–63; HTHSC, *ch.* 170, pp. 1a–15b; SS, *ch.* 414, pp. 12419–23.

118 *Sung-shih chi-shih pen-mo, ch.* 91.

119 Surprisingly, the gap separating Shih Mi-yüan and his critics on foreign policy issues grew increasingly narrow during the 1230s. Prominent officials such as Chen Te-hsiu and Wei Liao-weng, who had previously opposed his laissez-faire policy toward the north, actually came to oppose any attempt at invasion by the 1230s. These changing views are discussed in Huang K'uan-ch'ung, "Nan-sung ch'ao-ch'en," pp. 16, 34–40.

120 HTC, *ch.* 165, p. 4501, and ch. 166, p. 4524.

121 SS, *ch.* 414, pp. 12417–18; HTC, *ch.* 166, p. 4525.

122 SS, *ch.* 41, pp. 798–99, and *ch.* 414, pp. 12417–18; SSCW, *ch.* 32, pp. 8a–9a; HTC, *ch.* 167, pp. 4549–50.

123 SS, *ch.* 414, p. 12417.

124 SHY: CK, 77, 23a. He was suddenly given fiefs of maintenance representing the taxable income of some four thousand households. Although chiefly nominal, it was nonetheless a substantial allotment for an official whose career was just beginning to blossom. In time, the number grew in proportion to his political influence. By the time of his death in 1233, he undoubtedly held many tens of thousands. For more on this practice, see n. 71 of chap. 3 of this book.

125 SHY: CK, 77, 24a. Statements that he was not given this home untill 1221 (SS, *ch.* 109, p. 2634) are erroneous.

126 SHY: L, 11 (b), 1b and 10b; SS, *ch.* 109, p. 2634, and *ch.* 414, p. 12417; HTC, *ch.* 162, p. 4398. Actually, an ancestral temple was built in 1178 in honor of Shih Hao, but we do not know whether it was located in Lin-an or Ming-chou. That built to honor Shih Mi-yüan was not only located in the capital, but received special recognition as

an official, government-sponsored structure.

127 ss, *ch.* 41, pp. 798–99; sscw, *ch.* 32, pp. 8b–9a. It was extremely rare for the offspring of a meritorious official to receive the special conferral of *chin-shih* status, especially while the official in question remained alive. It was equally uncommon that imperial favor could enable them suddenly to secure executive posts in the bureaucracy.

128 sscw, *ch.* 32, p. 8b; hhyhc, *ch.* 14, p. 34a. Under the protection system, as many as three relatives of a chief councillor were permitted entrance to the bureaucracy upon his retirement and another five permitted to do so after his death (ss, *ch*, 170, p. 4099). In the case of Shih Mi-yüan, a much larger number of kinsmen appear to have benefited from his merit.

129 ss, *ch.* 41, pp. 798–99, and *ch.* 414, p. 12418; sscw, *ch.* 32, p. 9a.

130 sscw, *ch.* 32, p. 9a; Wei Liao-weng, *Ho-shan hsien-sheng ta ch'üan-chi, ch.* 20, pp. 10a–12a; Yüan Fu, *Meng-chai chi, ch.* 5, pp. 11a–14a; Chou Mi, *Ch'i-tung yeh-yü, ch.* 14, pp. 5b–6a; hhyhc, *ch.* 14, p. 40a. The exact nature of *pao-ch'üan* is uncertain because of its extremely rare implementation. We merely know that it was designed to protect Shih Mi-yüan's family from suffering any hardship in the aftermath of his death. This was of special concern to the throne due to the highly controversial nature of the chief councillor's tenure and the possibility that his enemies might someday attack his family in retribution.

The only other court official of the Sung whose family is known to have received similar protection was that of Ch'in Kuei, but official pressure ultimately compelled Kao-tsung to repeal the order. No doubt, it was for this reason that Li-tsung forbade officials to so much as discuss the guaranty given to the family of Shih Mi-yüan. Although this interdiction did not prevent them from complaining, the emperor ignored these complaints all the same.

At the very end of the Sung, a military leader also received *pao-ch'üan* for his noble resistance against the Mongols, but even less is known about the nature of his guaranty. For information on him, see Yao Tsung-wu, "Sung-meng tiao-yü-ch'eng chan-yi-chung hsiung-erh fu-jen chia-shih chi wang li yü ho-chou huo-te pao-ch'üan k'ao," in *Sung-shih yen-chiu chi* 2 (1964), pp. 123–40.

131 The special favor enjoyed by Shih Mi-yüan is better appreciated when compared with that enjoyed by other prominent Sung officials who died with honor rather than in disgrace. Chao P'u (921–91) was chief councillor to the two founding emperors of the Sung and is commonly held to be the dynasty's most accomplished official. Upon his death, the emperor suspended court for five days, gave his two daughters honorific titles, provided his family with silk and cotton, personally composed his tomb inscription, and had a tablet for him placed in the sacrificial temple of Sung T'ai-tsu. Chao P'u also shared with Shih Mi-yüan the posthumous title of "loyal and accomplished" *(chung-hsien)*. Although he had two sons, they either failed to survive him or the court, for unknown reasons, chose not to elevate them following his death (ss, *ch.* 256, pp. 8939–41).

Ts'ao Pin (931–99) was a highly accomplished general of the early Sung. Just before his death, the court provided him with ten thousand Chinese ounces of silver (literally "white gold"). Subsequently, over ten relatives, retainers, and close associates were given official rank (ss, *ch.* 256, pp. 8982–83).

Wang Ch'in-jo (d. 1025), a meritorious official of Emperor Jen-tsung's era (r. 1022–1063), is said by his biographers to have received the best posthumous treatment of any previous Sung official. His family was given five thousand ounces of silver, with over twenty relatives and close associates receiving official appointments (ss, *ch.* 283, p. 9563).

The case of Li Hang (947–1004) is one of the few during the Northern Sung in which, in recognition of a deceased official's merit, the court conferred *chin-shih* degrees upon his sons (ss, *ch.* 282, pp. 9540–41).

During the Northern Sung, there were a number of officials who enjoyed similar favor, but none exceeded Chao P'u, Ts'ao Pin, and Wang Ch'in-jo. With the advent of the Southern Sung, the court reduced the size of its monetary gifts and restricted the number of persons given official rank through merit of an ancestor. The fact that Shih Mi-yüan and his family fared so well in spite of these changes, reveals much about his special position at the court of Li-tsung.

132 HHYHC, *ch.* 14, p. 33a.

133 Ch'in Kuei, for example, allegedly groomed his son to succeed himself as chief councillor, only to have the emperor dismiss the son on the very night of Ch'in Kuei's death. In addition, Kao-tsung also changed his former councillor's posthumous title from "loyal and accomplished" to "delusive and repugnant" (ss, *ch.* 473, pp. 13764–65; HTC, *ch.* 130, pp. 3457–59). In the case of Han T'o-chou, not only did he lose his own life, but his only adopted son was stripped of official status and sent into exile (ss, *ch.* 474, p. 13778).

Chia Ssu-tao was equally unfortunate. Following his fall from power, he suffered banishment and his family property was confiscated. For months, he moved from one place to another before eventually being assassinated by a sheriff in Fukien, apparently on orders from the palace (ss, *ch.* 474, pp. 13786–87).

134 ss, *ch.* 474.

135 Compilers of *Sung shih* make this assertion, as do a host of other historians. See ss, *ch.* 414, p. 12418; sscw, *ch.* 32, p. 9a; sshp, *ch.* 151, p. 56; HTC, *ch.* 167, p. 4550.

136 For more on Chia Ssu-tao's political failures, see Herbert Franke, "Chia Ssu-tao (1213–1275): A 'Bad Last Minister'?" in Arthur F. Wright and Denis Twitchett, eds., *Confucian Personalities* (Stanford: Stanford University Press, 1962), pp. 217–34.

137 Little is known about these three, save that they were the chief councillor's "hawks and dogs," responsible for tracking down and eliminating his critics in the bureaucracy (ss, *ch.* 414, p. 12418).

138 Indeed, all three were dismissed immediately after Shih Mi-yüan's death. See Wu Yung, *Ho-lin chi*, *ch.* 21, pp. 4a–7a, 14b–16a; HTC, *ch.* 167, pp. 4550–57.

139 HTHSC, *ch.* 170, pp. 1a–15b.

140 HTC, *ch.* 163, pp. 4439, 4443–44.

141 ss, *ch.* 419, pp. 12551–52.

142 See ss, *ch.* 414, pp. 12419–23; *ch.* 417, pp. 12489–95; *ch.* 419, pp. 12551–52, respectively.

143 One source indicates that Shih Hao had yet another son, Shih Mi-mao, but this cannot be corroborated elsewhere (HHYHC, *ch.* 14, p. 33b).

144 This and subsequent information on the life of Shih Mi-ta derives from KKC, *ch.* 93,

p. 16a; CCTC, *ch.* 31, pp. 7b–8a; HHYHC, *ch.* 27, p. 37b.

145   The date of Shih Mi-ta's death is uncertain, but it was probably during the latter half
      of the 1180s.

146   Biographical information for Shih Mi-cheng is from KKC, *ch.* 74, p. 13b; *ch.* 83, p.
      10a; *ch.* 93, p. 16a; *(Chia-ting) Ch'ih-ch'eng chih,* *ch.* 5, p. 8a; HHYHC, *ch.* 27, p.
      37b.

147   KKC, *ch.* 83, p. 10a.

148   Biographical information for Shih Mi-chien is from KKC, *ch.* 74, p. 13b; Wu Yung,
      Ho-lin chi, *ch.* 10, pp. 7b–8b; YYSMC, *ch.* 5, pp. 27b–28a; SYHA, *ch.* 74, pp.
      1406–7; CCTC, *ch.* 45, p. 24b; HHYHC, *ch.* 29, pp. 26b–30a.

149   *Che-chiang t'ung-chih,* *ch.* 113, p. 22b; HHYHC, *ch.* 29, p. 26b.

150   HHYHC, *ch.* 29, pp. 26b–28a.

151   *(Hsien-ch'un) Lin-an chih,* *ch.* 48, pp. 10b–11a, and *ch.* 50, p. 9b; *Che-chiang
      t'ung-shih,* *ch.* 114, p. 14b; HHYHC, *ch.* 29, pp. 26b–27a.

152   YYSMC, *ch.* 5, pp. 27b–28a.

153   HSSSTP, *ch.* 35a–35b.

154   YYWSC, *ch.* 43, p. 16a; HSSSTP, *ch.* 5, pp. 30b–31a, 35a.

155   On the offspring of Shih Yüan [II], see HSSSTP, *ch.* 5, pp. 35b–37a; CCTC, *ch.* 31, pp.
      8b–9b; SKTY, *ch.* 31, p. 52.

156   HHYHC, *ch.* 29, pp. 9b–10a; HSSSTP, *ch.* 5, p. 38b.

157   HHYHC, *ch.* 29, pp. 9b–10a; SYIIA, *ch.* 74, pp. 1407–8.

158   *(Ch'ung-hsiu) Ch'in-ch'uan chih,* *ch.* 3, p. 17b; HHYHC, *ch.* 29, pp. 9b–10a; HSSSTP,
      ch. 5, p. 39a.

159   *(Ching-tiñg) Chien-k'ang chih,* *ch.* 27, p. 18b.

160   HSSSTP, *ch.* 5, pp. 37a–38a.

161   General biographical information on the sons of Shih Chün can be found in KKC, *ch.*
      105, pp. 10a–11b; HHYHC, *ch.* 28, p. 45a.

162   YYSMC, *ch.* 6, p. 16b; HSSSTP, *ch.* 5, p. 41a.

163   HSSSTP, *ch.* 5, pp. 41a–41b.

164   Ibid., pp. 42a–43a.

165   YYSMC, *ch.* 6, p. 24b; HSSSTP, *ch.* 5, p. 43a.

166   HSSSTP, *ch.* 5, p. 41b.

167   Ibid., pp. 40a–43a.

168   Biographical information for Shih Mi-chung is from YYSMC, *ch.* 5, pp. 21a–22a;
      YYWSC, *ch.* 38, p. 12b; SYHA, *ch.* 74, p. 1406; HHYHC, *ch.* 29, pp. 8b–9a.

169   SS, *ch.* 419, p. 12561, and *ch.* 437, p. 12963.

170   YYSMC, *ch.* 5, p. 21b.

171   Ibid. The exact source of this tension is uncertain, but it may have focused on the
      war-peace issue. Shih Mi-chung was reportedly much less inclined toward a peace
      policy. For more, see HTC, *ch.* 168, p. 4571.

172   HTC, *ch.* 170, p. 4631.

173   Biographical information for Shih Mi-kung is from SHHSC, *ch.* 22, p. 20b; SS, *ch.* 423,
      pp. 12637–38; *(Chih-cheng) Ssu-ming hsü-chih,* *ch.* 2, pp. 21b–23a; CJCSC, *ch.* 28,
      p. 27a; SYHA, *ch.* 74, p. 1407; HHYHC, *ch.* 30, pp. 14a–15b.

174   Many biographers of Shih Mi-kung contend that Shih Mi-yüan used his position as

chief councillor to prevent his cousin from securing a *chin-shih* degree earlier than 1217, allegedly because of the long-standing animosity that existed between them. Such an accusation is impossible either to prove or disprove, but it appears to be no more than an attempt at vilifying Shih Mi-yüan by the loyal opposition. After all, Shih Mi-kung was just one of many kinsmen critical of the chief councillor. Almost invariably, Shih Mi-yüan ignored such critics and there is little reason to believe that he should have been especially vindictive in this particular case.

175 *(Ching-ting) Chien-k'ang chih, ch.* 27, pp. 24a–24b.

176 HTC, *ch.* 169, pp. 4603–4.

177 *Che-chiang t'ung-chih, ch.* 115, pp. 11b, 33a; *ch.* 190, p. 22a.

178 A long-time critic of Shih Mi-yüan, Chen Te-hsiu, referred to Shih Mi-kung as "pure and without blemish" for sacrificing his own career in order to speak out against his cousin's treachery (SYHA, *ch.* 74, p. 1407). Many others shared this opinion.

179 SHHSC, *ch.* 22, p. 20b; HSSTP, *ch.* 5, pp. 53b–54a.

180 *(Ch'ung-hsiu) P'i-ling chih, ch.* 8, p. 12a.

181 *(Chih-shun) Chen-chiang chih, ch.* 17, p. 30a.

182 SHHSC, *ch.* 22, p. 20b; YYWSC, *ch.* 43, p. 12a; *Che-chiang t'ung-chih, ch.* 115, p. 21b; HSSSTP, *ch.* 5, p. 55a.

183 YYWSC, *ch.* 38, p. 12b; HHYHC, *ch.* 30, pp. 5b–6a; HSSSTP, *ch.* 5, pp. 55b–56a.

184 SHHSC, *ch.* 22, p. 20b; HSSSTP, *ch.* 5, p. 53a.

185 HSSSTP, *ch.* 5, p. 54b.

186 Ibid., pp. 43b–44b.

187 Ibid., pp. 45a–46a.

188 HHYHC, *ch.* 20, pp. 18b–19a; HSSSTP, *ch.* 5, pp. 58a–58b.

189 HSSSTP, *ch.* 5, pp. 57a–58b.

190 Ibid., pp. 59a–59b.

191 KKC, *ch.* 83, p. 10a, and *ch.* 93, pp. 16a–16b; YYSMC, *ch.* 5, p. 10b; SYHA, *ch* 40, pp. 756–57.

192 The only prominent exceptions to this are Shih Hao's two eldest sons, who were considerably older than most of their cousins and matured too early to consider Yang Chien and Yüan Hsieh to be their teachers. Eldest son Shih Mi-ta is especially interesting because he proved to be scholastically the most accomplished son of Shih Hao. A specialist of the *Yi-ching*, he wrote extensively on Northern Sung interpretations of the work (CCTC, *ch.* 31, pp. 8a–9b). In light of his father's lack of expertise in this area, it can be inferred that the younger Shih studied under others, although historical records fail to indicate just who these may have been.

193 Younger brother Shih Mi-chien and cousins Shih Mi-chung, Shih Mi-kung, and Shih Mi-ying all are known to have urged the chief councillor to resign. See YYSMC, *ch.* 5, p. 21b; HHYHC, *ch.* 29, p. 8b, 28b, and *ch.* 30, p. 6a.

194 Undoubtedly the most prolific was the imperial Chao clan. After it came the Lou and Shih. For more, see Walton-Vargo, "Education, Social Change, and Neo-Confucianism," pp. 45, 47, 48, 90, 94. Also see chap. 1 above.

5. ECLIPSE

1   HTC, *ch.* 170, p. 4623.

2   Tu Fan, *Ch'ing-hsien chi*, *ch.* 9, pp. 2b–11a; HTC, *ch.* 170, pp. 4625–26.

3   SS, *ch.* 45, p. 889, and *ch.* 418, p. 12515; SSHP, *ch.* 14, p. 52b; HTC, *ch.* 177, p. 4849.

4   SS, *ch.* 45, p. 889.

5   SSCW, *ch.* 31, pp. 1a–1b; HTC, *ch.* 162, pp. 4406–7.

6   HTC, *ch.* 163, pp. 4439–41.

7   Ibid., p. 4439.

8   SS, *ch.* 46, pp. 892–93, and *ch.* 246, pp. 8735–38; HTC, *ch.* 181, p. 4954, and *ch.* 182, p. 4969.

9   It is reported that the emperor wished to elevate his favorite, Lady Chia, to empress, but Dowager Yang forced him to marry Lady Hsieh instead. The selection of Lady Hsieh apparently stemmed from a political debt that the dowager owed her grandfather, one that she sought to repay by marrying the old man's granddaughter to the young emperor. Although Li-tsung appears to have harbored no resentment against the dowager for her interference, this nonetheless must have left him terribly frustrated. For more on this selection, see SS, *ch.* 243, pp. 8658–60; HTC, *ch.* 165, p. 4494.

10   The biography of Cheng Ch'ing-chih indicates that it was he who made arrangements for their recall, rather than the throne (SS, *ch.* 414, p. 12420). If this is true, then it suggests that the political differences between Shih Mi-yüan and his protégé were probably much greater than is generally realized. I am convinced that no single individual is entirely responsible for the revival; rather, it appears to have been the inevitable outcome of pressures being applied to the court from many quarters.

11   For more on this, see memorial by Ts'ui Yü-chih in HTC, *ch.* 168, pp. 4574–76.

12   In fact, the Mongols appear to have been disinclined to remain at war with the Sung. During the 1230s and 1240s, they sent several peace missions to South China, but Lin-an refused to make any significant compromises. At one point, the Sung government proved so indifferent to these overtures that one of its border officials actually imprisoned a Mongol emissary. See HTC, *ch.* 167, p. 4568, and *ch.* 170, pp. 4625, 4636.

13   Chen Tê-hsiu, *Chen wen-chung-kung wen-chi*, *ch.* 21, pp. 1b–2a; HSSSTP, *ch.* 8, p. 18a; HHYHC, *ch.* 14, p. 34a.

14   YYSMC, *ch.* 5, p. 10b.

15   CCTC, *ch.* 45, p. 22b.

16   CCTC *ch.* 45, pp. 22b–23a; HHYHC, *ch.* 14, p. 40a.

17   SS, *ch.* 41, p. 799.

18   There are several possible explanations for Shih Chai-chih being given regional assignments following his revival as an official. First, his previous experience had been confined to the capital and the court may have deemed it wise first to supplement this with regional experience before summoning him to serve once again as a metropolitan official. The second possibility is that the rise of cousin Shih Sung-chih to power had made it desirable to delay Shih Chai-chih's appointment there for fear of generating rivalry or collusion. A third possibility is that the emperor feared that his recall might aggravate elements at court opposed to the late Shih Mi-yüan and might rekindle old

flames of controversy. Whatever his motives, the action does not reflect a loss of imperial favor, for Shih Chai-chih retained high official rank throughout this period.

19 *Wu-chün chih*, *ch.* 11, p. 23a; ss, *ch*, 42, p. 821; *Che-chiang t'ung-chih*, *ch.* 114, p. 21a, and *ch.* 115, p. 39a; HHYHC, *ch.* 14, pp. 38b–40b.

20 ss, *ch.* 416, p. 12484.

21 ss, *ch.* 43, p. 839; HTC, *ch.* 172, p. 4696.

22 Ch'üan Tsu-wang (CCTC, *ch.* 45, p. 23a) also suspected that Li-tsung was preparing to name Shih Chai-chih chief councillor at the time of his death.

23 For biographical information on Shih Yü-chih, see HTHSC, *ch.* 65, pp. 11a–11b; YYSMC, *ch.* 5, pp. 11b–12a; *Ssu-ming wen-hsien chi*, *ch.* 5, pp. 41b–46a; CCTC, *ch.* 45, pp. 22b–24a; HHYHC, *ch.* 30, pp. 26b–27b.

24 CCTC, *ch.* 45, p. 23a.

25 Ch'üan Tsu-wang suggested that Shih Yü-chih's career came to an end after 1260 principally due to the rise to political prominence of Chia Ssu-tao. The new chief councillor, a native of southern Chekiang's T'ai-chou, was allegedly jealous of the imperial favor enjoyed by officials from Ming-chou and sought to break their hold on the court. As a result, he allegedly blocked the advancement, not only of Shih Yü-chih, but of other Ming-chou provincials as well. A modern historian confirms this report. See CCTC, *ch.* 45, p. 23b; Chang Ch'i-yün, "Sung-tai ssu-ming chih hsüeh-feng," p. 35.

26 HHYHC, *ch.* 14, p. 40a.

27 Ibid.; CCTC, *ch.* 45, p. 23a.

28 Shih Mi-yüan had apparently chosen a wife for young Shih Yü-chih before his own death in 1233. Surnamed Hung, she was from a prominent family that married her off to the chief councillor's son simply for the additional prestige that it lent them. In reality, she proved to be an independent woman who held no great affection for her husband.

Shih Yü-chih's mother, née Lin, was originally a concubine of Shih Mi-yüan. A young and profligate woman, she took advantage of her special appeal to and influence over the chief councillor to dominate his household, consequently alienating many members of his family. Rather than live with her son in the aftermath of Shih Mi-yüan's death, she chose to reside in disreputable quarters of the capital, where she could indulge herself "as she pleased." When Shih Yü-chih and his wife finally separated, rumor had it that his mother's overbearing and lewd conduct was chiefly to blame. In time, the controversy generated by the entire incident prompted Tu Fan to memorialize the throne requesting that it admonish Shih Yü-chih to perform his filial responsibilities by restricting his mother's amorous activities and reuniting with his wife. For more on the affair, see YYWSC, *ch.* 37, pp. 19a–21a; CCTC, *ch.* 45, pp. 22b–24a.

29 YYSMC, *ch.* 5, pp. 11b–12a.

30 CCTC, *ch.* 45, p. 23b.

31 For biographical information, see KKC, *ch.* 93, p. 16b; SYHA, *ch.* 74, pp. 1409–10, and *ch.* 75, p. 1435; *Nan-sung tsa-shih shih*, *ch.* 1, p. 40b; CCTC, *ch.* 45, p. 25a; HHYHC, *ch.* 30, pp. 17a–17b.

32 *Che-chiang t'ung-chih*, *ch.* 114, p. 21b, and *ch.* 115, p. 21a; SYHA, *ch.* 74, p. 1410, and *ch.* 75, p. 1435; HHYHC, *ch.* 30, pp. 17b–18b; HSSSTP, *ch.* 5, pp. 15b–16b.

33 KKC, *ch.* 93, p. 16b; *(Ch'ung-hsiu) P'i-ling chih, ch.* 8, p. 12a; HHYHC, *ch.* 30, pp. 18b–19a; HSSSTP, *ch.* 5, pp. 15a, 16b–17a.

34 HSSSTP, *ch.* 5, pp. 17b–18a.

35 CJCSC, *ch.* 30, p. 25a; HHYHC, *ch.* 30, p. 18b; HSSSTP, *ch.* 5, pp. 17a–18a.

36 SYHA, *ch.* 79, p. 1494; CCTC, *ch.* 45, p. 25b; HHYHC, *ch.* 29, pp. 28b–30a; HSSSTP, *ch.* 5, pp. 27b–28a.

37 HHYHC, *ch.* 29, p. 29b; HSSSTP, *ch.* 5, pp. 26a–26b.

38 On the sons of Shih Mi-kao, see HSSSTP, *ch.* 5, pp. 30b–35a; YYWSC, *ch.* 43, p. 16a; HHYHC, *ch.* 30, p. 44b.

39 On the grandsons of Shih Chüan, see HSSSTP, *ch.* 5, pp. 37a–40a.

40 HSSSTP, *ch.* 5, pp. 35a–37a.

41 SHHSC, *ch.* 22, pp. 18b–20b.

42 PCSMC, *ch.* 9, p. 3a.

43 Hellmut Wilhelm, "From Myth to Myth: the Case of Yüeh Fei's Biography," in Arthur Wright and Denis Twitchett, eds., *Confucian Personalities*, pp. 150–51.

44 See their biographies in SS, *ch.* 361, pp. 11297–311, and *ch.* 418, pp. 12533–40.

45 The principal sources of biographical information for Shih Sung-chih are SS, *ch.* 414, pp. 12423–28; YYSMC, *ch.* 5, pp. 23a–23b; HHYHC, *ch.* 14, pp. 35b–39b. For additional information, see HTHSC, *ch.* 80, pp. 3b–6a, 7a–8a, 10a–10b, 12b–17a; *Kuei-hsin tsa-chih, ch.* 6, pp. 16a–18b, 31a–32b.

46 HHYHC, *ch.* 14, p. 36a. Other, less reliable, accounts suggest that Shih Sung-chih hardly knew his uncle, the chief councillor; see *Sung-jen yi-shih hui-pien, ch.* 18, p. 90ff.

47 *Che-chiang t'ung-chih, ch.* 110, p. 24b.

48 For a brief discussion of the strategic importance of the region to the Southern Sung empire, see Herbert Franke, "Siege and Defense of Towns in Medieval China," in Frank A. Kiermann, Jr., ed., *Chinese Ways in Warfare* (Cambridge, Mass.: Harvard University Press, 1974), pp. 151–201 (esp. 181–85); HTC, *ch.* 134, p. 3565.

49 HTC, *ch.* 166, p. 4528; *ch.* 167, p. 4546.

50 Huang K'uan-ch'ung, "Meng kung nien-p'u," *Shih yüan,* no. 4 (Oct. 1973), pp. 79–135 (esp. 95–104); SS, *ch.* 412, pp. 12369–80; HTC, *ch.* 167, pp. 4546–49, 4555–57.

51 HTC, *ch.* 167, pp. 4557–59.

52 On the 1234 offensive, see Charles A. Peterson, "Old Illusions and New Realities: Sung Foreign Policy, 1217–1234," in Morris Rossabi, ed., *China among Equals; the Middle Kingdom and Its Neighbors, 10th–14th Centuries* (Berkeley: University of California Press, 1983), pp. 204–39 (esp. 218–30); SS, *ch.* 417, p. 12502; *Sung-shih chi-shih pen-mo, ch.* 92. HTC (*ch.* 167, p. 4563) indicates that Sung forces were also ordered to take a "third capital," apparently Ch'ang-an. While this may have been the initial plan, there is little to indicate that troops actually headed in that direction.

53 HTC, *ch.* 167, p. 4566.

54 *Che-chiang t'ung-chih, ch.* 110, p. 24b.

55 SS, *ch.* 214, p. 5617.

56 SS, *ch.* 417, pp. 12489–95; HTC. *ch.* 167, p. 4564.

57 SS, *ch.* 406, pp. 12257–64.

58 HTC, *ch.* 168, p. 4596, and *ch.* 169, pp. 4606–7, 4611.

59 One writer suggests that Ögödei lacked enthusiasm for the Sung conquest, preoccupied as he was with consolidating gains made in Russia and North China, including Korea. Far more important, I suspect, is a strong Sung defense; no doubt, Ögödei had come to realize that he had greatly underassessed the fortitude of the Sung army. See Luc Kwanten, *Imperial Nomads: A History of Central Asia, 500–1500* (Philadelphia: University of Pennsylvania Press, 1979), p. 133.

60 HTC, *ch.* 169, p. 4611; HHYHC, *ch.* 14, p. 38a.

61 HTC, *ch.* 168, p. 4571, and *ch.* 169, pp. 4601–2.

62 HTC, *ch.* 169, p. 4611.

63 Admittedly, this was only partially due to the success of Sung forces at repulsing them. Perhaps more important was Mongol preoccupation with a host of domestic problems, including a messy succession issue, which prevented them from concentrating their energies against the Sung.

64 SS, *ch.* 412, pp. 12369–80; HTC, *ch.* 169, pp. 4618–21. General Meng Kung was much more instrumental in regaining these areas but, with Shih Sung-chih as chief councillor, most of the credit went to him instead.

65 Mongol demands in early 1238 for "peace payments" from the Sung were unquestionably the principal reason for the mission's failure (HTC, *ch.* 169, p. 4611). Actually, the sum they requested was considerably lower than that given to the Jurchen during the reigns of Kao-tsung and Ning-tsung. By the time of Li-tsung, however, circumstances had changed. A succession of natural calamities, combined with disruptions along the border, had wreaked havoc upon the Sung economy, negatively affecting government revenues in the process. What in the past represented a reasonable demand must have been considered excessive during the 1230s and 1240s. Another reason for the Sung refusal to make such payments may be related to the fear that, once initiated, they might become a permanent element in north-south relations, no less of a political sore-spot than they were previously under Sung-Chin treaties.

66 Within one year after his elevation to chief councillor, censors and policy monitors had already begun viciously to attack him (HTC, *ch.* 170, p. 4624).

67 SS, *ch.* 416, pp. 12484–85, and *ch.* 423, pp. 12628–34.

68 HTC, *ch.* 170, p. 4631.

69 HTC, *ch.* 171, pp. 4656–59.

70 Fu Pi served as chief councillor during an era of peace and felt that circumstances did not warrant his official restoration at that time. He did not, however, condemn the practice per se. For more on his refusal to accept the emperor's recall, see SS, *ch.* 313, p. 10254.

71 Both Cheng Chü-cheng and Wang Fu were high-ranking officials at the court of Hui-tsung. Like Fu Pi, Wang Fu resigned to mourn the death of his mother. At the time, he was serving as censor and accepted the throne's restoration to that post. Cheng Chü-cheng was special commissioner at the Bureau of Military Affairs when the throne recalled him to service following the death of his father. Both men lived during a period of political and military instability, a time of intense factionalism when the Jurchen threat to the Sung had already become critical. There is little to indicate that contemporaries were especially critical of the two merely for having

accepted the emperor's recall, although they may have been unpopular for other reasons. Indeed, the practice was widely used throughout the Sung and drew little criticism in general. For more, see ss, *ch.* 351, pp. 11103–6, and *ch.* 470, pp. 13681–84.

The Ching-k'ang era represents the one-year reign of Emperor Ch'in-tsung, which preceded the fall of K'ai-feng to the Jurchen.

72 This is in reference to the houses of Wang Mang (45 B.C.–A.D. 23) and Ssu-ma Yen (d. 290).

73 Both Chao P'u and Chu Sheng-fei lost their mothers while serving as chief councillor. Neither of their restorations appear to have created much of a controversy (ss, *ch.* 256, p. 8932, and *ch.* 362, p. 11318).

74 T'ung-chou is in present-day Kiangsu and Shou-ch'un is in Anhwei. For further information on these two incidents, see HTC, *ch.* 170, p. 4642; *ch.* 171, p. 4654. The translation is based on the text contained in HTC, *ch.* 171, pp. 4656–59.

75 HTC, *ch.* 171, p. 4662.

76 ss, *ch.* 423, pp. 12633–34; HTC, *ch.* 172, pp. 4682–84.

77 During the early years of his tenure, Shih Sung-chih appears to have spent much of his time away from the capital. His return to Lin-an in the spring of 1240, what seems to have been his first time there since being appointed chief councillor, was so noteworthy that historians took the unusual step of recording the actual day when he "was ordered to return to the capital" and then "entered its gates" (HTC, *ch.* 170, pp. 4623–24). It cannot be determined with any certainty that his absences in subsequent years were equally prolonged, but this is very probable in light of his multitude of responsibilities.

78 *Kuei-hsin tsa-chih*, pp. 18a–20a; ss, *ch.* 414, pp. 12425–27, and *ch.* 415, pp. 12457–58; HTC, *ch.* 171, pp. 4669–71. It is noteworthy that accusations of treachery on the part of Shih Sung-chih did not begin to surface until *after* he had left the capital. I suspect that they were largely fabricated by the opposition to tarnish his reputation. At least one other historian holds a similar view. See HHYHC, *ch.* 14, p. 39a.

79 The only biography for Shih Yen-chih is contained in HHYHC, *ch.* 29, pp. 9a–9b.

80 Both *Che-chiang t'ung-chih* (*ch.* 114, p. 15a) and HHYHC (*ch.* 29, pp. 9a–9b) state that he received this appointment in 1236. HTC (*ch.* 167, p. 4558) indicates that he was already prefect of Lin-an by early 1234.

81 (*Hsien-ch'un*) *Lin-an chih*, *ch.* 49, p. 3b.

82 *Che-chiang t'ung-chih*, *ch.* 114, p. 21a; HHYHC, *ch.* 29, p. 9a.

83 ss, *ch.* 44, p. 867.

84 HTC (*ch.* 176, p. 4812) suggests that Shih Yen-chih's dismissal was actually part of a larger scheme by Chia Ssu-tao to prevent still another person from receiving credit for the Mongol retreat; in a struggle for power between the two, Shih Yen-chih became one of its casualties. It is also possible that the dismissal is related to Chia Ssu-tao's general bias against natives of Ming-chou (see n. 25 above). Regardless of his motives, it is ironic that Chia Ssu-tao should have been responsible for the ouster of Shih Yen-chih. In 1234, when Shih Yen-chih was already prefect of Lin-an and Chia Ssu-tao a mere granary inspector, the former reportedly said of the latter, "Although

[Chia] Ssu-tao has the habits of the young (that is, being carefree), his talents are nonetheless capable of extensive use" (SS, *ch.* 474, p. 13780; HTC, *ch.* 167, p. 4558). Shih Yen-chih was apparently among the first to recognize Chia Ssu-tao's political potential.

85 There also exist allegations that Shih Yen-chih, like his brother before him, once conspired to assassinate a former critic. See *Tung-nan chi-wen, ch.* 2, pp. 7b–8a. The source, however, is not especially reliable.

86 HSSSTP, *ch.* 5, pp. 49b–50a, 52a–52b.

87 CJCSC, *ch.* 28, p. 27a; HHYHC, *ch.* 30, pp. 25a–25b. The official biography of Shih Mi-kung (SS, *ch.* 423, p. 12638) states that he also served as executive at the Ministry of Justice (3b), an assertion unsubstantiated by other biographical materials and apparently erroneous. His posthumous rank—which customarily is set somewhat higher than that held during an official's lifetime—was merely 4b. Under normal circumstances, it is unlikely that an official with the rank of 3b would posthumously be assigned 4b.

88 HHYHC, *ch.* 30, p. 15a.

89 Ibid.; *Ssu-ming wen-hsien chi, ch.* 5, pp. 46b–47a.

90 HTHSC, *ch.* 67, p. 14a; (*Ch'ung-hsiu*) *P'i-ling chih, ch.* 8, p. 14b; HHYHC, *ch.* 30, p. 25b.

91 HHYHC, *ch.* 20, p. 35a, *ch.* 20, p. 15b.

92 *Che-chiang t'ung-chih, ch.* 115, p. 36b.

93 HHYHC, *ch.* 31, p. 23b; YYWSC, *ch.* 43, p. 12a.

94 HSSSTP, *ch.* 5, p. 55a.

95 YYWSC, *ch.* 38, p. 12b; HSSSTP, *ch.* 5, p. 55b.

96 (*Ching-ting*) *Chien-k'ang chih, ch.* 27, p. 19a; HSSSTP, *ch.* 5, p. 56a.

97 HSSSTP, *ch.* 5, p. 56b.

98 Like so many other prominent houses during the Sung, the Shih had a methodical system of ordering the personal names of its many kin (*p'ai-ming*), whereby an individual's generation and often kinship branch were indicated through easily identifiable elements in his personal name. Allegedly formulated by Shih Hao, it was strictly followed by most kinsmen from the fifth through eleventh generations (HSSSTP, *ch.* 2, pp. 10a–10b). All members of the fifth generation reportedly changed their names to conform to this scheme, with each of their one-character personal names containing the water radical (KKC, *ch.* 74, pp. 13a–13b). For members of the sixth generation, identification came through the first character in their two-character personal names, which was fixed as *mi*. For the seventh generation, the identifying element was *chih*; for the eighth, it was *ch'ing*; for the ninth, it was *sun* or *po*; for the tenth, *kung*; and the eleventh had *tsu*. Although some kinsmen appear to have abandoned the old scheme of ordering personal names as early as the eighth generation, most waited until generation XI to do so. At that point, two-syllable names gave way to one-syllable names. This suggests that the Shih had, by this time, come officially to recognize the fragmentation that had already begun to occur generations earlier.

99 HSSSTP, *ch.* 5, pp. 19a–25b.

100 Ibid., pp. 18b–19a, 20a–20b.

101 (*Chih-shun*) *Chen-chiang chih, ch.* 15, p. 14b; *Ssu-ming wen-hsien chi, ch.* 5, p. 45b.

102　For a slightly more detailed discussion of the development of Shih Hao's line, see Davis, "Political Success and the Growth of Kin Groups."

103　HSSSTP, *ch.* 5, pp. 46a–48b; HHYHC, *ch.* 14, p. 39b.

104　HSSSTP, *ch.* 5, pp. 60a–64b; HHYHC, *ch.* 30, pp. 14a–15b.

105　For a discussion of the trend among scholar-officials toward eremitism during this period, see Frederick W. Mote, "Confucian Eremitism in the Yüan Period," in Arthur Wright, ed., *The Confucian Persuasion*, pp. 202–40.

106　YYWSC, *ch.* 38, p. 13a, and *ch.* 43, pp. 15b–18a; CCTC, *ch.* 45, p. 25b; HHYHC, *ch.* 30, p. 44b.

107　CCTC, *ch.* 45, p. 25b; HHYHC, *ch.* 30, p. 29a.

108　CJCSC, *ch.* 28, pp. 25b–28b; *Sung-shih yi, ch.* 34, pp. 14a–15b; *Hsin yüan shih, ch.* 235, pp. 6b–7a; SYHA, *ch.* 87, pp. 1645–46; CCTC, *ch.* 45, p. 25b; HHYHC, *ch.* 30, pp. 44b–45b.

109　*Sung-shih yi, ch.* 34, pp. 14a–15b; CCTC, *ch.* 45, p. 25b; HHYHC, *ch.* 30, p. 45b.

110　Grandson of Shih Mi-yüan and son of Shih Yü-chih, Shih Hsi-ch'ing does not appear to have received an official assignment either during the Sung or subsequently. The biographer of his son merely states, "When the Yüan began, he did not serve." See Sung Lien, *Sung wen-hsien-kung ch'üan-chi, ch.* 23, pp. 11a–12a.

111　HHYHC, *ch.* 31, p. 9a.

112　CJCSC, *ch.* 30, pp. 24a–25a; HHYHC, *ch.* 30, pp. 49a–49b.

113　YYWSC, *ch.* 43, p. 12a; HHYHC, *ch.* 31, p. 23b.

114　YYWSC, *ch.* 43, pp. 11b–15b; *Che-chiang t'ung-chih, ch.* 192, p. 14b; HHYHC, *ch.* 31, pp. 23b–24a.

115　*Chao-chung lu,* p. 7a.

116　HHYHC, *ch.* 29, pp. 29b–30a; HSSSTP, *ch.* 5, pp. 28a–28b.

117　HHYHC, *ch.* 14, p. 39b; HSSSTP, *ch.* 5, pp. 46a–46b.

118　CCTC, *ch.* 45, p. 25b; HHYHC, *ch.* 30, p. 45b; HSSSTP, *ch* 5, pp. 62a–62b.

119　HSSSTP, *ch.* 5, pp. 20a–20b, 28a–28b, 50a–50b. Remaining Yüan officials are: Shih Chang-sun, Shih Ch'i-sun [V], Shih Ching-sun, Shih Hsien-sun [IV], Shih Fu-po [II], and Shih K'an-po.

120　John W. Dardess, *Confucianism and Autocracy: Professional Elites in the Founding of the Ming Dynasty* (Berkeley: University of California Press, 1983).

121　*(Chih-cheng) Ssu-ming hsü-chih, ch.* 2, p. 27a; HHYHC, *ch.* 30, p. 15b; HSSSTP, *ch.* 5, p. 64a.

122　HSSSTP, *ch.* 5, p. 35b.

123　The migrants in branch A were: Shih Shun-ch'ing [II], Shih Chih-sun, Shih Ju-sun, Shih Liu-sun, Shih Na-sun, Shih Yü-sun [VII], Shih Ying-sun [III], and Shih Kung-hsien [II]. The two migrants in branch C were Shih Yi-sun [III] and Shih Yüan-sun [II] (see appendix 4).

124　Besides Shih Kung-hsien [II] in generation 10 (HSSSTP, *ch.* 5, p. 39a), an eleventh- or twelfth-generation descendant of Shih Mi-yüan, Shih Heng, is said to have migrated to Hsiao-shan and there founded a new kin group (HSSSTP *ch.* 9, pp. 1a–1b).

125　Cf. n. 110.

126　Tai Piao-yüan, *Shan-yüan chi, ch.* 11, pp. 13b–14a.

127　Shih Yi-sun [IV], son of Shih Hsi-ch'ing and great grandson of Shih Mi-yüan, is said to have been a mere "commoner," despite his literary training. After his death, however, son Shih Ting-tsu (n.d.) became a midlevel official of the Ming court (cf. n. 110). This would suggest that Shih Yi-sun [IV], although lacking official privileges and engaged in agriculture like most commoners, was nonetheless distinguished from that group by the education he held and his transmission of this to offspring.

128   HSSSTP, *ch.* 5, p. 28b.
129   For his biography, see Ch'en Chi, *Yi-pai-chai kao, ch.* 34, pp. 2b–4a; HHYHC, *ch.* 31, pp. 30b–31a.
130   HHYHC, *ch.* 31, p. 31a.
131   With the Ming dynasty, several kinsmen of eremetic bent returned to government service. Besides Shih Ting-tsu (see n. 127), three other eleventh-generation scions are known to have done so. Shih Ching-tsu (fl. 1371–82), Shih Ch'un-tsu, and Shih Sheng-tsu all served the Ming. See YYWSC, *ch.* 43, pp. 11a, 14b; HTHSC, *ch.* 64, pp. 15a–15b; HHYHC, *ch.* 21, p. 2b, and *ch.* 31, p. 24a. Also see appendix 4.

After the eleventh generation, data become scant and the relationship of kinsmen to one another is blurred. HHYHC (*ch.* 31–41) contains the biographies of numerous individuals of the Ming-Ch'ing period who claim to have descended from the great Shih house of Sung times. Two received *chin-shih* degrees during the Ming and one during the early Ch'ing. Again, none became especially prominent.

CONCLUSION

1   YYSMC, *ch.* 6.
2   The kin group's only teacher of note is Shih Meng-ch'ing, who flourished largely under Yüan rule. Earlier kinsmen like Shih Hao and Shih Mi-kung may have won recognition for their scholarship, but appear to have taught few persons outside their own kin group.
3   HSSSTP, *ch.* 5.
4   E. A. Kracke, Jr., "Family vs. Merit in the Chinese Civil Service Examinations under the Empire," *Harvard Journal of Asiatic Studies*, 10, no. 2 (Sept. 1947), pp. 103–123.
5   Later generations had to rise to 7a before themselves becoming eligible to protect their own sons and grandsons. This generally required years of service and the passing of screening examinations. See Davis, "Political Success and the Growth of Kin Groups," fn. 2.
6   The exact dates for Shih Ts'ai were never recorded. It is known, however, that he died in 1162, forty-four years after earning *chin-shih* status. Even if he were exceptionally precocious and received the degree before thirty, this would still mean that he was in his late sixties or early seventies when death came.
7   Stone, *Crisis of the Aristocracy*, pp. 166–74; P'an, *Ming-ch'ing liang-tai chia-hsing ti wang-tsu*, pp. 131–35.
8   In Chinese society, where such stress is placed upon having male heirs, it is common for those who first have several daughters to continue procreation until either a male is born or restrictions of wealth or age force them to adopt. Well-to-do families that have the resources, in contrast with the peasantry, are likely simply to expand the procreation period and have more children. Assuming that the wealthy tended to keep

their daughters (unlike the poor, who frequently either committed infanticide or sold them into slavery), one can expect to find a somewhat larger number of female offspring among them.

9 The suddenness of the Shih leap from poverty to riches is best illustrated by an anecdote of the Sung dynasty relating to Shih Hao. Admittedly poor before receiving his *chin-shih* degree, on one New Year's Eve he reportedly dreamed of receiving gifts of gold and silver totaling some 470 items, these being bestowed upon him in a palace. Upon awakening, he related this to his wife, who scoffed at him saying, "Last night [there occurred] the great new year's festivities and our home lacked [both] liquor and sliced meat, [necessitating that we] meaninglessly pass the [most] splendid [time of] year. How could [we ever] possess wealth such as gold and silver? [No doubt, you] simply encountered a ghost and it played tricks on you." As it was, Shih Hao's dream became a reality several decades later, but this development was inconceivable even as a middle-aged man. See Ting Ch'uan-ching, *Sung-jen yi-shih hui-pien, ch.* 18, pp. 898–99.

10 Anthropologist Maurice Freedman notes, "The members of a successfully installed local lineage were driven on by the desire to expand their strength . . . up to the limits imposed on them by the extent of their agricultural land." See Freedman, *Chinese Lineage and Society: Fukien and Kuangtung* (London: Athlone, 1966), p. 37. This is confirmed by Robert M. Marsh, *The Mandarins: The Circulation of Elites in China, 1600–1900* (New York: Free Press, 1961), pp. 16–17.

11 For more on the rule of partible inheritance in China, see Jack M. Potter, "Land and Lineage in Traditional China," in Maurice Freedman, ed., *Family and Kinship in Chinese Society* (Stanford: Stanford University Press, 1970) pp. 121–38.

12 Ho, *Ladder of Success,* chap. 5.

13 Ibid., p. 212.

14 Jacques Gernet, *Daily Life in China on the Eve of the Mongol Invasion, 1250–1276,* trans. H. M. Wright (Stanford: Stanford University Press, 1962), pp. 228–29.

15 For more on these men and their private libraries, see Ch'en Ch'i-shou, "Sung mu-lu hsüeh-chia ch'ao kung-wu ch'en chen-sun chuan," *Kuo-ts'ui hsüeh-pao,* 68, no. 6 (1910), pp. 3883–93; SS, *ch.* 291, pp. 9736–37; *Sung-shih yi, ch.* 29, pp. 17b–18b.

16 Ho, *Ladder of Success,* pp. 168–71.

17 Yeh Hung-sa, "Lun sung-tai shu-yüan chih-tu," pp. 431–33.

18 For further discussion of the popularization of "charitable estates" during the latter half of Chinese imperial history, see Twitchett, "The Fan Clan's Charitable Estates"; Hu Hsien-chin, *The Common Descent Group in China and Its Functions,* Viking Fund Publications in Anthropology, no. 10 (New York: Viking Fund, 1948), pp. 72–80.

19 See Fukuda, "Sōdai gishō shōkō."

20 A modern biographer of Shih Hao has asserted that the Shih did indeed have such an estate, but this assertion is not adequately substantiated. See Chiang Yi-pin, "Shih hao yen-chiu," M.A. thesis, Chung-kuo wen-hua University (Taipei), 1980, pp. 170–72.

21 A host of writers have discussed the impact of dynastic change on the political and social orders. See Wilbur, *Slavery in China,* pp. 41–46; Ch'ü, *Han Social Structure,* pp. 83–84; Ho, *Ladder of Success,* pp. 215–19; Ch'en Yi-yen, "Pei-sung t'ung-chih

chieh-ts'eng," pp. 29ff; Mao Han-kuang, "Liang-chin nan-pei-ch'ao," pp. 165–78.

22   Hilary J. Beattie, *Land and Lineage in China: A Study of T'ung-ch'eng County,
     Anhwei, in the Ming and Ch'ing Dynasties* (Cambridge: Cambridge University Press,
     1979), pp. 42–43.

23   Robert M. Hartwell, "Demographic, Political, and Social Transformation of China,
     750–1550," *Harvard Journal of Asiatic Studies* 42, no. 2 (Dec. 1982), pp. 365–442;
     Robert P. Hymes, "Prominence and Power in Sung China: The Local Elite of Fu-chou,
     Chiang-hsi," Ph.D. diss., University of Pennsylvania, 1979; Walton-Vargo, "Education,
     Social Change, and Neo-Confucianism."

24   Davis, "Political Success and the Growth of Kin Groups."

25   Hymes, "Prominence and Power," chap. 1.

26   Hartwell, "Demographic, Political, and Social Transformation of China," p. 416ff.

27   Ibid., p. 416.

28   Ibid., p. 419. Emphasis mine.

29   KKC, *ch.* 93, p. 16a; *ch.* 105, p. 1b.

Bibliography

Western-Language Materials

Aoyama, Sadao. "The Newly-Risen Bureaucrats in Fukien at the Five-Dynasty-Sung Period, with Special Reference to Their Genealogies." *The Memoirs of the Toyo Bunko* 21 (1962): 1–48.

Beattie, Hilary J. *Land and Lineage in China: A Study of T'ung-ch'eng County, Anhwei, in the Ming and Ch'ing Dynasties.* Cambridge: Cambridge University Press, 1979.

Bielenstein, Hans. "The Restoration of the Han Dynasty." *The Museum of Far Eastern Antiquities, Bulletin* no. 26 (1954).

Chaffee, John W. "Education and Examinations in Sung Society (960–1279)." Ph.D. diss., University of Chicago, 1979.

Chang, Chung-li. *The Chinese Gentry: Studies on Their Role in Nineteenth-Century Chinese Society.* Seattle: University of Washington Press, 1955.

Chang, Fu-jui. *Les Fonctionnaires des Song: Index des titres.* Matériaux pour le manuel de l'histoire des Song (Sung Project). Paris: École Pratique des Hautes Études, 1962.

Ch'ü, T'ung-tsu. *Han Social Structure.* Edited by Jack L. Dull. Seattle: University of Washington Press, 1972.

———. *Local Government in China under the Ch'ing.* Stanford: Stanford University Press, 1962.

Dardess, John W. *Confucianism and Autocracy: Professional Elites in the Founding of the Ming Dynasty.* Berkeley: University of California Press, 1983.

Davis, Richard L. "Political Success and the Growth of Kin Groups: The Shih of Ming-chou during the Sung." In *Kinship Organization in Late Imperial China,* edited by Patricia Ebrey and James Watson. Berkeley: University of California Press, 1985.

———. "The Shih Lineage at the Southern Sung Court: Aspects of Socio-political Mobility in Sung China." Ph.D. diss., Princeton University, 1980.

———. "Shih Mi-yüan at the Hands of Traditional Historians: The Succession of 1224." Paper presented at the 1985 International Symposium on Song History, Hangzhou University, May 1985.

Dennerline, Jerry. *The Chia-ting Loyalists: Confucian Leadership and Social Change in Seventeenth-Century China.* New Haven: Yale University Press, 1981.

Eberhard, Wolfram. *Social Mobility in Traditional China.* Leiden: E. J. Brill, 1962.

Ebrey, Patricia Buckley. *The Aristocratic Families of Early Imperial China.* Cambridge: Cambridge University Press, 1978.

Franke, Herbert. "Chia Ssu-tao (1213–1275): A 'Bad Last Minister'?" In *Confucian Personalities,* edited by Arthur F. Wright and Denis Twitchett, 217–34. Stanford: Stanford University Press, 1962.

————. "Siege and Defense of Towns in Medieval China." In *Chinese Ways in Warfare,* edited by Frank A. Kiermann, Jr., 151–201. Cambridge, Mass.: Harvard University Press, 1974.

————. "Treaties between Sung and Chin." In *Études Song: In mémóriam Étienne Balazs,* edited by Francoise Aubin, 55–82. Paris: Mouton & Co., 1970.

————, ed. *Sung Biographies.* 4 vols. Wiesbaden: Steiner, 1976.

Freedman, Maurice. *Chinese Lineage and Society: Fukien and Kuangtung.* London: Athlone Press, 1966.

Fung, Yu-lan. *A History of Chinese Philosophy.* Translated by Derk Bodde. 2 vols. Princeton: Princeton University Press, 1952.

Gernet, Jacques. *Daily Life in China on the Eve of the Mongol Invasion, 1250–1276.* Translated by H. M. Wright. Stanford: Stanford University Press, 1962.

Hartwell, Robert M. "Demographic, Political, and Social Transformation of China, 750–1550." *Harvard Journal of Asiatic Studies* 42, no. 2 (December 1982): 365–442.

Ho, Ping-ti. "An Estimate of the Total Population of Sung-Chin China." In *Études Song: In mémóriam Étienne Balazs,* edited by Francoise Aubin, 33–53. Paris: Mouton & Co., 1970.

————. *The Ladder of Success in Imperial China: Aspects of Social Mobility, 1368–1911.* New York: Columbia University Press, 1962.

Hu, Hsien-chin. *The Common Descent Group in China and Its Functions.* Viking Fund Publications in Anthropology, no. 10. New York: Viking Fund, 1948.

Hucker, Charles O. "An Index of Terms and Titles in 'Governmental Organization of the Ming Dynasty.'" In *Studies of Governmental Institutions in Chinese History,* edited by John L. Bishop, 127–51. Cambridge, Mass.: Harvard University Press, 1968.

Hymes, Robert P. "Prominence and Power in Sung China: The Local Elite of Fu-chou, Chiang-hsi." Ph.D. diss., University of Pennsylvania, 1979.

Johnson, David. "The Last Years of a Great Clan: The Li Family of Chao Chün in Late T'an and Early Sung." *Harvard Journal of Asiatic Studies* 37, no. 1 (June 1977): 5–102.

————. *The Medieval Chinese Oligarchy.* Boulder, Colo.: Westview Press, 1977.

Kracke, E. A., Jr. *Civil Service in Early Sung China, 960–1067.* Cambridge, Mass.: Harvard University Press, 1953.

————. "Family vs. Merit in Chinese Civil Service Examinations under the Empire." *Harvard Journal of Asiatic Studies* 10, no. 2 (September 1947): 103–23.

————. *Translation of Sung Civil Service Titles.* Matériaux pour le manuel de l'histoire des Song (Sung Project). Paris: École Pratique des Hautes Études, 1957.

Kwanten, Luc. *Imperial Nomads: A History of Central Asia, 500–1500*. Philadelphia: University of Pennsylvania Press, 1979.

Legge, James. *The Chinese Classics*. 2d rev. ed. 7 vols. Shanghai, 1935.

Liu, James T. C. "How Did a Neo-Confucian School Become the State Orthodoxy?" *Philosophy East & West* 23, no. 4 (October 1973): 483–505.

———. "The Sung Views on the Control of Government Clerks." *Journal of Economic and Social History of the Orient* (Leiden) 10, pt. 2/3 (1967): 317–44.

McKnight, Brian. "Administrators of Hangchow under the Northern Sung: A Case Study." *Harvard Journal of Asiatic Studies* 30 (1970): 185–211.

———. *Village and Bureaucracy in Southern Sung China*. Chicago: University of Chicago Press, 1971.

Marsh, Robert M. *The Mandarins: The Circulation of Elites in China, 1600–1900*. New York: Free Press of Glencoe, 1961.

Mote, Frederick W. "Confucian Eremitism in the Yüan Period." In *The Confucian Persuasion*, edited by Arthur F. Wright, 202–40. Stanford: Stanford University Press, 1960.

Pan, Ku. *The History of the Former Han Dynasty*. Translated by Homer H. Dubs. 2 vols. Baltimore: Waverly Press, 1935.

Pareto, Vilfredo. *The Mind and Society*. Edited by Arthur Livingston. Translated by Andrew Bongiorno and Arthur Livingston. 4 vols. New York: Harcourt, Brace & Co., 1935.

Peterson, Charles A. "First Sung Reactions to the Mongol Invasion of the North, 1211–17." In *Crisis and Prosperity in Sung China*, edited by John Winthrop Haeger, 215–52. Tucson: University of Arizona Press, 1975.

———. "Old Illusions and New Realities: Sung Foreign Policy, 1217–1234." In *China among Equals: The Middle Kingdom and Its Neighbors, 10th–14th Centuries*, edited by Morris Rossabi, 204–39. Berkeley: University of California Press, 1983.

Potter, Jack M. "Land and Lineage in Traditional China." In *Family and Kinship in Chinese Society*, edited by Maurice Freedman, 121–38. Stanford: Stanford University Press, 1970.

Pulleyblank, Edwin G. *The Background of the Rebellion of An Lu-shan*. London: Oxford University Press, 1955.

Schirokauer, Conrad. "Neo-Confucians under Attack: The Condemnation of Wei-hsüeh." In *Crisis and Prosperity in Sung China*, edited by John W. Haeger, 163–98. Tucson: University of Arizona Press, 1975.

Shiba, Yoshinobu. "Ningpo and Its Hinterland." In *The City in Late Imperial China*, edited by G. William Skinner, 391–439. Stanford: Stanford University Press, 1977.

———. "Urbanization and the Development of Markets in the Lower Yangtze Valley." In *Crisis and Prosperity in Sung China*, edited by John W. Haeger, 13–48. Tucson: University of Arizona Press, 1975.

Ssu-ma, Ch'ien. *Records of the Grand Historian*. Translated by Burton Watson. New York: Columbia University Press, 1961.

Stone, Lawrence. *The Crisis of the Aristocracy, 1558–1641*. Glasgow: Oxford University Press, 1965.

Tao, Jing-shen. *The Jurchen in Twelfth-Century China: A Study of Sinicization*. Seattle: University of Washington Press, 1976.

Twitchett, Denis. "The Composition of the T'ang Ruling Class: New Evidence from Tun-huang." In *Perspectives on the T'ang*, edited by Arthur F. Wright and Denis Twitchett, 47–85. New Haven: Yale University Press, 1973.

———. "The Fan Clan's Charitable Estates." In *Confucianism in Action*, edited by David Nivison and Arthur F. Wright, 97–133. Stanford: Stanford University Press, 1959.

———. *Financial Administration under the T'ang Dynasty*. Cambridge: Cambridge University Press, 1963.

———, ed. "Sui and T'ang China, 589–906." Vol. 3, part 1 of *The Cambridge History of China*. Cambridge: Cambridge University Press, 1979.

Walton-Vargo, Linda Ann. "Education, Social Change, and Neo-Confucianism in Sung-Yüan China: Academies and the Local Elite in Ming Prefecture (Ningpo)." Ph.D. diss., University of Pennsylvania, 1978.

Wang, Gungwu. *The Structure of Power in North China during the Five Dynasties*. Kuala Lumpur: University of Malaya Press, 1963.

Wilbur, Martin C. *Slavery in China during the Former Han Dynasty, 206 B.C.–A.D. 25*. Anthropological Series, vol. 34. Chicago: Field Museum of Natural History, 1943.

Wilhelm, Hellmut. "From Myth to Myth: The Case of Yüeh Fei's Biography." In *Confucian Personalities*, edited by Arthur F. Wright and Denis Twitchett, 146–61. Stanford: Stanford University Press, 1962.

Williamson, Henry R. *Wang An-shih: A Chinese Statesman and Educationalist of the Sung Dynasty*. 2 vols. London: A. Probsthain, 1935.

Worthy, Edmund H. "The Founding of Sung China, 950–1000: Integrative Changes in Military and Political Institutions." Ph.D. diss., Princeton University, 1976.

Chinese- and Japanese-Language Materials

Aoyama, Sadao. "Zui-Tō-Sō san-dai ni okeru kosū no chiiki teki kōsatsu" (An areal study of population for the Sui, T'ang, and Sung dynasties). *Rekishigaku kenkyū* 6, no. 5 (1936): 411–46; no. 6:529–54.

青山定雄. 隋唐宋三代における戸數の地域的考察. 歷史學研究.

Chang, Ch'i-yün. "Sung-tai ssu-ming chih hsüeh-feng" (Intellectual milieu of Ssu-ming during the Sung dynasty). In *Sung-shih yen-chiu chi* 3:33–71. Taipei: Chung-hua ts'ung-shu, 1966.

張其昀. 宋代四明之學風. 宋史研究集.

Chang, Chia-chü. *Liang-sung ching-chi chung-hsin ti nan-yi* (Gravitation of the economy southward during the Sung). Wuhan, Hupei: Jen-min, 1957.

張家駒. 兩宋經濟中心的南移.

Chang, Chin-chien. *Chung-kuo wen-kuan chih-tu shih* (History of the Chinese civil service system). Taipei: Hua-kang, 1977.

張金鑑．中國文官制度史．

Chang, Hao. *Yün-ku tsa-chi*. In *Sung-jen cha-chi pa chung*. Taipei: Shih-chieh, 1963.

張淏．雲谷雜記．宋人劄記八種．

Chang, Tuan-yi. *Kuei-erh chi. Pai-pu ts'ung-shu chi-ch'eng*.

張端義．貴耳集．百部叢書集成．

Chao chung lu. Pai-pu ts'ung-shu chi-ch'eng.

昭忠錄．百部叢書集成．

Chao, T'ieh-han. "Sung-tai ti chou-hsüeh" (Prefectural schools of the Sung dynasty). In *Sung-shih yen-chiu chi* 2:343–62. Taipei: Chung-hua ts'ung-shu, 1964.

趙鐵寒．宋代的州學．宋史研究集．

———. "Sung-tai ti hsüeh-hsiao chiao-yü" (The schools and education of the Sung dynasty). *Hsüeh-shu chi-k'an* 3, no. 2 (December 1954): 36–47.

趙鐵寒．宋代的學校教育．學術季刊．

Chao, Yi. *Nien-erh shih cha-chi*. Rev. ed. Taipei: Ting-wen, 1978.

趙翼．廿二史劄記．

Che-chiang t'ung-chih. 1736. Compiled by Shen Yi-chi et al. Academia Sinica rare edition.

浙江通志．沈翼機等修．

Ch'en, Chi. *Yi-pai-chai kao. Ssu-pu ts'ung-k'an*.

陳基．夷白齋藁．四部叢刊．

Ch'en, Ch'i-shou. "Sung mu-lu hsüeh-chia ch'ao kung-wu ch'en chen-sun chuan" (Biography of Ch'ao Kung-wu and Ch'en Chen-sun, bibliographers of the Sung). *Kuo-ts'ui hsüeh-pao* 68, no. 6 (1910): 3883–93.

陳祺壽．宋目錄學家晁公武・陳振孫傳．國粹學報．

Chen, Te-hsiu. *Chen wen-chung-kung wen-chi. Ssu-pu ts'ung-k'an*.

真德秀．真文正公文集．四部叢刊．

Ch'en, Teng-yüan. "Ch'in kuei p'ing" (Critique on Ch'in Kuei). *Chin-ling hsüeh-pao* 1, no. 1 (May 1931): 27–46.

陳登原．秦檜評．金陵學報．

———. "Han p'ing-yüan p'ing" (Critique on Han P'ing-yüan [Han T'o-chou]). *Chin-ling hsüeh-pao* 4, no. 1 (November 1934): 89–142.

陳登原．韓平原評．金陵學報．

Ch'en, Yi-yen. "Pei-sung t'ung-chih chieh-ts'eng she-hui liu-tung chih yen-chiu" (Study of the ruling class and social mobility during the Northern Sung). Master's thesis, National Cheng-chih University (Taipei), 1971.

陳義彥. 北宋統治階層社會流動之研究.

Ch'en, Yin-k'o. "T'ang-tai cheng-chih-shih shu-lun kao" (Narrative on the political history of the T'ang dynasty). In *Ch'en yin-k'o hsien-sheng ch'üan-chi*, 151–304. Taipei: Chiu-ssu, 1978.

陳寅恪. 唐代政治史述論稿. 陳寅恪先生全集.

Cheng, Chen. *Hsing-yang wai-shih chi. Ssu-k'u ch'üan-shu chen-pen*.

鄭真. 滎陽外史集. 四庫全書珍本.

Ch'eng, Pi. *Ming-shui chi. Ssu-k'u ch'üan-shu chen-pen*.

程珌. 洺水集. 四庫全書珍本.

(*Chia-ching*) *Ning-po fu chih*. 1560. Compiled by Chang Shih-ch'e et al. National Palace Museum, Taipei, rare edition.

嘉靖寧波府志. 張時徹撰.

(*Chia-t'ai*) *K'uai-chi chih*. 1201. Compiled by Shih Su. In *Sung-yüan ti-fang-chih ts'ung-shu*. Taipei: Chung-kuo ti-chih yen-chiu hui, 1978.

嘉泰會稽志. 施宿撰. 宋元地方志叢書.

(*Chia-ting*) *Ch'ih-ch'eng chih*. 1223. Compiled by Ch'en Ch'i-ch'ing. In *Sung-yüan ti-fang-chih ts'ung-shu*. Taipei: Chung-kuo ti-chih yen-chiu hui, 1978.

嘉定赤城志. 陳耆卿撰. 宋元地方志叢書.

Chiang, Yi-pin. "Shih hao yen-chiu" (Research on Shih Hao). Master's thesis, Chung-kuo Wen-hua University (Taipei), 1980.

蔣義斌. 史浩研究.

Ch'ien, Shih-sheng. *Nan sung shu*. N.d.

錢士升. 南宋書.

(*Ch'ien-tao*) *Ssu-ming t'u-ching*. 1169. Compiled by Chang Chin et al. In *Sung-yüan ti-fang-chih ts'ung-shu*. Taipei: Chung-kuo ti-chih yen-chiu hui, 1978.

乾道四明圖經. 張津等撰. 宋元地方志叢書.

(*Chih-cheng*) *Ssu-ming hsü-chih*. 1342. Compiled by Wang Yüan-kung et al. In *Sung-yüan ti-fang-chih ts'ung-shu*. Taipei: Chung-kuo ti-chih yen-chiu hui, 1978.

至正四明續志. 王元恭等撰. 宋元地方志叢書.

(*Chih-shun*) *Chen-chiang chih*. 1332. Compiled by Yü Hsi-lu et al. In *Sung-yüan ti-fang-chih ts'ung-shu*. Taipei: Chung-kuo ti-chih yen-chiu hui, 1978.

至順鎮江志. 俞希魯纂. 宋元地方志叢書.

(*Chih-yüan*) *Chia-ho chih*. 1288. Compiled by Hsü Shuo. In *Sung-yüan ti-fang-chih ts'ung-shu*. Taipei: Chung-kuo ti-chih yen-chiu hui, 1978.

至元嘉禾志. 徐碩撰. 宋元地方志叢書.

Chin shih (History of the Chin). Compiled by T'o-t'o et al. Peking: Chung-hua, 1975.
金史．脫脫等撰．

(Ching-ting) Chien-k'ang chih. 1261. Compiled by Ma Kuang-tsu. In *Sung-yüan ti-fang-chih ts'ung-shu*. Taipei: Chung-kuo ti-chih yen-chiu hui, 1978.
景定建康志．馬光祖修．宋元地方志叢書．

Chiu t'ang shu (Old history of the T'ang). Compiled by Liu Hsü et al. Peking: Chung-hua, 1975.
舊唐書．劉昫等撰．

Chou, Mi. *Ch'i-tung yeh-yü*. In *Sung-yüan-jen shuo-pu-shu*. Shanghai: Shang-wu, 1919.
周密．齊東野語．宋元人說部書．

———. *Kuei-hsin tsa-chih. Pai-pu ts'ung-shu chi-ch'eng*.
周密．癸辛雜識．百部叢書集成．

Chou, Pi-ta. *Wen-chung chi. Ssu-k'u ch'üan-shu chen-pen*.
周必大．文忠集．四庫全書珍本．

Chou, Tao-chi. "Sung-tai tsai-hsiang ming-ch'eng yü ch'i shih-ch'üan chih yen-chiu" (Study of the title of chief councillor during the Sung dynasty and his *de facto* authority). In *Sung-shih yen-chiu chi* 3:245–63. Taipei: Chung-hua ts'ung-shu, 1966.
周道濟．宋代宰相名稱與其實權之研究．宋史研究集．

Chu, Hsi. *Hui-an hsien-sheng wen-kung wen-chi. Ssu-pu ts'ung-k'an*.
朱熹．晦庵先生文公文集．四部叢刊．

Ch'üan, Tsu-wang. *Chieh-ch'i-t'ing chi (Wai-pien). Ssu-pu ts'ung-k'an*.
全祖望．鮚埼亭集．外編．四部叢刊．

(Ch'ung-hsiu) Ch'ang-chou fu chih. 1618. Compiled by T'ang Ho-cheng et al. National Palace Museum, Taipei, rare edition.
重修常州府志．唐鶴徵等撰．

(Ch'ung-hsiu) Ch'in-ch'uan chih. 1365. Compiled by Lu Chen. In *Sung-yüan ti-fang-chih ts'ung-shu*. Taipei: Ta-hua, 1978.
重修琴川志．盧鎮纂修．宋元地方志叢書．

(Ch'ung-hsiu) P'i-ling chih. 1268. Compiled by Shih Neng-chih. In *Sung-yüan ti-fang-chih ts'ung-shu*. Taipei: Ta-hua, 1978.
重修昆陵志．史能之纂修．宋元地方志叢書．

Fu, Ts'eng. *Nan-sung tsa-shih-shih. Ssu-k'u ch'üan-shu chen-pen*.
符曾．南宋雜事詩．四庫全書珍本．

Fukuda, Ritsuko, "Sōdai gishō shōkō, Minshū rōshi o chūshin to shite" (Examination into charitable estates of the Sung dynasty, with special reference to the Lou house of

Ming-chou). *Chūgoku kankei ronsetsu shiryo*, no. 14, pt. 3b (1972): 188–206.

福田立子. 宋代義莊小考；明州樓氏を中心として. 中國關係,論説資料.

Hang-chou fu chih. 1784. Compiled by Shao Chin-han. Reprint. Taipei: Ch'eng-wen, 1970.

杭州府志. 邵晉涵纂.

Hsiao-shan shih-shih tsung-p'u. Pa-hsing t'ang edition. In East Asian Collection, Starr Library, Columbia University.

蕭山史氏宗譜. 八行堂.

(*Hsien-ch'un*) *Lin-an chih*. 1268. Compiled by Ch'ien Shuo-yu. In *Sung-yüan ti-fang-chih ts'ung-shu*. Taipei: Chung-kuo ti-chih yen-chiu hui, 1978.

咸淳臨安志. 潛説友撰. 宋元地方志叢書.

(*Hsin-hsiu*) *Yin-hsien chih*. 1887. Compiled by Tai Mei et al. Academia Sinica rare edition.

新修鄞縣志. 戴枚等撰.

Hsin yüan shih (New history of the Yüan). Compiled by K'o Shao-min et al. Taipei: Yi-wen, 1956.

新元史. 柯邵忞等撰.

Hu, Meng-yü, Hu Chih-jou. *Hsiang-t'ai shou-mo*. *Pai-pu ts'ung-shu chi-ch'eng*.

胡夢昱, 胡知柔. 象台首末. 百部叢書集成.

Hu-chou fu chih. 1874. Compiled by Chou Hsüeh-chün, Tsung Yüan-han et al. Taipei: Ch'eng-wen, 1970.

湖州府志. 周學濬. 宗源瀚等修.

Huang, K'uan-ch'ung. "Lüeh-lun nan-sung shih-tai ti kuei-cheng-jen" (Brief discussion of loyalist-refugees during the Southern Sung era). *Shih-huo yüeh-k'an* (Taipei) 7, no. 3 (June 1977): 111–20; 7, no. 4 (July 1977): 172–83.

黃寬重. 略論南宋時代的歸正人. 食貨月刊.

———. "Meng kung nien-p'u" (Chronological biography of Meng Kung). *Shih yüan* (Taipei) 4 (October 1973): 79–135.

黃寬重. 孟珙年譜. 史原.

———. "Nan-sung shih-tai k'ang chin yi-chün chih yen-chiu" (Study of righteous armies resisting the Chin in Southern Sung times). Ph.D. diss., National Taiwan University, 1980.

黃寬重. 南宋時代抗金義軍之研究.

———. "Wan-sung ch'ao-ch'en tui kuo-shih ti cheng-yi; Li-tsung shih-tai ti ho-chan, pien-fang, yü liu-min" (Polemics among late Sung officials concerning government policy; war-peace, border defense, and refugees during the era of Li-tsung). Master's thesis, National Taiwan University, 1974.

黃寬重．晚宋朝臣對國是的爭議：理宗時代的和戰．邊防與流民．

Huang, Tsung-hsi. *Sung-yüan hsüeh-an. Sung-yüan hsüeh-an pu-yi.* Taipei: Shih-chieh, 1973.

黃宗義．宋元學案．宋元學案補遺．

Ihara, Hiroshi. "Nan sō shisen ni okeru goshi no seiryoko; go sei no ran zenshi" (The might of the Wu house in Southern Sung Szechwan: a history prior to the rebellion of Wu Hsi). In *Aoyama hakushi koki kinen. Sōdai shi ronsō,* 1–33. Tokyo: Seishin, 1974.

伊原弘．南宋四川における吳氏の勢力：吳曦の亂前史．青山博士古稀紀念．宋代史論叢．

———. "Sōdai minshū ni okeru kanko no kon-in kankei" (Affinal relationships among official households in Ming-chou during the Sung dynasty). *Chūo daigaku daigakuin kenkyū nenpō* 1 (March 1972): 157–68.

伊原弘．宋代明州における官戶口婚姻關係．中央大學大學院研究年報．

Jui, Ho-cheng. "Lun sung t'ai-tsu chih ch'uang-yeh k'ai-kuo" (Discussion of Sung T'ai-tsu's founding of the empire). In *Sung-shih yen-chiu chi* 5:429–77. Taipei: Chung-hua ts'ung-shu, 1970.

芮和蒸．論宋太祖之創業開國．宋史研究集．

(*K'ai-ch'ing*) *Ssu-ming hsü-chih.* 1259. Compiled by Mei Ying-fa et al. In *Sung-yüan ti-fang-chih ts'ung-shu.* Taipei: Chung-kuo ti-chih yen-chiu hui, 1978.

開慶四明續志．梅應發等撰．宋元地方志叢書．

Kinugawa, Tsuyoshi. "Chin kai no kōwa seisaku o megute" (Concerning Ch'in Kuei's peace policy). *Tōhō gakuhō* (Kyoto) 45 (September 1973): 245–94.

衣川強．秦檜の講和政策をめぐって．東方學報．

———. "Sōdai no meizoku; kanan roshi no baai" (A famous clan of the Sung dynasty: the case of the Lü house of Honan). *Chūgoku kankei ronsetsu shiryo* 15, pt. 3a (1973): 37–53.

衣川強．宋代の名族：河南呂氏の場合．中國關係論說資料．

K'o, Wei-ch'i. *Sung-shih hsin-pien.* Taipei: Hsin wen feng, 1974.

柯維騏．宋史新編．

Li, Cheng-fu. *Sung-tai k'o-chü chih-tu yen-chiu*. Taipei: Cheng-chih University, Chiao-yü yen-chiu ts'ung-shu, 1963.

李正富．宋代科舉制度研究．

Li, Hsin-ch'uan. *Chien-yen yi-lai hsi-nien yao-lu*. In *Sung-shih tzu-liao ts'ui-pien*, edited by Chao, T'ieh-han. Taipei: Wen-hai, 1968.

李心傳．建炎以來繫年要錄．趙鐵寒主編．宋史資料萃編．

Li, Yu-wu. *Ssu-ch'ao ming-ch'en yen-hsing lu*. In *Sung-shih tzu-liao ts'ui-pien*. Taipei: Wen-hai, 1968.

李幼武．四朝名臣言行錄．宋史資料萃編．

Liang-ch'ao kang-mu pei-yao. In *Sung-shih tzu-liao ts'ui-pien*. Taipei: Wen-hai, 1968.

兩朝綱目備要．宋史資料萃編．

Lin, T'ien-wei. "Sung-tai ch'üan-hsiang hsing-ch'eng chih fen-hsi" (Analysis of the molding of powerful councillors during the Sung). In *Sung-shih yen-chiu chi* 8:141–70. Taipei: Chung-hua ts'ung-shu: 1976.

林天蔚．宋代權相形成之分析．宋史研究集．

Lin, Tzu-hsü. "Sung-tai ti-fang chiao-yü ti fa-chan" (Development of local education during the Sung dynasty). *Hua-kang hsüeh-pao* (Taipei) 2 (December 1965): 155–76.

林子勳．宋代地方教育的發展．華岡學報．

Liu, K'o-chuang. *Hou-ts'un hsien-sheng ta ch'üan-chi*. *Ssu-pu ts'ung-k'an*.

劉克莊．後村先生大全集．四部叢刊．

Liu, Tsai. *Man-t'ang wen-chi*. *Chia-yeh-t'ang ts'ung-shu*.

劉宰．漫塘文集．嘉業堂叢書．

Liu, Tzu-chien [James T. C. Liu]. "Lüeh-lun sung-tai ti-fang kuan-hsüeh ho ssu-hsüeh ti hsiao-chang" (Brief discussion of the rise and decline of local public and private schools during the Sung dynasty). *(Kuo-li) Chung-yang yen-chiu-yüan. Li-shih yü-yen yen-chiu-so chi-k'an* 36, pt. 1 (1965): 237–48.

劉子健．略論宋代地方官學和私學的消長．國立中央研究院．歷史語言研究所
集刊．

Liu, Tz'u-fu. *Ssu-ming jen-chien*. In *Ssu-ming ts'ung-shu*. Taipei, 1964.

劉慈孚．四明人鑑．四明叢書．

Lou, Yüeh (Yao). *Kung-k'uei chi*. *Ssu-pu ts'ung-k'an*.

樓鑰．攻媿集．四部叢刊．

Lu, Hsin-yüan. *Sung-shih yi*. Taipei: Ting-wen, 1978.

陸心源．宋史翼．

Ma, Tuan-lin. *Wen-hsien t'ung-k'ao*. Shanghai: Shang-wu, 1936.

馬端臨．文獻通考．

Mao, Han-kuang. "Chung-kuo chung-ku she-hui-shih lüeh-lun kao" (Framework for the social history of medieval China). *(Kuo-li) Chung-yang yen-chiu-yüan. Li-shih yü-yen yen-chiu-so chi-k'an* 47, pt. 3 (1976): 341–431.

毛漢光．中國中古社會史略論稿．國立中央研究院．歷史語言研究所集列．

———. "Liang-chin nan-pei-ch'ao shih-tsu cheng-chih chih yen-chiu" (Study of the politics of eminent families during the Wei, Chin, and Nan-pei-ch'ao period). 2 vols. Master's thesis, National Cheng-chih University (Taipei), 1966.

毛漢光．兩晉南北朝士族政治之研究．

———. "T'ang-tai ta shih-tsu ti chin-shih ti" (*Chin-shih* data on the most prominent families of the T'ang dynasty). *(Kuo-li) Chung-yang yen-chiu-yüan. Ch'eng-li wu-shih chou-nien chi-nien lun-wen chi* (June 1977): 593–614.

毛漢光．唐代大族的進士第．國立中央研究院．成立五十周年紀念論文集．

———. "Wo kuo chung-ku ta shih-tsu chih ko-an yen-chiu: Lang-ya wang-shih" (A case study of eminent families in medieval China: the Wang of Lang-ya). *(Kuo-li) Chung-yang yen-chiu-yüan. Li-shih yü-yen yen-chiu-so chi-k'an* 37, pt. 2 (1967): 577–610.

毛漢光．我國中古大士族之個案研究：瑯玡王氏．國立中央研究院．歷史語言研究所集列．

Ming shih (History of the Ming). Compiled by Chang T'ing-yü et al. Peking: Chung-hua, 1975.

明史．張廷玉等撰．

Moriya, Mitsuo. *Riku-chō mombatsu no ichi kenkyū* (Study of prominent families of the six dynasties). Tokyo: Tōyō Daigaku, 1951.

守屋美都雄．六朝門閥の一研究．

Niida, Noboru. "Tōdai no hōshaku oyobi shoku hōsei" (The T'ang dynasty systems of ennoblement and fiefs of maintenance). *Tōhō gakuhō* (Tokyo), no. 10, pt. 1 (1939): 1–64.

仁井田陞．唐代の封爵及び食封制．東方學報．

Nishikawa, Masao. "Kahoku godai ōchō no bunshin kanryō" (Civilian officials in North China under the five dynasties' regimes). *Tōyō bunka kenkyūjo kiyō* 27, pt. 3 (March 1962): 211–61.

西川正夫．華北五代王朝の文臣官僚．東京大學．東洋文化研究所紀要．

Ou-yang, Hsiu. *Chi-ku-lu pa-wei.* In *Shih-k'o shih-liao ts'ung-shu* 24. Taipei: Hsin wen feng, 1966.

歐陽修．集古錄跋尾．石刻史料叢書．

———. *Hsin t'ang shu* (New history of the T'ang). Peking: Chung-hua, 1975.

歐陽修．新唐書．

Pan, Ku. *Han shu* (History of the Han). Peking: Chung-hua, 1962.

班固．漢書．

P'an Kuang-tan. *Ming-ch'ing liang-tai chia-hsing ti wang-tsu* (Eminent families of Chia-hsing during the Ming and Ch'ing dynasties). Shanghai: Shang-wu, 1947.

潘光旦．明清兩代嘉興的望族．

(*Pao-ch'ing*) *Ssu-ming chih.* 1227. Compiled by Lo Chün et al. In *Sung-yüan ti-fang-chih ts'ung-shu.* Taipei: Chung-kuo ti-chih yen-chiu hui, 1978.

寶慶四明志．羅濬等撰．宋元地方志叢書．

P'eng, Kuei-nien. *Chih-t'ang chi. Ssu-k'u ch'üan-shu chen-pen.*

彭龜年．止堂集．四庫全書珍本．

Pi, Yüan. *Hsü tzu-chih t'ung-chien.* Peking: Ku-chi, 1958.

畢沅．續資治通鑑．

Shao-hsing fu chih. 1586. Compiled by Chang Yüan-pien et al. National Central Library, Taipei, rare edition.

紹興府志．張元忭等撰．

Shiba, Yoshinobu. "Sōdai minshū no toshika to chiiki kaihatsu" (Urbanization and regional development of Sung-dynasty Ming-chou). *Machikaneyama ronsō,* no. 3 (December 1969): 127–48.

斯波義信．宋代明州の都市化と地域開發．待兼山論叢．

Shih, Hao. *Mou-feng chen-yin man-lu. Ssu-k'u ch'üan-shu chen-pen.*

史浩．鄮峯真隱漫錄．四庫全書珍本．

Ssu-k'u ch'üan-shu tsung-mu t'i-yao. Taipei: Shang-wu, 1971.

四庫全書總目提要．

Ssu-ma, Ch'ien. *Shih chi* (Records of the grand historian). Peking: Chung-hua, 1959.

司馬遷．史記．

Ssu-ma, Kuang. *Tzu-chih t'ung-chien* (Comprehensive mirror to aid in governing). Peking: Chung-hua, 1956.

司馬光．資治通鑑．

Su-chou fu chih. 1368–98. Compiled by Lu Hsiung et al. National Palace Museum, Taipei, rare edition.

蘇州府志．盧熊等輯．

Sun, K'o-k'uan. *Meng-ku han-chün yü han wen-hua yen-chiu* (Study of Chinese armies under the Mongols and Chinese culture). Taipei: Wen-hsing, 1958.

孫克寬．蒙古漢軍與漢文化研究．

Sun, Kuo-tung. "T'ang-sung chih chi she-hui men-ti chih hsiao-jung" (The demise of the socially prominent during the T'ang-Sung period). *Hsin-ya hsüeh-pao* 4, no. 1 (1959): 211–304.

孫國棟．唐宋之際社會門第之消融．新亞學報．

Sung-chi san-ch'ao cheng-yao. Pai-pu ts'ung-shu chi-ch'eng.

宋季三朝政要．百部叢書集成．

Sung hui-yao chi-kao. Taipei: Hsin wen feng, 1976.

宋會要輯稿．

Sung, Lien. *Sung wen-hsien-kung ch'üan-chi. Ssu-pu pei-yao.*

宋濂．宋文憲公全集．四部備要．

Sung shih (History of the Sung). Compiled by T'o-t'o et al. Peking: Chung-hua, 1977.

宋史．脫脫等撰．

Sung-shih chi-shih pen-mo. Compiled by Ch'en Pang-chan et al. Rev. ed. Taipei: Ting-wen, 1978.

宋史紀事本末．陳邦瞻纂輯．

Sung-shih ch'üan-wen hsü tzu-chih t'ung-chien. In *Sung-shih tzu-liao ts'ui-pien.* Taipei: Wen-hai, 1969.

宋史全文續資治通鑑．宋史資料萃編．

(*Ta-te*) *Ch'ang-kuo-chou t'u-chih.* 1298. Compiled by Feng Fu-ching et al. In *Sung-yüan ti-fang-chih ts'ung-shu.* Taipei: Chung-kuo ti-chih yen-chiu hui, 1978.

大德昌國州圖志．馮福京等撰．宋元地方志叢書．

Tai, Piao-yüan. *Shan-yüan chi. Pai-pu ts'ung-shu chi-ch'eng.*

戴表元．剡源集．百部叢書集成．

T'ang, Ch'ang-ju. *Wei-chin nan-pei ch'ao shih lun ts'ung.* Peking: San-lien, 1955.

唐長孺．魏晉南北朝史論叢．

T'ao, Chin-sheng. *Chin hai-ling-ti ti fa sung yü ts'ai-shih chan-yi ti k'ao-shih* (The campaign of Chin emperor Hai-ling against the Sung and the battle at Ts'ai-shih—an investigation). Taipei: National Taiwan University, 1963.

陶晉生．金海陵帝的伐宋與采石戰役的考實．

Teng, Ssu-yü. *Chung-kuo k'ao-shih chih-tu shih* (History of the Chinese examination system). Taipei: Hsüeh-sheng, 1967.

鄧嗣禹．中國考試制度史．

Ting, Ch'uan-ching. *Sung-jen yi-shih hui-pien.* Peking: Shang-wu, 1958.

丁傳靖. 宋人軼事彙編.

Ts'ui, Tun-shih. *Ts'ui she-jen yü-t'ang lei-kao. Pai-pu ts'ung-shu chi-ch'eng.*

崔敦詩. 崔舍人玉堂類藁.

Tu, Fan. *Ch'ing-hsien chi. Ssu-k'u ch'üan-shu chen-pen.*

杜范. 清獻集. 四庫全書珍本.

T'ung, Chao-hsiung. *Nan-sung wen-lu.* N.d.

童兆熊, 南宋文錄.

Tung-nan chi-wen. Pai-pu ts'ung-shu chi-ch'eng.

東南紀聞. 百部叢書集成.

Umehara, Kaoru. "Sōdai no onin seido" (The Sung dynasty's system of favor and protection). *Tōhō gakuhō* (Kyoto) 52 (March 1980): 501–36.

梅原郁. 宋代の恩蔭制度. 東方學報.

———. "Sōdai sensen no hitokoma" (Aspects of placement selection in the Sung dynasty). *Tōyōshi kenkyū* 39, no. 4 (March 1981): 79–114.

梅原郁. 宋代銓選のひとこま. 東洋史研究.

Wang, An-shih. *Lin-ch'uan chi. Ssu-pu pei-yao.*

王安石. 臨川集. 四部備要.

Wang, Chien-ch'iu. "Sung-tai t'ai-hsüeh yü t'ai-hsüeh-sheng" (The imperial university and imperial university students during the Sung). Master's thesis, Fu-jen University (Taipei), 1965.

王建秋. 宋代太學與太學生.

Wang, Shih-p'eng. *Mei-hsi wang hsien-sheng wen-chi. Ssu-pu ts'ung-k'an.*

王十朋. 梅溪王先生文集. 四部叢刊.

Wang, Teh-yi. "Sung hsiao-tsung chi ch'i shih-tai" (Sung Hsiao-tsung and his times). In *Sung-shih yen-chiu chi* 10:245–302. Taipei: Chung-hua ts'ung-shu, 1978.

王德毅. 宋孝宗及其時代. 宋史研究集.

———. *Sung-tai tsai-huang ti chiu-chi cheng-ts'e* (Disaster-relief programs during the Sung dynasty). Taipei: Chung-kuo hsüeh-shu, 1970.

王德毅. 宋代災荒的救濟政策.

Wang, Yi-t'ung. *Wu-ch'ao men-ti* (The socially prominent of the five kingdoms). Nanking, 1943.

王伊同. 五朝門第.

Wang, Ying-lin. *Ssu-ming wen-hsien chi.* In *Ssu-ming ts'ung-shu.* Taipei: Chung-kuo ti-chih yen-chiu hui, 1964–66.

王應麟. 四明文獻集. 四明叢書.

Wei, Liao-weng. *Ho-shan hsien-sheng ta ch'üan-chi. Ssu-pu ts'ung-k'an.*

魏了翁. 鶴山先生大全集. 四部叢刊.

Wu chün chih. 1229. Compiled by Fan Ch'eng-ta. In *Sung-yüan ti-fang-chih ts'ung-shu.* Taipei: Chung-kuo ti-chih yen-chiu hui, 1978.

吳郡志. 范成大撰. 宋元地方志叢書.

Wu, Yung. *Ho-lin chi. Ssu-k'u ch'üan-shu chen-pen.*

吳泳. 鶴林集. 四庫全書珍本.

Yang, Lien-sheng. "Tung-han ti hao-tsu" (Great families of the Eastern Han). *Ch'ing-hua hsüeh-pao* 11, no. 4 (October 1936): 1007–31.

楊聯陞. 東漢的豪族. 清華學報.

Yang, Shih-ch'i. *Li-tai ming-ch'en tsou-yi.* Taipei: Hsüeh-sheng, 1964.

楊士奇. 歷代名臣奏議.

Yang, Shu-fan. *Chung-kuo wen-kuan chih-tu shih* (History of the Chinese civil service system). Taipei: San-min, 1976.

楊樹藩. 中國文官制度史.

———. "Sung-tai kung-chü chih-tu" (The Sung dynasty system of official selection). In *Sung-shih yen-chiu chi* 4:239–73. Taipei: Chung-hua ts'ung-shu, 1969.

楊樹藩. 宋代貢舉制度. 宋史研究集.

Yao, Tsung-wu. "Sung-meng tiao-yü-ch'eng chan-yi-chung hsiung-erh fu-jen chia-shih chi wang li yü ho-chou huo-te pao-ch'üan k'ao" (Examination into the Sung-Mongol battle of Tiao-yü: background of the Lady Hsiung-erh, the battle of Ho-chou, and the conferral of *pao-ch'üan* upon Wang Li). In *Sung-shih yen-chiu chi* 2:123–40. Taipei: Chung-hua ts'ung-shu, 1964.

姚從吾. 宋蒙釣魚城戰役中熊耳夫人家世及王立與合州獲得保全考. 宋史研究集.

Yeh, Hung-sa. "Lun sung-tai shu-yüan chih-tu chih ch'an-sheng chi ch'i ying-hsiang" (Discussion of the inception and influence of the Sung system of academies). In *Sung-shih yen-chiu chi* 9:417–73. Taipei: Chung-hua ts'ung-shu, 1977.

葉鴻灑. 論宋代書院制度之產生及其影響. 宋史研究集.

Yeh, Shih. *Shui-hsin hsien-sheng chi. Ssu-pu ts'ung-k'an.*

葉適. 水心先生集. 四部叢刊.

(*Yen-yu*) *Ssu-ming chih.* 1320. Compiled by Yüan Chüeh. In *Sung-yüan ti-fang-chih ts'ung-shu.* Taipei: Chung-kuo ti-chih yen-chiu hui, 1978.

延祐四明志. 袁桷撰. 宋元地方志叢書.

Yin-hsien t'ung-chih. 1935. Reprint. Taipei: Ch'eng-wen, 1974.

鄞縣通志.

Yüan, Chüeh. *Ch'ing-jung chü-shih chi. Ssu-pu ts'ung-k'an.*

袁桷．清容居士集．四部叢刊．

Yüan, Fu. *Meng-chai chi. Ssu-k'u ch'üan-shu chen-pen.*

袁甫．蒙齋集．四庫全書珍本．

Yüan shih (History of the Yüan). Compiled by Sung Lien et al. Peking: Chung-hua, 1976.

元史．宋濂等撰．

Glossary of Chinese Terms

Names and Terms

an-fu shih 安撫使

Chang Chiu-ch'eng 張九成

Ch'ang-chou 常州

Chang Chün 張浚

Ch'ang-shu 常熟

Chang Tsai 張載

Chang Tzu 張鎡

Chao Fan 趙范

Chao Hsiung 趙雄

Chao Hsün 趙詢

Chao Hung 趙竑

Chao Ju-yü 趙汝愚

Chao K'ai 趙愷

Chao K'uei 趙葵

Ch'ao Kung-wu 晁公武

Chao K'uo 趙擴

Chao P'u 趙普

Chao Ting 趙鼎

Chao Tun 趙惇

Chao Yi 趙翼

Chao Yün 趙昀

Ch'en Chen-sun 陳振孫

Chen-chiang 鎮江

Chen-chou 真州

Ch'en-chou 郴州

Ch'en Chün-ch'ing 陳俊卿

Ch'en Fu-liang 陳傅良

Ch'en K'ang-po 陳康伯

Ch'en shih 陳氏

Chen Te-hsiu 真德秀

Ch'en Tzu-ch'iang 陳自強

Cheng Chen 鄭真

Cheng Ch'ing-chih 鄭清之

Cheng Chü-cheng 鄭居正

Ch'eng Hao 程顥

cheng-p'in 正品

Ch'eng Yi 程頤

Ch'eng Yüan-feng 程元鳳

Chi-chou 吉州

ch'i-chü lang 起居郎

Chi-nan 濟南

chia-hsüeh 家學

Chia She 賈涉

Chia Ssu-tao 賈似道

Chiang-chou 江州

Chiang Fei 蔣芾

Chiang-ning 江寧

chiang-tso shao-chien 將作少監

Chiang Wan-li 江萬里

Chiang-yin 江陰

Ch'iao Hsing-chien 喬行簡

chieh-tu-shih 節度使

chien-chü 薦舉

Ch'ien Hsiang-tsu 錢象祖

Chien-k'ang 建康

Chien-ning 建寧

ch'ien-shu shu-

    mi-yüan shih 簽書樞密院事

chien-tu chin-

    tsou-yüan 監都進奏院

chih-chiang 直講

chih-chih fu-shih 制置副使

Ch'ih-chou 池州

chih-hsien 知縣

chih-k'o 制科

chih pi-ko 直祕閣

Chin-chiang 晉江

Ch'in-chou 秦州

Ching T'ang 京鏜

Ch'ing-yüan-fu 慶元府

Ch'iu Ch'ung 丘崈

Chiu-yüan 九原

chou 州

chou-hsüeh 州學

Chou Pi-ta 周必大

Chou Tun-yi 周敦頤

Chu Cho 朱倬

Ch'u-chou,

    Chekiang 處州

Ch'u-chou,

    Kiangsu 楚州

Chu Hsi 朱熹

chu-k'o 諸科

chu-pu 主簿

Chu Sheng-fei 朱勝非

Chu-wang-kung ta hsiao hsüeh chiao-shou

    諸王宮大小學教授

Ch'ü-chou 衢州

Ch'üan-chou 泉州

ch'üan-shih 銓試

Ch'üan Tsu-wang 全祖望

chün-ch'i-chien 軍器監

chung-hsien 忠獻

Chung-shu she-jen 中書舍人

Chung-tu 中都

chung-yi chün 忠義軍

E-chou 鄂州

Fan Chung 范鐘

Fan Tsung-yin 范宗尹

Fang Hsin-ju 方信儒

feng-chih tai-fu 奉直大夫

Fu-chou 福州

Fu Pi 富弼

Hai-ling wang 海陵王

Hai-yen 海鹽

Han Ch'i 韓琦

Han-chou 漢州

Han-lin shih-tu 翰林侍讀

Han T'o-chou 韓侂胄

Hang-chou 杭州

Hao-chou 濠州

Heng-shan 衡山

Hsia Chen 夏震

Hsia-chou 峽州

Hsiang-chou 相州

Hsiang-shan 象山

Hsiang-yang 襄陽

Hsiao-shan 蕭山

Hsiao-tsung 孝宗

Hsieh-chou 解州

Hsieh Fang-shu 謝方叔

Hsieh Shen-fu 謝深甫

hsien 縣

hsien-ch'eng 縣丞

hsien-hsüeh 縣學

Hsin-chou 信州

Hsing-hua 興化

Hsing-pu shih-lang 刑部侍郎

Hsü Hsi-chi 徐晞稷

Hsü Kuo 許國

Hu-chou 湖州

Hu-pu shih-lang 戶部侍郎

hu-ts'ao 戶曹

Huang Ch'ien-shan 黃潛善

hui-cheng-jen 回正人

Hui-chou 徽州

Hui-tsung 徽宗

Hung Kua 洪适

Hung shih 洪氏

Hung Tzu-k'uei 洪咨夔

Jao-chou 饒州

Jen shih 任氏

Jui-an 瑞安

K'ai-feng 開封

Kao-tsung 高宗

Ko-men shih 閤門事（使）

Ko Pi 葛邲

kuan-p'in 官品

Kuang-chou 廣州

Kuang-tsung 光宗

kuei-cheng-jen 歸正人

kung-chü 貢舉

Kung-pu shang-shu 工部尚書

Kung-pu shih-lang 工部侍郎

Li Chih-hsiao 李知孝

Li Ch'üan 李全

Li Hang 李沆

Li Kang 李綱

Li Kuang 李光

Li Pi 李璧

Li-pu shang-shu
(Personnel) 吏部尚書

Li-pu shang-shu
(Rites) 禮部尚書

Li-pu shih-lang
(Rites) 禮部侍郎

Li-shui 溧水

Li-tsung 理宗

Li Tsung-mien 李宗勉

Li-yang 溧陽

Liang Ch'eng-ta 梁成大

Liang K'o-chia 梁克家

Liang-k'o-yüan 糧科院

Lien-chou 連州

Lin-an 臨安

Lin Ta-chung 林大中

Lin Ta-nai 林大鼐

Liu Cheng 留正

Liu Cho 劉琸

Liu Pang 劉邦

Lo-yang 洛陽

Lou Yü 樓郁

Lou Yüeh 樓鑰

Lu Chiu-yüan 陸九淵

Lü Yi-hao 呂頤浩

Lung-hsing 隆興

Ma T'ing-luan 馬廷鸞

Meng Kung 孟珙

Mien-chou 沔州

ming-ching 明經

Ming-chou 明州

Mo Tse 莫澤

Nan-k'ang 南康

Ni Ssu 倪思

Ning-kuo chün 寧國軍

Ning-po 寧波

Pa 巴

pa-fen 八分

pa-hsing hsien-sheng 八行先生

p'ai-ming 排名

pao-ch'üan 保全

Pei shih 貝氏

Pi-shu-sheng
cheng-tzu 秘書省正字

Pi-shu-sheng
chiao-shu lang 秘書省校書郎

p'ing-chang chün-kuo (chung) shih
平章軍國（重）事

Ping-pu 兵部

Ping-pu shang-shu 兵部尚書

san-she-fa 三舍法

san-sheng 三省

Shang-shu yu p'u-yeh t'ung chung-shu
men-hsia p'ing-chang-shih
尚書右僕射同中書門下平章事

Shao-hsing 紹興

Shao-wu 邵武

Shao Yung 邵雍

Shen Kai 沈該

sheng-shih 省試

shih-feng 食封

Shih Han 史翰

Shih Heng 史亨

Shih-lu chien-t'ao 實錄檢討

Shih-lu-yüan t'ung hsiu-chuan
實錄院同修撰

Shih-shih chia-chuan 史氏家傳

shih-shih-feng 食實封

Shih Shu 史書

Shih Sui 史璲

Shih Wei-tse 史惟則

shih-yi 食邑

Shu 蜀

Shu-mi-yüan fu tu ch'eng-chih
樞密院副都承旨

Shu-mi-yüan pien-hsiu-kuan
樞密院編修官

Shu-mi-yüan shih 樞密院事

Soochow, Kiangsu 蘇州

Ssu-ma Yen 司馬炎

Ssu-ming 四明

Ssu-nung ch'eng 司農丞

Ssu-nung shao-ch'ing 司農少卿

Su-chou,
Anhwei 宿州

Su Shih-tan 蘇師旦

Sui-ch'ang 遂昌

Sui-chou 隨州

sun-tzu 孫子

Sung Min-ch'iu 宋敏求

Sung P'u 宋樸

Ta-li shao-ch'ing 大理少卿

Ta-li-ssu-chih 大理司直

Ta tsung cheng 大宗正

T'ai-ch'ang
chu-pu 太常主簿

tai-chih 待制

T'ai-chou 台州

T'ai-fu ch'eng 太府丞

T'ai-fu chu-pu 太府主簿

T'ai-fu shao-ch'ing 太府少卿

T'ai-hsüeh 太學

T'ai-hsüeh cheng 太學正

T'ai-hsüeh po-shih 太學博士

T'ai-she-ling 太社令

T'ai-tsu 太祖

T'ai-tsung 太宗

t'ai-tzu chan-shih 太子詹事

t'ai-tzu pin-k'o 太子賓客

t'ai-tzu shao-fu 太子少傅

t'ai-tzu shao-pao 太子少保

t'ai-tzu tso shu-tzu 太子左庶子

t'ai-tzu yu shu-tzu 太子右庶子

T'an-chou 潭州

T'ang-chou 唐州

T'ang Ssu-t'ui 湯思退

Tao-hsüeh 道學

Te-shun chün 德順軍

Teng Jo-shui 鄧若水

Teng Yu-lung 鄧友龍

t'i-chü ch'ang-p'ing ch'a-yen kung-shih 提舉常平茶鹽公事

t'i-tien hsing-yü 提點刑獄

tien-shih 殿試

Ting Ta-ch'üan 丁大全

tsa-chü 雜劇

Ts'ai-chou 蔡州

ts'an-chih
   cheng-shih 參知政事

ts'an-chün 參軍

Ts'ao Pin 曹彬

Tsao-yang 棗陽

Tseng Huai 曾懷

Ts'ui Yü-chih 崔與之

Tsung-cheng ch'eng 宗正丞

Tsung-cheng
   shao-ch'ing 宗正少卿

Tsung-cheng ssu 宗正司

tsung-p'in 從品

Tu Ch'ung 杜充

Tu Fan 杜範

t'un-t'ien 屯田

t'ung-chih shu-mi-yüan shih 同知樞密院事

Tung Huai 董槐

t'ung-p'an 通判

Tzu-chou 梓州

Tzu-shan-t'ang chih-chiang 資善堂直講

Wan-ssu Hsieh 万俟卨

Wang Ch'in-jo 王欽若

Wang Fu 王黼

Wang Huai 王淮

Wang Mang 王莽

Wang Po-yen 汪伯彥

Wang Tz'u-weng 王次翁

wei 尉

Wei Ch'i 魏杞

Wei-chou 咸州

Wei Liao-weng 魏了翁

Wen-chou 溫州

Wen T'ien-hsiang 文天祥

Wu Ch'ien 吳潛

Wu-chou 婺州

Wu Hsi 吳曦

Wu-hu 蕪湖

Wu-kang chün 武岡軍

Wu Lin 吳璘

Wu Ping-hsin 吳秉信

Yang An-erh 楊安兒

Yang Chien 楊簡

Yang-chou 揚州

Yang Shao-yün 楊紹雲

Yang Shih 楊時

Yang Tz'u-shan 楊次山

Yao Ch'ung 姚翀

Yeh Heng 葉衡

Yeh Meng-ting 葉夢鼎

Yeh Shih 葉適

Yeh shih 葉氏

Yeh Yung 葉顒

Yen-chou 嚴州

yen-hai chih-shih ssu 沿海制置司

Yen-yu 延祐

yi-chuang 義莊

yi-t'ien 義田

Yin-hsien-nan 鄞縣男

yin-pu 蔭補

Ying-chou 郢州

Ying Ch'un-chih 應純之

yu ch'eng-hsiang 右丞相

yu cheng-yen 右正言

yu chien-yi tai-fu 右諫議大夫

Yu Ssu 游似 (侶)

Yü-hang 餘杭

Yü T'ien-hsi 余天錫

Yü Tuan-li 余端禮

Yü-yao 餘姚

Yü Yün-wen 虞允文

Yüan Chüeh 袁桷

Yüan Hsieh 袁燮

Yün-chung 雲中

Yung-chia 永嘉

Shih Kinsmen[1]

GENERATIONS I–V

Shih Chan 史湛

Shih Ch'eng 史成

Shih Ch'eng [II][2] 史澄

Shih Chi 史濟

Shih Chien 史簡

Shih Chien [II] 史漸

Shih Chüan 史涓

Shih Chün 史浚

Shih Hao 史浩

Shih Ho 史永

Shih Hung 史浤

Shih Jo-ch'ung 史若冲

Shih K'o 史溶

Shih Kuang 史光

Shih Mu 史木

Shih P'u 史溥

Shih Shih-chung 史師仲

Shih Ts'ai 史才

Shih Yüan 史漸

Shih Yüan [II] 史源

GENERATION VI

Shih Mi-chang 史彌彰

Shih Mi-cheng 史彌正

Shih Mi-chien 史彌堅

Shih Mi-ch'ien 史彌謙

Shih Mi-chin 史彌謹

Shih Mi-chin [II] 史彌進

Shih Mi-chiu 史彌久

Shih Mi-chu 史彌春

Shih Mi-chuang 史彌壯

Shih Mi-chuang [II] 史彌莊

Shih Mi-chün 史彌俊

Shih Mi-chung 史彌忠

Shih Mi-hou 史彌厚

Shih Mi-hsing 史彌性

Shih Mi-hsiung 史彌迥

Shih Mi-huan 史彌煥

Shih Mi-kao 史彌高

Shih Mi-kuang 史彌廣

Shih Mi-kung 史彌鞏

Shih Mi-kung [II] 史彌恭

Shih Mi-k'uo 史彌廓

Shih Mi-liang 史彌亮

Shih Mi-lin 史彌林

Shih Mi-lun 史彌綸

Shih Mi-lung 史彌隆

Shih Mi-mao 史彌戊

Shih Mi-min 史彌忞

Shih Mi-ming 史彌明

Shih Mi-nien 史彌年

Shih Mi-ning 史彌寧

Shih Mi-ping 史彌炳

Shih Mi-shao 史彌邵

Shih Mi-shu 史彌恕

Shih Mi-sun 史彌遜

Shih Mi-ta 史彌大

Shih Mi-tai 史彌逮

Shih Mi-tsan 史彌贊

Shih Mi-tsun 史彌遵

Shih Mi-tzu 史彌資

Shih Mi-wen 史彌文

Shih Mi-yeh 史彌曄

Shih Mi-ying 史彌應

Shih Mi-yü 史彌禽

Shih Mi-yüan 史彌遠

Shih Mi-yüan [II] 史彌愿

Shih Mi-yüeh 史彌的

GENERATION VII

Shih An-chih 史安之

Shih Chai-chih 史宅之

Shih Ch'ang-chih 史常之

Shih Chi-chih 史及之

Shih Chi-chih [II] 史即之

Shih Chieh-chih 史介之

Shih Chieh-chih [II] 史節之

Shih Ch'ih-chih 史持之

Shih Ch'in-chih 史懂之

Shih Ching-chih 史敬之

Shih Chou-chih 史冑之

Shih Chü-chih 史舉之

Shih Chü-chih [II] 史居之

Shih Ch'uan-chih 史傳之

Shih Ch'üan-chih 史佺之

Shih Ch'üan-chih [II] 史全之

Shih Ch'üan-chih [III] 史全之

Shih Chün-chih 史準之

Shih Ch'ung-chih 史寵之

Shih Fu-chih 史阜之

Shih Heng-chih 史衡之

Shih Hsi-chih 史希之

Shih Hsi-chih [II] 史爨之

Shih Hsiao-chih 史肖之

Shih Hsien-chih 史憲之

Shih Hsüan-chih 史宣之

Shih Hsün-chih 史訓之

Shih Hsün-chih [II] 史循之

Shih Hua-chih 史華之

Shih Huai-chih 史懷之

Shih Huan-chih 史寰之

Shih Hui-chih 史撝之

Shih Hui-chih [II] 史翬之

Shih Kai-chih 史改之

Shih K'en-chih 史肯之

Shih K'uan-chih 史寬之

Shih K'uei-chih 史撥之

Shih K'uei-chih [II] 史蘻之

Shih Kung-chih 史拱之

Shih Lin-chih 史麟之

Shih Mao-chih 史袤之

Shih Neng-chih 史能之

Shih Ni-chih 史嶷之

Shih Pai-chih 史百之

Shih Pao-chih 史襃之

Shih Pen-chih 史本之

Shih Piao-chih 史表之

Shih Pin-chih 史賓之

Shih Sa-chih 史撒之

Shih Shen-chih 史審之

Shih Shen-chih [II] 史申之

Shih Sheng-chih 史聖之

Shih Shih-chih 史實之

Shih Shih-chih [II] 史十之

Shih Shou-chih 史守之

Shih Shou-chih [II] 史受之

Shih Sui-chih 史寯之

Shih Sun-chih 史損之

Shih Sung-chih 史嵩之

Shih Tao-chih 史衜之

Shih Te-chih 史得之

Shih Ting-chih 史定之

Shih T'ing-chih 史挺之

Shih Tsai-chih 史在之

Shih Ts'ai-chih 史寀之

Shih Ts'ao-chih 史慥之

Shih Tsung-chih 史宗之

Shih Wang-chih 史望之

Shih Wei-chih 史偉之

Shih Wu-chih 史悮之

Shih Wu-chih [II] 史鏌之

Shih Yao-chih 史嶢之

Shih Yen-chih 史巘之

Shih Yen-chih [II] 史衍之

Shih Yi-chih 史宜之

Shih Yi-chih [II] 史一之

Shih Yi-chih [III] 史栁之

Shih Yi-chih [IV] 史怡之

Shih Yi-chih [V] 史懌之

Shih Ying-chih 史郢之

Shih Yu-chih 史有之

Shih Yü-chih 史宇之

Shih Yü-chih [II] 史愉之

Shih Yü-chih [III] 史育之

Shih Yüan-chih 史元之

Shih Yung-chih 史永之

GENERATION VIII

Shih Chang-ch'ing 史璋卿

Shih Ch'ang-ch'ing 史昌卿

Shih Ch'ang-ch'ing [II] 史長卿

Shih Ch'ang-ch'ing [III] 史常卿

Shih Chao-ch'ing 史昭卿

Shih Chen-ch'ing 史震卿

Shih Chen-ch'ing [II] 史真卿

Shih Chen-ch'ing [III] 史珍卿

Shih Chen-ch'ing [IV] 史瑱卿

Shih Chen-ch'ing [V] 史鎮卿

Shih Chi-ch'ing 史吉卿

Shih Chi-ch'ing [II] 史汲卿

Shih Ch'i-ch'ing 史齊卿

Shih Ch'i-ch'ing [II] 史頎卿

Shih Ch'i-ch'ing [III] 史祺卿

Shih Ch'i-ch'ing [IV] 史琦卿

Shih Chia-ch'ing 史嘉卿

Shih Chieh-ch'ing 史玠卿

Shih Chih-ch'ing 史直卿

Shih Chih-ch'ing [II] 史賨卿

Shih Chin-ch'ing 史晉卿

Shih Ching-ch'ing 史璟卿

Shih Ching-ch'ing [II] 史靖卿

Shih Ch'iu-ch'ing 史裘卿

Shih Chou-ch'ing 史周卿

Shih Chü-ch'ing 史椇卿

Shih Ch'uan-ch'ing 史傳卿

Shih Ch'un-ch'ing 史椿卿

Shih Chün-ch'ing 史俊卿

Shih Fan-ch'ing 史范卿

Shih Fang-ch'ing 史芳卿

Shih Fu-ch'ing 史甫卿

Shih Fu-ch'ing [II] 史輔卿

Shih Fu-ch'ing [III] 史傅卿

Shih Han-ch'ing 史漢卿

Shih Hsi-ch'ing 史熹卿

Shih Hsi-ch'ing [II] 史習卿

Shih Hsia-ch'ing 史夏卿

Shih Hsiang-ch'ing 史相卿

Shih Hsien-ch'ing 史顥卿

Shih Hsien-ch'ing [II] 史遜卿

Shih Hsin-ch'ing 史信卿

Shih Hsin-ch'ing [II] 史莘卿

Shih Hsiu-ch'ing 史修卿

Shih Hsü-ch'ing 史須卿

Shih Hsü-ch'ing [II] 史序卿

Shih Hu-ch'ing 史琥卿

Shih Hu-ch'ing [II] 史瑚卿

Shih Huai-ch'ing 史槐卿

Shih Huang-ch'ing 史黃卿

Shih Hui-ch'ing 史會卿

Shih Hui-ch'ing [II] 史回卿

Shih Jen-ch'ing 史仁卿

Shih Jen-ch'ing [II] 史任卿

Shih Jih-ch'ing 史日卿

Shih Jui-ch'ing 史瑞卿

Shih K'an-ch'ing 史侃卿

Shih Kao-ch'ing 史杲卿

Shih Kuan-ch'ing 史貫卿

Shih Kuan-ch'ing [II] 史管卿

Shih Kuei-ch'ing 史珪卿

Shih Kuei-ch'ing [II] 史桂卿

Shih K'uei-ch'ing 史葵卿

Shih Kung-ch'ing 史琪卿

Shih Lai-ch'ing 史來卿

Shih Lai-ch'ing [II] 史萊卿

Shih Li-ch'ing 史理卿

Shih Li-ch'ing [II] 史立卿

Shih Li-ch'ing [III] 史鯉卿

Shih Liang-ch'ing 史良卿

Shih Lien-ch'ing 史璉卿

Shih Lin-ch'ing 史璘卿

Shih Lu-ch'ing 史魯卿

Shih Man-ch'ing 史曼卿

Shih Mao-ch'ing 史茂卿

Shih Meng-ch'ing 史蒙卿

Shih Meng-ch'ing [II] 史孟卿

Shih Min-ch'ing 史閔卿

Shih Ming-ch'ing 史明卿

Shih Nai-ch'ing 史仍卿

Shih P'ei-ch'ing 史裴卿

Shih Pen-ch'ing 史本卿

Shih P'eng-ch'ing 史彭卿

Shih Pi-ch'ing 史璧卿

Shih Pi-ch'ing [II] 史玼卿

Shih P'u-ch'ing 史普卿

Shih Sen-ch'ing 史森卿

Shih Shan-ch'ing 史善卿

Shih Shang-ch'ing 史商卿

Shih Shang-ch'ing [II] 史裳卿

Shih Shao-ch'ing 史紹卿

Shih Shao-ch'ing [II] 史韶卿

Shih Shen-ch'ing 史申卿

Shih Sheng-ch'ing 史昇卿

Shih Shih-ch'ing 史世卿

Shih Shih-ch'ing [II] 史仕卿

Shih Shih-ch'ing [III] 史侍卿

Shih Shih-ch'ing [IV] 史奭卿

Shih Shou-ch'ing 史壽卿

Shih Shu-ch'ing 史書卿

Shih Shun-ch'ing 史辭卿

Shih Shun-ch'ing [II] 史順卿

Shih Ssu-ch'ing 史尋卿

Shih Ssu-ch'ing [II] 史偲卿

Shih Ssu-ch'ing [III] 史似卿

Shih Su-ch'ing 史蘇卿

Shih Sun-ch'ing 史巽卿

Shih Sung-ch'ing 史松卿

Shih T'ai-ch'ing 史泰卿

Shih T'an-ch'ing 史坦卿

Shih T'an-ch'ing [II] 史曇卿

Shih T'ang-ch'ing 史唐卿

Shih Te-ch'ing 史德卿

Shih Teng-ch'ing 史登卿

Shih Tsao-ch'ing 史璪卿

Shih Tseng-ch'ing 史曾卿

Shih Tso-ch'ing 史佐卿

Shih Tsung-ch'ing 史琮卿

Shih Tuan-ch'ing 史端卿

Shih T'ung-ch'ing 史同卿

Shih Wan-ch'ing 史萬卿

Shih Wei-ch'ing 史喜卿

Shih Wei-ch'ing [II] 史衞卿

Shih Wei-ch'ing [III] 史位卿

Shih Wen-ch'ing 史文卿

Shih Wu-ch'ing 史伍卿

Shih Ya-ch'ing 史亞卿

Shih Yao-ch'ing 史堯卿

Shih Yeh-ch'ing 史燁卿

Shih Yen-ch'ing 史儼卿

Shih Yen-ch'ing [II] 史琰卿

Shih Yen-ch'ing [III] 史晏卿

Shih Yi-ch'ing 史沂卿

Shih Yi-ch'ing [II] 史益卿

Shih Yi-ch'ing [III] 史伊卿

Shih Yi-ch'ing [IV] 史頤卿

Shih Yi-ch'ing [V] 史昊卿

Shih Yi-ch'ing [VI] 史庡卿

Shih Yi-ch'ing [VII] 史儀卿

Shih Ying-ch'ing 史穎卿

Shih Yu-ch'ing 史佑卿

Shih Yü-ch'ing 史與卿

Shih Yü-ch'ing [II] 史瑜卿

Shih Yüan-ch'ing 史元卿

Shih Yüeh-ch'ing 史月卿

Shih Yün-ch'ing 史允卿

Shih Yün-ch'ing [II] 史雲卿

Shih Yung-ch'ing 史泳卿

Shih Yung-ch'ing [II] 史雍卿

GENERATION IX

Shih Ai-po 史藹伯

Shih Ang-sun 史昂伯

Shih Chang-po 史章伯

Shih Ch'ang-po 史昌伯

Shih Ch'ang-po [II] 史瑒伯

Shih Chang-sun 史暲孫

Shih Ch'ang-sun 史昌孫

Shih Ch'ao-po 史超伯

Shih Chen-po 史震伯

Shih Ch'en-po 史晨伯

Shih Chen-sun 史震孫

Shih Chen-sun [II] 史真孫

Shih Chen-sun [III] 史辰孫

Shih Chen-sun [IV] 史鎮孫

Shih Ch'eng-po 史承伯

Shih Ch'eng-po [II] 史試伯

Shih Cheng-sun 史振孫

Shih Chi-po 史紀伯

Shih Ch'i-po 史耆伯

Shih Ch'i-po [II] 史起伯

Shih Chi-sun 史紀孫

Shih Chi-sun [II] 史繼孫

Shih Chi-sun [III] 史墍孫

Shih Chi-sun [IV] 史曁孫

Shih Ch'i-sun 史祺孫

Shih Ch'i-sun [II] 史奇孫

Shih Ch'i-sun [III] 史圻孫

Shih Ch'i-sun [IV] 史祁孫

Shih Ch'i-sun [V] 史昕孫

Shih Ch'i-sun [VI] 史錡孫

Shih Ch'iang-sun 史鎗孫

Shih Chieh-sun 史提孫

Shih Ch'ien-po 史潛伯

Shih Ch'ien-po [II] 史謙伯

Shih Chien-sun 史絨孫

Shih Chien-sun [II] 史鑑孫

Shih Chih-po 史志伯

Shih Chih-sun 史賀孫

Shih Chih-sun [II] 史指孫

Shih Chih-sun [III] 史臺孫

Shih Chih-sun [IV] 史至孫

Shih Chin-po 史進伯

Shih Chin-po [II] 史晉伯

Shih Ch'in-po 史芹伯

Shih Chin-sun 史縉孫

Shih Chin-sun [II] 史搢孫

Shih Chin-sun [III] 史僅孫

Shih Ch'ing-po 史清伯

Shih Ching-sun 史經孫

Shih Ching-sun [II] 史俓孫

Shih Ch'iu-sun 史坒孫

Shih Chou-po 史舟伯

Shih Ch'ou-po 史疇伯

Shih Ch'ou-sun 史儔孫

Shih Ch'ou-sun [II] 史田孫

Shih Chu-sun 史鑄孫

Shih Chü-po 史巨伯

Shih Chü-sun 史舉孫

Shih Ch'üan-po 史全伯

Shih Ch'üan-sun 史佺孫

Shih Chuang-sun 史壯孫

Shih Ch'ui-sun 史坐孫

Shih Chün-po 史鈞伯

Shih Chün-po [II] 史俊伯

Shih Chün-sun 史均孫

Shih Chung-po 史仲伯

Shih Chung-sun 史鍾孫

Shih Fang-po 史方伯

Shih Fang-sun 史昉孫

Shih Feng-po 史鳳伯

Shih Fu-po 史孚伯

Shih Fu-po [II] 史復伯

Shih Fu-sun 史福孫

Shih Fu-sun [II] 史傅孫

Shih Heng-sun 史鎬孫

Shih Ho-po 史盍伯

Shih Ho-sun 史賀孫

Shih Ho-sun [II] 史龢孫

Shih Ho-sun [III] 史鼚孫

Shih Hou-sun 史窐孫

Shih Hsi-po 史熙伯

Shih Hsi-po [II] 史莲伯

Shih Hsi-po [III] 史㑴伯

Shih Hsi-sun 史錫孫

Shih Hsi-sun [II] 史禧孫

Shih Hsi-sun [III] 史璽孫

Shih Hsiang-po 史湘伯

Shih Hsiang-po [II] 史章伯

Shih Hsiang-po [III] 史庠伯

Shih Hsiang-sun 史祥孫

Shih Hsiao-sun 史曉孫

Shih Hsien-po 史㨂伯

Shih Hsien-sun 史顗孫

Shih Hsien-sun [II] 史遄孫

Shih Hsien-sun [III] 史賢孫

Shih Hsien-sun [IV] 史顯孫

Shih Hsin-po 史信伯

Shih Hsing-po 史興伯

Shih Hsing-sun 史興孫

Shih Hsing-sun [II] 史性孫

Shih Hsü-po 史緒伯

Shih Hsü-po [II] 史需伯

Shih Hsüan-sun 史暄孫

Shih Hsüeh-sun 史璺孫

Shih Hsün-po 史塤伯

Shih Hsün-sun 史塤孫

Shih Hsün-sun [II] 史郇孫

Shih Huan-po 史煥伯

Shih Hui-po 史憝伯

Shih Hui-sun 史巘孫

Shih Hui-sun [II] 史暉孫

Shih Jao-po 史饒伯

Shih Jen-sun 史仁孫

Shih Jen-sun [II] 史仁孫

Shih Ju-sun 史儒孫

Shih Jui-sun 史銳孫

Shih Jun-po 史潤伯

Shih Jung-sun 史鏷孫

Shih K'ai-sun 史愷孫

Shih K'ai-sun [II] 史暟孫

Shih K'ai-sun [III] 史壇孫

Shih K'an-po 史侃伯

Shih K'ang-po 史康伯

Shih Kang-sun 史綱孫

Shih K'ang-sun 史抗孫

Shih Kao-sun 史杲孫

Shih K'o-po 史可伯

Shih Kuan-po 史觀伯

Shih Kuei-po 史畦伯

Shih K'uei-po 史奎伯

Shih K'uei-po [II] 史蔡伯

Shih K'uei-po [III] 史逵伯

Shih Kuei-sun 史桂孫

Shih Kuei-sun [II] 史貴孫

Shih K'uei-sun 史奎孫

Shih K'uei-sun [II] 史圭孫

Shih K'uei-sun [III] 史葵孫

Shih Lan-sun 史蘭孫

Shih Le-po 史樂伯

Shih Lei-sun 史壘孫

Shih Li-po 史禮伯

Shih Li-po [II] 史璨伯

Shih Li-sun 史里孫

Shih Liang-po 史良伯

Shih Lien-po 史蒹伯

Shih Lin-po 史麟伯

Shih Liu-sun 史鏐孫

Shih Lü-po 史呂伯

Shih Lü-po [II] 史履伯

Shih Lun-po 史綸伯

Shih Lun-po [II] 史倫伯

Shih Lun-sun 史倫孫

Shih Lung-po 史龍伯

Shih Meng-po 史夢伯

Shih Meng-po [II] 史孟伯

Shih Mien-sun 史冕孫

Shih Ming-po 史明伯

Shih Ming-sun 史明孫

Shih Mo-po 史蓦伯

Shih Mou-po 史鄮伯

Shih Na-sun 史昀孫

Shih Ning-sun 史甯孫

Shih Pao-sun 史寶孫

Shih P'ei-sun 史培孫

Shih Pi-sun 史壁孫

Shih Pi-sun [II] 史駓孫

Shih Pien-sun 史抃孫

Shih Pin-po 史斌孫

Shih Pin-sun 史邠孫

Shih P'ing-po 史平伯

Shih Ping-sun 史邴孫

Shih Po-sun 史柏孫

Shih Shan-po 史善伯

Shih Shen-po 史伸伯

Shih Shen-po [II] 史紳伯

Shih Shen-sun 史神孫

Shih Sheng-po 史盛伯

Shih Sheng-po [II] 史聲伯

Shih Sheng-po [III] 史升伯

Shih Sheng-po [IV] 史繩伯

Shih Sheng-sun 史晟孫

Shih Sheng-sun [II] 史昇孫

Shih Shih-sun 史時孫

Shih Shih-sun [II] 史實孫

Shih Shou-sun 史綬孫

Shih Shu-sun 史俶孫

Shih Shu-sun [II] 史塾孫

Shih Ssu-sun 史俍孫

Shih Sui-po 史遂伯

Shih Sui-sun 史隨伯

Shih Ta-po 史達伯

Shih Tai-po 史逮伯

Shih T'ai-po 史台伯

Shih T'ai-po [II] 史泰伯

Shih T'ai-sun 史童孫

Shih Tan-sun 史旦孫

Shih T'ang-sun 史鏜孫

Shih Te-sun 史得孫

Shih Ti-sun　史悌孫

Shih Ti-sun [II]　史昭孫

Shih Tien-sun　史典孫

Shih Ting-po　史定伯

Shih Ting-sun　史定孫

Shih Tsai-po　史宰伯

Shih Ts'ang-po　史蒼伯

Shih Tse-sun　史擇孫

Shih Tseng-po　史瓚伯

Shih Tso-po　史佐伯

Shih Tsung-po　史綜伯

Shih T'u-sun　史塗孫

Shih Tung-sun　史暕孫

Shih T'ung-sun　史通孫

Shih Tzu-sun　史資孫

Shih Tzu-sun [II]　史鎡孫

Shih Tz'u-sun　史塗孫

Shih Wang-po　史玨伯

Shih Wang-sun　史綱孫

Shih Wei-po　史渭伯

Shih Wei-sun　史緯孫

Shih Wei-sun [II]　史暐孫

Shih Wen-sun　史旼孫

Shih Wu-po　史午伯

Shih Wu-sun　史倈孫

Shih Yang-sun　史揚孫

Shih Yao-sun　史曜孫

Shih Yeh-sun　史曄孫

Shih Yen-po　史彥伯

Shih Yen-po [II]　史演伯

Shih Yen-sun　史衍孫

Shih Yen-sun [II]　史儼孫

Shih Yi-po　史儀伯

Shih Yi-po [II]　史益伯

Shih Yi-sun [II]　史伊孫

Shih Yi-sun [III]　史億孫

Shih Yi-sun [IV]　史佾孫

Shih Yin-sun　史鄞孫

Shih Yin-sun [II]　史壄孫

Shih Ying-po　史英伯

Shih Ying-po [II]　史瑛伯

Shih Ying-sun　史應孫

Shih Ying-sun [II]　史郢孫

Shih Ying-sun [III]　史映孫

Shih Yu-po　史佑伯

Shih Yu-po [II]　史侑伯

Shih Yu-sun　史佑孫

Shih Yu-sun [II]　史偱孫

Shih Yü-sun　史譽孫

Shih Yü-sun [II]　史嶼孫

Shih Yü-sun [III]　史郁孫

Shih Yü-sun [IV]　史昱孫

Shih Yü-sun [V]　史鈺孫

Shih Yü-sun [VI]　史儻孫

Shih Yü-sun [VII]　史輿孫

Shih Yüan-sun　史援孫

Shih Yüan-sun [II]　史垣孫

Shih Yüeh-po　史越伯

Shih Yüeh-sun　史鉞孫

Shih Yün-po　史韞伯

Shih Yung-po 史壖伯

Shih Yung-sun 史鏞孫

GENERATION X

Shih Jen-sou 史仁叟

Shih Kung-an 史公安

Shih Kung-ch'ai 史公茝

Shih Kung-chang 史公彰

Shih Kung-chang [II] 史公璋

Shih Kung-chang [III] 史公暲

Shih Kung-chang [IV] 史公鄣

Shih Kung-chao 史公肇

Shih Kung-chen 史公振

Shih Kung-ch'eng 史公誠

Shih Kung-ch'eng [II] 史公儞

Shih Kung-ch'eng [III] 史公郕

Shih Kung-chi 史公機

Shih Kung-chi [II] 史公濟

Shih Kung-chi [III] 史公積

Shih Kung-chi [IV] 史公紀

Shih Kung-chi [V] 史公曁

Shih Kung-chi [VI] 史公廣

Shih Kung-chi [VII] 史公稷

Shih Kung-ch'i 史公麒

Shih Kung-ch'i [II] 史公祺

Shih Kung-ch'i [III] 史公碕

Shih Kung-ch'i [IV] 史公啓

Shih Kung-ch'i [V] 史公綮

Shih Kung-ch'i [VI] 史公昕

Shih Kung-ch'i [VII] 史公奇

Shih Kung-ch'i [VIII] 史公祁

Shih Kung-chiao 史公郊

Shih Kung-chieh 史公節

Shih Kung-chieh [II] 史公傑

Shih Kung-ch'ien 史公謙

Shih Kung-ch'ien [II] 史公芡

Shih Kung-chih 史公止

Shih Kung-chih [II] 史公至

Shih Kung-chih [III] 史公直

Shih Kung-chih [IV] 史公襄

Shih Kung-chih [V] 史公址

Shih Kung-chih [VI] 史公芷

Shih Kung-ch'ih 史公糦

Shih Kung-chin 史公瑾

Shih Kung-ch'in 史公裹

Shih Kung-ch'in [II] 史公芹

Shih Kung-ching 史公敬

Shih Kung-ching [II] 史公靜

Shih Kung-ching [III] 史公曔

Shih Kung-ching [IV] 史公靖

Shih Kung-ch'ing 史公清

Shih Kung-ch'ing [II] 史公慶

Shih Kung-ch'o 史公繛

Shih Kung-chou 史公晝

Shih Kung-ch'ou 史公疇

Shih Kung-chu 史公埣

Shih Kung-ch'u 史公塙

Shih Kung-ch'u [II] 史公髓

Shih Kung-ch'u [III] 史公初

Shih Kung-chü 史公舉

Shih Kung-chü [II] 史公莒

Shih Kung-ch'üan 史公權

Shih Kung-chuang 史公裝

Shih Kung-ch'un 史公純

Shih Kung-chung 史公忠

Shih Kung-chung [II] 史公仲

Shih Kung-chung [III] 史公鐘

Shih Kung-e 史公鄂

Shih Kung-fan 史公梵

Shih Kung-fang 史公方

Shih Kung-fang [II] 史公昉

Shih Kung-fei 史公芾

Shih Kung-fen 史公瀵

Shih Kung-fu 史公輔

Shih Kung-fu [II] 史公福

Shih Kung-fu [III] 史公富

Shih Kung-fu [IV] 史公復

Shih Kung-fu [V] 史公黼

Shih Kung-fu [VI] 史公福

Shih Kung-heng 史公亨

Shih Kung-hou 史公厚

Shih Kung-hou [II] 史公垕

Shih Kung-hsi 史公憙

Shih Kung-hsi [II] 史公龕

Shih Kung-hsi [III] 史公禧

Shih Kung-hsi [IV] 史公錫

Shih Kung-hsi [V] 史公熙

Shih Kung-hsi [VI] 史公禧

Shih Kung-hsia 史公夏

Shih Kung-hsiang 史公祥

Shih Kung-hsieh 史公爕

Shih Kung-hsien 史公絃

Shih Kung-hsien [II] 史公詵

Shih Kung-hsin 史公信

Shih Kung-hsing 史公興

Shih Kung-hsing [II] 史公馨

Shih Kung-hsiu 史公秀

Shih Kung-hsü 史公序

Shih Kung-hsüan 史公亘

Shih Kung-hsüan [II] 史公桓

Shih Kung-hsüan [III] 史公璿

Shih Kung-hsüeh 史公壆

Shih Kung-hsün 史公循

Shih Kung-hsün [II] 史公塤

Shih Kung-hsün [III] 史公勛

Shih Kung-hsün [IV] 史公郇

Shih Kung-hu 史公祜

Shih Kung-hua 史公華

Shih Kung-hui 史公惠

Shih Kung-hung 史公竑

Shih Kung-jang 史公讓

Shih Kung-jen 史公仁

Shih Kung-jo 史公若

Shih Kung-jui 史公瑞

Shih Kung-jun 史公閏

Shih Kung-jung 史公裕

Shih Kung-kai 史公垓

Shih Kung-k'ai 史公愷

Shih Kung-kang 史公剛

Shih Kung-k'ang 史公康

Shih Kung-kao 史公皋

Shih Kung-ko 史公輅

Shih Kung-kuei 史公貴

Shih Kung-kuei [II] 史公圭

Shih Kung-k'uei 史公裒

Shih Kung-k'uei [II] 史公奎

Shih Kung-k'uei [III] 史公夔

Shih Kung-kung 史公巽

Shih Kung-lei 史公壘

Shih Kung-li 史公禮

Shih Kung-liang 史公亮

Shih Kung-lien 史公廉

Shih Kung-lin 史公麟

Shih Kung-lin [II] 史公鄰

Shih Kung-lu 史公祿

Shih Kung-lung 史公隆

Shih Kung-lung [II] 史公龍

Shih Kung-mai 史公邁

Shih Kung-man 史公滿

Shih Kung-mao 史公懋

Shih Kung-mao [II] 史公戊

Shih Kung-mei 史公美

Shih Kung-meng 史公孟

Shih Kung-min 史公敏

Shih Kung-ming 史公明

Shih Kung-mo 史公默

Shih Kung-mo [II] 史公謨

Shih Kung-mou 史公謀

Shih Kung-mou [II] 史公襄

Shih Kung-mou [III] 史公侔

Shih Kung-mou [IV] 史公鄮

Shih Kung-mu 史公暮

Shih Kung-nai 史公耐

Shih Kung-nai [II] 史公褦

Shih Kung-nei 史公倆

Shih Kung-ni 史公儗

Shih Kung-ning 史公甯

Shih Kung-pang 史公邦

Shih Kung-pao 史公寶

Shih Kung-pao [II] 史公葆

Shih Kung-p'ao 史公袍

Shih Kung-pi 史公弼

Shih Kung-piao 史公禠

Shih Kung-pien 史公弁

Shih Kung-pin 史公彬

Shih Kung-sai 史公賽

Shih Kung-shan 史公善

Shih Kung-shan [II] 史公鄯

Shih Kung-shang 史公裳

Shih Kung-shao 史公卲

Shih Kung-shen 史公慎

Shih Kung-shen [II] 史公紳

Shih Kung-sheng 史公升

Shih Kung-sheng [II] 史公勝

Shih Kung-sheng [III] 史公生

Shih Kung-shih 史公式

Shih Kung-shih [II] 史公詩

Shih Kung-shih [III] 史公釋

Shih Kung-shou 史公壽

Shih Kung-shou [II] 史公綬

Shih Kung-shu 史公樞

Shih Kung-shu [II] 史公恕

Shih Kung-shu [III] 史公庶

Shih Kung-shu [IV] 史公述

Shih Kung-shu [V] 史公俶

Shih Kung-sou 史公廋

Shih Kung-ssu 史公芭

Shih Kung-ssu [II] 史公氾

Shih Kung-sui 史公璲

Shih Kung-sui [II] 史公隨

Shih Kung-sun 史公巽

Shih Kung-sung 史公竦

Shih Kung-ta 史公達

Shih Kung-t'ai 史公泰

Shih Kung-tan 史公旦

Shih Kung-t'an 史公郯

Shih Kung-t'ang 史公堂

Shih Kung-t'ao 史公燾

Shih Kung-te 史公德

Shih Kung-ti 史公迪

Shih Kung-ti [II] 史公棣

Shih Kung-t'i 史公褆

Shih Kung-tien 史公點

Shih Kung-ting 史公定

Shih Kung-ting [II] 史公鼎

Shih Kung-t'ing 史公珽

Shih Kung-t'ing [II] 史公廷

Shih Kung-to 史公鐸

Shih Kung-tsai [II] 史公在

Shih Kung-tsai [III] 史公戴

Shih Kung-tsan 史公瓚

Shih Kung-ts'e 史公策

Shih Kung-tso 史公佐

Shih Kung-ts'ung 史公聰

Shih Kung-tu 史公庋

Shih Kung-tu [II] 史公都

Shih Kung-tuan 史公端

Shih Kung-tzu 史公稹

Shih Kung-wang 史公望

Shih Kung-wei 史公瑋

Shih Kung-wei [II] 史公為

Shih Kung-yao 史公垚

Shih Kung-yao [II] 史公藥

Shih Kung-yeh 史公頊

Shih Kung-yeh [II] 史公埜

Shih Kung-yeh [III] 史公鄴

Shih Kung-yeh [IV] 史公曄

Shih Kung-yen 史公衍

Shih Kung-yen [II] 史公郾

Shih Kung-yi 史公頤

Shih Kung-yi [II] 史公益

Shih Kung-yi [III] 史公翼

Shih Kung-yi [IV] 史公義

Shih Kung-yi [V] 史公怡

Shih Kung-yi [VI] 史公禩

Shih Kung-yi [VII] 史公禥

Shih Kung-yi [VIII] 史公繹

Shih Kung-yi [IX] 史公翊

Shih Kung-yi [X] 史公彞

Shih Kung-yi [XI] 史公异

Shih Kung-yin 史公裀

Shih Kung-ying 史公英

Shih Kung-ying [II] 史公廳

Shih Kung-ying [III] 史公盈

Shih Kung-ying [IV] 史公郢

Shih Kung-yu 史公佑

Shih Kung-yu [II] 史公祐

Shih Kung-yu [III] 史公友

Shih Kung-yü 史公響

Shih Kung-yü [II] 史公玉

Shih Kung-yü [III] 史公餘

Shih Kung-yü [IV] 史公裕

Shih Kung-yü [V] 史公禹

Shih Kung-yü [VI] 史公虞

Shih Kung-yü [VII] 史公輿

Shih Kung-yüan 史公元

Shih Kung-yüeh 史公的

Shih Kung-yüeh [II] 史公説

Shih Kung-yüeh [III] 史公論

Shih Kung-yung 史公詠

GENERATION XI

Shih Ching-tsu 史景祖

Shih Ch'un-tsu 史純祖

Shih Mao-tsu 史懋祖

Shih Sheng-tsu 史晟祖

Shih Ting-tsu 史定祖

1. This list of Shih kinsmen, based upon *Hsiao-shan shih-shih tsung-p'u*, contains three duplicate names: Shih Jen-sun [I, II], Shih Kung-fu [II, VI], and Shih Kung-hsi [III, VI]. These apparently represent copy errors.

2. Bracketed numerals, as in the case of Shih Ch'eng [II], are used to distinguish homonymic personal names.

Index

abdication of throne: Hsiao-tsung, 84; Kao-tsung, 55, 57; Kuang-tsung, 84–86
academician-in-waiting, *tai-chih*, 118, 119
adoption: imperial clan, 55, 58, 89, 96, 267 n. 9; kin group, 158
affinal ties: of Shih kinsmen, 12, 120, 186–87, 256 n. 32; source of kinship strength, xii, 5, 181–82, 186
aliens. *See* Jurchen; Mongols; Tanguts
alliance, military: Sung/Mongol, 111, 130, 144–47
Analects, of Confucius, 274 n. 15
ancestral temples: for Shih Hao, 37, 279 n. 126; for Shih Mi-yüan, 112, 279 n. 126
ancestry: of branches D and E, 76; of Shih, 35–36, 39–40; of Sung elite, 33–35
an-fu shih. *See* civil and military commissioner
Anhwei province, 21, 66, 83, 117
An Lu-shan (T'ang rebel), 7
anthropology, xiii, 292 n. 10
Aoyama Sadao, on social mobility, 256 n. 33
arbiter system, *chiu-p'in chung-cheng*, 4, 253 n. 6
aristocracy: British, 175; for China, *see* powerful families
assassination: attempt against Shih Mi-yüan, 92; of Chao Hung, 97, 103; of Chia Ssu-tao, 281 n. 133; of Han T'o-chou, 89–93; of Kuang-tsung's concubine, 84; perpetrated by Shih Sung-chih, 156;

by Shih Yen-chih, 289 n. 85
assistant councillor, *ts'an-chih cheng-shih*: ascent of Shih Mi-yüan, 93; at court of Hsiao-tsung, 72; demise of Li Pi, 91; natives of Ming-chou, 29, 31; nomination of Shih Sung-chih, 148, 157; Shih Hao, 55; Shih Ts'ai, 49, 78, 265 n. 56; tenure of Li Kuang, 46–47; translation by Kracke, 265 n. 56
autocratic leadership, absolutism: of Ch'in Kuei, 47–48, 50, 80; of Han T'o-chou, 86–87; under Hsiao-tsung, 72–73, 80; of Shih Mi-yüan, 104; of Shih Sung-chih, 148–49; at Southern Sung court, 80, 115–16, 134–35, 180
avoidance (bureaucratic practice): compliance of Shih Yen-chih, 157; exemption for Shih Chai-chih, 137; negative effect, 126

ban: on poetry, 104, 277 n. 93; *Tao-hsüeh*, 87, 94
bandits, banditry: in central plains, 131; in guise of loyalists, 61; near the capital, 105; "redcoats" in Shantung, 107–8
baron of Yin, *Yin-hsien-nan*, 144
Basic Annals, *Pen-chi*, 98
Beattie, Hilary, 181–82
Book of Changes, *Yi-ching*, 74
border wars. *See* foreign policy
branch, kinship divisions, 53
Buddhism, 23, 25

Library of Congress Cataloging-in-Publication Data
Davis, Richard L., 1951–
Court and family in Sung China (960–1279)
Bibliography: p.
Includes index.
1. Elites (Social sciences)—China—Case studies.
2. Yin-hsien (China)—Official and employees—History—
Case studies. 3. Family—China—Yin-hsien—Case
studies. 4. China—History—Sung dynasty, 960–1279.
I. Title.
HN740.Z9E434 1986   306.8'5'0951   85-20656
ISBN 0-8223-0512-7